HISTORIES OF THE NON-COOPERATION AND KHILAFAT MOVEMENTS

Histories of the Non-Cooperation and Khilafat Movements

P.C. BAMFORD

MANOHAR
2026

First published 1925
Reprinted 2021, 2022, 2023, 2024, 2025, 2026

ISBN 978-93-88540-88-9

Published by
Ajay Kumar Jain *for*
Manohar Publishers & Distributors
4753/23 Ansari Road, Daryaganj
New Delhi 110 002

Printed at
Replika Press Pvt. Ltd.

ORIGINAL TITLE PAGE

Histories of the Non-Co-operation and Khilafat Movements

by

P. C. BAMFORD

Deputy Director, Intelligence Bureau,
Home Department, Government of India.

DELHI
GOVERNMENT OF INDIA PRESS
1925

CONTENTS.

APPENDICES.

CONTENTS.

PART I.

THE NON-CO-OPERATION MOVEMENT.

CHAPTER I.

CHAPTER II.

PART II.

THE KHILAFAT MOVEMENT.

CHAPTER I.

CHAPTER II.

CHAPTER III.

CHAPTER V.

PREFACE.

The success which attended the Non-co-operation and Khilafat Movements in India is undoubtedly attributable to the Great War, for neither agitation could have attained the dimensions which it did but for the economic pressure to which the people were subjected in consequence of the prolonged and wide-spread hostilities. This pressure aggravated and magnified local grievances and spread the spirit of unrest, thus making, for a time, the work of agitators easy. There is, however, no greater proof of the hollowness of these agitations than the manner in which they succumbed to improved economic conditions. The crops during the years 1922 and 1923 were good and financial stability was beginning to re-appear. The result was the total failure of the agitations to survive the set-backs they incurred in 1922, and in consequence, by 1924, they were confined (except in Burma) to the comparatively small irreconcilable elements from which every country, to a greater or lesser extent, suffers.

Although the Khilafat Movement ostensibly had the purely religious object of compelling the maintenance of spiritual and temporal Muslim control over the Holy Places of Islam, yet there is no doubt that the real aim of its most revolutionary and active leaders was the destruction of British rule in India: an aim which was justified on the ground that Britain is the most powerful rival to Muslim influence in the Near East. Gandhi quickly realised this and, appreciating the value of a common object for the Non-co-operation and Khilafat Movements, provided them with a common platform, *i.e.*, the Punjab and Khilafat wrongs, from which to appeal to the feelings of people of all denominations. The Annual Congress and Khilafat Conferences were always held at the same time and place, and some of the personnel were generally common to the committees of both. These committees, during the period of their greatest activity in the years 1920 and 1921, were very closely associated.

In consequence of Gandhi's influence the two organisations became, for a time, largely interdependent; and although each maintained separate machinery, yet their methods and products were identical. It is therefore often very difficult to distinguish between the results of the two movements, when considering them in retrospect, and the history of one would be incomplete without the history of the other. This is particularly applicable to Chapter III of Part I, *viz.*, "The results of Non-co-operation propaganda", much of which could, with equal ease, have been incorporated in Part II, since it contains matter which might be attributed as much to Khilafat as to Non-co-operation agitation.

In these histories Burma has not been mentioned because—owing to its geographical, religious and racial distinctions—the agitation there ran a different course. A history of the Non-co-operation and Khilafat Movements in Burma, as prepared by the Government of that Province, has been included at Appendix A, and it shows that a "no-tax" campaign came to a head in 1924, which led to much violent crime and caused the local authorities considerable anxiety before it was suppressed.

P. C. BAMFORD.

INTELLIGENCE BUREAU

SIMLA;

June 22nd, 1925.

Histories of the Non-Co-operation and Khilafat Movements.

PART I.

A History of the Non-Co-operation Movement.

CHAPTER I.

The Inception of the Non-co-operation Programme, 1919-20.

1. **Origin of Non-co-operation.**—Leading Non-co-operators have claimed that "from times immemorial"* the refusal to assist a government which will not listen to their grievances has been regarded as the highest duty of the people in India. They have referred to speeches made by Gokhale in 1905 and Lokmanya Tilak in 1907 to show that Non-co-operation was a live policy in those years. For the purposes of this history, however, Non-co-operation in India may be taken as commencing with the *Satyagraha* Campaign organised by Mahatma Gandhi after his return from South Africa, where he had adopted a policy of passive resistance in order to improve the position of Indians in that Colony.

Mr. Gokhale, in 1909, defined this South African Passive Resistance Campaign as follows:—

> "It is essentially defensive in its nature and it fights with moral and spiritual weapons. A passive resister resists tyranny by undergoing suffering in his own person. He pits soul-force against brute force; he pits the divine in man against the brute in man; he pits suffering against oppression, pits conscience against might; he pits faith against injustice; right against wrong."

2. **The advent of Mahatma Gandhi.**—After a stormy career as an agitator in South Africa, Gandhi returned to India in January 1915. He spent some time after his arrival in studying the political situation and in religious observances, and it was not until 1916 that he began to take an active part in propaganda. He soon obtained

---

**Vide* the Civil Disobedience Enquiry Committee Report.

great influence among the masses by his reputation for sanctity and by taking up the cause of the tenants in Bihar in their quarrel with the planters in 1917. It was at about this time that he was given the title of "Mahatma". In 1918 he organised a passive resistance movement in the Kaira District, in the Presidency of Bombay, and advised the ryots not to pay land revenue on account of the poorness of their crops. This may be regarded as one of the first indications in India of his inclination towards the policy of Non-co-operation.

Before proceeding further it is necessary to review very briefly the effect which the general unrest caused by the War had on India, and the political machinery available to Gandhi. The machinery was the Indian National Congress which had been initiated at a time when such articulate public opinion as existed in India was moderate in tone. At Surat in 1907, however, Tilak caused a schism as the leader of an extremist section which established a strong footing and ultimately asserted, at Lucknow in 1916 (where incidentally the Hindu-Muslim Pact* was passed), its predominance which it has maintained ever since.

3. **Extremists Capture the Congress.**—The reason for the reversal in the position of the Parties was the War, and is explained in "India in the years 1917-18" in the following words:—

> "As a consequence of the outbreak of hostilities, and of the rallying of the Dominions to the Mother Country, the readjustment of the constitutional relations between the component parts of the British Empire had been brought into the forefront of public discussion. In this readjustment, Indian political leaders were vitally interested in India's loyal response to the Empire's call had aroused a generous echo in the hearts of the British public; and British Ministers had solemnly pledged the Empire's gratitude. These pledges were now more than two years old, and while there were continual rumours of schemes to hasten on Imperial federation, there had been no indication as to the place which would be found for India in the new scheme. Indian opinion, it must be remembered, was still smarting under the treatment of Indian settlers in some parts of the Empire, and it was widely feared that the projected adjustment of the Imperial constitution would give the Dominions some share in the control of Indian affairs. The long postponement of any announcement as to the future position of India had perplexed all shades of Nationalist opinion. The Moderates had recently lost two of their most influential leaders in Mr. Gokhale and Sir Pherozeshah Mehta, and they had no plan of campaign ready to oppose the Extremists, who had taken the

*Part II, paragraph 24.

opportunity afforded by the delay to set up their own standard of political demand. Having thus a clear field, the Home Rule movement in Madras under Mrs. Besant and the corresponding movement in the Bombay Presidency under Mr. Tilak had gone ahead very fast."

From this it is apparent that the change of atmosphere caused by the War was directly responsible for the rapid hardening of opinion in India. It hastened the ascendancy of the extremist faction in the Congress and thus made it available to Gandhi for the production of his policy of Non-co-operation. Similarly the economic pressure adduced by the war reacted on the masses in India, making it difficult to obtain necessities and aggravating any temporary grievance which happened to exist. The people of India were consequently fertile soil for the seed of unrest at the time when Gandhi began his agitation.

4. **Problems resulting from the War.**—The War also provided two new problems for the solution of which the Non-co-operation policy ostensibly came into existence. These were (1) the Khilafat Question and (2) the Punjab disturbances. The connection between the Khilafat question and the War is obvious, but the link with the Punjab disturbances needs elucidation.

When War broke out the *ultra*-extremists in India undoubtedly hoped for a British defeat which would enable them to throw off the foreign yoke. This hope was amply manifested in Bengal where the anarchical element entered into conspiracy with Germany to bring about a revolution in India. To cope with this revolutionary movement the Defence of India Act was widely used in Bengal, with considerable success. This Act, however, automatically expired six months after the termination of the War, and in order to have something on the Statute Book to take its place if necessary, the Rowlatt Bills were introduced in the beginning of 1919. Under the provisions of these Bills, they could only be enforced in specified areas for specified periods to cope with emergencies; and the freedom of law-abiding citizens was fully protected. These limitations and safeguards were, however, ignored by Gandhi and his followers who engineered an agitation which, as will be shown hereafter, was directly responsible for the Punjab disturbances.

5. **Gandhi's Satyagraha Campaign.**—In February 1919, at Ahmedabad where he resided, Gandhi initiated a campaign of passive resistance against the Rowlatt Bills and drew up a *Satyagraha* vow which opponents of the Bills were invited to sign. This vow read as follows:—

" Being conscientiously of opinion that the Bills known as the Indian Criminal Law (Amendment) Bill No. I of 1919 and the Criminal Law (Emergency Powers) Bill No. II of 1919, are unjust, subversive of the principles of liberty and justice and destructive of the elementary rights of individuals on which the safety of the community, as a whole, and the State itself, is based, we solemnly affirm that, in the event of these Bills becoming law and until they are withdrawn, we shall refuse civilly to obey these laws and such other laws as a Committee, to be hereafter appointed, may think fit, and we further affirm that in this struggle we will faithfully follow truth and refrain from violence to life, person or property."

It was published in the *Bombay Chronicle* of the 2nd of March with a manifesto signed by Gandhi which is quoted below:—

"The step taken is probably the most momentous in the history of India. I give my assurance that it has not been hastily taken. Personally, I have passed many a sleepless night over it. I have endeavoured duly to appreciate Government's position but I have been unable to find any justification for the extraordinary Bills. I have read the Rowlatt Committee's report. I have gone through its narrative with admiration. Its reading has driven me to conclusions just the opposite of the Committee's. I should conclude from the Reports that secret violence is confined to isolated and very small parts of India and to a microscopic body of people. The existence of such men is truly a danger to society. But the passing of the Bills, designed to affect the whole of India and its people and arming the Government with powers out of all proportion to the situation sought to be dealt with, is a greater danger. The Committee utterly ignores the historical fact that the millions in India are by nature the gentlest on earth.

"Now look at the setting of the Bills. Their introduction is accompanied by certain assurances given by the Viceroy, regarding the civil service and the British commercial interests. Many of us are filled with the greatest misgivings about the Viceregal utterance. I frankly confess I do not understand its full scope and intention. If it means that the civil service and the British commercial interests are to be held superior to those of India and its political and commercial requirements, no Indian can accept the doctrine. It can but end in a fratricidal struggle within the Empire. Reforms may or may not come. The need of the moment is a proper and just understanding upon the vital issue. No tinkering with it will produce real satisfaction. Let the great Civil Service corporation understand that it can remain in India only as its trustee and servant, not in name but in deed, and let the British commercial houses understand that they can remain in India only to supplement her requirements and not to destroy indigenous art, trade and manufacture; and you have two measures to replace the Rowlatt Bills. They, I promise, will successfully deal with any conspiracy against the State.

"Sir George Lowndes simply added fuel to the fire when he flouted public opinion. He has forgotten his Indian History or he would have known that the Government he represents has, before now, surrendered its own considered opinion to the force of public opinion.

"It will be now easy to see why I consider the Bills to be an unmistakable symptom of a deep-seated disease in the Governing body. It needs therefore to be drastically treated. Subterranean violence will be the remedy applied by impetuous hot-headed youths who will have grown impatient of the spirit underlying the Bills and the circumstances attending their introduction. The Bills must intensify the hatred and ill-will against the State, of which the deeds of violence are undoubtedly an evidence. The Indian Covenanters by their determination to undergo every form of suffering make an irresistible appeal to the Government towards which they bear no ill-will and provide the believers in the efficiency of violence as a means of securing redress of grievances, with an infallible remedy, and withal a remedy that blesses those that use it and also those against whom it is used. If the covenanters know the use of this remedy, I fear no ill from it. I have no business to doubt their ability. They must ascertain whether the disease is sufficiently great to justify the strong remedy and whether all milder ones have been tried. They have convinced themselves that the disease is serious enough, and that milder measures have utterly failed. The rest lies in the lap of the gods."

With the Manifesto was published the first list of signatories to the vow and these were confined almost entirely, as was natural, to inhabitants of the Bombay Presidency, *i.e.*, the province of origin.

Gandhi's next step was to form a *Satyagraha Sabha* for which certain rules were published. The object of this Association was "to oppose until they are withdrawn, the Bills popularly known as the Rowlatt Bills (Acts I and II of 1919) by resort to *Satyagraha* in terms of the pledge"— which was a reproduction of the *Satyagraha* vow already quoted. The rules went on to create the requisite machinery for the working of the *Sabha*, which included a Committee as contemplated in the *Satyagraha* vow.

6. **Satyagraha Propaganda.**—In order to give publicity to the *Satyagraha* campaign, Gandhi set forth on a propaganda tour throughout India and visited first the United Provinces and then Madras.

From Madras on the 24th March 1919, he sent the following letter to the press:—

" *Satyagraha*, as I have endeavoured to explain at several meetings, is essentially a religious movement. It is a process of purification and penance. It seeks to secure reforms or redress of grievances by self-suffering. I therefore venture to suggest that the second Sunday after the publication of the Viceregal assent to Bill No. II of 1919 may be observed as a day of humiliation and prayer. As there must be effective public demonstration in keeping with the character of the observance, I beg to advise as follows:— A twenty-four hours fast counting from the last meal on the preceding night should be observed by all adults unless prevented from so doing by consideration of religion or health. The fast is not to be regarded in any shape or form in the nature of a hunger-strike or designed to put any pressure upon Government. It is to be regarded for *Satyagrahis* as a necessary discipline to fit them for the civil disobediency contemplated in their pledge and for all others as some slight token of the intensity of their wounded feelings.

"All work except such as may be necessary in the public interest should be suspended for the day. Markets and other business places should be closed. Employees who are required to work even on Sundays may only suspend work after obtaining previous leave. I do not hesitate to recommend these two suggestions for adoption by public servants for though it is an unquestionably right thing for them not to take part in political discussions and gatherings, in my opinion they have the undoubted right to express upon vital matters their feelings in the very limited manner herein suggested. Public meetings should be held on that day in all parts of India not excluding villages at which a resolution praying for the withdrawal of the measures should be passed. If my advice is deemed worthy of acceptance the responsibility will lie in the first instance on various *Satyagraha* associations for undertaking the necessary work of organisation, but all other associations will, I hope, join hands in making this demonstration a success."

7. Delhi Riots, March 1919.—The suggestion to fast contained in this letter was responsible for the Delhi riots on Sunday the 30th March 1919, for that disturbance was caused by the violent manner in which food vendors were prevented from selling their wares, after the news of the Viceregal assent to the Rowlatt Bills had been received. This result must have given Gandhi a fair working idea as to how far non-violence was compatible with his *Satyagraha* campaign.

but his subsequent conduct shows that the lesson did not deter him, on future occasions, from exciting the populace, by means of an ostensibly non-violent agitation, up to a point at which non-violence became impossible.

After the riots Gandhi published in the *Bombay Chronicle* on 3rd March 1919 the following letter which is an interesting apologia for the violence of the mob, disguised as a warning against mob-violence:—

" To the Editor of the " Chronicle "

" Sir,—I venture to seek the hospitality of your columns to make a few remarks on the Delhi tragedy. It is alleged against the Delhi people who were assembled at the Delhi Railway Station:—

1. that some of them were trying to coerce the sweatmeat sellers into closing their stalls;
2. that some of them were forcibly preventing people from boarding tramcars and other vehicles;
3. that some of them threw brickbats;
4. that the whole crowd that marched to the station demanded the release of the men who are said to be the coercers and who were for that reason arrested at the instance of the Railway authorities;
5. that the crowd declined to disperse when the Magistrate gave the order to disperse.

'I have read Sanyasi Swami Shraddanandji's account of the tragedy. I am bound to accept it as true, unless it is authoritatively proved to be otherwise, and his accounts seem to me to deny allegations 1, 2 and 3. But assuming the truth of all the allegations, it does appear to me that the local authorities in Delhi have made use of a Nasmyth hammer to crush a fly. On their action, however, in firing on the crowd, I shall seek another opportunity of saying more.

My purpose in writing this letter is merely to issue a note of warning to all *Satyagrahis*. I would therefore like to observe that the conduct described in allegations 1 to 4, if true, would be inconsistent with the *Satyagraha* pledge. The conduct described in allegation 5, can be consistent with the pledge but if the allegation is true, the conduct was premature, because the committee contemplated in the pledge has not decided upon the disobedience of orders that may be issued by Magistrates under the Riot Act. I am anxious to make it as clear as I can that in this movement, no pressure can be put upon the people who do not wish to accept our suggestions and advice. The movement being essentially one to secure the greatest freedom for all, *Satyagrahis* cannot forcibly demand the release of those who might be arrested, whether justly or unjustly. The essence of the pledge is to invite imprisonment. And until the committee decides upon the breach of the Riot Act it is the duty of *Satyagrahis* to obey, without making the slightest ado, magisterial orders to disperse, etc., and thus to demonstrate their law-abiding nature. I hope that next Sunday at *Satyagraha* meetings, all speeches will be free from passion, anger or resentment. The movement depends for its success entirely upon perfect self-possession, self-restraint, absolute adherence to Truth and an unlimited capacity for self-suffering.

" Before closing this letter, I would add that in opposing the Rowlatt legislation, the *Satyagrahis* are resisting the spirit of terrorism which lies behind it and of which it is a most glaring symptom. The Delhi tragedy imposes an added responsibility upon *Satyagrahis* of steeling their hearts and going on with their struggle until the Rowlatt legislation is withdrawn."

This letter together with Gandhi's *Satyagraha* pronouncements have been given in full to avoid any possibility of mis-representation of his ideas regarding passive resistance which formed the basis of the resulting Non-co-operation movement, and to show how outbreaks of violence were regarded by him. After the riots Gandhi announced his intention of proceeding to Delhi to investigate the cause of the trouble, but orders were issued under the Defence of India Act externing him from the Delhi Province and this was followed by similar orders, first externing him from the Punjab, and subsequently confining him to the Presidency of Bombay. These orders were withdrawn in the following October.

8. **The agitation in the Punjab.**—Gandhi's disciples throughout India had been interpreting his doctrine and policy according to their own lights, and the manner in which *anti*-Rowlatt Act propaganda was carried on in the early part of 1919 in the Punjab, can best be shown by quoting *in extenso* from the History of Non-co-operation in that Province.

"On the 6th February 1919 Mr. Jinnah had said in the Imperial Legislative Council at Delhi that, if the Rowlatt Bills vere passed, " You will create in the country from one end to the other a discontent and agitation, the like of which you have not witnessed ". The prophecy was speedily to be fulfilled. At Lahore, on the 4th February, there was a meeting of protest, at which Chaudhri Ram Bhaj Datt declared " With this disgraceful Bill no patriot is safe. Will India after the lesson she has learnt render any assistance to Government? Never!" At Amritsar, on the 9th February, Dr. Gokal Chand Narang likened the Bill to snakes and scorpions let loose in Indian houses. On the 11th, at the same place, Dr. Satya Pal said: "The policy of passive resistance as started by Mr. Gandhi should be followed, as it is a sin to put up with oppression". At Multan, on the 23rd February, Dr. Choit Ram, a well-known Sindhi agitator, declared that a black law was being enacted against them against which they should fight with all their might: "You die of cholera, plague, influenza and other diseases, but would it not be better to die nobly the death of a hero and lion than as a dog?" At Amritsar, on the 28th February, and Lahore, on the 9th March, there were large meetings, with speeches of the same tenor.

"So far, nevertheless, audiences were mostly confined to the politically-minded, and the intention was probably only to promote a general demonstration against the Bills, mainly by adhesion to the passive resistance movement. But sacrifice of an advanced type was demanded:—

> "Let the sword fall: they should not move an eye. If hands were cut, let them be cut. Let fetters and handcuffs adorn their body. Let prisons be their temples and mosques: then would freedom kiss their feet."*

"On the 23rd, 29th and 30th March there were mass meetings at Amritsar, attended by crowds numbering as many as 40,000 persons. Speeches, it is true, were less provocative, but only because they were more subtle. The support of the masses, the weekly wage-earner, the small householder and the man in the street was to be won by appeal to history, tradition and sentiment. The Bill was described as a Nadir Shahi order, and there could be no more telling comparison than this in the Punjab; nearly two crores of Indians had died of starvation: the stores of grain were not in their hands: Hindus and Musalmans were now walking on common ground, but the Government sought to keep them apart; if they had the blood of the old *rishis*† in their veins, they should follow their *rishis*; one thing only their motherland required of them, that they should give her their hearts—and so on in similar strain.

"The Press was naturally more guarded, but no less uncompromising in its opposition:—

> "No civilized Government would adopt a policy of repression in the teeth of opposition from the public. There are now two ways open to us. One is that we should, like the dead, put the noose of this law round our necks, bury in oblivion for ever our fair name, as also that of our great men, and sound the death-knell of the so-called liberty of India. The other is that we should afford proof of our life by refusing to accept the law in question"

("Tribune", issue of the 11th March 1919.)

*Pandit Dina Nath at Amritsar on the 23rd March 1919.
†"Sages"

'Government by its deliberate contempt for the Indian point of view has shown that it is not in a mood to be sympathetic towards our aspirations. It is now our duty to put Government to trouble in every constitutional way. Unless Government repents of its unwisdom, as it had to do in the partition of Bengal case, we should do our utmost so to confuse the authorities as to render their work in the country almost impossible ".

(" *New Herald* ", *issue of 23rd March 1919.*)

'It is absurd to seek to minimize the character of the demonstrations by saying that the multitude which took part in it did not know what the Rowlatt Act was. It was not necessary for them to know the detailed provisions of the Act. No multitude ever knew the details of any Act. It was enough for them to be told by their leaders, by men in whom they had the fullest confidence, that the Government had passed a measure by which one of their most fundamental rights, a right which was the chief security for all their other rights, had been considerably curtailed "

(" *Tribune* ", *issue of the 8th April 1919.*)

" The effect of those and other publications was widespread in persuading people who usually took no interest in political questions that a dangerous weapon was being prepared against their liberty and peace of mind. Intelligent criticism of the Bills there was none. The *Tribune*, it will be observed, did not even think fit to distribute accurate information as to its provisions. It is to be regretted that even the Government waited till the 6th April before taking steps to publish and explain the Act to the people at large. The uneducated remained unaware that it could only be put in operation in districts where anarchical crimes were being perpetrated, after the sanction of the Government of India. To them the Rowlatt Act was the Black Act and as rumour distorted its provisions, so public indignation waxed.

" There is a curious analogy between this agitation and that which centred round the Colony Bill of 1907. In each case the intentions of Government were grossly travestied and the details of the Bill itself practically ignored. In 1919 nothing was too crude to pass current. Catch-words were invented; " *tang amad, bejang amad* ",* said a speaker at Multan: " *na vakil, na dalil, na* appeal " was another. It was genuinely believed that the police would have power to invade the sanctity of the home; that the Bill would penalize with pecuniary exactions the ceremonies accompanying marriage and death; that four men sitting together could be arrested; that no landholder would be allowed to keep more than a few acres of land. Anything more damaging to the *bona fides* of Government could not well be imagined

*" One who is pressed must fight ".

than this sort of propaganda. But the posters were worse. One found at Lahore on the 12th April read as follows:—

"We are the Indian nation whose bravery and honour have been acknowledged by all the kings of the world. The English are the worst lot and are like monkeys whose deceit and cunning are obvious to all, high and low. Have these monkeys forgotten their original conditions? Now these faithless people have forgotten the loyalty of Indians, are bent upon exercising limitless tyranny. O brethren, gird up your loins and fight. Kill and be killed. Do not lose courage and try your utmost to turn those mean monkeys from your holy country"

"At Lyallpur the following appeared:—

"What time are you waiting for now? There are many ladies here to dishonour. Go all round India, clear the country of the ladies and these sinful creatures and then will be the time when we can all say together: 'Blessed be the Hindus, Muhammadans and Sikhs'"

"At Hissar, not otherwise conspicuous at this time, one of the worst of these papers was found:—

"You know that some Englishmen came as merchants to India in the days of Jehangir. But what do you see now? They are the masters of India in these days. They carried on an excellent business indeed, for they made India their slaves, converted part of it to Christianity and used the knife of irreligion. The Punjabis have vowed to go on fighting till Emperor George V and other Englishmen die. Kill with the sword whenever you come across them"

"The posters have a special importance because they conveyed a direct incentive to violence, hitherto lacking in the products of the Press and platform. But, inflammatory and widely read as they undoubtedly were, it is probably correct to regard them as the work of isolated fanatics, rather than organized societies.*

"It is to be observed that, although the appeal both in the Press and at public meetings was almost invariably for peaceful resort to passive resistance, the idea of civil disobedience did not commend itself as an active principle. Few in Amritsar, and it is alleged no one in Lahore, took the *Satyagraha* vow. But for resort to the time-honoured custom of *hartal*, the agitation might have died down. *Hartal* is a characteristically Indian institution, its liberal meaning is the closing of shops in token of mourning, but it has an insidious suggestion of violence, for "by immemorial tradition the first

---

*Disorders Enquiry Committee, Minority Report, page 106.

symptom of a popular outbreak in India is uneasiness lest the bazaars should be looted by the disorderly elements of the urban population ".* Mourning tempered by excitement may be assumed as the key-note, added to which is the ominous fact that it immobilizes large masses of people who roam about with nothing to do. Nor were *hartals* of common occurrence prior to these disturbances. Later on, they became so, and in time the announcement of a *hartal* meant nothing but a certain amount of trouble for the authorities and a certain dislocation of trade, not always acceptable to those who had to close down their businesses. But in 1919 the idea of a *hartal* was still portentous and a far greater instrument of mischief than any abstract principle of resistance. It is impossible to say whether those who organized the mass meetings of this period had any idea that violence would ensure, but it is clear from a perusal of speeches that every rhetorical device was employed to awaken strong feeling short of actual incitement to violence. With Punjabis the transition from words to deeds is short and direct; indeed it was recognised even by those who advocated passive resistance at this time. Thus a speaker at Lahore on the 6th April delivered himself as follows:—

> " Passive resistance was not mainly a matter of undergoing physical suffering, but it was a question of soul force, and for that reason it might not be easy for Punjabis. For them it was the easiest thing to lay down their lives in a just cause, but to bear every humiliation, to undergo every indignity, to put up with every suffering, not to lift the little finger and not to let the heart feel the slightest resentment, that was a task indeed and required that the heart should undergo a transformation. For the other provinces it was easy to resort to passive resistance, but for the Punjab it was far more difficult "
>
> (*" Tribune ", issue of the 3th April 1919.*)

" Be this as it may, *hartals* took place on the 30th March, again on the 6th April and thereafter the situation developed disastrously and with great rapidity."

9. **The Punjab Disturbances.**—It is unnecessary to describe the serious disturbances which broke out as a result of the intensive propaganda in the Punjab and Bombay, for they have been fully dealt with elsewhere. In order to quell the trouble in the former province, Martial Law had to be declared and deterrent steps were taken at Jallianwallah Bagh and elsewhere, the necessity for which was subsequently the subject of much violent controversy. Acts of repression were greatly exaggerated and soon came to be known in Congress circles as the " Punjab Atrocities " and, in response to a demand for an enquiry, Government appointed a Committee, presided over by Lord Hunter, in October 1919 to report on the disorder and the action

*India in 1919, page 32.

taken to quell it. At about the same time the Congress also appointed a committee, of which Gandhi was a member, to enquire into the same matter, and both Committees were engaged in their investigations at the end of 1919. As the Punjab extremist leaders in prison, among whom were Dr. Kitchlew and Lala Har Kishen Lal, were not allowed to appear in person to give evidence, the Congress declined to give evidence before the Hunter Committee, and this act of omission was subsequently claimed by the Civil Disobedience Enquiry Committee (appointed by the Congress in June 1922) to be the first step in Non-co-operation.

10. **The rumoured Turkish Peace Terms.**—In the meantime the Muhammadan situation had deteriorated, for of course the followers of all creeds suffered in common from the economic pressure and from the disturbing effect of the upheaval in the Punjab. In consequence, the publication of rumours regarding the Turkish Peace Terms towards the end of 1919 was a signal for an outburst of religious feeling among Muhammadans throughout India, for the alleged control of the Holy Places of Islam by foreigners, and the curtailment of the temporal power of the Khalifa had been used, for some time previously, by Muhammadan extremists to stir up *anti*-British feeling among their co-religionists.* All through the war *pro*-Turkish agitators had been busy and the activity of the brothers, Muhammad and Shaukat Ali, had led to their internment as early as May 1915. The ground had been prepared, therefore, for the reception of any Peace Terms, at all detrimental to the status of the Khalif, as indicative of British disregard for the religion and feelings of Muhammadans. The All-India Khilafat Conference held in Delhi in November 1919 resolved to withdraw co-operation from Government unless the Khilafat question was satisfactorily settled, and this resolution was framed on the advice of Gandhi who was one of the first of the Hindu leaders definitely to associate himself with the Khilafat cause. Since at this time he was establishing himself as the leader of the Congress, his support was valuable.

11. **The Reforms Act.**—At the end of 1919 it was clear that Gandhi's policy of passive resistance was gaining a considerable following among extremists of all religious denominations, as the result of the skilful manner in which he had utilised the feeling engendered by the "Punjab atrocities" and the Khilafat question. At this stage, however, on the 24th December 1919, came the Royal assent to the Reforms Act and the Royal Amnesty to political prisoners not guilty of actual violence. So definite a step on the part of the British Government towards meeting the aspirations of the Nationalist Party in India and such clear tokens of good will, could not be ignored.

12. **Amritsar Congress, Christmas 1919.**—Immediately afterwards, the annual meeting of the Congress took place at Amritsar in X'mas

*Part II, Chapter II.

week 1919, and among the most welcome attendants were the Ali Brothers and the Punjab leaders who had been released under the Amnesty. It was soon apparent, however, that the sense of the Congress was in no way disposed to meet the Reforms Act in the spirit in which it had been granted, and that the released prisoners generally considered that both their release and the Reforms, were due solely to the agitation they had engineered. Consequently they were encouraged to agitate still more. According to the Civil Disobedience Enquiry Committee Report, " the Congress felt itself insulted at this poor half-hearted measure, but in response to the earnest appeal of Mahatma Gandhi and the Moderate leaders, resolved for the time being, that while the Reforms were ' inadequate, unsatisfactory and disappointing ' the Congress would work them for what they were worth." The Committee were undoubtedly correct in attributing this consent to work the reforms to the personal influence of Gandhi, and it was clear that the consensus of extremist opinion was to accept nothing short of Swaraj which, up to this point, seems to have meant self-government within the British Empire. This uncompromising attitude must have been, to a great extent, the outcome of Gandhi's own propaganda and it is probable that his advocacy of tolerance at the Amritsar Congress was governed mainly by his own personal instinct towards benevolence which he never succeeded in conveying to his followers. The shallowness of the desire of the Congress to work the Reforms was very soon apparent by its seizure of the first possible excuse to withdraw from the Amritsar resolution.

13. **The Punjab enquiry reports.**—This excuse was afforded by the publication in March 1920 of the Report of the Congress Enquiry Committee into the repressions in the Punjab. The report was a very bulky publication and included a mass of statements of witnesses giving greatly exaggerated accounts of various incidents, which were in no way watered down in the body of the Report. This production came into the hands of the public before the Report of the Hunter Committee and the Government despatches thereon, and served to ensure for the latter a very antagonistic reception in extremist circles. This antagonism was, of course, enhanced by the issue of a Minority Report by the Indian members of the Hunter Committee which criticised the action of the authorities in the Punjab more severely than did the Majority Report. Public feeling ran high and the All-India Congress Committee considered that a meeting of the Congress should be held to give vent to it, so a special session was summoned which met at Calcutta in September 1920.

14. **The Leaders' Conference.**—In May the publication of the Turkish Peace Terms, emanating from the Conference at San Remo, caused excitement in India and seems to have been the cause of a meeting of the leaders of all parties at Allahabad which, on the 2nd June 1920, after some very acrimonious discussion, passed the resolution given below. The personnel of the committee mentioned therein

indicates the nature of the voting—the resolution being opposed by most of the Hindu leaders other than Gandhi:—

"This meeting re-affirms the movement of Non-co-operation in accordance with the four stages already approved by the Central Khilafat Committee and appoints a sub-committee consisting of the following gentlemen with power to add to their number, to give practical effect to the movement without further delay:—

Mahatma Gandhi, Maulana Abul Kalam Azad, Maulvi Muhammad Ali, Mr. Ahmad Haji Siddik Khattri, Maulana Shaukat Ali, Dr. Kitchlew and Maulana Hasrat Mohani"

The four stages of Non-co-operation* referred to were:—

(1) the resignation of titles and honorary posts.

(2) the resignation of posts in Civil services of Government, the Police being excluded.

(3) the resignation of service in the Police and the Army.

(4) the refusal to pay taxes.

For some time prior to this it had been apparent that Gandhi had realised that his advocacy of co-operation at Amritsar had weakened his hold on his followers and had severely tested the loyalty of his Muhammadan allies; and that he had either changed his attitude on the subject, or had considered it wise ostensibly to do so, in order to re-establish his position. Hence his abandonment (mainly on the excuse of the unredressed Khilafat wrongs) of the policy he had forced through the Amritsar Congress, and his presence on a committee engaged in drawing up a non-co-operation programme, which was issued in July 1920 and included the boycott of schools, colleges and law courts. He realised that this change of attitude required some elucidation, so he wrote a letter to H. E. the Viceroy in June 1920 explaining his connection with the Khilafat question. This letter is given at Appendix B.

His position was consolidated in the following month in consequence of the death of Mr. Tilak who was too big a figure to play a minor part, but whose demise left Gandhi indubitably the leading actor in the Indian National Drama.

15. **Calcutta Congress, September 1920.**—The account of the special session of the Congress at Calcutta as given in the Civil Disobedience Enquiry Committee Report reads as follows:—

"In the meantime the political situation had become worse. The attitude of the Government had become clearer in regard to the Punjab, the Khilafat and the Reforms, and the

*Part II, paragraph 56.

Punjab debate in both Houses of Parliament had destroyed the last vestige of faith in the Government. It was generally agreed that the time had come for vigorous action. The Special Congress, which met at Calcutta in September 1920, was called upon to consider the programme as well as the policy of Non-co-operation. In the Subjects Committee all Muhammadan members, except Mr. Jinnah, voted with the Mahatma, while many prominent non-Muslim Nationalists supported Mr. Das, who led the opposition to Mahatmaji. It is noteworthy that in the Subjects Committee and, to a lesser extent in the open Congress, Mahatmaji was met with no inconsiderable opposition on the question of this triple boycott. But the extreme disappointment in the country in the matter of the redress of the Punjab and Khilafat wrongs and the illusory nature of the Reforms, coupled with the towering personality of Mahatmaji enabled him to carry his programme through the Congress."

The actual resolution passed was:—

"In view of the fact that on the Khilafat question both the Indian and Imperial Governments have signally failed in their duty towards the Mussalmans of India, and the Prime Minister has deliberately broken his pledged word given to them and that it is the duty of every non-Moslem Indian in every legitimate manner to assist his Mussalman brother in his attempt to remove the religious calamity that has overtaken him.

And in view of the fact that in the matter of the events of April 1919 both the said Governments have grossly neglected or failed to protect the innocent people of the Punjab and punish officers guilty of unsoldierly and barbarous behaviour towards them, and have exonerated Sir Michael O'Dwyer who proved himself, directly or indirectly, responsible for most of the official crimes and callous to the sufferings of the people placed under his administration, and that the debate in the House of Commons and specially in the House of Lords betrayed a woeful lack of sympathy with the people of India and showed virtual support of the systematic terrorism and frightfulness adopted in the Punjab, and that the latest Viceregal pronouncement is proof of an entire absence of repentance in the matters of the Khilafat and the Punjab;

This Congress is of opinion that there can be no contentment in India without the redress of the two aforementioned wrongs, and that the only effectual means to vindicate national honour and to prevent a repetition of similar wrongs in future is the establishment of Swarajya. This

Congress is further of opinion that there is no course left open for the people of India but to approve of and adopt the policy of progressive non-violent Non-co-operation inaugurated by Mr. Gandhi until the said wrongs are righted and Swarajya is established.

And inasmuch as a beginning should be made by the classes who have hitherto moulded and represented public opinion, and inasmuch as Government consolidates its power through titles and honours bestowed on the people, through schools controlled by it, its law-courts and its Legislative Councils, and inasmuch as it is desirable in the prosecution of the movement to take the minimum risk and to call for the least sacrifice compatible with the attainment of the desired object, this Congress earnestly advises:—

(*a*) surrender of titles and honorary offices and resignation from nominated seats in local bodies;

(*b*) refusal to attend Government levees, durbars and other official and semi-official functions held by Government officials or in their honour;

(*c*) gradual withdrawal of children from Schools and Colleges owned, aided or controlled by Government, and in place of such Schools and Colleges, establishment of National Schools and Colleges in the various Provinces;

(*d*) gradual boycott of British courts by lawyers and litigants, and establishment of private arbitration courts by their aid, for the settlement of private disputes;

(*e*) refusal on the part of the military, clerical and labouring classes to offer themselves as recruits for service in Mesopotamia;

(*f*) withdrawal by candidates of their candidature for election to the Reformed Councils and refusal on the part of the voters to vote for any candidate who may, despite the Congress advice, offer himself for election;

(*g*) boycott of foriegn goods;

And inasmuch as Non-co-operation has been conceived as a measure of discipline and self-sacrifice without which no nation can make real progress, and inasmuch as an opportunity should be given in the very first stage of Non-co-operation to every man, woman and child, for such discipline and self-sacrifice, this Congress advises adoption of Swadeshi in piece-goods on a vast scale, and inasmuch as the existing mills of India with indigenous capital and control do not manufacture sufficient yarn and sufficient cloth for the requirements of the nation, and are not likely to do so for long time to come, this Congress advises

> immediate stimulation of further manufacture on a large scale by means of reviving hand spinning in every home and hand weaving on the part of the millions of weavers who have abandoned their ancient and honourable calling for want of encouragement.

The passing of this resolution was a personal triumph for Gandhi who was opposed by most of the Congress leaders. It was adopted by a majority of over 2 to 1, but it is interesting to note that out of nearly 6,000 delegates present, less than one-third voted.

This session of the Congress appointed a sub-committee to draft instructions as to how to give effect to the resolution on Non-co-operation. The All-India Congress Committee considered the draft instructions at a meeting held at Bombay on the 2nd October and the result of their deliberations is given at Appendix C.

16. **Gandhi captures the All-India Home Rule League.**—Having captured the Congress, at any rate for the time being, Gandhi then set himself to win over the All-India Home Rule League, of which he was the President. He was advised by many not to add to the complexity of the situation by unnecessarily alienating several of the leading members of the League, but he paid no attention to this and forced his views on the meeting of that body held in Bombay on October 3rd, and the League was re-named the Swaraj Sabha. When Article No. 1, commencing with " The object of the Swaraj Sabha is to secure complete Swaraj for India according to the wishes of the people of India " came up for discussion, several of the members, headed by Mr. Jinnah, demurred. The chief objection of Mr. Jinnah was that the new constitution omitted the mention of the British connection and that it was permissive of " unconstitutional and illegal activities ". In reply Mr. Gandhi said:—

> " I want my country to have Swaraj with or without the British connection. I am not opposed to that connection by itself but I do not wish to make a fetish of it. By clause 3 we have limited our ambition in order that we may carry the Congress with us and be thus enabled to remain affiliated to that body. As regards the words ' unconstitutional ' and ' illegal ' they are highly technical terms. An ex-Advocate-General of Madras considers non-co-operation to be unconstitutional; I think Mr. Jinnah considers it to be perfectly constitutional. The President of the Special Congress gave it as his considered ruling that my resolution was not unconstitutional. It is difficult for me to conceive an illustration under the British constitution of unconstitutional activity, except violence; and violence has been specifically eschewed from the Sabha's constitution. Similarly, about the word ' illegal ', jurists have differed in its interpretation. It is a most dangerous thing for a

country, fighting for its very life, its honour and its religion, to tie itself down in a knot of indefinable expressions. I personally hate unconstitutionalism and illegalities, but I refuse to make a fetish of these as I refuse to make a fetish of the British connection."

Not approving of this change in the constitution of the Sabha, Mr. Jinnah and several others tendered resignation of their membership.

17. **The Elections 1920.**—The elections to the Reformed Councils took place after the Calcutta Congress, and with respect to them Gandhi issued the following manifesto*:—

"THE DUTY OF VOTERS."

"The Special Session of the Congress by an overwhelming majority has decided in favour of complete boycott of the Reformed Councils. It is therefore your duty *not to vote for any candidate for election* to the Reformed Councils. It is however necessary for any candidate who wishes to stand in your name to know that you do not wish him or anybody else to represent you. For that purpose you should sign the form that has been prepared for your signature. It is your duty also to tell your co-voters what they should do.

You know why it is wrong to enter the Councils. The Government have declined to grant justice to the Punjab. British Ministers have broken their pledged word to the Mussalmans and otherwise ignored the deepest Mussalman sentiments regarding the Khilafat.

We must get these wrongs righted, and in order to prevent a recurrence of such injustice or bad faith we must obtain full *Swaraj* and must get rid of the badge of inferiority. We cannot do this by going to the Councils, nor can we gain Swaraj by going there. On the contrary although our representatives may vote against unjust Government measures and thus (*sic*) be unwilling instruments of injustice. The best way therefore for conserving our honour, hastening the advent of Swaraj and righting those wrongs is for the voters not to send any representatives to the Councils."

In pursuance of the Non-co-operation policy formulated at the Calcutta Congress extremists generally refrained from either standing for election or voting, but they were unable to prevent the Councils from being filled. Some exceptions were made with the object of throwing ridicule on these bodies and Non-co-operators succeeded in electing a *muchi* to represent a Noakhali constituency in the Bengal

******Vide* **the History of the N. C. O. movement in Bombay City.**

Council, and a sweetmeat seller to represent Delhi in the Legislative Assembly. The supporters of these candidates evidently intended that they should not occupy their seats, but both of them discovered that there were certain financial benefits involved of which they made full use, and the experiment of returning illiterates was not repeated at the next election.

CHAPTER II

Non-co-operation gains strength, 1921.

18. **Congress machinery.**—The subsidiary machinery which the Congress had at its disposal for carrying on the Non-co-operation agitation consisted of the All-India Congress Committee, which was ostensibly an assembly of representatives elected by the members of the National Congress; and the Working Committee, which was a small executive body of fifteen Congress leaders, whose duty it was, under the supervision of the All-India Congress Committee, to guide and control the execution of the policy in the various phases dictated, from time to time, by the central body. In each province Congress activities were regulated and controlled by the Provincial Congress Committees, which transmitted the policy and directions of the Working Committee to the District Congress Committee while co-ordinating and generally supervising their work. The organisation was, as intended, an effective machine for carrying on Non-co-operation agitation. It was also designed to provide a framework of National Government which was to be set up in supersession of the Imperial Government in the event of the failure of the latter to accede to the demands of the National Congress.

In taking a retrospect of the Non-co-operation Movement probably the best method of reviewing its progress and development will be to consider the various pronouncements and declarations of policy embodied in the resolutions passed by the National Congress and by the All-India Congress Committee and the Working Committee at the periodic sessions of those bodies.

19 **The Nagpur Congress, Christmas 1920.**—The annual session of the National Congress held at Nagpur in X'mas week 1920, having amended the Congress creed so as to define the object of the Indian National Congress as " the attainment of Swaraj by the people of India by all legitimate and peaceful means ", gave to the country the programme which will now be outlined. Before proceeding to the programme, the point must be emphasised that henceforth the object of the National Congress was no longer the attainment of self-government within the British Empire, but merely the attainment of self-government. Whether within or without the British Empire was left for events to decide, because any attempt to define the meaning of that self-government would have split the Congress into as many factions as each had a different nostrum to offer. The failure to face so important a question is indicative of the difficulty which the Congress has invariably experienced in maintaining even a semblance of unity within its ranks.

To proceed to the details of the programme laid down at Nagpur. The Congress reaffirmed the resolution on Non-co-operation passed at the Special Session at Calcutta and declared that the entire or any part or parts of the scheme of non-violent Non-co-operation, (with the renunciation of voluntary association with the present government at one end and the refusal to pay taxes at the other) should be put into force at a time to be determined by either the Indian National Congress or the All-India Congress Committee, and that in the mean-time the country should be prepared for that scheme by continuing to take effective steps to:—

Educational: (1) call upon the parents and guardians of school children under the age of 16 years to make greater efforts to withdraw them from schools, owned, aided or controlled by the Government, and concurrently to provide for their training in National Schools or by other means;

(2) call upon students aged 16 or over to withdraw without delay, irrespective of consequences, from the institutions mentioned above, if they felt it against their conscience "to continue in institution dominated by a system of Government which the Nation had solemnly resolved to end". Such students were advised either to devote themselves to some special service or to continue their education in National institutions;

(3) call upon trustees, managers and teachers of Government affiliated or aided schools, and municipalities and local boards to help to nationalise them;

Legal: (4) call upon lawyers to make greater effort to suspend their practice and to devote their attention to the national service including the boycott of Law-courts by litigants and fellow-lawyers and the settlement of disputes by private arbitration;

Commercial Boycott: (5) call upon merchants and traders to carry out a gradual boycott of foreign trade relations, to encourage hand spinning and weaving and to have a scheme of economic boycott planned and formulated by a committee of experts to be nominated by the All-India Congress Committee;

Popular Appeal: (6) call upon every section and every man and woman in the country to make the utmost possible contribution of self-sacrifice to the national movement;

Organisation: (7) organise committees in each village or group of villages with a provincial central organisation in the principal cities of each province to accelerate the progress of Non-co-operation;

(8) organise a band of national workers for a service to be called the Indian National Service;

Finance: (9) take effective steps to raise a National Fund to be called the All-India Tilak Memorial Swaraj Fund to finance the Indian National Service and the Non-co-operation Movement in general.

The National Congress also trusted that all persons who had been elected to the Reformed Council would resign their seats.

20. **Government Services.**—Its attitude towards the Government services was defined as follows: The Congress, while recognising the growing friendliness between the Police and soldiery on the one hand and the people on the other, hoped that the former would refuse to subordinate their creed and country to the fulfilment of the orders of their officers. The Congress appealed to all persons in Government service, pending the call of the nation, to resign their service, to help the national cause by imparting greater kindness and stricter honesty to their dealings with the people, and fearlessly and openly to attend all popular gatherings while refraining from taking any active part in them, and more especially by openly rendering financial assistance to the national movement.

21. **Non-violence and Religious Tolerance.**—The National Congress next laid special stress on the observance of the principle of non-violence and called on all public associations to advance and foster Hindu-Moslem Unity. To Hindus it appealed for the settlement of all disputes between Brahmins and non-Brahmins and for a special effort to rid Hinduism of the reproach of the untouchability of certain of its castes. It also urged the heads of the Hindu religion to reform Hinduism in the matter of the treatment of its "suppressed classes"

22. **Exploitation of Exchange Disputes.**—Not content with this already comprehensive programme of unification and composition of its own religious and caste differences, combined with active hostility, non-violent though it was, to the Imperial Government, the Congress next turned its attention to the question of exchange which by its fluctuations had caused many Indian merchants to refuse to fulfil their commercial contracts with British exporters. Relations were already very strained between the parties concerned so the Congress thought this might be useful fuel for the fire they were arranging to kindle. Accordingly it passed a resolution accusing H. M.'s Government and the Government of India of manipulating the exchanges to their own advantage and declared its opinion that Indian importers, merchants, etc., of British goods would be entirely justified in refusing to complete their contracts at the rates of exchange then current. It also appointed a committee "to deal effectively with the situation." The report of this Committee, when eventually published, was neither useful nor important to the agitation and need not be referred to again.

23. **Boycott of H. R. H. the Duke of Connaught's visit.**—As a further mark of its displeasure with the Government and all its doings, the Congress called on the Indian people to refrain from taking any part in functions or festivities in honour of H. R. H. the Duke of Connaught during his visit to India.

24. **Labour Policy.**—After these digressions, the Congress defined its attitude and policy regarding the organisation of the Labour Force of India. This resolution is worth recording in detail. The Congress

expressed its fullest sympathy with the workers of India in their struggle to secure their legitimate rights by the organisation of Trade Unions, and condemned the brutal policy of treating the lives of Indian workers as of no account under the false pretext of preserving law and order. It also expressed its opinion that Indian Labour should be organised in order to improve and promote its well-being and to secure its just rights as well as to prevent the exploitation (1) of Indian Labour, (2) of Indian resources by foreign agencies. It appointed a sub-committee " to take active steps in this behalf."

This resolution was important in that a potentially effective labour organisation, the All-India Trade Union Congress, had already been inaugurated at Bombay in October 1919 which, through its Secretary, Diwan Chaman Lal, maintained the closest touch with a pro-Communist group in London—the Workers Welfare League of India. Through this London group it was connected with British Labour extremists and Communists, who in their turn were in communication with Moscow; to which place they looked for guidance and financial help. The first part of this resolution on Labour was moved by Diwan Chaman Lal (Punjab)—

Seconded by	...	V. Chakkarai Chetti (Madras).
Supported by	...	K. P. S. Sinha (Behar).
Supported by	...	E. L. Iyer (Madras).
Supported by	...	D. D. Sathaye (Bombay).
Supported by	...	Jitendra Lal Banarji (Bengal).

The Second part was proposed by Lajpat Rai (Punjab).

Seconded by	...	C. R. Das (Bengal).
Supported by	...	Swami Govindand (Sindh).

Most of these, and the organisations with which they are concerned, will again be conspicuous when the time comes to consider the effects of the influence of the Non-co-operators on the Indian Labour Movement and the use to which they have sought to put that movement. It is interesting to note that the Congress Labour Sub-Committee consisted of—

1. Lajpat Rai, *President*.
2. Joseph Baptista.
3. E. L. Aiyar.
4. L. G. Khare.
5. C. R. Das.
6. G. B. Deshpande.
7. Mrs. Anasuya Ben,
8. Pandit Ram Bhaj Dutt Chowdhury.
9. Dr. N. Singh, *Secretary*.

of whom the first four also figured on the Standing Committee of the All-India Trade Union Congress of which Lajpat Rai and J. Baptista were President and Vice-President, respectively.

25. **Effect of the Nagpur Resolutions.**—The next event of importance in the Non-co-operation Movement was the session of the All-India Congress Committee at Bezwada in the Madras Presidency on the 1st of April. The interval between this meeting and the close of the National Congress at Nagpur had been devoted to propaganda tours by Gandhi and the Ali Brothers while provincial Congress leaders were busy explaining and promulgating in their respective provinces the resolutions passed at Nagpur. In Bengal C. R. Das with B. C. Pal, and in the Punjab, Lajpat Rai, made determined efforts to "empty" Government and Government-aided schools and colleges. Both met with considerable, though temporary, success. The success was temporary because, firstly, they had no Congress substitute to offer for the institutions they persuaded the students to leave and, secondly, because they had no organised national employment to offer enthusiastic young Nationalists. When this became clear to the students, most of them returned to work more or less disgusted at this reckless and unscrupulous attempt to exploit their enthusiasm. Another factor in the failure of this attempt to stampede the student community was the opposition of parents and guardians who were not disposed to see their sons and charges lose a year of their educational career under the plea that "education could wait but Swaraj could not"

This movement was reflected in the other Provinces, notably Bombay and Bihar and Orissa, but more feebly and with still less ultimate success. In Madras and Assam little was done, but Bihar and Orissa showed much activity in spreading a net-work of local bodies called "panchayats" in the rural tracts and both Bihar and Orissa and the United Provinces devoted much attention to the fostering and propagating of *Kisan Sabhas* or "Peasants' Associations". In this aspect of the movement Non-co-operators, while initiating peasants into the new Congress doctrine, fomented their grievances against their landlords and the Government which, they were taught to believe, existed to support and protect the former. In the United Provinces both at the end of 1920 and the beginning of 1921 the *Kisan Sabha* movement, which was under the guidance of Moti Lal Nehru and Jawahar Lal Nehru, had been, in conjunction with some actual oppression of tenants, responsible for serious agrarian disturbances.

By this time in all Provinces a systematic agitation against the Government had commenced under the two pretexts—the "Punjab Atrocities" and the "Khilafat Wrongs". The organisation of village propaganda particularly through 'panchayats' and arbitration courts had made its appearance and the other features of the agitation, *e.g.*, the renunciation of honorary posts and honours, suspension of practice by lawyers, the temperance movement, etc., were already becoming familiar. Originally the salient idea in adding temperance to the list was, following the Irish Sein Fein example, to deprive the Government of its Excise Revenue. The moral and religious aspect was a minor consideration, though naturally for propaganda purposes it was made to appear the only one. Thus the Government became the protagonist of drink and all its evils, while Gandhi and his followers waged a righteous battle against the Government and its iniquitous traffic.

26. **Bezwada Session of the All-India Congress Committee, 1st April 1921.**—At Bezwada the All-India Congress Committee estimated the progress made and appreciated the general situation in the following resolutions:—

(1) It congratulated the country on the rapid progress made in organising *panchayats* and expected still greater efforts to boycott Government Law Courts.

(2) It congratulated the country on taking up the temperance campaign and hoped to see the habit of intoxicating drink and drugs totally disappear.

(3) It adopted civil disobedience in principle but the terms of a resolution on this point were left to be drafted by Gandhi.

(4) (*a*) The Committee was of opinion that the orders (under section 144 C. P. C.) of officials in various provinces against Non-co-operators in pursuit of the policy of repression were totally unwarranted by the situation in the country and were, in most cases, pronounced by the highest legal opinion to be illegal.

(*b*) The Committee believed the country had responded in a wonderful manner, and in face of grave provocation by the Government, to the principle of non-violence enjoined by the Congress.

(*c*) The Committee was of opinion that, apart from the fact that civil disobedience was not expressly prescribed in the Congress Resolution on Non-co-operation, the country was not yet sufficiently disciplined, organised and ripe for the immediate taking up of civil disobedience.

(*d*) The Committee by way of preparation advised all those upon whom orders might be served, voluntarily to conform to them, and trusted that new workers would take the place of those who might be disabled by the Government, and that the people at large would not be disheartened or frightened by such orders and would continue the work of quiet organisation and construction outlined by the Congress.

The Committee, sensible of the need adequately to finance their activities and to increase and organise the number of their supporters, resolved further that:—

All Congress organisations and workers should concentrate their energies chiefly upon:—

(a) bringing the Tilak Swaraj Fund to one crore of rupees before the 30th of June. Each Congress Province to collect in ratio to its population;

(b) registering one crore of Congress members before the 30th of June. Provinces to contribute in ratio to population;

(c) introducing into villages and houses 20 lakhs of spinning wheels in good working order before 30th June. Each Province to introduce wheels in ratio to population.

The qualifications of a Congress member were laid down as follows:—(1) The recruit must be over 20 years of age. (2) He or she must subscribe to the Congress creed: and (3) must pay an annual subscription of 4 annas.

The recruiting ground was thus the adult population of India able to pay 4 annas per annum, without any further qualification.

The ratios fixed for each Province were as under. This list will also serve to show the territorial distribution of Indian Provinces under the Congress. The distribution was fixed mainly on a linguistic basis:—

List of Congress Provinces.

—	Men.	Money.	Charkas.
Madras	6,50,000	6,50,000	1,30,000
Andhra	6,82,000	6,82,000	1,36,000
Karnatak	3,90,000	3,90,000	78,000
Kerala	2,27,000	2,27,000	45,000
Bombay	32,500	32,500	6,000
Maharashtra	3,90,000	3,90,000	78,000
Gujrat	3,57,000	3,57,000	71,000
Sindh	1,30,000	1,30,000	26,000
United Provinces	15,92,000	15,92,000	3,18,000
Punjab	8,77,000	8,77,000	1,76,000
North-West Frontier Province	97,500	97,500	20,000
Delhi	32,500	32,500	6,000
Ajmer-Merwara	6,17,000	6,17,000	1,23,000
C. P. (Hindi)	2,92,000	2,92,000	58,000 (78,000 "Young India" 15-6-21)
C. P. (Marathi)	97,500	97,500	19,400
Berar	97,500	97,500	19,400
Behar	9,42,000	9,42,000	1,88,000
Utkal	4,87,000	4,87,000	97,000
Bengal	15,27,000	15,27,000	3,05,000
Assam	1,30,000	1,30,000	26,000
Burma	3,90,000	3,90,000	78,000
Surma Valley	97,000	97,000	19,200
	101,34,500	101,34,500	20,23,000

According to confidential information, in addition to the above resolutions, which were published in the press, the Working Committee of the All-India Congress Committee at a secret session resolved that efforts should be made (1) to hinder recruitment in the Army, (2) to approach persons employed in the Army, the Police and the Civil Services to induce them to resign from the service of the Government, (3) to organise volunteer Corps to spread Non-co-operation and the Congress creed, (4) to enlist the service of Sadhus and religious ascetics for the above purposes, (5) to uplift the depressed classes, (6) to establish arbitration courts in all towns and villages.

27. **Congress leaders' views on the Bezwada Meeting.**—As to the inner meaning of the proceedings of the All-India Congress Committee the following authoritative dicta are illuminating. C. R. Das said that what they had to do was to collect men, money and munitions for their peaceful campaign. The *Independent* of Allahabad, a journal owned and directed by Pandit Moti Lal Nehru, considered the activities of the Bezwada Session might be summed up under two heads:—(1) Consolidation. (2) The determination to create an alternative National Government.

If, the paper argued, they could constitute an electorate on a franchise wider and more equal than that of the Government such an electorate would be more authoritative than the Government's and would be more representative than the Reformed Councils. After June 30th this electorate could vote on and pass civil disobedience and the non-payment of taxes with the prospect of carrying them out immediately. In other words a Special Session of the Congress meeting after June the 30th would be representative and would have the authority of a true legislative body. The Working Committee would then have the power of a true Government executive against which the authority of the Reformed Councils and their mixed Cabinets could not avail. A genuine alternative Government would come into being, the sanction of its existence being the consent of the electorate and its readiness to sustain its opinion through suffering, and if need be, to death.

Regarding the call for the introduction of the spinning wheel the *Independent* thought that this would mark the end of the country's economic dependence. "More than all, the revolutionary employment of the people in the work of the spinning wheel will band them all in a spiritual brotherhood going out to do bloodless battle for the nation's freedom."

The Tilak Swaraj Fund it regarded as the Nation's strike fund against the day of the National Strike.

28. **Muhammad Ali's Speech *re* an Afghan invasion.**—After the Bezwada meeting, Gandhi and the Ali Brothers made a propagandist tour in the Madras Presidency. This tour was chiefly remarkable for an indiscreet speech by Muhammad Ali at Madras on the 2nd April 1921 on the duties of Muslims in the event of an

Afghan invasion. He said that if the Amir of Afghanistan or any outside power were to invade India to subjugate its people it was the duty of Muslims to resist the attack. But if the Amir of Afghanistan were to invade India, not with a view to its subjugation, but to attack those who wished to subjugate his people, who held the Holy Places of Islam, who wished to crush Islam and to destroy the Muslim faith and the Khilafat, then it would be the duty of Muslims not merely to refuse to assist the Government but to gird up their oins and fight the good fight for Islam.

This declaration caused uneasiness to Hindus who had no illusions as to how they were likely to fare in the event of such an invasion, the object of which might be interpreted by Muhammad Ali and his brother Moslems as they thought fit. This uneasiness was not calculated to cement the ties of Hindu-Moslem Unity and, for some time, in order to distract attention from it, the extremist press continued to agitate, and to minimise what it decided to label the "Afghan Bogey". The views of the Hindu leaders of Non-co-operation on this matter were announced in speeches at the Allahabad District Conference early in May. Some of these views are reproduced as showing the lengths to which Hindu leaders were compelled to go in order to preserve their principle of Hindu-Moslem Unity and also the bitterness they openly exhibited towards the Government.

Gandhi said* that if Afghanistan should invade India he would tell Indians not to assist the Government. At the time of such an invasion the Government should expect no assistance from them unless it promised them Swaraj. They wanted to mend or end the Government which had ordered the Punjabis to crawl (at Amritsar). Lajpat Rai, speaking on the same question, said they could never co-operate with this Government under any circumstances. It would be better for Hindus to be the slaves of Muslims rather than of another nation. It was preferable to die fighting one another than to live under foreign rule.

29. **Working Committee Meeting, Allahabad, 12th May.**—The Working Committee next met at Allahabad and its members attended the Allahabad District Conference. No copies were published of any formal resolutions passed but the meeting was notable as it considered the matter of Gandhi's then forthcoming interview with H. E. the Viceroy. As the discussions of the Committee were private, there is naturally no authentic record of what passed at them, but according to confidential and reliable information, Gandhi and Moti Lal Nehru were in favour of effecting a compromise with the Government at that stage, but were opposed by Muhammad Ali and Lajpat Rai on the ground that the Government would not permit the continuance of the agitation while the compromise was under discussion, and if the agitation were allowed to subside, it would not be possible to revive it to the strength and the dimensions it had

---

*Part II, paragraph 83.

attained. As regards the minimum demands acceptable, Lajpat Rai is reported to have expressed his willingness to accept Home Rule within the British Empire provided substantial reforms were granted at once and repression was stopped immediately. Muhammad Ali held that there could be no settlement of the Khilafat question which did not include Palestine.

Shortly after this Gandhi left for Simla where he had a series of private interviews with H. E. the Viceroy. He left Simla on the 19th of May.

30. **Working Committee Meeting, Bombay, 14th and 15th June.**—The Working Committee again met at Bombay on the 14th and 15th of June. The principal items on the agenda were:—

(1) The situation in respect of the collections for the Tilak Swaraj Fund.

(2) To consider a request by the Lahore City Congress Committee to start civil disobedience in the matter of the refusal of the District Authorities under the Seditious Meetings Act to permit meetings of the Committee.

(3) The duty of Non-co-operators proceeded against under the law.

(4) Congress elections.

(5) The duty of Indians in the event of hostilities being re-opened between the British Government and the Turkish Government at Angora.

The Working Committee promulgated the following decisions:—

(1) Collections made for, or donations given to local institutions or for local needs arising out of Non-co-operation may be retained wholly by the organisers concerned and at their instance might be considered part of the Tilak Swaraj Fund. It was open to donors to the Fund to earmark their donations for specific purposes so long as these purposes were not inconsistent with the objects of the Fund.*

(2) Permission to the Lahore City Congress Committee to start civil disobedience was refused until the All-India Congress Committee decided on that step.

(3) Non-co-operators in the event of prosecution should not participate in the proceedings beyond making to the Court a full statement of the facts in order to establish their innocence before the public. If security was demanded from Non-co-operators under the Criminal Procedure Code, they should refuse to offer security and should offer to

*Note.—At that time it appeared extremely improbable that the collections for the Tilak Swaraj Fund would approach anything like the total of a crore of rupees which had been fixed at Bezwada and this resolution was tantamount to permitting all collections, made since the beginning of the movement to be reckoned towards that total.

undergo imprisonment. The Working Committee was also of opinion that lawyers were precluded from appearing as counsel with or without payment.

(4) In order to secure adequate representation of Muslims, all Congress bodies were advised to give full effect in Congress elections to the proportion fixed in the Lucknow Pact of 1916.

(5) With reference to the propriety of Indians assisting the British Government in the event of hostilities being re-opened by the British Government against the Turkish Government at Angora, the Working Committee was of opinion that, consistently with the Non-co-operation Resolution adopted by the special session of the Congress at Calcutta, it was the duty of every Indian to refrain from helping the British Government in the prosecution of such hostilities in direct defiance of Muslim opinion and it was, therefore, the duty of every Indian to decline to serve in connection therewith.

31. **Situation on the 30th June in regard to the Bezwada Resolutions.**—When the 30th of June arrived it was triumphantly announced by Gandhi after a very strenuous personal canvass in Bombay, that the crore of rupees fixed at Bezwada had been collected The Provincial contributions announced were as follows:—

Province.	Rupees in lakhs.
Bombay City	37½
Bengal	25
Gujerat and Kathiawar	15
Punjab	5
Madras and Andhra	4
Central Provinces and Berar	3
Maharashtra (including Bombay suburbs)	3
Behar	3
Sind	2
Burma	1¼
United Provinces	2½
Karnatak	1
Delhi	2
Ajmer and Merwara	½
Orissa, Assam, etc.	¼
Total	105

There is good ground to discount a considerable proportion of these claims but, after making all allowance for exaggeration and mis-statement, the fact unquestionably remains that the sums collected in the time were sufficiently large to constitute a notable achievement and a record in Indian agitation. Of the other items of the Bezwada programme little was said because little had been done.

32. **Session of the All-India Congress Committee, Bombay, 28th to 30th July.**—The All-India Congress Committee met at Bombay on the 28th to the 30th of July.

It passed resolutions that:—

(1) If the British Government persisted in bringing to India the Prince of Wales in spite of the growing unrest and discontent, it was the duty of everyone to refrain from participating in, or assisting in, any welcome to H. R. H., or in any functions organised officially or otherwise in connection with the visit.

(2) In order to attain Swaraj, and to secure redress of the Punjab and Khilafat grievances during the year, the Committee advised all Congress organisations to concentrate on attaining a complete boycott of foreign cloth by the 30th of September, and on the manufacture of country-made cloth by stimulating hand-spinning and hand-weaving. Accordingly it called on all persons belonging to the Congress to discard foreign cloth from the 1st day of August and advised all Congress organisations:—

(1) To utilise all national institutions as far as possible for hand-spinning and hand weaving.

(2) To introduce spinning wheels in such homes as did not yet possess them.

(3) To take a census in every district of weavers and to induce them to use hand-spun yarn as far as possible, and otherwise Indian mill-spun yarn.

(4) To open depots for the supply of country-made cloth, spinning wheels, hand-looms and accessories.

(5) To collect foreign cloth from consumers for destruction, or use outside India according to option.

The Committee invited mill-agents and shareholders in Indian cloth mills to support the national effort by regulating the price of their products, so as to bear a proportion to the wages of the mill hands and other expenditure, so that the products might be within the reach of the poorest. It trusted that in no case would prices be raised above the rates then prevailing. The Committee further invited importers of foreign cloth and yarn to co-operate with the nation by immediately stopping all foreign orders and by endeavouring to dispose of their stocks, as far as possible, outside India.

The Committee deplored the mob excesses that had been committed at Malegaon and at Aligarh " even though under great provocation ", and congratulated the Indian people on the complete self-restraint they had exhibited, notwithstanding grave provocation, at several places named, including Dharwar. The attitude of the Congress and the relation of Non-co-operation to the numerous instances of mob violence and intimidation which occurred during the year will be discussed elsewhere. As regards those who had lost their lives, the Committee reserved its sympathy entirely for the rioters and the following passage is instructive:—" The Committee tenders sympathy and congratulations to the families of those who lost their lives by unprovoked fire opened by local auhorities at several places; and congratulates all brave and innocent citizens who have been wounded or suffering imprisonment." Of those unfortunate Police Officers who had been savagely done to death and burnt at Malegaon there was no word beyond the perfunctory deprecation of mob excesses.

The Congress Committee held that the way to freedom lay only " through the imprisonment, without defence, of innocent men and women ".

The All-India Congress Committee also considered its position in relation to the sanctioning of civil disobedience. Towards this matter the attitude of the delegates was interesting. Reliable information shows that, though most Provinces had asked for its initiation in one form or another, most of the delegates at Bombay were actually opposed to it. The Resolution on the subject noted the reasonable desire of workers in various parts of the country to take up civil disobedience in answer to the repressive measures of Local Governments. In order to test, however, the measure of influence attained by the Congress over the people, and also to retain on the part of the nation, an atmosphere free for the proper and swift prosecution of the Khaddar campaign, the Committee was of opinion that civil disobedience should be postponed till after the completion of the programme relating to foreign and homespun cloth. After this programme had been successfully carried through, the Committee would not hesitate, if necessary, to recommend a course of civil disobedience. Nevertheless, the Committee declared it open to any province or place to adopt civil disobedience, subject to the approval of the Working Committee, to be obtained through the Provincial Congress Committees concerned.

Another important step taken by the All-India Congress Committee at this session was its authorisation of the Working Committee to " take all such action as may be necessary to give effect to the resolutions of the Congress and of the All-India Congress Committee, and to deal with all matters with which the All-India Congress Committee is empowered to deal, and which may arise while this Committee is not sitting and which may require urgent attention ". Thus, in effect, complete control of the movement was formally handed over to the Working Committee, a step which caused considerable misgiving even to ardent Non-co-operators.

The following composed the Working Committee at that time:—

Ex-officio	1. C. Bijoyraghavachariar	President.
	2. Pandit Motilal Nehru	General Secretaries.
	3. Dr. M. A. Ansari	
	4. C. Rajgopalachariar	
	5. Seth Jamnalal Bajaj	Treasurers.
	6. Umar Sobhani	
	7. M. K. Gandhi	Bombay.
	8. Lajpat Rai	Punjab.
	9. C. R. Das	Bengal and Assam.
	10. Muhammad Ali	Khilafat.
	11. N. C. Kelkar	Maharashtra (Bombay.)
	12. Hakim Ajmal Khan	Khilafat.
	13. K. Venkalappaya	Andhra (Madras.)
	14. Rajendra Prasad	Bihar and Orissa.
	15. V. J. Patel	Maharashtra (Bombay).

This meeting of the All-India Congress Committee expressed its attitude towards the temperance movement, in connection with which the use of coercion and violence by its adherents was conspicuous. The Committee noted with deep satisfaction the growth of public opinion against the use and sale of intoxicating liquors or drugs as shown by the peacefully picketting shops licensed for the purpose of selling them, and it noted with concern the undue and improper interference, commenced by the Government in various parts of the country, with the recognised right of the public to wean weak members from temptations to visit such shops In the event of such interference being persisted in, the Committee would be prepared to recommend the continuance of picketting in disregard of such interference. What the methods of weaning weak members from temptation included will appear when considering the general propaganda and methods of the movement.

38. **Committee for Propaganda in the Army.**—Up to this time there had been no open and organised campaign to seduce the Army from its duty* but it now appeared, from confidential information regarding the unpublished doings of the Working Committee, that a committee for propaganda in the Army was formed consisting of:—

M. K. Gandhi,
Muhammad Ali,
Abul Kalam Azad, and
Lajpat Rai.

It appeared from the proceedings also that it was claimed that successful work had been carried on among Jat regiments from a propaganda centre at Aligarh, and that Sardul Singh Cavessiur, a

*Part II, paragraph 94.

Sikh malcontent, had been at work among Sikh Regiments. This man acted as the link between the Congress extremists and the Sikh extremist organisations and had been convicted and imprisoned shortly before this Bombay Session of the Committee. It was stated that though his conviction would hamper the work, two other good men were working and Lajpat Rai expected to get more. Work among Pathans had been satisfactory but they had no one to work among the Gurkhas. Soldiers were asked not to resign, nor to mutiny, nor to raise any trouble in their units, but when the message came they should not fire on their countrymen.

As will appear later the organised campaign against the Army and the Police was opened by a religious *fatwa** issued by extremist Ulemas from Delhi, and the Congress supported the campaign under the pretext of challenging and denouncing the Government's right to interfere in what it sought to represent as a purely religious matter. At the close of the year a similar exploitation of Hinduism was contemplated on the score of protection of the cow.

Another small item and this resumé of the proceedings of the All-India Congress Committee at Bombay may be closed. Much was made of the fact, in the Extremist press, that C. R. Das was unanimously elected by Provincial Congress Committees to be President of the Session of the National Congress at Ahmedabad in December. It subsequently appeared, however, that confidential letters had issued from the Working Committee to Provincial organisations requesting that C. R. Das might be so elected and the elections were declared in accordance with this inspiration.

34. **Meeting of the Working Committee, Patna, 17th August.**—Little of interest occurred at this meeting of the Working Committee. The real reason for the selection of Patna as a meeting place was the necessity of guarding against trouble between Hindus and Muslims during the festival of the Bakr-Id. Gandhi and others made special tours in the areas where riots were most feared by the Provincial Congress and Khilafat leaders, to appeal for the preservation of peace and non-violence. Thanks to special precautions by the Government and these efforts by non-co-operators, the festival passed without disturbance.

The Working Committee resolved that, to effect a complete boycott of foreign cloth by the 30th of September, it was necessary that foreign cloth from every house should be collected by volunteers, under proper control, to be specially set apart for the purpose.

It also called on all Provincial Committees to spend on Swadeshi not less than one-fourth of its contributions to the Tilak Swaraj Fund.

35. **Meeting of the Working Committee, Calcutta, 9th September.**—During the interval between the Patna meeting and the re-assembly of the Committee at Calcutta, Gandhi and Muhammad Ali had been on a propaganda tour in Assam and a part of Bengal. The peace of

---

***Part II, paragraph 75 and Appendix G.**

their progress was rudely shattered by the news of the Moplah outbreak in Malabar, which was widely and very naturally believed to be a direct outcome of Khilafat propaganda. Since there was little to choose between the leaders of Non-co-operation and the leaders of Khilafat it behoved both to repudiate responsibility and inconvenient facts as early as might be. Accordingly a resolution was published to the following effect by the Working Committee:—

The Working Committee deeply regretted the acts of violence committed by the Moplahs—such acts being evidence of the fact that there were still people in India who had not understood the message of the National Congress and the Central Khilafat Committee. It called every Congress and Khilafat worker to spread the message of non-violence—even under the gravest provocation—throughout the length and breadth of India. The Working Committee desired it to be known that evidence in its possession showed that provocation beyond endurance had been given to the Moplahs, and that the reports published by and on behalf of the Government, gave a one-sided and highly exaggerated account of the wrongs done by the Moplahs and an understatement of the needless destruction of life resorted to by the Government in the name of peace and order.

The Working Committee regretted to find that there had been instances of so-called forcible conversions (of Hindus to Islam) by some fanatics among the Moplahs, but warned the public against believing the Government's inspired versions of such happenings. it then quoted a report supplied by its local organisation which stated that the organisation had only heard of 3 cases of such conversion and that these were the acts of a fanatic gang which was always opposed to the Khilafat and Non-co-operation movements, and further that disturbances had taken place only in areas in which Congress and Khilafat activities had been prohibited by the authorities.

Perhaps the pithiest commentary on this laboured and disingenuous defence was that in certain Taluks, where the rebels obtained a temporary sway, they declared that they had set up Khilafat Kingdoms, while the campaign of murder, violence and loot against the Hindu population continued with unabated zeal.

The Working Committee also empowered Gandhi to sanction civil disobedience in respect of the grazing tax in certain parts of Andhra, should the situation warrant it and if such a step were consistent with non-violence. It does not appear that Gandhi ever did sanction this particular form of disobedience in Andhra, but that made little difference to the local leaders of Non-co-operation who successfully incited the peasantry to disregard the Forest laws, to graze their crops on forest lands, and to carry off forest produce in defiance of the law and the forest officials.

36. **Meeting of the Working Committee, Bombay, the 5th October.**—When the Working Committee next met at Bombay on the 5th October an important event had taken place in the arrest of the

Ali Brothers* and five other leaders as the result of a Resolution they had been instrumental in passing at the Khilafat Conference in Karachi† on July 10th. This resolution declared it unlawful for any Muslim to serve in the Army or to assist in recruiting for the Army; also that, should the British Government fight openly or secretly with the Turkish Government at Angora, the Muslims of India would start civil disobedience and would declare complete independence at the next session of the Congress at Ahmedabad where an Indian Republic would be declared. For this the Ali Brothers and 5 others were arrested just after the Calcutta Session of the Working Committee and proceedings were instituted against them, under section 120B read with section 131 and under section 505 read with sections 109 and 117 of the Indian Penal Code, for attempting to seduce Mussulman officers and soldiers in the Army from their duty. The reply of the Working Committee to this prosecution was to congratulate those arrested on their prosecution, to declare that the subject matter of the prosecution virtually reaffirmed the principle already laid down by the Congress at Calcutta and Nagpur and that it was contrary to the national interest and the national dignity for any Indian to engage or remain in the service of the Government in any capacity whatsoever—a Government that had used the Army and Police to repress the just aspirations of the people and to crush the national spirit of the Egyptians, the Turks, the Arabs and other nations.

The Working Committee declared further that it had been deterred from calling out soldiers and civilians in the name of the Congress only because the Congress was not yet ready to support those who left the service of Government and who were without other means of livelihood. Nevertheless the Committee declared its opinion that it was the clear duty of every Government employee whether soldier or civilian, able to support himself without Congress assistance, to leave the service of Government. The Committee pointedly drew the attention of all Indian soldiers and police to its statement that hand-spinning and hand-weaving offered them an honourable means of independent livelihood. Lastly the Committee declared its opinion that the reasons given for the prosecution of the Ali Brothers and their co-accused constituted an undue interference with religious liberty.

So, at this stage, the object of the Congress-Khilafat campaign was to paralyse the executive force of the Government under the cry that "Government was unduly interfering with their religion." Had no action been taken by the Government the campaign would still have been carried on by the Khilafat Party by the exploitation and dissemination of the religious *fatwa* of the Muslim extremist divines which declared service in the Police and the Army religiously unlawful. Now that the Government had acted both organisations called on their subordinate branches to carry on this portion of the campaign with redoubled vigour; the Congress by demanding the

*Part II, paragraph 98.
†Part II, paragraph 92.

adoption at public meetings of the resolution outlined above; the Khilafat by the reaffirmation of the Karachi resolution on similar occasions and by the general dissemination of leaflets containing the proscribed *fatwa* Combined action by the Hindus and Muslim leaders was taken on this occasion at Bombay in the preparation and publication of an artfully worded manifesto over the signature of 50 leaders. This document stated that the signatories, speaking in their individual capacity, declared it to be the inherent right of every-one to express his opinion without restraint on the propriety of citizens offering their services to, or remaining in the employ of the Government in the Civil or Military Departments. The signatories declared that it was contrary to the national dignity for any Indian to serve as a civilian or more especially as a soldier, and that it was the duty of every Indian soldier and civilian to sever his connection with the Government and to find some other means of livelihood.

37. **The comments of the "Tribune".**—The remarks of the *Tribune* of Lahore (11th October) on this manifesto are worthy of reproduction. This journal consistently maintained a friendly attitude to Non-co-operators and Non-co-operation, though not hesitating to offer amicable criticism at times. It is pre-eminently a Nationalist organ sympathising with and in touch with Nationalist politics and politicians, and as such the following passage has peculiar significance. After pointing out various defects in the manifesto and its implications the paper continued:—

"Let us hasten to add that from the point of view of the signatories to the manifesto as well as the Working Committee, all this is of no account. They, or at any rate many of them, believe in the first place that this system of government that we have in India, is the worst of all possible evils and secondly and consequently that anything would be better than it, be it anarchy, chaos, confusion and widespread disorders".

This assertion was not put forward as a mere deduction, however obvious, from the tactics of the Non-co-operators, but was definitely made as if from the knowledge and information of one well-qualified to speak.

38. **Resolutions regarding Boycotts and Civil Disobedience.**—To return to the proceedings of the Working Committee. Regarding the boycott of foreign cloth the Committee had to regret, that in spite of considerable progress, it had not been completed in the two months allowed for its completion by the All-India Congress Committee. The Working Committee called for special efforts on the part of all subordinate organisations to complete the boycott by the end of October.

As to civil disobedience which most of the members were desirous of voting, Gandhi secured the passage of a resolution declaring it not possible to authorise any general plan of civil disobedience in any Congress district or province where the effective boycott of foreign cloth had not been completed, and sufficient country-made cloth was not manufactured by hand-spinning and hand-weaving for the wants of the District or Province concerned. But the Committee authorised civil disobedience by individuals who might be hindered in the prosecution of the Swadeshi propaganda, provided that it was done under the authority of the Provincial Congress Committee and that the Provincial Committee were assured of the non-violent atmosphere being retained.

In the matter of the attitude of Non-co-operators to the visit of H. R. H. the Prince of Wales, the Working Committee advanced beyond their former position and now recommended a general voluntary *hartal* throughout India with " an effective boycott " of any public welcome to H. R. H. during his visit to India. The Working Committee left the necessary arrangements to the Provincial Congress Committees concerned. This step was to have disastrous consequences at Bombay when H. R. H. landed in India, while in Calcutta this behest was to be utilised to produce so intolerable a state of coercion and intimidation, together with an almost general suspension of the business of the city, that action against the organisation responsible could be no longer delayed.

39. **Foreign Policy.**—At this meeting the Working Committee adopted and published, for public criticism and for submission to the All-India Congress Committee, its long delayed resolution on the Foreign Policy of the Congress. The Working Committee recommended that the Congress should let it be known to the neighbouring and other States—

(1) That the Government of India in no way represents Indian opinion. Its traditional policy has been more to hold India under subjection than to protect her borders.

(2) That India, as a self-governing country, can have nothing to fear from any state and has no intention of establishing trade relations inimical or unacceptable to any State.

(3) That India considers most of the treaties entered into by the Imperial Government with neighbouring states as mainly designed to perpetuate the exploitation of India by the Imperial power. It, therefore, urges all friendly disposed states to refrain from entering into any treaty with the Imperial power.

(4) That when India has attained self-government Mussalman states should feel assured that her foreign policy will always be guided so as to respect Mussalman religious obligations.

40. **Retirement of the President of the Working Committee.**—After the last session of the All-India Congress Committee at Bombay at the end of July, the Working Committee had shed its President Bijoyraghavachari of Madras. The manner in which the Congress elections had been conducted in Bengal and Madras had been challenged at the previous session; and though the President ruled that the elections had been improperly held he very inconsistently

permitted the delegates concerned to participate in the proceedings. The Working Committee had considered the matter further and in the voluntary absence of the Chairman passed a resolution shelving the constitutional question involved and requesting aggrieved parties, for the sake of the urgent work in hand, to lay aside their grievances and devote their whole energies to the campaign.

The President apparently disliked the way events were tending and returned to the charge later by circularising Provincial organisations to regard the session of the A. I. C. Committee as cancelled, pending the holding of new elections, as the events under consideration were so important that the electorate should have the opportunity to express its views again. The Working Committee issued opposing circulars and the President accordingly dropped out of the Committee and its activities, having met with negligible support from the subordinate organisations.

41. **Delhi Session of the All-India Congress Committee, 4th and 5th Novomber.**—The All-India Congress Committee met at Delhi on the 4th and 5th of November, to take stock of the situation and to consider the further action to be pursued during the period before the session of the National Congress at Ahmedabad at the end of December. The feature of this Delhi session was the restiveness displayed by a large proportion of the delegates against Gandhi's shyness of declaring mass civil disobedience immediately. The result of the struggle was a curious resolution which, while permitting civil disobedience, in effect forbade it by the strictness and extent of the limitations it imposed. The explanation of its acceptance by an impatient assembly lay in Gandhi's announcement that he hoped to start civil disobedience personally, in the Bardoli Taluk of the Surat District, Bombay Presidency, by November the 23rd. This was to be a crucial test besides affording a valuable object-lesson for imitators. It seems correct to say that the Committee gave a grumbling assent to the scheme, mainly out of personal regard for Gandhi and a feeling that he should be allowed to have his own way in his own movement till the end of the year within which he had promised " Swaraj ". It seemed clear that after that time Gandhi would have served his turn and if he failed to produce Swaraj as promised he would have to make way for other leaders and other methods. The treatment accorded to Bijoyraghavachari, and even to B. C. Pal earlier in the year, showed that the Nationalist machine would ruthlessly reject old and trusted leaders who could not or would not keep up with its reckless career. B. C. Pal as President of the Bengal Provincial Conference had pleaded for a definition of the Swaraj the Congress was striving for, and had defined his own ideal as a democratic Swaraj founded on village institutions, which by representation on elected District and Provincial Governments would express itself in the elected Central Government. The effort immediately cost him his place in the Non-co-operation party which cast him out with contempt.

42. **Resolutions Passed.**—The resolutions passed by the Committee at Delhi were to the following effect:—

Whereas not much more than one month remained for the establishment of Swaraj before the end of the year and the Nation had demonstrated its capacity to observe complete non-violence over the arrest of the Ali Brothers, the All-India Congress Committee authorised every Provincial Committee, on its own responsibility, to undertake civil disobedience including the non-payment of taxes, but subject to the following conditions:—

Any person offering individual civil disobedience must:—

(*a*) Have completely fulfilled the part of the Swadeshi programme applicable to him.

(*b*) Be a believer in Hindu-Moslem Unity and in the unity of the other communities in India professing different religions.

(*c*) Believe in non-violence as absolutely essential for the redress of the Punjab and Khilafat wrongs and the attainment of Swaraj.

(*d*) If a Hindu, show by personal conduct that he regarded untouchability as a blot upon Nationalism.

For purposes of mass civil disobedience a District or Tahsil should be treated as a unit and therein a vast majority of the population must have adopted full Swadeshi and must be clothed in cloth hand-spun and handwoven in the District or Tahsil, and must believe in and practise all the other items of the Non-co-operation programme. The Working Committee was empowered to relax any of these conditions at its discretion. Civil resisters and their dependents were enjoined to expect no support from Congress funds and it was resolved that the families of civil resisters sentenced to imprisonment must support themselves by handspinning or handweaving or by other means.

The Committee expressed dissatisfaction at the progress made with the Swadeshi programme and the cloth boycott, and called on all workers to devote exclusive attention to boycott of foreign cloth so as to enable the country to offer civil disobedience.

It endorsed the resolution of the Working Committee regarding the duty of Government employees, and declared it to be the inherent right of every citizen to appeal in an open manner to the soldier and the civilian to sever his connection with a Government which had forfeited the confidence and support of the vast majority of the population in India.

It adopted the draft resolution of the Working Committee on the Foreign policy of the Congress, and instructed the Working Committee to appoint, as soon as the time had arrived to do so, a Commission to proceed to Malabar "to investigate the causes of the Moplah riots," the extent of the outrages alleged to have been committed by the rioters, the forcible conversion of Hindus to Islam and certain other matters. It also published the amount actually collected for the Tilak Swaraj Fund under the Bezwada Resolutions. This amount was now said to be 99,87,145 rupees—still short of the crore so triumphantly announced as collected at the end of June.

43. **Bombay riots 17th to 21st of November.**—The precise value of the All-India Congress Committee's injunctions regarding the observance of the principle of non-violence, was almost immediately apparent in the serious rioting which occurred at Bombay from the 17th to the 21st of November. In accordance with the Working Committee's directions regarding the visit of H. R. H. the Prince of Wales, the Bombay Provincial Congress Committee, in common with other Provincial Committees, had arranged for a "general voluntary *hartal*" As a counter attraction to the ceremonies attending the landing at Bombay of H. R. H. the Prince of Wales a public meeting was arranged which was addressed by Gandhi himself. The crowd on dispersing after the meeting, went into the city and commenced violent interference with persons who were not observing the *hartal* in accordance with its desires, burnt tramcars and motor-cars, assaulted Europeans, Anglo-Indians and Parsees of whom 2 were murdered and one severely wounded with a bayonet. The trouble developed into sustained inter-sectarian rioting attended with arson and serious loss of life, due both to assault and the action of the military and the Police in suppressing the disturbances.

Gandhi seems at first to have been appalled at this revelation of the results of his movement and the worth of his propaganda He published some frank, if inadequate, statements regarding his own responsibility for the disaster and his incapacity to control the mobs which the Congress and himself had called into being on this occasion. He also summoned a meeting of the Working Committee to consider the situation.

44. **Working Committee's Resolution on the Riots.**—Gandhi's repentance and confessions must have been both distasteful and embarrassing to his colleagues on the Working Committee. At any rate, the resolutions published showed that they were not going to permit themselves to be deterred from proceeding with their programme. Basing their resolution on the audaciously false assumption that peace had been restored without any Government aid whatsoever, they actually expressed their opinion that the riots had proved by the response of the people to their natural leaders, that the masses had advanced in their adherence to the principle of non-violence. Further, that this outbreak of violence had shown the necessity of further educating the masses, and the Working Committee seized on this pretext to order the re-organisation, co-ordination and strengthening of the National Volunteers under their own supreme control.

45. **Calcutta Hartal, 17th November.**—Meantime at Calcutta the *hartal* of the 17th of November had been made so complete, through the objectionable methods of the Congress and Khilafat Volunteers, that

the business and legitimate activities of the citizens were in effect suspended and an intolerable state of affairs prevailed. The volunteers by persuasion, and in default by picketing and coercion, largely succeeded in withdrawing labour from road transport and industry. They interfered even with private domestics and attempted to usurp the functions of the regular Police in the control of traffic.

46. **Local Government forced to take action.**—The Bengal Government were forced to act and declared the Congress and Khilafat volunteers unlawful associations under the Criminal Law Amendment Act of 1908, and action was taken to raid and search Congress and Khilafat offices throughout the Province. This example was imitated in rapid succession by the Governments of the United Provinces, Assam, Bihar and Orissa and the Punjab, in the latter the Seditious Meetings Act being also applied to certain districts.

To this action by these Governments the Provincial Congress leaders concerned at once showed open defiance, and having published their intention to continue the formation of the National Volunteer Corps proceeded to put it into execution. This left the Provincial Governments concerned no alternative but to enforce the law, and the arrests of Lajpat Rai in the Punjab, C. R. Das in Bengal and Moti Lal Nehru in the United Provinces, with others of lesser note, took place within a few days of each other. The issue had thus shifted from mass civil disobedience and individual disobedience to non-moral laws, to civil disobedience to enforce the right of the subject to freedom of association and public meeting—a change of the greatest tactical value to the Non-co-operators.

While Gandhi's intention to launch civil disobedience, mass and individual, may have commanded a certain amount of sympathy outside the ranks of Non-co-operators, to a greater extent it caused alarm and misgiving, particularly after the Bombay riots; but the resentment caused by the application of the Criminal Law Amendment Act of 1908 and of the Seditious Meetings Act soon warmed these waverers into outspoken opposition to the Government's action. Moderate politicians and members of Legislative Councils joined in the chorus of protest that was raised, and were at pains to emphasise the gravity of the situation that had been produced.

47. **Attitude of the Moderates.**—This speedy descent of the Moderates on Gandhi's side of the fence (upon which they had sat so long) may appear puzzling at first sight, particularly if it be recalled that in Bengal they had joined in calling on the Government for strong action after the *hartal* of the 17th of November. It is readily intelligible, however, if it be realised that the film dividing the Moderate from the Extremist is one merely of method—not of aim. So long as Gandhi proceeded on his perilous course towards mass civil disobedience their commonsense condemned him but they felt no overwhelming impulse to thwart him. They were content to wait on events—probably in the hope that something would happen

to postpone the issue indefinitely. However, when Gandhi and his lieutenants were able to change the issue to the rights of public association and public meeting and, when the sons and relatives of Moderates began to fill the prisons, the Moderates very quickly made themselves heard.

48. **Proposal for a Round Table Conference.**—A deputation headed by Pandit Madan Mohan Malaviya waited on H. E. the Viceroy at Calcutta on December 21st, to suggest the summoning of a Round Table Conference with a view to finding some way of bridging the breach between the Government and the Nationalists. The address read by this deputation made it clear (1) that while acknowledging what the Government had done to redress the Punjab and Khilafat wrongs, the deputation was of opinion that " all that should have been done has not yet been done "; (2) that while one section of the people regarded the Reforms as inadequate and unsatisfactory, and while another section had co-operated with the Government in working the Reforms, both sections were agreed in asking that full responsible Government should be established as speedily as possible.

Pending the summoning of a Conference the deputation suggested the withdrawal of the notifications and proclamations under the Criminal Law Amendment Act of 1908 and the Seditious Meetings Act, in order to allay existing excitement and to relieve the political tension. It will be observed that nothing was said of any suspension by Non-co-operators of those activities which had called the above Acts into force. In the face of this omission H. E. the Viceroy was unable to accept the suggestions of the deputation and the project fell through for the time being, while Pandit M. M. Malaviya and Mr. M. A. Jinnah gathered their energies for an appeal to the Congress itself at Ahmedabad.

49. **The Ahmedabad Session of the Indian National Congress.**—The Annual Session of the Indian National Congress took place at Ahmedabad from the 24th to the 27th of December, under the acting Presidency of Hakim Ajmal Khan *vice* C. R. Das who had been elected President before his arrest. The resolutions showed the intention to exploit for all it was worth the ferment among the Moderates and co-operators. The first resolution appealed to all who, while not believing in full Non-co-operation, yet consider it essential to national self-respect to insist on the redress of the Khilafat and Punjab wrongs and the immediate establishment of Swaraj, to co-operate in the following items of the non-co-operation programme:—

(1) The promotion of unity between different religious communities.
(2) The popularisation of hand-spinning and hand-weaving and ancillary industries.
(3) The total prohibition of liquor and drugs.
(4) The removal of untouchability and the improvement of the submerged classes.

Gandhi was also careful to plead for tolerance of all who disagreed with the Non-co-operation programme, even tolerance of Government servants. In fact everything was done to encourage the advance of the wary Moderate towards the Non-co-operation Camp. In effect he was told " If you cannot fully co-operate in our Non-co-operation then co-operate just as far as you feel you can. Meantime we will do our best to make you feel at ease in your new surroundings ".

50. **Its determination to continue non-violent Non-co-operation.**—The same policy was visible in the fifth resolution—the main resolution of the Session. This confirmed the resolutions of non-violent non-co-operation, passed at Calcutta and Nagpur, as having caused the country to advance greatly in fearlessness, self-sacrifice and self-respect, and as having " greatly damaged the prestige of the Government." It determined to continue the programme of non-violent non-co-operation with greater vigour than heretofore " in such manner as each Province may determine till the Punjab and the Khilafat wrongs are redressed and Swaraj is established and the control of the Government of India passes into the hands of the people from those of an irresponsible corporation." Here was a long step forward in devolution of powers to the Provincial organisations.

51. **Resolution *re* Civil Disobedience.**—It then proceeded to raise in the forefront of the battle the newly-acquired slogan of " Freedom of speech, Freedom of the Press, Freedom of Association and Freedom of public meeting." The wording was as follows:—

"And whereas by reason of the threat uttered by H. E. the Viceroy in his recent speeches and the consequent repression started by the Government of India in the various Provinces by way of disbandment of Volunteer Corps and forcible prohibition of public and even Committee meetings in an illegal and high-handed manner, and whereas this repression is manifestly intended to stifle all Congress and Khilafat activities * * * this Congress resolves that all activities of the Congress be suspended as far as necessary and appeals to all quietly and without any demonstration to offer themselves for arrest by belonging to the Volunteer organisations to be formed throughout the country * * * * * * Notwithstanding the proclamations prohibiting public meetings, and inasmuch as even Committee meetings have been attempted to be construed as public meetings, this Congress advises the holding of Committee meetings and of public meetings, the latter in enclosed places and by tickets * * * care being taken in every case to avoid risk of provocation and possible violence by the public in consequence.

" This Congress further is of opinion that Civil Disobedience is the only civilized and effective substitute for an armed rebellion whenever every other remedy for preventing arbitrary, tyrannical and emasculating use of authority by individuals or corporations has been tried, and, therefore, advises all Congress workers and others who believe in peaceful methods and are convinced that there is no remedy save some kind of sacrifice to dislodge the existing Government from its position of perfect irresponsibility * * * * to organise individual and mass Civil Disobedience when the mass of the people have been sufficiently trained in the methods of non-violence.

* * * * *

This Congress is of opinion that in order to concentrate attention upon Civil Disobedience * * * * all other Congress activities should be suspended whenever and where-ever and to the extent to which it may be found necessary "

52 **Gandhi Predominant.**—In the same resolution the Congress hoped that every person of the age of 18 and over would immediately join the Volunteer organisation, and it made a pointed appeal to all students of suitable age to join the Volunteer Corps at once. It also prescribed an amended form of pledge for Volunteers requiring each to declare his belief that " as India is circumstanced non-violence alone can help the Khilafat and the Punjab and result in the attainment of Swaraj * * * * " and to promise that so long as he remained a member of the Corps he would remain non-violent in word and in deed and would earnestly endeavour to be so in intent. Further, in view of impending arrests of Congress workers, it appointed Gandhi dictator of the Congress with plenary powers except in the settlement of terms of peace with the Government and in the alteration of the creed of the Congress.

Pandit M. M. Malaviya and Mr. M. A. Jinnah attended the Congress with the intention of inducing that body to pass a resolution extending a formal welcome to the idea of a Round Table Conference In this, in spite of strenuous efforts to persuade Gandhi to accept their view, they were unsuccessful, and the Congress followed Gandhi without demur. In opposing a motion, by Pandit M. M. Malaviya before the All-India Congress Committee, to delete from the main resolution the portion relating to aggressive civil disobedience and to place before the open session a resolution expressing the desire of the Congress for a Round Table Conference on reasonable and honourable terms, Gandhi urged that it would be undignified for the Congress to pass such a resolution when there had been nothing in the Viceregal pronouncements to show the change of heart so necessary for the success of such a conference.

In the open session Gandhi explained with much emphasis that the fifth resolution did not close the door to a Round Table Conference, but it must be a real conference where only equals were to sit and the Viceroy must be prepared to do justice and nothing but justice. That resolution was an irrevocable challenge to the authority which, to save itself, wished to crush freedom of opinion and freedom of association. Briefly Gandhi was opposed to a conference unless he were in a position to dictate terms, and to that position Non-co-operation had not yet attained. If any conference were arranged it must be arranged by parties other than Non-co-operators who could have nothing to say to the proposal unless the Government showed clearly a change of attitude and views. The aims and objects of Non-co-operation were well-known and had been many times defined and till such time as the Government saw fit to move in the desired direction Non-co-operators could do no less than proceed on the path they had appointed. If approached in a manner consonant with the dignity and prestige of the Congress they would not object to consider a proposal, but they could make no spontaneous move in that direction.

53. **Attempt to find a common platform.**—To bridge this gulf between the Government and the Congress Pandit M. M. Malaviya and Mr. Jinnah set about preparations to convene a non-party conference early in the following January, with a view to devising a platform, acceptable to all parties, from which a proposal might be made to the Government for a Round Table Conference. These activities and the general situation had been very largely influenced by the course of events in Ireland where a Round Table Conference had just been the means of reconciling apparently irreconcilable differences between the British Government and the Sinn Feiners.

54. **Appearance of Violence Party.**—Another most important feature of the Ahmedabad Congress was the appearance in the open of a party in favour of the formal adoption of violence, as a means to achieve the aims of the National Congress. Hasrat Mohani both in the Subjects Committee and the open session of the Congress pressed for the alteration of the Congress creed so as to include the attainment of complete independence " by all possible and proper means ", while in his speeches in support of his motion he made open reference to violence and guerilla warfare—references he subsequently attempted to explain away.

Allusion has been made already to the amended Volunteer pledge contained in the fifth resolution whereby the Volunteer was to declare his belief that " as India is circumstanced " non-violence alone could assist in attaining the ends of the Congress. This pledge, it is to be borne in mind, superseded that prescribed by the All-India Working Committee at its special session after the Bombay riots wherein a pledge of adherence to non-violence was prescribed "so long as the policy of non-violence is continued by the Nation." The speeches of Gandhi and others on the amended form of the pledge made it clear that non-violence was not to be regarded as an unalterable tenet of the Congress creed and in the case of Gandhi, his attitude appeared to be that, if after fair and full trial of his methods, those methods failed to achieve their purpose, he would make way for those who had other methods to try. It did not appear, however, that he could himself abandon his principle of non-violence and participate in such a venture.

Hasrat Mohani secured but small support in the voting on his motion, which in the open session was defeated by a majority of about 10 to 1. The fact must not be overlooked, however, that this result was only achieved after Gandhi had made a strenuous appeal to the Congress to retain his principle of non-violence. Previous to that appeal the volume of sentiment in favour of Hasrat Mohani's motion was very much larger, if it did not actually predominate in the Assembly. The supporters of Hasrat Mohani's motion comprised all the Andhra delegates, the Bengal delegates, all the delegates from the Central Provinces, 3 from the United Provinces, a few from Bombay and all the Sikh delegates except one from Delhi.

55. **Position at the end of 1921.**—Thus, at the close of 1921 the Congress were carrying on the fight with Gandhi as Dictator and the new slogan of " Freedom of Association, Freedom of Meeting and Freedom of the Press ". To this new slogan a large and vocal part of the Co-operators had responded in all parts of India; while, on the other wing, a tendency to discard the principle of " non-violence " was apparent.

CHAPTER III.

Non-co-operation propaganda and its effect on the masses, 1921.

It is necessary at this point to digress in order to give some account of the actual methods and propaganda employed in agitating the masses and the effect which this propaganda had on uneducated people such as the industrial and agrarian labouring classes.

56 **Gandhi and the Ali Brothers tour India.**—Until the arrest of Muhammad and Shaukat Ali in September, Gandhi, with one or other of the two brothers, was constantly touring the various Provinces of India, preaching and agitating. Usually they attracted large, and often vast crowds, who came mainly to have a glimpse of the Mahatma about whom unscrupulous agitators were circulating to the credulous masses stories of divine attributes and miraculous powers. These were readily believed and thus the Mahatma's influence was strengthened by a spurious divinity. Some extracts of the speeches they delivered to these mixed, and often completely ignorant and uneducated audiences will now be given.

57. **Gandhi's Speeches.** *Jhansi, November 1920.*—" We must regard as impure the Courts of a Government which has become demoniacal and satanic in its nature. It must be an unholy act for us to go to the Courts established by the Government which prosecuted, imprisoned and even put to death our great Punjab leaders who were innocent."

Lucknow, February 1921.—" To-day the whole of India understands that reading in Government schools, practising in Government courts and holding Government titles are dirty things. Swadeshi is our creed; it is our duty. I want to tell you if you want to solve the Khilafat question that though you believe Englishmen to be your enemies you must not call them enemies, but you must dislike their manners. They are casting evil eyes on your religion. To-day we are ruling India. The Government cannot cajole anybody. Our influence is increasing even over the C. I. D. * * I positively assert that we are ruling India to-day ".

Cuttack, March 1921.—" I used to co-operate with the Government and entertain the belief that co-operation would do good, but I find I was mistaken. No good can be had of a satanic system of Government ".

Puri, March 1921.—" As for cow protection, if you wish to protect the cow you should either mend or end this Government ".

Jubbulpore, March 1921.—" The present Government is satanic and wants you to become drunkards. It keeps you under subjection with the forces maintained from the Excise revenue. It is *Ravan*

Raj * * * The Government meets the education charges out of Excise revenue which is 17 crores * * * If we give up drinking it means we can educate our children and attain Swaraj ".

Aligarh, August 1921.—" The attainment of Swaraj means that the whole of Hindusthan should come under our control. Just as at present control can be established all over the Indian Empire by means of gunpowder, shots and aeroplanes, so we proclaim our non-violence by means of Non-co-operation and there is no need to fear the aeroplanes and machine guns of the Government. We cannot fear a lakh of Englishmen however powerful they may be if thirty crores of men and women are fully convinced of the fact that they cannot be coerced by anyone ".

Pilibhit, August 1921.—" We innocents want to go to jail and we wish to be hanged. This is the meaning of Non-co-operation * * * "

Lucknow, August 1921.—" By successfully carrying out the boycott of Foreign goods we would gain sufficient strength to carry out another final step, *viz.*, asking the *Kisans* (peasants) to suspend paying their land revenue * * Civil Disobedience is such a mighty weapon that no power can dare defy it. If we decide to do Civil Disobedience against the Government, to defy the law and order established by the Government, then I say 50,000 such men who would do Civil Disobedience are enough to wipe out this Government. There is no question of our being wiped out by this Government; the Government itself would be wiped out before long. * * * I only want to fill the jails of the Government with our innocent men, and then you would find you had acquired sufficient strength to win the Khilafat and take Swaraj ".

Madras, September 1921.—" For do we not claim and do we not say from a thousand platforms that the present Government is a Kingdom of Satan and do we not claim that we seek to substitute the Kingdom of Satan by the Kingdom of God ".

58. **The general trend of Gandhi's Propaganda.**—Gandhi repeatedly said that the Government was a satanic Government, that it was the duty of Non-co-operators openly to preach disaffection to the Government which they must mend or end. Mending he explained consisted in compelling the Government to accede to their demands. Sedition was the creed of the Congress and Non-co-operation deliberately aimed at the overthrow of the Government. It was a sin for a single Indian to serve in the Army or the Civil Departments of the Government. It was a sin for anybody to serve this Government. For example, in his *Young India* in October 1921, he wrote, " We must declare from a thousand platforms that it is sinful for any Mussalman or Hindu to serve the existing Government whether as a soldier or in any capacity whatsoever ".

At Bombay he said that the picketing of liquor shops must be maintained even if rivers of blood should flow, and again he wrote in *Young India* that he clearly saw the time coming when he must refuse obedience to every state-made law even though a certain amount of bloodshed might result. These latter references to violence are isolated ones, and merely described his determination to adhere to his principles even at the cost of bloodshed. Usually abuse of the Satanic Government, its myrmidons and all relating to it, were carefully qualified with appeals for non-violence; for hatred of the Government, but love for the individuals who compose it; for complete Non-co-operation with all institutions of the Government and with its officials, but only in their official capacity.

One explanation of the open virulence of these attacks is contained in an article in *Young India* where Gandhi remarked, regarding the arrest of the Ali Brothers: " it was common cause (*sic*) tha. so long as the movement remained non-violent nothing would be done to interfere with it." Undoubtedly this impression was widespread and an inspection of casual specimens of Non-co-operation oratory from all parts of India strengthens the view that agitators were convinced that so long as some reference was made to non-violence, there need be no bounds to abuse, vilification and expressions of detestation and contempt.

59. **Gandhi's Promises.**—During the years 1920-21 Gandhi made number of promises as to the date by which Swaraj would be obtained, and although these are of little historical value, yet they give an interesting side-light on his mentality. These prophesies are dealt with rather severely by Sir Sankaran Nair in his book "Gandhi and Anarchy". He points out that in moving the resolution on Non-co-operation in the National Congress held at Calcutta in September 1920, Gandhi said, "If there is sufficient response to my scheme, I make bold to reiterate my statement that we can gain Swaraj in the course of one year." On the 29th of December 1920, *i.e.*, three months afterwards, he said, "My experience during the last months fills me with the hope that within the nine months that remain of the year in which I have expected Swaraj for India we shall redress the two wrongs and we shall see Swaraj (Parliamentary) established in accordance with the wishes of the people of India." After about a month—on the 21st January—he again confirmed his previous statement saying, "Four months of this one year have already gone by and my faith has never burnt as brightly as it burns to-night as I am talking to the young men of Bengal." He added that in the event of his death before the expiry of the eight months he was satisfied that the people of India would secure Swaraj before the year was out. A few days later, while appealing to the merchants of Calcutta on the 30th of January for funds, he again mentioned the attainment of Swaraj if the requisite money was coming, and on the same day, while addressing a meeting of students, he said, "If the

response continues as it has begun there is no doubt of Swaraj coming within the time prescribed."

In March 1921, he stated, "The last Congress has given a constitution whose working is in itself calculated to lead to Swaraj. It is intended to secure in every part of India representative committees working in conjunction with, and under willing and voluntary submission to a central organisation—the All-India Congress Committee. It establishes an adult suffrage open to men and women and subject only to two qualifications, *viz.*, the signing of the creed and a nominal payment of four annas. It is intended to secure due representation of the parties and communities, if then, it is honestly worked, and commands confidence and respect, it can oust the present Government without the slightest difficulty. For the latter has no power except through the co-operation, willing or forced, of the people. The force it exercises is mostly through our own people. One lac of Europeans without our help, can only hold less than one-seventh of our villages each and it would be difficult for a man, even when physically present, to impose his will on, say four hundred men and women—the average population of an Indian village". He stipulated that it was necessary to concentrate up to the 30th of June on getting—

(1) One crore of rupees for the Tilak Swaraj Fund.

(2) One crore of members on the Congress Register.

(3) The spinning wheel introduced in 20 lakhs of homes.

He added, however, "This programme does not mean cessation of the other activities of Non-co-operation. They go on. Drink and untouchability must vanish. The education movement is steadily going forward. The National institutions that have sprung up will, if they are efficiently managed, make headway and attract students who are still hesitating. The pleaders, always a cautious and calculating class by training, will, as they see the movement progressing more and more, fall in line with the rest of the country. Boycott of law courts by the public is making fair progress. These things do not now require concentration of universal effort. They apply to special classes. But the three things mentioned by me are the most essential: they must be done now, and without them the movement, as a mass movement must be pronounced a failure." The crore of rupees was reported to have been collected, but as Swaraj showed no immediate signs of arriving he postponed the date from time to time on the grounds that the other stipulations he had made had not been fulfilled.

He subsequently fixed other dates, *i.e.*, the 1st September, the 1st of October, the 31st of October and the 13th of December 1921 for the attainment of Swaraj; but after 1921, he refrained from making further promises on this subject. These promises of Swaraj, which Gandhi obviously knew that he could not fulfil, were made with the object of stimulating excitement in the masses by giving them something tangible to which to look forward. When it is remembered that for the purposes of Non-co-operation propaganda Swaraj was synonymous with Utopia it is not surprising that the cry of "Gandhi ke Raj ki jai" became common among the ignorant people who were his dupes.

Sir Sankaran Nair also points out Gandhi's failure to comply with a vow to retire to the Himalayas in the event of violence. The terms of this vow were not very clear and Gandhi ultimately explained it away by saying that he meant universal violence throughout India. As will be shown later, the violence induced by his propaganda during 1921 was more than sufficient to ensure his disappearance from the political stage had he been really sincere.

60. **Muhammad Ali's Speeches.**—Muhammad Ali was no less outspoken and he always emphasised in addition that the use of the sword in religious war (*jehad*) is not only permissible to, but incumbent on, Muslims. Owing to the lack of armed force, however, he admitted that it was more expedient to adopt Non-co-operation. The following are casual specimens of his propaganda:—

Bareilly, October 1920.—"Then let me know what is right for us. Can we teach our boys in Aligarh with the money of these who we know are the enemies of our religion, who have enslaved our Khalifa, who have desecrated our Kaaba, our Medina, our Jerusalem and our Jazirat-ul-Arab, who are the enemies of our country, who snatched the veils of our women in the Punjab, who made our Indian brethren crawl like earth-worms on their bellies? * * * * Can I say you should go for property worth a few pennies to the law courts of those unjust people who have treated our Turkish brethren unjustly and have done injustice to our Khalifa?"

Lucknow, October 1920.—Referring to the murder of the Deputy Commissioner of Kheri by a Muslim fanatic he said, "In other words this (British) nation has remained unmindful of all that has been passing in our hearts until one of its members forfeited his life. They have shown us that murder is the method which opens their eyes to the history of our suffering. To-day we have come to know it, and it has been exposed to the world how the Englishmen's hearts are filled with the sentiments of hate, tyranny and treachery. * * * * * * I tell you that in addition to the ghi, rice and meat, females are also supplied to the armies. Those females belong to your nation."

Aligarh, October 1920.—"If Muslims wish to maintain Islam they should join hands with the Hindus and free their country first * * * * * If Hindus wished to free their country they should maintain the freedom of neighbouring countries Egypt was enslaved because the British wished to strengthen the fetters of India * * * * * If Indian troops went to-day to enslave Mesopotamia the time would come when Mesopotamian troops would come to trample on Indians when they raised their heads."

"In case of necessity I will be the first man to inform the Government that the sword has been drawn and I would not then draw back until either I or the Government were killed. * * * * * We are not drawing the sword, not from fear of being hanged, but because the necessity of India and Islam demands that we should not do so * * * * * The success obtained in Ireland is not due to the murder of 150 policemen but to the fact that three-fourths of Ireland has its own courts."

Delhi, November 1920—"The snake of the British bureaucracy is obstructing the door of entrance to the house of freedom."

Fyzabad, 10th February 1921.—"The Mussalmans wanted to seek the alliance of Gandhiji * * in the work of the Khilafat but I told them * * that we could not make him our ally as he wanted us to banish from our hearts all thought of using the sword. I declared that God had given me the right to use the sword against my adversary when I had the power to do so and that no one could then stop me. This is our creed. But now we know and * * * we see that our country does not possess that power and so long as we do not have that power we will be his (Gandhi's) associates * * * we are, therefore, standing to-day on the same platform,—he for reasons of principle and we for those of policy."

"Who will laugh to-morrow when the flow of sixty crores of rupees to Europe is stopped and the cotton of India is spun and woven in India? On that day we will laugh and they will weep. They have lost their senses and do not know how to arrest this man (Gandhi) He surely says that this is *Ravan Raj*, and a rule of demons. I also say so."

"I have asked the Government to change their ways. I have asked them whether or not they wish to have any connection with us and whether they want to have any connection with India or to keep away from it." * * * When both these questions (Punjab and Khilafat) are decided our connection with you would be possible But such a relationship as exists between a slave or a servant and a master can exist no longer. If this is not done we shall take Swaraj and sever our connection with the British Government * * * * * * If you do not possess sufficient power to face your enemy and get rid of him * * * * you will regard your enemy as your enemy. I do not refer to the English nation or any particular official belonging to it. I am simply referring to the methods of the British Government. I say we cannot call the English our friends. This rule is like Ravana's. This rule is not a rule * * * * * You cannot tame a snake by keeping it within your sleeve * * * Would you give a wolf meat to encourage him in future to eat your own flesh?"

61. **Other Propaganda.**—During 1921, in addition to the well known leaders, numerous other agitators were at work, who were by no means temperate in their language as is apparent from the specimens, selected at random, of district propaganda, given below.

Bengal, August 1921.—"God has divided religions into two classes, *viz.*, those who fight against Islam and those who fought for Islam and did not help its enemies. The former should have their hands and feet cut off or be killed somehow. For the attainment of Swaraj great sacrifices are necessary and the shedding of blood is not impossible. We cannot be loyal to a foreign government."

Madras, August 1921.—"The British are a race of cowards and the state of affairs at Mocherla (in the Guntur District) shows there is no Government. If foreign cloth were not destroyed shops selling it would be burnt. It is most necessary to refuse to pay taxes. In case of combine resistance to the payment of taxes the Government would be helpless. We have already succeeded to a very large extent in shaking the foundation of the British power and the rest must follow as day follows night. Foreign cloth is prepared with the fat of cows and pigs".

As a further instance of the unscrupulous depths to which minor agitators did not hesitate to stoop, must be catalogued the widespread and repeated allegations that the British had ravished some women in the Punjab during the disturbances of 1919 and had outraged the modesty of others.

The mention of violence was frequent particularly by Muhammadan speakers. Close attention was focussed on Sinn Fein and its tactics, and references to the example of Ireland and the lessons to be drawn from it were fairly numerous. As was to be expected, the party of violence derived much encouragement from Sinn Fein and found in it a valuable weapon with which to rout the supporters of non-violence.

Prominent items of propaganda which may be reckoned as failures were:—

(1) The campaign against educational institutions aided, and controlled by Government and their replacement by National institutions.

(2) Boycott of law courts by lawyers and litigants and the settlement of disputes by National Courts.

(3) Renunciation of titles, honours and honorary offices.

(4) Boycott of the Reformed Legislative Councils.

But the appeal of Non-co-operation was made frankly to the masses rather than to the educated classes, and it was not surprising to find that a large measure of success, though mainly temporary, attended the formation of panchayats, kisan sabhas and arbitration courts, and also the temperance movement and, by December 1921, the enforcement of the boycott of foreign cloth. All these items lent themselves readily to the treatment of the unscrupulous demagogue and to enforcement by the universal weapon of social boycott and coercion, wielded mainly through the volunteers.

62. **The result of intensive agitation.**—Briefly it may be said that by means of persistent and unscrupulous propaganda, vilifying the Government and encouraging the formation of rival institutions, much was done to engender contempt for authority and a tendency to open lawlessness on the part of the more ignorant masses. The times were hard for the lower classes in particular, and this too was utilised to place Non-co-operation in a favourable light by means of promises of no taxes and no rent under a Swaraj Government. A beginning was made in the no-tax campaign by inciting refusal to pay minor taxes such as Municipal, Chaukidari and Local Board Taxes. This met with considerable success in parts of Madras and Bengal, and in the former Province there was a widespread disregard of Forest regulations and laws. Violence was offered to Forest officials and the assistance of Armed Police was necessary to support their authority. The most striking feature of Non-co-operation in its varying aspect was the constant and intentional tendency to disintegrate existing law and order, if not society, without constructing any remotely adequate machinery with which to replace them

This aspect of the movement was most apparent in the concentration of effort, in the last months of 1921, on the disintegration of the Police and Army. These were attacked with social pressure, appeals to religious susceptibilities and the ever-ready social boycott, and an organised attempt was made to make life in those services miserable.

63. **Pressure on Government Officials.**—The boycott of Government officials was adopted in several places, and in most provinces they were, to a greater or less extent, harassed in the performance of their duty and pressure was brought to bear on them to force them to resign. Generally speaking, however, the results obtained by the Non-co-operators in this direction were negligible in spite of the fact that in Bengal and the United Provinces particularly, certain Government servants suffered considerably. The attack was directed principally against the Police—both district and rural—and when it is remembered that it occurred at a time of great economic distress, the meagre results obtained reflected great credit on the loyalty of the force. In some districts in Bengal and Bihar, a considerable number of village police, who are poorly paid, resigned, and difficulty was experienced in filling their places; but the regular Police, although their morale was occasionally shaken, with rare exceptions, withstood all the attacks made on them in spite of the fact that they were boycotted with respect to their food supply, socially ostracised and harassed in every conceivable way. For example, in one instance, medical attendance was refused to the sick child of a Sub-Inspector.

The Education Department also suffered and school masters were stoned and schools which failed to "nationalize" were, in places, burnt down. No class of Government servant escaped persecution, and when this was directed against village officials who were particularly exposed to attack, it is not surprising that in Madras and elsewhere a number resigned.

As was to be expected, Indians were the chief sufferers in this campaign, but Europeans were by no means exempted, and touring officers were frequently insulted and, on occasions, were the victims of personal violence.

64. **Pressure on the Public.**—The co-operating public was similarly subjected to persecution and the vendors of foreign cloth and liquor were the victims of boycott and picketing, while it was not uncommon for their shops to be burnt and their goods destroyed. Their customers were often garlanded with shoes, forcibly shaved, made the target of missiles of dung, or otherwise molested. In Bengal—with the object of embarrassing the European mercantile community—an anti-jute campaign was initiated. Cultivators who persisted in growing this crop on occasions found that it had been wilfully destroyed by Non-co-operators.

Sometimes funeral rites were refused to co-operators who were compelled to dispose of their dead under the most harrowing circumstances. A recitation of instances of this nature might be prolonged indefinitely to make the point that during the height of the Non-co-operation Movement the life of a loyal British Indian subject was a burden.

65. **The National Congress and the All-India Trade Union Congress.**—In addition to the propaganda campaign outlined above the Congress devoted considerable attention to existing labour organisations. An account has been given of the resolution on labour policy passed by the National Congress at Nagpur* and of the organisation set up to give effect to that policy. At the same time attention was drawn to the fact that several members of the Congress Labour Sub-Committee were also members of the All-India Trade Union Congress. The question remained as to how far the Trade Union Congress was identical in aim and activity with the National Congress.

The labour creed of the Trade Union Congress was, to put it conservatively, an advanced type of socialism. It taught the labourers that they were the producers of wealth and therefore the product should be theirs. Through its Secretary—Diwan Chaman Lal—it also indulged in markedly anti-capitalist propaganda, but in the main it did not openly identify itself with the cult of Non-co-operation. There were, however, indications that it was an active sympathiser and co-operator in the general Non-co-operation Movement.

* Paragraph 24.

On the 23rd of September Chaman Lal, as Secretary of the Trade Union Congress, issued a manifesto to the Labourers of India notifying them that it was not the wish of the arrested leaders, the Ali Brothers and their co-accused, that workers should indulge in *hartals* as a protest against their arrest. Whatever, therefore, their individual feelings might be they should subordinate them to the general will and there should be no strikes. It may be presumed then that the converse of this instruction also held good.

Another indication was afforded by the proceedings of the All-India Trade Union Congress at its second session at Jharia at the end of November. It was plain that the Congress had a decided tinge of politics of the Non-co-operation variety. The Pandal, where the Congress was held, was decorated in Khadi cloth and a press account stated that a large proportion of the people present wore Khadi clothes and Gandhi caps. The President, J. Baptista, was also garbed in Non-co-operation uniform. As was to be expected from the composition of the Standing Committee of the A. I. T. U. Congress, the names of several prominent Non-co-operators, *e.g.*, C. R. Das, D. N. Singh and Shyam Sundar Chakravarty, appeared in the proceedings.

The following political resolutions were among those passed:—

(*a*) That this Congress considers that the country is ready for Swaraj.

(*b*) That this Congress recommends the country to adopt Swadeshi and to encourage hand-spinning and hand-weaving.

Political subjects which were stock items of Non-co-operation propaganda, were also freely imported into the addresses of the speakers. The All-India Trade Union Congress thus showed a benevolent attitude to current aspects of Non-co-operation.

66. **Labour organisation—General Lines of.**—In considering the general lines of the labour organisation set up by the All-India Trade Union Congress the fact is conspicuous that leading Non-co-operators occupied important positions in the Executive of this organisation.

A central labour organisation affiliated to the All-India Trade Union Congress was started at each of the following industrial centres:—

Bombay.—The Bombay Central Labour Federation.

Calcutta.—The Bengal Central Labour Federation.

Madras.—The Central Labour Board.

Cawnpore.—The Mazdur Sabha.

The policy pursued was to secure affiliation of existing labour unions and associations to the Provincial Central organisation and to the All-India Trade Union Congress, while fostering the further organisation of labour. From the resolutions of the All-India Trade Union

Congress at Jharia it was plain that an extension of this policy was contemplated.

In surveying the results attained in the organisation of labour during 1921 another fact is conspicuous, *viz.*, that the Labour Sub-Committee of the National Congress had done nothing to this end in its individual capacity, but had remained content with the activities of the A. I. T. U. C. and its subordinate organisations. Considering how fully the National Congress was represented on the A. I. T. U. C. this was not surprising.

Without proceeding to details it may briefly be said that the organisation of Trade Unions and their affiliation to the central body made considerable progress in the places named, especially in Calcutta, Bombay and Madras. It now remains to consider the action of these labour organisations in labour disputes handled by them. The fact must be emphasised at the outset that in any case the year would have been one of great economic unrest. The world-wide after-effects of the War had been felt severely in India and trade had suffered. The bare cost of living, far from showing any reduction, had continued to rise and labour of all classes had been severely pinched, while anti-capitalist propaganda assiduously preached by the labour agitator, was correspondingly welcome. In such a combination of circumstances it was but natural that each week should have brought its unrest and its crop of strikes in all parts of India.

At the same time another general symptom must be noticed showing that the mass of labourers were affected by the Non-co-operation agitation, however vaguely they may have understood its causes or its teachings. It was a universal practice throughout India for labour crowds convened for definitely labour purposes, to raise shouts of "Gandhi Maharaj-ki-Jai" and other political cries. The appeal of Non-co-operation to the masses was heard at any rate by the industrial population of the larger cities.

67. **Agrarian.**—The same appeal was received sympathetically by the Agricultural classes in Oudh, in the United Provinces, in the Andhra Districts of the Madras Presidency, and in Bombay, Bihar and Orissa. Non-co-operation lent the support of its best leaders to fostering the Kisan Sabha Movement in the United Provinces where real grievances of the peasantry against the landlords made their task easy. At the commencement of the year serious agrarian outbreaks occurred in parts of Oudh and these were reflected in the movement against European landlords in the planting areas of Bihar—a movement which resulted in serious instances of incendiarism and necessitated the strengthening of the local constabulary by a force of regular cavalry. In Madras and Assam the peasantry were successfully incited to defy the Forest Laws and the non-payment of revenue was vigorously preached. In Bengal, where the number of European landlords is very small, the movement, besides being directed against those who existed, was turned with considerable success to-

wards the refusal to pay minor taxes such as Union Board and Chaukidari taxes. The peasantry were also led to believe that under a Swaraj Government, which was to come into being in 1922, the payment of rent and revenue would be no longer required of them. When the economic pinch was so severe and the listener so ignorant and gullible, it need be no matter for surprise that the propaganda proved effective.

68. **The Assam Tea Garden Coolies.**—The consideration of agrarian propaganda leads to the most important example during the year of agrarian labour unrest and its fomentation and exploitation by Non-co-operators. This was the successful stampeding of the Tea Garden Coolies from the Chargola Valley Tea Estates in Assam. A communiqué issued by the Assam Government shows that on May 2nd strikes commenced on Tea Gardens in the Chargola and Longai Valleys when the coolies demanded large increases in their pay. Increases were offered ranging from 30 per cent. to 50 per cent. These were rejected and by the middle of the month between six and seven thousand coolies left the gardens and assembled at Karimganj. Here food was at first provided by the Government, but the coolies were led to believe that acceptance of Government food would entail their being sent back to the Gardens. The communiqué also stated definitely that persons unconnected with the tea industry had made efforts to foment discontent among the coolies for some time previously with the intention of causing ill-will against Europeans and the Government. It was also clear that Tea Gardens in that part of Assam, owing to trade depression, had been very hard hit and the opportunities afforded to coolies to supplement their daily wage with "overtime" work had suffered accordingly. Both the Government and the tea industry had for some time previously realised that some readjustment of wages was called for and the only reason why a commission had not been appointed to deal with the matter was the depressed state of the industry.

At this stage it was already plain that Non-co-operators had seized on genuine economic discontent and had fomented and exploited it for their own purposes. Further light is thrown in this aspect of the trouble by statements in the Press issued by the Tea Industry. Representatives of the Calcutta Agency houses visited the gardens affected and promised to enquire into all grievances and to redress any found to be well-grounded. In the majority of cases the labourers refused to listen to any terms saying they had been instructed not to work on any European-owned Estate.

It was found that the coolies were under the impression that Gandhi had chartered a steamer to take them to their homes and the evidence also proved that Non-co-operation meetings had been held in the neighbourhood of tea gardens and that at these meetings, which were largely attended by coolies, they were incited to strike work. The religious susceptibilities of the coolies were fully exploited and they were told that the day of the British Raj was over and that Gandhi Raj had succeeded it The coolies were informed that Gandhi had issued orders that coolies were no longer to work for European employers and must leave the gardens in a body, on pain, amongst other things, of being turned into mud or stone. Representatives of Tea firms were told by coolies that their reason for leaving the gardens was the order of Mahatma Gandhi to do so. All this was borne out by an article in a local Non-co-operation newspaper which said that the coolies had received the message of Mahatma Gandhi with a sincerity and a whole heartedness which the paper correctly described as "simply amazing." "Mahatma's name is in their mouths. Mahatma's image is in their hearts" . . . So much for the successful propaganda employed. Now for its effects.

It at once became evident that the coolies had the open official support of the Bengal Congress organisation. From the commencement of the exodus, when the Karimganj Congress Committee assumed charge of arrangements for their food and accommodation, the coolies were supported by the Congress organisation and its funds. Serious trouble, as was to be expected, soon ensued. The coolies, who were mainly without means to pay railway fares, managed to assemble to the number of several thousands at Chandpur, the terminus of the A. B. Railway, whence the journey had to be continued by river steamer. The coolies successfully rushed one steamer, which had to transport them free of cost to Goalundo where the land journey had to be resumed. In order to avoid a repetition of this lawlessness and also to clear the coolies from the Chandpur Railway Station, which they absolutely refused to leave, the services of a party of Military Police were requisitioned by the Commissioner of the Division. Under his orders the Military Police cleared the station using no weapons other than unloaded rifles without bayonets. This action, which had been also rendered necessary by the insanitary condition of the Railway Station precincts, was the signal for a unanimous howl of indignation from Non-co-operators and their press, combined with characteristically false allegations of the use of bayonets, and the infliction of serious wounds including fractured limbs and bones by the Government's cruel soldiery. These allegations were promptly inquired into on the spot by the Hon'ble Home Member of the Bengal Government whose challenge to produce the persons alleged to be so injured met with no response other than shuffling and evasion.

The Non-co-operators, having now manufactured a fresh grievance successfully, exploited it and a general strike was caused among the staff of both the Assam Bengal Railway and Steamer services in Bengal. *Hartals* were observed at numerous places in East Bengal and Non-co-operators actually succeeded in gaining such control over shopkeepers at Chandpur and some other places that persons without a Congress permit could not be served. This necessitated the direct importation of supplies. These strikes lasted till September and caused intense misery among the strikers, particularly on the Assam

Bengal Railway. Both failed and the strikers had eventually to surrender at discretion after having tried, under their Non-co-operation leaders, all means fair and foul, including even train-wrecking, to force the authorities to capitulate. Throughout the strikers were led by Non-co-operators and supported by the funds of the Congress organisation. In the meantime the garden coolies after losing some 300 of their number from cholera at Chandpur, were repatriated with funds raised from the charitable, mainly through Moderate agency, in Calcutta. The object of the Non-co-operators in exploiting the Railway and Steamer strikes was to force the Bengal Government to assume responsibility for the repatriation of the coolies and on this political issue it was a direct trial of strength. C. R. Das fully supported this policy and spent over a lakh of rupees from Provincial Congress funds to finance it. Gandhi opposed the exploitation of labour for political purposes and for some time there was a split in the Congress camp over this question.

This whole transaction may be briefly summed up in four stages:—

(*a*) Anti-European propaganda among the tea-garden coolies with a view to damaging the interests and prestige of European capital.

(*b*) The stampeding of the coolies *en masse*.

(*c*) The inevitable occurrence of lawlessness.

(*d*) The exploitation of the Railway and Steamer Labour to paralyse communications in order to compel the Bengal Government to accede to the demands of the Non-co-operators. This was responsible for the death of many of the coolies whose sole means of transport was cut off. Even when funds and steamers were available Non-co-operation leaders refused to call off the strike, even temporarily.

69. **The Madras Mills Strikes.**—The next prominent example of interference by Non-co-operators in labour affairs took place at Madras in the fomenting and subsequent conduct of the protracted and disastrous strikes in the Buckingham and Carnatic Mills. Labour in Madras had shown itself restive in January and there were several strikes one of which took place in the Buckingham Mills. Even in these, Madrassi Non-co-operators were conspicuous. It was also evident that these strikes, in which the Carnatic Mills, also joined, had the support of the Madras Congress and Khilafat Committees. The management of the Mills came to terms with the strikers and the two mill strikes terminated at the end of January.

At this time the Madras Labour Union was under the guidance of B. P. Wadia of whom it may be said that he is a genuine sympathiser with Labour first, and a politician afterwards. He now resigned from the Madras Provincial Congress Committees as he differed from the extreme political doctrines it laid down. He also resigned the office of President of the Madras Labour Union preparatory to an extended tour in Europe. Early in March it was noticed that in Madras City the Madras Labour Union with a membership of 10,000 and three other Unions, led by E. L. Aiyer, Kumaraswami Chetti and a few other Non-co-operators, mustered strong at the "*Hartal*" meeting on what was known as "Yakub Hassan's day." The object of the meeting was to demonstrate and protest against the action taken against Yakub Hassan and his Non-co-operation-Khilafat activities in Malabar.

At the end of March the Madras C. I. D. reported that the labour movement in Madras City, as well as in the mofussil, was remarkably quiet in spite of the persistent efforts of political agitators to exploit it for political ends. But after Wadia's departure the hold of the Non-co-operators on the Madras Labour Union gained in strength and they began to visit the Labour Union and address meetings. By May Wadia and his Assistant—Miss Chattopadhya—had resigned the posts of President and Secretary, respectively, of the Madras Central Labour Board. They were succeeded by Chakarai Chetti and E. L. Aiyer and the control of the Board passed to the Non-co-operators. These began to enlist Labourers for the Congress and to preach Non-co-operation and hand-spinning.

In June the Buckingham and Carnatic Mills again made common cause and entered on a combined strike. The Carnatic Mills struck first and the Buckingham Mills followed suit avowedly to enforce the demands of the strikers in the Carnatic Mills. The Madras Labour Union conducted both strikes and Non-co-operators immediately planned to supply the strikers with handlooms and spinning wheels. The conduct of the strikers soon took an ugly turn and a regular reign of violence, terrorism and lawlessness began in the Mill area. It is unnecessary for the purposes of this review to describe in detail the incidents of this period. It will suffice to say that special military measures were necessary with the repeated use of armed forces both by the military and the Police to suppress the frequent outbursts of violence.

At the end of June the Madras C. I. D. reported that Kalyana Sundara Mudaliar and other Non-co-operators were trying to induce sympathetic strikes in other industrial concerns. At the end of July, the Non-co-operation labour leaders were exhorting the strikers to hold out at any cost but it was evident that the strike had begun to weaken. The only alleviation proferred to the unfortunate strikers by the Non-co-operators was the offer of spinning wheels and hand-looms and resolutions of sympathy and support passed at public meetings. In spite of efforts by the Madras Government and various public bodies to find some basis for a settlement the strikes dragged on with increasing lawlessness and violence till the 21st of October when they collapsed. The Non-co-operators had then to allot funds and appeal to the public for further assistance to maintain some 5,000 strikers who were not reinstated in their posts.

His Excellency the Governor of Madras in reviewing the situation on one occasion plainly told a deputation from the Madras Labour Union and the strikers that the continuous unrest and indiscipline among the workmen of these mills were the outcome of deliberate efforts made mainly for political purposes. He also directed attention to the fact that a number of the executive officers of the Labour Union, who had directed the workers in successive strikes, were well-known Non-co-operators.

These two examples—the Madras Mills strikes and the A. B. Railway and Steamer Service strikes—sufficiently illustrate the motives and policy which have guided the Non-co-operator in his dealing with Labour.

70. **Other Riots and Disturbances.**—As was to be expected from the nature of the agitation and the propaganda by which it was carried on, the year 1921 was, apart from the strikes already dealt with, an abnormally disturbed one throughout India. In this connection may be quoted the Report of the Committee appointed to examine the repressive laws on the Statute Book, and the question of their repeal or amendment. The Report was dated September the 2nd and contained the following account of the general situation:—

"The first question then that we have to decide is whether with the conclusion of the war and the introduction of constitutional changes in the Government of India, there has been such an improvement in the general situation as to justify the repeal of all or any of these measures We have particularly to consider whether there exists such an anarchical movement as prevailed in Bengal during the last decade, or any probability of recrudescence of a movement, which at that time seriously disturbed the tranquillity of certain parts of India. On this point plain speaking is unavoidable."

"The evidence of many witnesses indicates that the constitutional reforms have produced a distinct change for the better in the attitude towards Government of the larger portion of the literate classes. As regards the illiterate masses, the position is much less satisfactory. It must be recognised that recent appeals to racial feeling, religious prejudice or economic discontent have in fact shaken respect for law, government and authority, and created an atmosphere of preparedness violence. Intimidation, social boycott and the establishment of courts, the jurisdiction of which is in some cases enforced by violence and insult, are among the methods employed to create a situation full of dangerous potentialities. Similarly, while many witnesses expressed the view that the general position had improved and that the cult of non-co-operation had generally failed to appeal to more thoughtful persons, we are forced to the conclusion that the leaders of this movement have succeeded in arousing a deep and widespread feeling of hostility towards Government. It is, however, as yet more marked in urban than in rural areas. The large number of serious riots during the past seven months cannot be regarded merely as passing ebullitions of temporary discontent. The disturbances in places so widely apart as Rai Bareli, Malegaon, Nagpur, Giridih, Dharwar, Aligarh and Matiari indicate a growing contempt for law and order. We have no doubt that economic and agrarian discontent has been exploited by agitators, and that these riots have in many cases disclosed a disregard of authority or an attempt to intimidate the courts or officers carrying out the orders of the courts, which justifies us in ascribing them to an active and malicious propaganda. In attempting any survey of the present political situation we cannot leave out of account further dangerous developments adumbrated by leaders of the Non-co-operation Party."

* * * * * *

"Taking into consideration all the evidence we have received, and the points to which we have adverted, and bearing in mind the still prevailing economic discontent, we cannot dismiss as improbable the danger of sudden sectarian, agrarian or labour disorder on a large scale culminating in riots."

Non-co-operation or Khilafat agitation was distinctly traceable in over 40 disturbances which occurred at various places in India during 1921. Special mention may be made of the riots at Malagaon (Bombay) Aligarh (U. P.) Bombay City and the Moplah rebellion,* where the Police, and in the last instance, all Government authority, were attacked and loss of life, more or less serious, occurred.

The tactics followed or attempted by Non-co-operators in all the cases of serious disturbances were to appoint a non-official committee of enquiry. These committees invariably published reports which sought to show that the officials of the Government were solely responsible for provoking the trouble and acted wrongly, if not criminally, in using armed force to quell them. Government communiqués which were issued as authoritative statements of fact were uniformly attacked as untrustworthy, one-sided, whitewashing documents, where they were not actually stigmatised as false.

This form of activity was an important factor in the campaign to weaken and challenge the authority of the Government. It cannot be said that leading Non-co-operators directly incited to violence where violence occurred, and they therefore, invariably disclaimed responsibility for it. But to their efforts and propaganda was due the gathering of mobs whose actions they were unable or unwilling to control. Further, the experience they gained early in their campaign can have left no doubt in their minds as to the ultimate outbreak of violence as the direct result of their methods.

---

* Part II, paragraph 96.

CHAPTER IV

Non-co-operation reaches and passes its zenith, 1922.

71. **Non-co-operation at its height.**—The period during, and immediately subsequent to, the meeting of the Congress at Ahmedabad may be regarded as the zenith of the Non-co-operation Movement. As shown in Chapter II, during 1921 Non-co-operation propaganda had resulted in widespread excitement throughout India and this had already forced some Local Governments to deal with volunteer associations under the Criminal Law Amendment Act of 1908. Since volunteers were the tools essential for all forms of Non-co-operation agitation, such as *hartals* and mass demonstrations, boycott of foreign goods and Government officials, picketting and preparation for civil disobedience, the Government action was immediately challenged, and, in pursuance of the Ahmedabad resolution, endeavours were made in most provinces to enlist volunteers in very large numbers. This endeavour was successful in Bengal, Madras and Bihar and, to a lesser extent, in the Punjab and Assam, while in Bombay and the Central Provinces, the recruitment of volunteers was meagre.

72. **Volunteers.**—In Bengal, particularly, volunteers were enlisted in very large numbers and resorted to activities which left the Government no option but to arrest them; and undoubtedly the idea underlying this movement was to form a mass too unwieldly to handle with which to fill the jails.* The situation caused the Local Government the greatest anxiety and they had to consider the question of preparing prison camps to accommodate the persons arrested. As can be imagined, before this stage was reached, the resources of the Congress were very severely taxed and they were finally compelled, in Calcutta, to enlist mill hands who were scarcely worthy of the title "volunteer" since they were paid in order to court arrest. Ultimately the supply failed—but not until the Local Government had been forced to convert a disused dockyard into a jail.

73. **Hartals.**—Another feature of this period was the series of *hartals* which took place wherever H. R. H. the Prince of Wales visited. These were attended in most places with a certain amount of success, but in spite of the efforts of the Non-co-operators, considerable crowds generally appeared and gave the Prince a hearty reception. In Calcutta, extensive picketting was expected on the day of the Prince's arrival, but this was countered by patrolling the streets during the preceding night by means of a civil guard, which had been formed for the purpose, and this method had a very salutary effect in that it prevented intimidation.

74. **Civil Disobedience.**—In accordance with the Ahmedabad resolution civil disobedience was adopted with respect to the Criminal Law Amendment Act and to the Seditious Meetings Act. In Bengal and Bihar and Orissa, the payment of the *chowkidari* tax was, in places,

*Paragraph 57.

withheld; while in Madras, the Central Provinces and Assam, forest laws were ignored. Generally, civil disobedience was widely discussed and most Provincial Congress Committees considered the selection of some area in which "aggressive civil disobedience", including refusal to pay all taxes, should be launched. At this stage it was apparent that the Congress leaders were being carried on a wave of enthusiasm, of their own raising, faster than they liked to go and much hesitation was apparent among them as to the actual introduction of this step which, they were perfectly aware, would most certainly lead to violence. For example, the District Congress Committee of Guntur, Madras, were anxious to start complete civil disobedience towards the end of December 1921, but permission was refused by the Andhra Provincial Congress Committee. In the following month, however, the Guntur District Congress Committee again raised the question and called for a suspension of payment of land revenue, pending the decision of the Andhra P. C. C. On this occasion, the Andhra Committee responded and directed, in its own jurisdiction, the withholding of taxes for a fortnight or as long as the District Congress Committee decided. The Government of Madras indicated that they would take steps to enforce the law, and Gandhi disapproved of the action of the Andhra Committee, with the result that the proposal seems to have been dropped, although Guntur, acting independently, caused a great deal of trouble.

75. **The Non-Party Conference, Bombay, 14th January 1922.**— Gandhi, in the meantime, had been preparing Bardoli for civil disobedience pending the decision with regard to the Round Table Conference. It will be remembered that Pandit M. M. Malaviya and Mr. Jinnah were endeavouring to arrange a non-party conference in order to find some ground common to all parties This conference assembled at Bombay on the 14th of January 1922 and purported to represent all shades of Indian opinion. According to press accounts, a certain amount of success was attained in finding a common platform, and this success found expression in a resolution deploring the action taken by Government in arresting volunteers and in encroaching upon the "elementary rights of citizenship, freedom of the press and liberty of speech and association." In order to explore all methods and to arrive at an honourable agreement, a conference between the Government and popular representatives was suggested. To create a favourable atmosphere for his conference it appeared that Gandhi was prepared to abandon *hartals*, picketing and civil disobedience; while the Government, on their part, were asked to withdraw all orders under the Criminal Law Amendment Act of 1908 and under the Seditious Meetings Act, to release all prisoners convicted under these Acts and also the *fatwa* prisoners (including the Ali Brothers), and to appoint a joint committee to consider the cases of prisoners who had been convicted under cover of the ordinary law for activities of an innocent nature. The points at issue in the Conference were to be the Punjab and Khilafat wrongs and the demand for

Swaraj or full responsible government on Dominion basis. H. M.'s Government were to be asked to clothe H. E. the Viceroy with the necessary powers for the conclusion of negotiations on these lines.

It was obvious that the Non-co-operators were giving very little away and what Gandhi was prepared to abandon were the points which were calculated to do him the most harm with public opinion in England, while not seriously interfering with the normal course of the agitation in India. It was equally obvious that the Government of India could not agree to surrender all the advantages they had gained without any guarantee of a cessation of hostilities, particularly as the attitude of their opponents was so thoroughly uncompromising that it was certain that no agreement could possibly be reached.

76. **Gandhi's Predicament.**—The failure to arrive at any negotiation with Government put Gandhi in an exceedingly difficult position. He could not close his eyes to the fact that civil disobedience was certain to result in violence, for, in addition to the actual outrages which had occurred during 1921, the activities of the Non-co-operation volunteers during the beginning of 1922 were a clear indication of the spirit of violence underlying the movement. The picketing with respect to the boycott of foreign goods, the methods resorted to in the furtherance of *hartals* and the intimidation adopted towards Government servants who refused to resign, continually furnished instances of violence, or threats of violence. In addition, the threat of violence by mobs excited by volunteers was constant, as was obvious from violent mass demonstrations directed against police stations in Bihar and Bengal and by numerous instances of the burning of toddy shops in the furtherance of the temperance movement in Madras. His position was in no way eased by an outbreak of hooliganism on the part of volunteers on the occasion of the visit of the Prince of Wales to Madras city in the middle of January 1922. Stones were thrown at motor cars and pedestrians, public streets were barricaded with dustbins and places of entertainment were damaged. Commenting on this the *Englishman* remarked:—"There was no repression in Bombay and Madras and riots followed. There was repression in Calcutta and there were no riots."

77. **Civil Disobedience to commence at Bardoli.**—Gandhi therefore was faced by the difficulty, after having brought the pot to the boil, of keeping it boiling without allowing it to boil over. He had seen the fate in the past of leaders who failed to lead, and he knew that unless he went on, his personal ascendancy would disappear. He had originally fixed the 23rd of November 1921 for the commencement of civil disobedience at Bardoli but had been able temporarily to shelve this programme in consequence of the disorder at the time of the arrival of H. R. H. the Prince of Wales. The resulting action taken by Local Governments had filled the jails in some parts of India, which condition had been pledge by Gandhi as an unfailing means of obtaining Swaraj. The Swaraj, however, had not yet come and it was perfectly apparent that Local Governments were quite prepared

to continue to deal with volunteers under the law as soon as they broke it. Gandhi, therefore, was forced to fix other dates for the commencement of civil disobedience, but on each occasion had been able to find some excuse to postpone it, pending a decision regarding the Round Table Conference. All this had not enhanced his reputation with his followers and to withdraw from the stand he had taken would have meant his political funeral. He had to do something and what he did was to issue a letter addressed to H. E. the Viceroy on the 4th February 1922 in which he announced his intention, failing certain concessions on the part of Government, to resort to aggressive civil disobedience at Bardoli within seven days' time. This action, he declared, had been forced upon him by the lawless repression of the Government and in defence of the rights of freedom of speech, freedom of press and freedom of association. He claimed that his offer, made through the Malaviya Conference, of suspending Non-co-operation activities in respect to *hartals*, picketing and civil disobedience, fulfilled all the conditions laid down by the Viceroy as the necessary preliminaries to the summoning of the Round Table Conference, and, as no response to this offer had been made, there was no alternative left him but to carry on his policy in order to enforce the Congress demands. He admitted that the lessons of non-violence had not yet been absorbed by the country, and he would have preferred to have postponed action, but his hand had been forced by the Government. He added that he would re-consider his decision if the Government released all political prisoners convicted for non-violent activities and gave him a guarantee that they would refrain from repressing non-violent activities of the Non-co-operation Party, even if they fell within the purview of the Indian Penal Code.

In a communiqué issued on the 6th February calling for the support of loyal citizens in any action which they might think fit to take to suppress mass civil disobedience, the Government of India had no difficulty in exposing the falsity and absurdity of Gandhi's statements and claims. To this Gandhi replied by accusing Government of being responsible for every *fracas* which occurred between the police and volunteers and made a grievance of the fact that officials did not stand aside to allow the volunteers to terrorise the country. He implied that Government would be to blame for any trouble which arose from aggressive civil disobedience, for which preparations had continued at Bardoli and some other places—with probably less success than was claimed by Non-co-operators.

78. **Chauri Chaura Massacre, February 1922.**—It seemed as if Gandhi would have no alternative to the declaration of mass civil disobedience, but an incident occurred which gave him the pretext to withdraw, which he undoubtedly wanted. On the 5th February 1922 at Chauri Chaura in the Gorakhpur district of the United Provinces, a mob of 2,000 villagers led by volunteers attacked a police station,

killing and burning the entire police staff, consisting of two Sub-Inspectors, 18 constables and one chowkidar. This gave Gandhi the requisite excuse and, on the ground that India was clearly not yet sufficiently non-violent to indulge in civil disobedience, he called a meeting of the Working Committee of the Congress at Bardoli on the 11th and 12th of February which passed the following resolutions:—

79. **Working Committee Resolutions at Bardoli.**—"(1) The Working Committee deplores the inhuman conduct of the mob at Chauri Chaura in having brutally murdered constables and wantonly burnt a police thana, and tenders its sympathy to the families of the bereaved.

"(2) In spite of the nations repeated warnings, every time mass civil disobedience has been imminent, some popular violent outburst has taken place, indicating that the atmosphere in the country is not non-violent enough for mass civil disobedience, the latest instance being the tragic and terrible events at Chauri Chaura near Gorakhpur. The Working Committee of the Congress, therefore, resolves that mass civil disobedience, as contemplated at Bardoli and elsewhere, be suspended and instructs the local Congress Committees forthwith to advise the cultivators to pay the land revenue and other taxes due to the Government, the payment of which might have been suspended in anticipation of mass civil disobedience, and instructs them to suspend every other preparatory activity of an offensive nature.

" (3) The suspension of mass civil disobedience shall be continued till the atmosphere is so non-violent as to ensure the non-repetition of popular atrocities, such as at Gorakhpur, or hooliganism, such as at Bombay and Madras, respectively, on November 17th, 1921, and January 13th last.

" (4) In order to promote a peaceful atmosphere, the Working Committee advises, till further instructions, all Congress organisations to stop activities especially designed to court arrest and imprisonment, save the normal Congress activities including voluntary *hartals*, wherever an absolutely peaceful atmosphere can be assured, and for that end all picketing shall be stopped, save for the *bona fide* and peaceful purpose of warning the visitors to liquor shops against the evils of drinking. Such picketing is to be controlled by persons of known good character and specially selected by the Congress Committee concerned.

" (5) The Working Committee advises, till further instructions, the stoppage of all volunteer processions and public meetings merely for the purpose of defiance of the notifications regarding such meetings. This, however, shall not interfere with the private meeting of the Congress and other Committees or public meetings which are required for the conduct of the normal activities of the Congress.

" (6) Complaints having been brought to the notice of the Working Committee that ryots are not paying rents to the zamindars, the Working Committee advises Congress workers and organisations to inform the ryots that such withholding of rent is contrary to the resolutions of the Congress and that it is injurious to the best interests of the Country.

" (7) The Working Committee assures the Zemindars that the Congress movement is in no way intended to attack their legal rights, and that even when the ryots have grievances, the Committee desires that redress should be sought by mutual consultation and by the usual recourse to arbitration.

" (8) Complaints having been brought to the notice of the Working Committee that in the formation of volunteer corps great laxity prevails in the selection, and that insistence is not laid on the full use of hand-spun and hand-woven khaddar, and on the full observance by the Hindus of the rule as to the removal of untouchability, nor is care being taken to ascertain that the candidates believe fully in the observance of non-violence in word and deed in terms of the Congress Resolution, the Working Committee calls upon all Congress organisations to revise their lists and remove from them the names of all such volunteers as do not strictly conform to the requirements of the pledge.

"(9) The Working Committee is of opinion that unless Congressmen carry out to the full the Congress Constitution and the Resolutions from time to time issued by the Working Committee, it is not possible to achieve its objects expeditiously or at all.

"(10) The foregoing Resolutions will have effect only pending the meeting, to be specially convened, of the All-India Congress Committee and thereafter subject to confirmation by it. The Secretary will call such a meeting as soon as possible after consultation with Hakim Ajmal Khan."

" WORKING OF CONGRESS ORGANISATION."

"Whereas the Gorakhpur tragedy is a powerful proof of the fact that the mass mind has not yet fully realised the necessity of non-violence as the integral active and chief part of mass civil disobedience, and whereas the reported indiscriminate acceptance of persons as volunteers in contravention of the Congress instructions betrays want of appreciation of the vital part of Satyagraha, and whereas in the opinion of the Working Committee the delay in the attainment of the national aim is solely due to the weak and incomplete execution in practice of the constitution of the Congress with a view to perfecting the internal organisation, the Working Committee advises all Congress organisations to be engaged in the following activities:—

" (1) To enlist at least one crore of the members of the Congress.

" *Note.*—(i) Since peace (non-violence and legitimateness) and truth are the essence of the Congress creed, no person should be enlisted who does not believe in non-violence and truth as indispensable for the attainment of Swaraj. The creed of the Congress must, therefore, be carefully explained to each person who is appealed to join the Congress " "(ii) The workers should note that none who does not pay the annual subscription can be regarded as a 'qualified Congressman. All the old members are, therefore, to be advised to re-register their names."

"(2) To popularise the spinning wheel and organise the manufacture of hand-spun and hand-woven khaddar.

"*Note*.—To this end, all workers and office-bearers should be dressed in khaddar, and it is recommended that with a view to encouraging others they should themselves learn hand-spinning."

"(3) To organise National schools.

"*Note*.—No picketting of the Government Schools should be resorted to. Best reliance should be placed upon the superiority of National Schools in all vital matters to command attendance."

"(4) To organise the depresse classes for a better life, to improve their social, mental and moral condition to induce them to send their children to the National Schools and to provide for them the ordinary facilities which other citizens enjoy.

"*Note*.—Whilst, therefore, where the prejudice against the untouchables is still strong in places, separate schools and separate wells must be maintained out of Congress funds, every effort should be made to draw such children to National Schools and to persuade the people to allow the untouchables to use the common wells."

"(5) To organise the temperance campaign amongst the people addicted to the drink habit by house-to-house visits and to rely more upon appeal to the drinker in his home than upon picketing.

"(6) To organise village and town "Panchayats" for the private settlement of all disputes, reliance being placed solely upon the force of public opinion, and the truthfulness of "Panchayat" decisions to ensure obedience to them.

"*Note*.—In order to avoid even the appearance of coercion, no social boycott should be resorted to against those who will not obey the Panchayat's decisions."

"(7) In order to promote and emphasise unity among all classes and races and mutual good-will, the establishment of which is the aim of the movement of non-co-operation, to organise a Social Service Department that will render help to all, irrespective of differences, in times of illness or accident.

"*Note*.—A Non-co-operator whilst firmly adhering to his Creed, will deem it a privilege to render personal service in case of illness or accident to every person, whether English or Indian."

"(8) To continue the Tilak Memorial Swaraj Fund and to call upon every Congressman or Congress sympathiser to save at least one hundredth part of his annual income for the year 1921. Every province to send every month 25 per cent. of its income from the Tilak Memorial Swaraj Fund to the All-India Congress Committee.

"(9) The above resolutions shall be brought before the forthcoming Session of the All-India Congress Committee for revision, if necessary.

"(10) In the opinion of the Working Committee, a project is necessary for the purpose of finding employment for those who may give up Government service, and to that end the Committee appoints Messrs. Mian Mahomed Haji Jan Mahomed Chotani, Jamnalal Bajaj and V. J. Patel to draw up a scheme for consideration by the said Special Meeting of the All-India Congress Committee."

These resolutions are given in full as they contain tacit admissions of violence on the part of volunteers apart from the instance of mob violence at Chauri Chaura. They also give an appreciation of the situation from the Congress point of view and show the programme on which it was proposed to employ Non-co-operators, in the hope that it would maintain their interest in the movement.

80. **Gandhi's Apologia.**—At the same time Gandhi in *Young India* explained his own view of the position in an article which commenced as follows:—

> "God has been abundantly kind to me. He has warned me the third time that there is not as yet in India that truthful and non-violent atmosphere which, and which alone, can justify mass disobedience which can be at all described as civil, which means gentle, truthful, humble, knowing, wilful yet loving, never criminal and hateful.
>
> He warned me in 1919 when the Rowlatt Act agitation was started. Ahmedabad, Viramgaum and Kheda erred, Amritsar and Kasur erred. I retraced my steps, called it a Himalayan miscalculation, humbled myself before God and man and stopped not merely mass Civil Disobedience but even my own which I knew was intended to be civil and non-violent. The next time it was through the events of Bombay that God gave a terrific warning. He made me eye-witness of the deeds of the Bombay mob on the 17th November. The mob acted in the interest of non-co-operation. I announced my intention to stop the mass Civil Disobedience which was to be immediately started in Bardoli. The humiliation was greater than in 1919. But it did me good. I am sure that the nation gained by the stopping. India stood for truth and non-violence by the suspension.
>
> But the bitterest humiliation was still to come. Madras did give the warning, but I heeded it not. But God spoke clearly through Chauri Chaura. I understand that the constables, who were so brutally hacked to death, had given much provocation. They had even gone back upon the word just given by the Inspector that the people

would not be molested, that when the procession had passed the stragglers were interfered with and abused by the constables. The foreman cried out for help. The mob returned. The constables opened fire. The little ammunition they had was exhausted and they retired to the thana for safety. The mob, my informant tells me, therefore, set fire to the thana. The self-imprisoned constables had to come out for dear life, and as they did so they were hacked to pieces and the mangled remains were thrown into the raging flames."

The article went on to imply that volunteers were not concerned in the Chauri Chaura outrage and that the mob had had great provocation owing to the high-handed tyranny of the police of that locality. Later on he said that the Congress did not "think of starting mass civil disobedience until we are sure of peace being retained in spite of such civil disobedience being started and in spite of Government provocation." He went on to make it clear that mass civil disobedience had merely been postponed, and added that he intended to mortify the flesh by imposing on himself a five days' continuous fast, but urged his co-workers not to follow his example.

81. **All-India Congress Committee confirms Bardoli Resolutions.**— The All-India Congress Committee met at Delhi on the 24th February 1922 to consider the Bardoli resolutions which it confirmed, but specified that individual civil disobedience, whether of a defensive or aggressive character, might be commenced in respect of particular places or particular laws at the instance of, and upon permission being granted therefor, by the respective Provincial Committees, provided that such civil disobedience should not be permitted unless all the conditions laid down by the Congress or the All-India Congress Committee or the Working Committee were strictly fulfilled.

The All-India Congress Committee went on to make it quite clear that the permanent abandonment of mass civil disobedience was not intended, and that it held civil disobedience to be the right and duty of the people to be exercised and performed whenever the State opposed the declared will of the people. Civil disobedience was defined as disobedience of orders or laws by a single individual or an ascertained number or group of individuals. Therefore, a prohibited public meeting where admission was regulated by tickets and to which no unauthorised admission was allowed, was an instance of individual civil disobedience; whereas a prohibited meeting to which the general public was admitted without any restriction was an instance of mass civil disobedience. Such civil disobedience was defensive when a prohibited public meeting was held to conduct a normal activity, although it might result in arrests. It would be aggressive, if it was held, not for any normal activity, but merely for the purpose of courting arrest and imprisonment.

In spite of the alterations made by the All-India Congress Committee in the Bardoli resolutions, the calling off at this juncture of civil disobedience had the effect, throughout India, of taking a boiling pot off the fire, and, undoubtedly, it was the beginning of the end of Non-co-operation.

82. **Result of Bardoli Resolution.**—At the beginning of 1922 reports from officials from all over India were steadily growing more pessimistic in tone and it was very apparent that the resources of Government were being taxed to their utmost. As soon as the Bardoli resolutions became generally known (a slow process in a country like India) a lull in the agitation was reported from all directions.

The resolutions were confirmed by Provincial Congress Committees, though it was clear that in many cases this confirmation was the result of the necessity to appear loyal to the Central Body and not from any real desire to refrain from civil disobedience, even though it was certain to lead to violence.

The lack of cohesion was apparent from the amount of criticism levelled at the suspension of civil disobedience by the more extreme members of the Congress; and this had the effect of re-opening the partially closed breach between them and the Moderates as well as creating schism in the ranks of the Non-co-operators themselves. This disunion was enhanced by the arrest of Gandhi on the 10th March 1922, and his removal from the political arena resulted in the disintegration of the various elements in the Congress which his personality had held together. The relations between Hindus and Muhammadans became strained, for it will be remembered that the Ali Brothers were in jail and it was their very close co-operation with Gandhi that had served to make Hindu-Muhammadan unity something more than a phrase.

83. **Gandhi's conviction and imprisonment, March 1922.**—Gandhi's arrest had been decided upon by the Government of India because it was apparent that, although civil disobedience had been postponed, there was no fundamental change in the policy of the Non-co-operation party. He had frequently offended under the law but Government had held their hand in the hope that his inclination towards non-violence would deter him from a path leading to violence. It was now clear that although he was perfectly aware of the direction which the path was taking yet he was determined to follow it—slowly, it is true, but surely. Nothing could be gained by giving him more rope, so he was prosecuted with respect to four seditious articles which he had published in the *Young India* during 1921 and 1922. He was convicted under section 124-A of the Indian Penal Code and sentenced to six years' simple imprisonment on the 18th of March 1922, at Ahmedabad. He made no defence, and said, "I do not ask for mercy. I do not plead an extenuating act. I am here, therefore, to invite and submit to the highest penalty that can be inflicted upon me for what in law is a deliberate crime and what appears to me to be the highest duty of a citizen."

84. **Non-co operation agitation wanes.**—The strife within the Congress, brought about by the withdrawal of civil disobedience and by the arrest of Gandhi, resulted in the Congress leaders having little time available for propaganda purposes as they were busily occupied in quarrelling with each other. In consequence of this, and of the loss of prestige from which Gandhi had suffered by reason of the Bardoli resolutions, his arrest and conviction caused extraordinarily little excitement*; and the visit of the Prince of Wales to the Punjab which took place about this time was very successful. A meeting of the Congress Working Committee at Ahmedabad on the 17th of March produced nothing novel and the official Congress programme remained as outlined by the Bardoli-Delhi resolution with emphasis on non-violence and the production of *khaddar*.

85. **Changes of policy suggested.**—In April 1922 various proposals to change the Non-co-operation policy appeared. In the Central Provinces, a suggestion was made to capture municipalities and this was shortly afterwards again mentioned by Mrs. C. R. Das at the annual meeting of the Bengal Provincial Conference, of which she was elected President in deference to her husband who was then in jail. Mrs. Das went on to suggest the consideration of the question of Non-co-operators entering the Councils. This proposal, which was also mooted in the Maharashtra Provincial Congress Committee, was a revolutionary one, as it was directly contrary to Gandhi's policy, and it was subsequently to lead to a very sharply defined split in the Congress.

86. **Sporadic Picketing.**—During this period such Congress activities as existed were concentrated mainly on the production of *khaddar* and the boycott of foreign goods which, during the middle of 1922, led to a certain amount of sporadic picketing in Bengal and the United Provinces. For this purpose some volunteers were recruited in Calcutta and their activities necessitated arrests at the end of July, but by September, picketing had ceased in Bengal, though it occurred again in the Bombay Presidency at the end of the year.

After Gandhi's conviction the Congress decided that the 18th of every month should be set aside as a day of prayer, on which all earnings should be devoted to the Tilak Swaraj Fund in his memory. In a very short time, however, Gandhi Day was celebrated more in the breach than in the observance.

87. **Revolutionaries and the Bengal Provincial Congress Committee.**—In Bengal another factor which appeared was an attempt on the part of the revolutionaries in that province to gain control of the management of the Bengal Provincial Congress Committee. Up to this point they had realised that the doctrine of non-violence had been accepted by the public and that it was hopeless to endeavour to change it, but after Bardoli they quickly grasped the fact that Gandhi's ascendency was on the wane, and they endeavoured to capture the local

* He had asked that there should be no *hartals* or demonstrations.

Congress Committee with the object ultimately of diverting it towards violence. These revolutionaries had, for some time past, been in touch with the renegade Indian—M. N. Roy—in Europe, who was the accredited agent for India of the Third International. Roy had been urging on them the hopelessness of any agitation in India which was not supported by the masses and had strongly advocated propaganda among agricultural and industrial labouring classes. The effect of Roy's propaganda, such as it was, will be shown later.

88. **All-India Congress Committee, Lucknow, June 1922.**—The most important event in the middle of 1922 was the appointment of a Civil Disobedience Enquiry Committee by the All-India Congress Committee at a meeting at Lucknow which was held on the 6th to 8th June 1922. For some time past, the Congress leaders had realised that the passive programme, on which the Congress was at that time officially embarked, had totally failed to provide the requisite excitement to keep the movement alive. At the same time, in view of past experience, they naturally hesitated to revert to civil disobedience as was being urged by their Left Wing, of which Mr. V. J. Patel of Bombay was one of the most outspoken members. They therefore decided to appoint a sub-committee in the hopes that it would find the solution to the problem which they could not solve themselves; so the All-India Congress Committee passed the following resolution:—

> "This Committee records its satisfaction that although, in spite of the suspension of all aggressive activities by the Congress Committees, repression in a most severe form has been resorted to by the Government in several parts of the country, the spirit of the Congress workers has not been daunted and the constructive programme laid down by the Committee is being loyally carried out at great sacrifice in every province.
>
> The Committee has taken note of the widespread feeling that, in view of the extremely unfair manner in which the policy of repression is being carried out by the Government, the country should be advised to resort to some form of civil disobedience to compel the Government to abandon their present policy and to agree to concede the Triple Demand of the Congress. But the Committee is of opinion that the carrying out of the Constructive Programme will be the best preparation for even mass civil disobedience while it will also be the most effective means of furthering the objects of the Congress. The Committee therefore earnestly appeals to the country to concentrate all its efforts upon carrying out the Constructive Programme to the fullest extent and to endeavour to complete it within the shortest period possible.
>
> That the further consideration of the question whether civil disobedience in some form or some other measure of a similar character should be adopted, should be taken up

at the next meeting of the Committee to be held at Calcutta on the 15th of August next.

That in the meantime the President be requested to nominate and authorise a few gentlemen to tour round the country and report on the situation to the next meeting."

In compliance with this resolution Hakim Ajmal Khan, the acting President of the Congress, appointed a committee consisting of himself as Chairman and the following members:—

Pandit Motilal Nehru.
Syt. C. Rajagopalachariar.
Dr. M. A. Ansari.
Syt. V. J. Patel.
Syt. S. Kasturiranga Iyengar.
Seth M. M. H. J. M. Chotani.*

89 **Civil Disobedience Enquiry Committee.**—The Civil Disobedience Enquiry Committee commenced its tour at the beginning of July, but it soon became apparent that they were experiencing great difficulty in finding a solution to the problem which had been set to them and that there was no hope of their report being ready by the 15th of August. In consequence the meeting of the All-India Congress Committee, fixed for that date, was postponed several times and actually it did not take place until the 20th of November at Calcutta. In the meantime, the difficulty experienced by the Civil Disobedience Enquiry Committee resulted in considerable internal friction and ultimately the Committee split on the question of council-entry. In this connection the pro-council entry members, in defence of their advocacy of a change of policy, pointed out in the following words how Gandhi himself had changed his course to suit the wind:—"In March 1919 Mahatma Gandhi gave to India and the world his noble conception of Satyagraha. After the disturbances of April he unhesitatingly admitted that he had misjudged the readiness of the people to wield such a mighty weapon. At the Amritsar Congress he earnestly pleaded for co-operation with the Government in the Councils and outside, and warmly thanked Mr. Montagu for the Reforms such as they were—satyagraha to co-operation, from one pole to the other, all in the brief space of 8 months. After another three months he began a march back from co-operation Six months more of mature consideration and non-co-operation including the boycott of Councils became the accepted creed of the Congress at Calcutta".

90. **The Committee's findings.**—The following is a summary of the Civil Disobedience Enquiry Committee s recommendations as given in their Report:—

" 1. CIVIL DISOBEDIENCE."

" (a) The country is not prepared at present to embark upon general Mass Civil Disobedience but in view of the fact that a situation may

* Chotani was unable to take part in the tour or meetings of the Committee.

arise in any part of the country demanding an immediate resort to Mass Civil Disobedience of a limited character, *e.g.*, the breaking of a particular law or the non-payment of a particular tax for which the people are ready, we recommend that provincial committees be authorised to sanction such limited Mass Civil Disobedience on their responsibility if the conditions laid down by the All-India Congress Committee in that behalf are fulfilled.

(Unanimous)

" (*b*) We recommend the restoration of the Resolution No. 2 passed by the All-India Congress Committee at Delhi on the 4th-5th November which gives Provincial Committees all the powers necessary to determine upon a resort to Civil Disobedience of any kind whatever, by cancelling Resolution 1, cl. 1, passed on the 24th-25th February to the extent it conflicts with that resolution; provided that general Mass Civil Disobedience is not permissible.

(Unanimous) "

" 2. Entry into Legislative Councils."

" (A) The Congress and the Khilafat at their Gaya Sessions should declare that in view of the fact that the working of the Legislative Councils during their first term has, besides proving a great obstacle to the redress of the Khilafat and Punjab wrongs and the speedy attainment of Swarajya, caused great misery and hardship to the people, it is desirable that the following steps should be taken in strict accordance with the principles of non-violent non-co-operation to avoid the recurrence of the evil:—

1. Non-co-operators should contest the election on the issue of the redress of the Punjab and Khilafat wrongs and immediate Swarajya, and make every endeavour to be returned in a majority.
2. If the non-co-operators are returned in a majority large enough to prevent a quorum they should after taking their seats leave the Council Chamber in a body and take no part in the proceedings for the rest of the term. They should attend the Council occasionally only for the purpose of preventing vacancies.
3. If non-co-operators are returned in a majority which is not large enough to prevent a quorum they should oppose every measure of the Government including the budget and only move resolutions, for the redress of the aforesaid wrongs and the immediate attainment of Swarajya.
4. If the non-co-operators are returned in a minority they should act as pointed out in No. 2, and thus materially reduce the strength of the Council.

As the new Councils will not assemble till January 1924, we further propose that the Congress Session of 1923 be held during the first instead of the last week of December and the matter be again brought up for the issue of a final mandate by the Congress in view of the election.

Recommended by Hakim Ajmal Khan.

Pt. Motilal Nehru.

Syt. V. J. Patel.

" (B) There should be no change of the Congress programme in respect of the boycott of Councils.

Recommended by Dr. M. A. Ansari.

Syt. C. Rajagopalachari.

Syt. S. Kasturiranga Iyengar."

" 3. LOCAL BODIES."

" We recommend that in order to clear the position it should be declared that it is desirable for Non-co-operators to seek election to Municipalities and District or Local Boards with a view to facilitate the working of the constructive programme but that no hard and fast rules be at present laid down to regulate or restrict the activities of Non-co-operating members beyond advising them to act in harmony with local or provincial Congress organisations.

(Unanimous)."

" 4. BOYCOTT OF GOVERNMENT EDUCATIONAL INSTITUTIONS."

" We recommend a strict adherence to the Bardoli resolution in regard to these, by suspending for the present active propaganda calling upon boys to come out of schools and colleges. As required by that resolution reliance should be placed upon the superiority of National schools for drawing scholars from Government Institutions and not upon picketing or other aggressive propaganda.

(Unanimous)."

" 5. BOYCOTT OF LAW COURTS BY LITIGANTS AND LAWYERS."

" Effort should be concentrated on the establishment of panchayats and cultivation of a strong public opinion in their favour. We further recommend that all existing disqualifications imposed on practising lawyers should be removed.

(Unanimous)."

" 6. ORGANISATION OF LABOUR."

" Resolution No. 8 passed by the Nagpur Congress should be carried out without further delay.

(Unanimous)."

" 7. RIGHT OF PRIVATE DEFENCE."

" (A) We recommend that individuals should be given full freedom to exercise the right within the limits defined by law, except when carrying on Congress work or on occasions directly arising therefrom, subject always to the condition that it is not likely to lead to a general outburst of violence.

Using force in private defence in gross cases, such as insults to religion, outrages on modesty of women or indecent assaults on boys and men is not prohibited under any circumstances.

(All members except Syt. V. J. Patel).

"(B) Full freedom to exercise the right within the limits defined by law should be reserved to non-co-operators subject only to the condition that it is not likely to lead to a general outburst of violence, and to no further conditions.

(Syt. V. J. Patel)."

" 8. BOYCOTT OF BRITISH GOODS."

"(A) We accept the principle and recommend that the whole question be referred to a committee of experts for a full report to be submitted before the next Congress meets.

(All members except Syt. C. Rajagopalachariar.)

"(B) There is no objection to the collection and examination of facts by experts, but the acceptance of the principle by the All-India Congress Committee would mislead the nation and injure the movement.

(Syt. C. Rajagopalachariar)."

It will be noticed that a step towards the provision of excitement was made by recommending limited mass civil disobedience and the right of private defence to non-violent Non-co-operators. Although this right was not permitted to the extent desired by Mr. V. J. Patel, yet the conditions were sufficiently loosely worded to allow an Indian agitator, who is always prepared to take a great deal of license with truth, occasionally to find an excuse for violence on the grounds that provocation was exceptional.

In the meantime such agitation as existed had centred mainly on Mr. Lloyd George's "steel frame" speech and the Akali trouble. The former was delivered on the 2nd August 1922 and served temporarily to create some excitement as most Indian politicians seemed to see in it some threat of withdrawal from the policy of advances towards self-government by progressive stages already promised by Parliament.

91. **The Congress takes up the Akali Question.**—At this period the Akali Movement in the Punjab had come into direct conflict with Government, and at Guru-ka-Bagh in August 1922, Akalis were deliberately offering themselves for arrest by trespassing on the property of the local *Mahant*. The Congress leaders realised the value of this in their campaign of creating agitation against the Government, so a meeting of the Congress Working Committee took place on the 17th of September at Amritsar and a Committee was appointed to enquire into the Akali question. This Committee did not produce its report until a couple of years had elapsed, by which time Non-co-operation was little more than a phrase.

92. **Mr. C. R. Das' attitude on release from jail, August 1922.**—While in Jail Mr. C. R. Das had been elected President of the All-India Congress which met at Gaya during X'mas week 1922. Mr. Das was actually released from jail at the beginning of August 1922 and in view of the fact that he was President-elect of the Congress, he, for a time, hesitated to announce openly his views on council-entry, although there was no doubt as to what his views were in consequence of the lead given by his wife. With other Congress leaders, Das attended the United Provinces Provincial Conference at Dehra Dun on the 29th of October and there made a speech outlining Swaraj for the masses and not for the classes, in which he indicated that he had no intention of playing into the hands of the bourgeoisie. Undoubtedly this idea came to him from M. N. Roy in Berlin *via* their common revolutionary friends in Bengal. It is interesting to note that on this occasion Mr. Das' speech regarding the masses was supported by Mr. Patel who, in view of his inclination towards violence, appreciated the value of having the masses behind him.

By November 1922 Mr. C. R. Das had come down on the council-entry side of the fence and had expressed his opinion that there was no objection to taking the oath of allegiance required from a member of the Legislative Council, in view of the fact that the Congress had not yet adopted a creed leading out of the British Empire. He conceived that it was his clear duty to end the Councils and considered that the only effective way was for Non-co-operators to enter them, and, by obstruction, render their continued working impossible. In a statement dated the 7th November 1922 giving expression to his views, he added to his programme the following points:—

(1) Congress propaganda to be carried on outside India.

(2) India should join the "Great Asiatic Federation"—the Union of the Oppressed Nationalities of Asia which, according to C. R. Das, was then in process of formation as an extension of the pan-Islamic Movement.

(3) The definition by the Congress of the system of **Government for which they were working.**

(4) Spread of *khaddar* as the "symbol of Swaraj" but not as a means of attaining Swaraj itself.

(5) Organisation of labourers and peasants.

93. **The Council-Entry Question.**—By the end of 1922 the Congress was so agitated by the question of council-entry that all other matters were shelved. The All-India Congress Committee met at Calcutta and discussed the problem at great length from the 20th to the 24th of November, and finally resolved that the elections should be contested; but it did not define subsequent policy which was referred to the Gaya Congress for decision.

The Bengal Provincial Congress Committee met on the 24th of November and declared itself very strongly against council-entry, and all the office-bearers elected, with the exception of C. R. Das who was President, were No-changers. Das thereupon resigned from the Bengal Provincial Congress Committee and his example was shortly afterwards followed by Pandit Motilal Nehru, who resigned from the United Provinces Congress Committee after 14 No-changers out of its 15 office-bearers, were elected on the 29th of November. At about the same time a meeting of the Maharashtra Congress Committee nearly came to blows in discussing the same subject.

At this period, external Congress activities were confined to some picketing in and near Ahmedabad in the Bombay Presidency, and to a call for volunteers in Bengal by Mr. C. R. Das immediately after the Local Government had, on the 29th of November, cancelled their orders making volunteer associations unlawful under the Criminal Law Amendment Act.

94. **Gaya Congress, December 1922.**—Those for and against council-entry endeavoured to consolidate their position before the Gaya Congress, and by the middle of December feeling on this subject was running so high that a split was almost certain. This was not desired by either faction, so just before the Congress assembled at Gaya during X'mas week, some ineffectual efforts were made towards conciliation.

Mr. Das, in his presidential address, outlined his plan of work as follows:—

(1) Insistence on non-violence.

(2) Necessity for foreign propaganda.

(3) India to join the "Great Asiatic Federation."

(4) Swaraj not to be a government of the middle classes but of the people.

(5) The "scheme of Swaraj" to be built up by developing the ancient village system of India, controlled in a manner which appeared to bear a family resemblance to the Russian Soviet system.

(6) Councils to be destroyed from within, *i.e.*, elections contested.

(7) Organisation of labour and peasantry.

In the Congress itself an attempt was made to arrive at a compromise, but this was unsuccessful, and the pro-council party ultimately were completely outvoted, both in the Subjects Committee and in the open Congress.

The Congress refused to pass a resolution advocating the boycott of British goods and adopted various others of a non-contentious nature. Of these the most interesting was one congratulating Mustapha Kemal Pasha on his victories over the Greeks and pledging Indian support for the movement to free the Jazirat-ul-Arab from non-Muslim control. Resolutions were also passed in favour of the organisation of labour, boycott of schools, law-courts and Government institutions, and repudiation of responsibility for any financial liability incurred, subsequent to 1922, by the Government of India. The policy of the Non-co-operation Movement for the future was outlined in a resolution advocating preparation for civil disobedience which was passed by the Congress and is quoted below in full:—

> "The Congress reaffirms its opinion that Civil Disobedience is the only civilised and effective substitute for an armed rebellion, when every other remedy for preventing the arbitrary, tyrannical and emasculating use of authority has been tried, and in view of the widespread awakening of the people to a sense of the general urgent need for Swarajya, and the general demand and necessity for Civil Disobedience in order that the National goal may be speedily attained, and in view of the fact that the necessary atmosphere of non-violence has been preserved in spite of all provocation, this Congress calls upon all the Congress workers to complete the preparations for offering Civil Disobedience by strengthening and expanding the National organisation and to take immediate steps for the collection of at least Rs. 25 lakhs for the Tilak Swarajya Fund and the enrolment of at least 50,000 volunteers, satisfying the conditions of the Ahmedabad pledge, by a date to be fixed by the All-India Congress Committee at Gaya, and empowers the Committee to issue necessary instructions for carrying this resolution into practical effect."

Amendments to this resolution suggesting an immediate introduction of civil disobedience were defeated.

CHAPTER V.

The Swaraj Party swamps orthodox Non-co operation, 1923-24.

95. **Formation of the Swaraj Party.**—After his defeat at Gaya, Mr. C. R. Das resigned the Presidentship of the Congress and formed a new party named the 'Congress-Khilafat-Swarajya' Party which, while remaining within the Congress, would endeavour to capture the Councils. In the formation of this party, with Mr. Das were associated Pandit Motilal Nehru, Hakim Ajmal Khan, Mr. V. J. Patel and several other well known individuals. Immediately after the Gaya Congress both parties defined their policy and each accused the other for the failure to bring about a compromise, and they both entered on propaganda campaigns in furtherance of their own particular views. The All-India Congress Committee urged the enlistment of 50 thousand volunteers and a collection of 25 lakhs of rupees for the Tilak Swarajya Fund by the end of April and decided that the no-change leaders should tour the country in order to attain these results. The Swaraj Party on the other hand, engaged in an extensive newspaper campaign in favour of council-entry—with considerable effect for the party had succeeded in gaining control of the majority of important vernacular papers in India. By the end of January, the No-change Party had worked up a certain amount of volunteer activity in Bengal and the Punjab, but Mr. Das' group undoubtedly gained ground, and the bitterness between the two sections of the Congress in no way diminished. Both parties, however, realised that the split ultimately would have the effect of killing Non-co-operation activity in any form, for, it served as an excuse for the people to refrain from subscribing money and enlisting as volunteers: consequently the question of compromise was continually considered and Abul Kalam Azad endeavoured to bring one about, but he failed, and resigned from the Working Committee. During February 1923 Mr. Das is believed to have put forward the following programme at a secret meeting of his followers held in Calcutta on the 8th of that month:—

(1) Their object was to attain Swaraj by peaceful and legitimate means.

(2) Members of their party would contest seats in the Councils.

(3) If elected, they should place a *moderate* demand before the Government and the British Parliament. By *moderate* demand was meant some sort of Dominion Home Rule. If this demand was not conceded, they should return to the electorate for a fresh mandate and advise the people to stop payment of taxes.

(4) No members of their party, elected for the Councils, would seek office under Government.

(5) In localities where their party possessed a majority in the local Congress Committee, the Congress organisation would be used for electioneering purposes; in other places parallel organisations would be formed.

(6) They should keep constant touch with Indians in foreign countries and obtain assistance from foreign sympathisers.

(7) They should boycott British goods."

Shortly afterwards Das produced an " Outline Scheme of Swaraj " in which he proposed that India should be divided into local, district, provincial and all-India *panchayats;* the unit for a local *panchayat* being an area with a population of ten thousand persons. This scheme is reproduced at Appendix D.

96. **A truce.**—At the end of February a meeting of leaders of both parties took place at Allahabad and although it appeared at first that a compromise was exceedingly improbable, ultimately a hollow truce was patched up in the following terms:—

(1) Suspension of propaganda relating to Councils on both sides till 30th April.

(2) Both parties to be at liberty to work the remaining items of their respective programmes in the interval without interfering with each other.

(3) The majority party would be at liberty to carry on their propaganda, in accordance with the Gaya programme, regarding money and volunteers.

(4) The minority party would co-operate with the majority party in appealing for, and raising, such funds and enlisting such workers as might be necessary for the constructive programme, and also in working the constructive programme and other common matters.

(5) Each party to adopt such course after 30th April as it might be advised.

(6) The above arrangement was subject to the condition that there was no dissolution of the existing Councils in any province before the expiry of the full term for which they have been constituted.

With these terms the following explanatory note was given to the Working Committee:—

" This proposal gives the majority party full latitude to carry on their propaganda for the collection of 25 lakhs and enlistment of 50 thousand volunteers for the next two months without hindrance from the minority party. If at the end of two months the majority party declare for individual Civil Disobedience throughout the country in such form, to such extent and on such issues as the minority party approves, the latter will join the Civil Disobedience; if not, each party will be at liberty to pursue its own course in its own way, but it is expected that the majority party will not obstruct the minority party in the latter's programme about Councils after 30th April in return for the latter offering no hindrance to the former in their propaganda about 25 lakhs money and 50 thousand volunteers during March and April. The minority party, however, does not bind the majority party to any particular line of action after 30th April and reserves itself similar freedom."

After this compromise endeavours were made to stimulate enlistment and collection by vigorous propaganda during a "Gandhi Week" which ended on 18th of March and a National Week from the 6th to the 13th of April. A partial *hartal* occurred in some places on the 18th of March, but on the whole the results were surprisingly poor as is apparent from the announcement by the No-change Party that only 3,900 volunteers and 3,62,000 rupees had been collected up to the end of Gandhi Week. In the meantime the Swaraj Party, which had not been observing the terms of the truce faithfully, had decided to contest the Municipal elections which took place in the United Provinces at about this time, and succeeded in gaining a majority in many places. The *swarajya* leaders visited Northern India to try to improve Hindu-Muhammadan unity which, at this time, had been severely strained by local causes as well as by the *Shuddhi* Movement, which meant originally the re-conversion of Rajput Muhammadans to Hinduism by Sadhu Shradhananda.

97. **All-India Congress Committee meet at Bombay, May 1923.**—As soon as the truce expired the Swaraj Party, which had already set up separate organisations in most provinces, set about an election campaign; while the No-changers, who still hoped to introduce some form of civil disobedience, considered the question of boycotting the Council elections which in no way reduced the animosity between the two parties. Meetings of the All-India Congress Committee and the Congress Working Committee took place at Bombay towards the end of May, and although the Swaraj Party were in the minority on the Working Committee they obtained a majority on the All-India Congress Committee which passed a so-called compromise resolution which, in reality, was a victory for C. R. Das, and read as follows:—

"In view of the fact that there was a strong body of opinion in the Congress in favour of contesting the elections and that the existing division amongst Congressmen had already led to a lessening of the influence of the Congress, the Committee deemed it absolutely necessary that the Congressmen should close their ranks and present a united front

> and that no propaganda should be carried on amongst the voters in furtherance of the Gaya Congress resolution relating to the boycott of the Council."

At about the same time the result of the No-change Party's appeal for money and volunteers was published in the press. They claimed to have obtained up to the 30th April, 15 lakhs of rupees and approximately 8 thousand volunteers as compared with their self-imposed goal of 25 lakhs of rupees and 50 thousand volunteers. During the same period the Swaraj Party had independently collected over two lakhs of rupees which; however, it retained for its own use.

98. **The Swaraj Party gains grounds.**—The Bombay result was achieved by the secession of several No-changers including Dr. Ansari, Mrs. Naidu and Abul Kalam Azad, who put forward the compromise resolution. This took Rajagopalachariar by surprise and he and his supporters resigned from the Working Committee and C. R. Das, while following their example, succeeded in packing the Working Committee with Congressmen who were inclined to support him. The No-changers were much incensed with the results and threatened active opposition at the coming elections. They also attempted to create trouble between the Swaraj Party and Muhammadans by publishing telegrams issued in connection with the proposed Round Table Conference in December 1921, which purported to show that Das and Abul Kalam Azad did not attach much importance to the release of the Ali Brothers as a preliminary to that Conference. Rajagopalachariar further commenced to canvass for Muhammad Ali, who was still in jail, as President of the next annual session of the Congress, hoping to gain his support to the no-change policy.

In the meantime Das had outlined his policy in the following words in a speech which he delivered on the 30th of May 1923 at Madras:—

> "I am going to take the people into the path of resistance. I know they will follow me. I have sixty lakhs of voters and I am going to appeal to them. I want you to enter the Councils and secure the majority of seats and to put forward the national demand. If it is not accepted I want to oppose the Government in every measure, good, bad and indifferent. What I do want is to fight the bureaucracy from all directions, from inside the Councils, trying to make Government impossible, and from outside the Councils by working the Non-co-operation programme more enthusiastically than now. The day will come when the outside and inside activities put together will be too much even for this bureaucracy."

In Madras, he also made some remarks disparaging Gandhi's policy, which were promptly seized upon by the No-changers to discredit him as an iconoclast, but in spite of this the Swaraj Party undoubtedly gained in strength.

99. **Nagpur National Flag Campaign.**—In the middle of 1923 a *Satyagraha* National Flag Campaign was initiated at Nagpur, the *modus operandi* being for a party of volunteers to carry national flags into the European quarter and there make themselves objectionable. The Local authorities countered by arresting them. This manifestation of Non-co-operation activity was doubtless responsible for the selection of Nagpur as the meeting place of the All-India Congress Committee on the 7th and 8th of July. At this meeting it was resolved to take up the Nagpur *Satyagraha* movement, which hitherto had been purely a local affair, as an all-India matter and to send volunteers from other provinces to offer themselves for arrest at Nagpur. It was also urged that similar demonstrations should be made elsewhere on the 18th of July which was declared to be a National Flag Day. The Bombay Compromise resolution was again considered by the All-India Congress Committee and an attempt was made to have it declared *ultra vires*, but this was defeated by 82 votes to 63. On the other hand, however, a proposal put forward by the Working Committee to censure such Provincial Congress Committees as had defied the compromise resolution was turned down; so the members of the Working Committee resigned, and the majority of their successors were No-changers.

The efforts of the All-India Congress Committee with respect to the National Flag Campaign was not successful and although a few volunteers came to Nagpur from other provinces, yet it was very soon apparent that the supply both of local and foreign volunteers was drying up. In this connection it is interesting to note that the agitators tried to enlist the sympathies of the *Mahar* or untouchable classes of Nagpur who, however, claimed religious equality before resorting to political *Satyagraha* and demanded that members of their community should be allowed to enter temples without restriction. The Nagpur National Flag Campaign was brought to an end on the 18th of August by means of a compromise with the Local Government to the mutual relief of both parties.

100. **All-India Congress Committee meet at Vizagapatam.**—The All-India Congress Committee next met on the 3rd of August at Vizagapatam and there provisionally selected Bombay for a special session of the Congress, which the Nagpur meeting had decided to call in connection with the question of council-entry. It also nominated Muhammad Ali as the President of the next annual session of the All-India Congress. At this period, certain restrictions placed on Indians by the Kenya Government were being used by agitators to create political excitement in India, and the All-India Congress Committee resolved that a peaceful *hartal* should be observed throughout the country on August the 25th in consequence of the Kenya decision.

The Working Committee assembled at Nagpur shortly afterwards and. as Bombay had intimated its inability to entertain the special session of the All-India Congress, Delhi was selected as the place of meeting.

At about this time feeling between the two factions in the Congress ran very high in Bengal, and both parties were trying to gain control of the Bengal Provincial Congress Committee. The Swaraj Party, which was receiving great assistance from the revolutionary element, summoned a meeting of the B. P. C. C. on the 11th of August and being in a majority, they dismissed all the office-bearers who, it will be remembered, were No-changers. The No-changers summoned another meeting of the Committee on the 15th of August which terminated in a free fight. They then refused to recognise the decision arrived at on the 11th on the grounds that the requisite 15 days notice, specified by the rules, had not been given when calling the meeting on that date, and they referred the question to the All-India Congress Committee for a decision. In the meantime each party formed a provincial Congress Committee of its own and separately arranged to send delegates to the special session of the Congress at Delhi. Similar trouble was apparent in the Punjab Provincial Congress Committee where the no-change office-bearers contemplated resigning in a body. Lala Lajpat Rai, in issuing a manifesto appealing for unity, said that mass civil disobedience on a large scale had, for the time being, to be indefinitely postponed and that in the absence of Gandhi their task consisted of "(*a*) securing his release, (*b*) discovering another personality who may, in course of time, take his place, (*c*) in the meantime keeping the Flag flying and (*d*) devising some other method to compel the Government to negotiate." He advocated that the Council boycott should be suspended and that the elections should be contested and candidates should follow the programme which would be laid down for them at the special session of the Congress at Delhi.

101. **The release of the Ali Brothers.**—Muhammad Ali was released from jail on 29th August and Shaukat Ali on 26th October 1923. The former was asked to persuade the Ulemas to withdraw the *fatwa* against council-entry which they had promulgated at Delhi in November 1920 at a conference of the Jamait-ul-Ulema. He, however, would not commit himself to this, and announced that he would not rest until he had found the key of the Yervada Prison* to set the Mahatma free and that, if Non-co-operation was *haram* two years previously, it could not become *halal* until the Jazirat-ul-Arab was once more under absolute, independent and exclusive Muslim sovereignty and the Khilafat relationship with the Muslim world was recognised according to Islamic Law.

Prior to the special session of the Congress at Delhi Hindu and Muhammadan leaders met on the 11th and 12th of September and explained their respective view-points regarding the *Shuddhi* and

*In which Gandhi was incarcerated.

Sangathan Movements and an agreement was reached with Swami Shradhananda, who consented to postpone the *Shuddhi* campaign provided the Muhammadans abandoned their counter movement. A committee consisting of 7 Muhammadans and 7 Hindus, with power to add to their number, was then appointed to formulate definite proposals to place before the Congress, and to become thereafter a permanent committee to decide inter-communal disputes.

102. **Special Session of the Congress Delhi, September 1923.**— The Special Session of the Congress met at Delhi on the 15th and 16th September with Abul Kalam Azad as President and, with respect to the Bengal dispute, decided in favour of the Swaraj Party so the 750 delegates sent by C. R. Das were admitted while the 250 brought by the opposition party were rejected and were not allowed inside the *pandal*. On the question of council-entry, Muhammad Ali, in the Subjects Committee, moved the following resolutions:—

> "While re-affirming its adherence to the principle of non-violent non-co-operation, this Congress declares that such Congressmen as have no religious or other conscientious objections against entry into legislatures are at liberty to stand as candidates and to exercise their right of voting at the forthcoming elections, and this Congress, therefore, suspends all propaganda against entry into legislatures. The Congress at the same time calls upon Congressmen to redouble their efforts to carry out the constructive programme of their great leader Mahatma Gandhi, and by united endeavours to achieve Swaraj at the earliest possible moment."

He made it clear that he had consented to this compromise solely because he realised that some change of programme was necessary and that it was contrary to his own inclination as he was personally against council-entry on the grounds of religious scruples. Further he was afraid of the Councils capturing the Swarajists instead of the reverse, but he had proposed the resolution with the object of retaining the existence of the Congress, which he did not consider could continue as a divided body. C. R. Das explained that he was going into the Councils to end them and to "hurl Non-co-operation on the Bureaucracy from within and from without." The resolution was carried by a large majority, but only three-quarters of the delegates voted. The Congress passed other resolutions as follows:—

> To form a strong and representative committee to advise on and organize civil disobedience for the attainment of Swaraj, release of Gandhi and freedom from non-Muslim control of the Jazirat-ul-Arab. It also condemned the "forced abdication" of the Maharaja of Nabha and the repressive policy of the Punjab Government against the Akalis in the Doaba."

This meeting of the Congress was the occasion for serious quarrels between Hindu and Muhammadan volunteers which, on the night of the 14th September, ended in a *fracas*. Internal friction was also evident from the withdrawal of all the Bombay delegates early in the session owing to their dissatisfaction with an alteration in the seating arrangements. Another feature of this meeting of the Congress was a marked tendency in favour of violence which encouraged speakers to make frequent references to it, or to revolution, which were always loudly cheered.

103. **Das revises his programme.**—After the Delhi meeting of the Congress, C. R. Das, in a speech in Calcutta on the 30th of September, revised the programme he had enunciated on the 30th of May and stated that impossible demands should not be made in the Councils, nor should Government resolutions for the public good be opposed. The object of this utterance was undoubtedly to gain the support of the waverers with moderate inclinations, in the approaching elections. After the Delhi Congress, warrants under Regulation III of 1918 were executed in Bengal against about 20 revolutionary leaders. As several of these were also important members of the Swaraj Party, this action was interpreted by Das and his followers as directed against themselves; and in this spirit and to retain the support of their revolutionary members, the Swaraj Party in Bengal made the repeal of all repressive laws one of the main planks of their political platform.

104. **The Civil Disobedience Committee and the Akali Movement.**—In the Punjab Dr. Kitchlew showed considerable activity in connection with the work of the Civil Disobedience Committee appointed at Delhi, but he met with little success. He was informed by several provincial Congress Committees that funds and enthusiasm were lacking and that the Congress programme must go further if enthusiasm was to be stimulated. The Civil Disobedience Committee which incidentally had been created at the instigation of Akalis, confined itself to the Akali Movement which, of course, was civil disobedience but not in pursuance of the Non-co-operation programme. The Committee, however, recommended to the Working Committee of the Congress that some leaders should remain at Amritsar to keep in touch with and advise the Akalis, and this proposal was accepted by the Working Committee at a meeting at Ahmedabad on the 25th of November where Dr. Kitchlew, Jawahar Lal Nahru and Gidwani were appointed to be liaison officers between the Akalis and the Congress. Dr. Kitchlew ultimately issued a report dealing mainly with the Akali Movement which, he urged, the Congress should prepare to assist. He stated his conviction that "if an effective campaign of civil disobedience is taken up by the Congress all these dissensions and communal frictions which are the result of national activity will at once disappear, focussing public attention on the one important issue before the country."

105. **The elections.**—In November 1923, the Bombay Provincial Congress Committee met at Bijapur and unanimously passed a resolution adhering to orthodox Non-co-operation. At this time there were other indications that the No-changers were rallying, but their efforts were negatived by the success which attended the Swarajists in the elections for the Legislative Assembly and the Provincial Councils. The Swarajists with their allies were returned in a majority in the Legislative Assembly and the Bengal Legislative Council, while the Swarajists alone had an absolute majority in the Council of the Central Provinces. In the Bombay, United Provinces and Assam Councils, they gained sufficient seats to establish themselves as a party to be reckoned with.

After the elections, the Bengal members of the Swaraj Party held a meeting *in camera* on the 16th of December, 1923 at Calcutta, at which it was unanimously decided not to accept ministerial office under Government until the minimum demands of the party had been granted. These demands were to be (1) the immediate release of political prisoners, (2) the repeal or withdrawal of all repressive laws, and (3) complete provincial autonomy. It was decided that if these demands were not conceded, the policy of the party would be one of consistent and continuous obstruction. At about the same time the B. P. C. C, which by then had been completely captured by the Swarajists, considered the advisability of deleting the word ' peaceful ' from the Congress creed and to enunciate that " The object of the Indian National Congress is the attainment of complete independence by all legitimate means." No conclusion, however, was reached and it was decided to raise the question at the Coconada Congress.

106. **The Bengal Hindu-Muslim Pact.**—In order to retain the allegiance of the Muhammadan *swarajya* M. L. C.'s, C. R. Das at this time framed a Bengal Hindu-Muslim Pact which was more favourable to Muhammadans than the Lucknow Pact of 1916. This Pact, however, resulted in considerable opposition from Hindus who considered that Das had sold himself to the Muhammadans in order to establish his majority in the Council. To meet this criticism, C. R. Das announced that the Pact was provisional and was subject to confirmation at the Coconada Congress.

107. **Annual Session of Congress Coconada, December, 1923.**—The All-India Congress assembled at Coconada in X'mas week 1923 under the presidentship of Muhammad Ali. At first it appeared that the differences between the Swarajists and No-changers were irreconcilable, but, mainly owing to the influence of Muhammad Ali, a compromise resolution was reached and this, which was proposed by Rajagopalachariar and seconded by C. R. Das, was ultimately passed by the Congress after much heated discussion. Rajagopalachariar was subjected to much criticism by his fellow No-changers for

consenting to this resolution and they considered that he had betrayed them. The resolution read as follows:—

> " This Congress reaffirms the Non-co-operation resolutions adopted at Calcutta, Nagpur, Ahmedabad, Gaya and Delhi
>
> Since doubts have been raised, by reason of the Non-co-operation resolution adopted at Delhi with regard to Council-entry, whether there has been any change in the policy of the Congress regarding the triple boycott, this Congress affirms that the principle and policy of that boycott remain unaltered.
>
> This Congress further declares that the said principle and policy form the foundation of constructive work and appeals to the nation to carry out the programme of constructive work as adopted at Bardoli and prepare for the adoption of Civil Disobedience. This Congress calls upon every Provincial Congress Committee to take immediate steps in this behalf with a view to the speedy attainment of our goal."

The Hindu-Muslim Unity Committee appointed at Delhi had. like C. R. Das in Bengal, framed a draft National Pact which amounted to a compromise between the Lucknow and Bengal Pacts. It was obvious that discussion of this subject would lead to a great deal of friction, so the Congress avoided the issue by appointing a sub-committee to consider the terms of the National Pact, but at the same time it gave a clear indication that it did not approve of the Bengal draft. The Bengal proposal to change the Congress creed was also turned down.

The Congress welcomed the formation of an all-India volunteer organisation—a movement which had been initiated shortly before by J. L. Nehru and N. S. Hardikar—and the Subjects Committee asked the Working Committee to co-operate with the originators to form a trained and disciplined band of workers. The object in view was undoubtedly mass civil disobedience.

One of the main features of the Coconada meeting of the Congress was the unrestrained language indulged in by the speakers which gave a further indication that the Congress was drifting from the policy of non-violence.

108. **Swarajya Meeting, Lucknow, January 1924.**—The *swarajya* leaders met at Lucknow early in January 1924 and decided to demand in the Councils, (1) the release of political prisoners, (2) the withdrawal of repressive laws and (3) the summoning of a Round Table Conference of selected members of the Assembly, the Swaraj Party and Government to determine the principles of a constitution for India in accordance with the policy of the Indian National Congress. In the Central

Provinces, the *swarajya* majority soon brought the Council to a standstill by passing a vote of no confidence in the Ministers, after which the Council was adjourned *sine die*. In Bengal when the supremacy of the Swarajists was established, H. E. the Governor invited C. R. Das to form a Ministry and there is no doubt that this invitation proved very tempting to him. Ho however dared not accept it in view of the declared policy both of Gandhi and his own party, so the Swarajists began operations by passing a resolution demanding the withdrawal of all repressive legislation.

109. **The All-India Congress Committee Meeting, Bombay, January 1924.**—The All-India Congress Committee, on which the No-changers still had a majority, met at Bombay and drew up a programme on the lines of the Coconada resolutions and resolved that a Gandhi Month should be observed from the 18th of February to the 18th of March for intensive National work, such as the production of *khaddar* and the collection of money for the Tilak Swaraj Fund. It also sanctioned the disbursement of 25 thousand rupees for the maintenance of families of Akalis in jail, and it was clear that it hoped for the declaration of mass civil disobedience at the earliest possible date. Soon afterwards, the Board of the Hindustani Seva Dal, as the volunteer organisation was called, met at Bombay and approved of a draft scheme of work prepared by J. L. Nehru. This scheme clearly indicated that the organisation was to be on military lines and provided for regiments of volunteers, sub-divided into battalions, companies and sections, each under its own commanders. All provincial Congress Committees were asked to organise accordingly but actually very little was done.

110. **The release of Gandhi.**—On the 5th February 1924, Gandhi was released from jail as Government were advised by medical authorities that further detention would be detrimental to his health. His release was greeted ostensibly with great joy by all sections of the Congress and was claimed to be a triumph for the agitation which had taken place to effect it.

The No-changers hoped that he would re-establish their position but actually they were disappointed, for while declining to commit himself publicly to any line of policy until he had studied the situation, he coquetted with the Swarajists. At the same time he clearly indicated his dis-approval of total obstruction in the Councils and considered that if the Swarajists insisted on entering the Legislatures, they should adopt a policy of responsive co-operation.

One of his first public acts after release was to ask the Akalis to refrain from sending further *jathas* to Jaiton (where they were coming into violent conflict with the authorities) and, in guarded language, he questioned their loyalty to the policy of non-violence. His interference was resented by the Sikhs and the departure of the *jatha* then being assembled was not postponed; but at the same time it clearly disturbed them, for they had no desire to lose the support of the Congress.

The next few months produced nothing of outstanding interest and both the *swarajya* and the no-change leaders devoted much of their time in trying to persuade Gandhi to come out into the open on their side. At first he seemed inclined to come to some compromise with the Swarajists, but in *Young India* on the 29th of May, he indicated that he had come down on the no-change side of the fence by stating that all those who did not believe in the five boycotts,* non-violence and truthfulness should resign from the Congress executive bodies. He laid stress on the importance of the boycotts as an integral part of the Congress programme and said that title-holders, lawyers, schoolmasters and members of the Assembly and Council should have nothing to do with the Congress Executive, for they represented, in his view, the voluntary branch of Government administration.

This announcement greatly disappointed the Swarajists who were further embarrassed by dissension in their own ranks. Pandit Motilal Nehru wished to serve on the Reforms Committee but his followers would not consent. He therefore tendered his resignation as leader of the party but it was not accepted. The result was a decided weakening in *swarajya* policy, and, at a meeting of the *swarajya* members of the Legislative Assembly at Simla, it was unanimously resolved to adopt responsive co-operation and to accept membership on Government committees and this example was followed by the Swarajists in the Central Provinces Council.

111. **The Gopi Saha Resolution.**—At about the same time, the Bengal Provincial Conference assembled at Serajgunj and there, mainly owing to the assistance he received from revolutionaries, C. R. Das gained a complete triumph and succeeded in passing, by a large majority, his proposed Bengal Hindu-Muslim Pact. In return, however, for the assistance which he had received from the revolutionaries, he was compelled to pass another resolution eulogising the revolutionary—Gopi Mohan Saha—who had shortly before been hanged for the unprovoked murder of a European named Day, whom he had mistaken for the Commissioner of Police, Calcutta. Soon afterwards Gandhi submitted certain resolutions for the consideration of the All-India Congress Committee, which was to meet at Ahmedabad, which amounted to an open challenge to the Swarajists. They were briefly (1) that officers of the Congress organization who do not personally observe the 'five boycotts' (foreign cloth, Government courts, schools, titles, and Legislative bodies) should vacate their seats; (2) That the All-India Congress Committee should strongly condemn the murder of Mr. Day and all such political murders as

* *Vide* next paragraph.

being inconsistent with the Congress creed; (3) That members of the various Congress organisations should spin for at least half an hour each day and send 10 tolas of twisted yarn to the Secretary of the All-India Congress Committee once a month. Any member failing to do this shall be deemed to have vacated office.

112. **All-India Congress Committee meet at Ahmedabad, June 1924.**—Gandhi's Khaddar resolution was strongly opposed by the Swarajists at the meeting of the All-India Congress Committee in the end of June at Ahmedabad. Motilal Nehru moved that the resolution was not in order and was inconsistent with the constitution of the Congress. He quoted certain articles of the constitution in support of his contention. The point was put to the vote and 68 voted with Nehru and 82 with Gandhi. The Khaddar resolution was then discussed and impassioned speeches were made, culminating in the withdrawal of Nehru and 50 of his followers as protest against the resolution, which, in a depleted ' House ', was carried only by 67 votes to 37. The unexpected departure of the Swarajists took Gandhi by surprise, and realising the distaste with which his resolution was regarded, he moved an amendment withdrawing the ' penalty clause ' (compulsory vacation of office by Congress officials on failure to spin and despatch a certain quantity of yarn for *khaddar*). After much discussion the amendment was carried unanimously, and the obnoxious clause removed. Das, Nehru and Abul Kalam Azad then induced Gandhi to modify his ' five boycotts ' resolution so as to permit Swarajists to retain executive control of Congress bodies. The modified resolution was passed in face of strong opposition from angry No-changers. Gandhi's resolution condemning the action of Gopi Mohan Shaha was carried by a narrow majority. At the close of the meeting Gandhi expressed bitter disappointment at the rupture in the Congress and burst into tears Muhammad Ali also broke down, and sobbingly implored Gandhi not to desert them in their hour of need.

Shortly afterwards, in an article in his paper *Young India*, Gandhi, commenting on the Ahmedabad meeting described himself as ' defeated and humbled '. He admitted that the excision of the ' penalty clause ' from his *khaddar* resolution left matters much as they were before, and that the mutilation of the original resolution was a concession to the victorious Swarajists. Similarly, the evasion of the strict letter of the ' boycotts ' resolution was nothing but a subterfuge enabling him to provide a loophole of escape for the pro-change party. Instead of insisting on the observance of the five boycotts, which would automatically exclude Swarajists from the Congress executives, Gandhi so amended the resolution as to make it merely a reiteration of the compromise agreed upon at Delhi and Coconada. The bare majority by which his resolution relating to Gopi Mohan Shaha was passed, completed Gandhi's discomfiture. That his policy of non-violence in thought and act should receive such half-hearted support, was a ' staggering revelation ', which disclosed the weakness of the foundations on which the Congress creed was based.

113. **The end of orthodox Non-co-operation.**—This may be regarded as the end of the orthodox non-violent Non-co-operation which was Gandhi's original creed. While Gandhi was in jail, his followers had found themselves in a steadily deteriorating position, but they had kept his flag flying in the hope that he would be able to retrieve the situation on his release. This hope had now to be abandoned for Gandhi himself had joined issue with the Swarajists at Ahmedabad, and in order to avoid defeat, he had been compelled to enter into a compromise with them which gave them complete license to carry on their policy in their own way. By September 1924 Gandhi had publicly announced his unwillingness to oppose the Swarajists and had said that he would completely surrender himself into their hands. He admitted that he had failed to realise the true position at Ahmedabad and that the dissensions within the Congress had greatly strengthened the hands of Government. He added that he wanted nothing but an atmosphere of peace at the meeting of the All-India Congress at Belgaum in X'mas week 1924, where, he trusted, the two parties would sink their differences and would strive to further the objects which he had himself at heart, namely, *khaddar*, removal of untouchability, and Hindu-Muhammadan unity. As was to be expected he came in for a good deal of heckling from prominent No-changers in consequence of this pronouncement and he had little consolation to offer them. He advised the temporary suspension of the five boycotts and concentration on the constructive programme, and urged the No-changers not to oppose the Swarajists who, he said were doing useful national work in the Councils. He emphasised the fact that during the last two years the No-changers had remained idle and had failed to take advantage of the opportunities offered to them, whereas the other wing of the Congress had worked enthusiastically and had many remarkable achievements to its credit. He finally announced that if he failed to bring about a peaceful atmosphere at Belgaum, he was determined to leave the Congress to its own devices and to pursue his constructive programme in a few selected villages, where he would prepare the ground for civil disobedience.

This was followed in November 1924 by a manifesto issued in Calcutta over the signatures of Messrs. Gandhi, C. R. Das and Motilal Nehru in which, among other things, the signatories strongly recommended the " following for the adoption of all parties and eventually by the Congress at Belgaum " ...... " The Congress should suspend the programme except in so far as it relates to the refusal to use or wear cloth made out of India "; and " No one shall be a member of any Congress Committee or organisation * * * * who does not contribute 2,000 yards of yarn per month of his own spinning or, in case of illness, unwillingness or any such cause, a like quantity of yarn by any other person ", *i.e.*, the Swarajists could spin by proxy.

This marked the final stage of Gandhi's surrender to the Swaraj Party and was the end of orthodox Non-co-operation. Non-co-operation still remained a popular catch word, but it had ceased to be practised, and the Swarajists had gained the support of the majority of extremists with a policy which was directly opposed to some of the fundamental principles of Gandhi's Non-co-operation programme.

At the Belgaum Congress the resolution regarding the "spinning franchise" was passed as a sop to Gandhi, whose feelings the delegates wished, as much as possible, to spare. There was, however, no desire to enforce the resolution nor was any real endeavour to do so apparent. Opposition to it soon appeared, particularly in Western India (for a prophet is without honour in his own country) and, by the middle of 1925, a strong demand for a Special Session of the Congress to cancel the "spinning franchise" had grown up. In voicing it, Gandhi's quondam followers had no hesitation in describing him as a "*khaddar* maniac", and a "spent force" although four short years before he had raised all India to a pitch of enthusiasm and united effort which it had never attained previously and which—with its widely divergent communal interests—it will possibly never reach again.

CHAPTER VII.

The effect of the non-co-operation Boycotts.

A history of the Non-co-operation Movement would be incomplete without some indication as to how far the various boycotts adopted during that movement were successful. It is extraordinarily difficult to give details of the results under most of the boycott heads for in very few instances are figures available; and such of these as exist generally refer to some particular locality at a time of stress, so are misleading when considering the situation as a whole. It is, however, possible to arrive at some general conclusions from the material available.

114. **Boycott of Foreign Cloth.**—There was undoubtedly a decrease in the importation of foreign cloth during the height of the Non-co-operation movement; but a number of other factors contributed to the general depression in trade at that time, so it is impossible to allocate the extent to which Non-co-operation was responsible for the decrease. This is apparent from the following extracts under the head "import of cotton manufactures" in the Review of the Trade of India in 1921-1922 published by the Commercial Intelligence Department:—"Reference was made in last year's *Review* to the conditions occasioned in Indian piecegoods markets by the fall of exchange and the inability of a number of piecegoods merchants in India to meet the heavy losses resulting from the combination of a fall in rupee prices and a fall in exchange. As a consequence of these difficulties Indian contributing centres were seriously overstocked at the beginning of the year and further shipments of goods purchased at high prices added to the congestion in the earlier months. And the leading piecegoods merchants' Associations, hoping against hope that the rupee would soon rise to the illusive two-shilling-level reiterated resolutions forbidding their members to settle contracts except at that rate, and imposing fines on any members who did so. Despite these resolutions settlements were arrived at in most cases during the course of the year and those left over at the end of 1921-22 consisted almost entirely of a small gambling residue from the post-war boom. Another factor which seriously affected piecegoods importations during the year under review was the vigorous revival, particularly on the Western side, of the campaign in favour of Indian-made piecegoods, reinforced by a further development in favour of the wearing of home-woven goods made from Indian handspun yarn. This latter development was reflected also in greater imports of twist and yarn, the imported yarns, spun from longer-stapled Egyptian and American cotton, being more suitable for handweaving than yarn spun from Indian cotton. But the out-

standing factor which really controlled the consumption of both imported and Indian-made piecegoods was the seriously reduced purchasing power of the country in general. reference has been made to this factor generally and piecegoods figures afford a striking illustration, as the bulk of the goods bought was of the grey (unbleached) variety and appreciable reductions in price produced very little increase in demand, thus showing that consumption was limited almost entirely to minimum clothing requirements."

In the Review for the subsequent year, the following appears:—
"During 1921-22 the combination of excessive stocks on hand and the reduced purchasing power of consumers rendered importations small. In the year under review most of the old stocks were cleared and the improvement in purchasing power combined with the collapse of the movement against the use of imported goods. led to a marked increase in importations."

The effect of this boycott was felt throughout India, to a greater or lesser extent, during the height of the movement. It attained considerable success in Bengal, Bombay, Madras and the United Provinces. A feature of this campaign was the bonfires of foreign cloths which were a frequent accompaniment to Non-co-operation meetings all over India.

115. **Boycott of Law Courts.**—To effect the boycott of Government courts, litigants were urged to refuse to use them and members of the legal profession were exhorted to give up their practices. To take place of Government courts, the Non-co-operation programme provided arbitration courts and these were set up in a few places. They had, however, generally a very short life for the justice they administered was indifferent and often tainted, while they had not sufficient authority to enforce their orders without recourse to violence. On occasions the requisite violence was forthcoming, but frequently their findings were ignored. Some barristers, *vakils* and *mukhtears* resigned their practices, but very few who were capable of earning anything maintained this attitude after the pinch of want was felt.

Perhaps the most striking result of this boycott was the refusal of Non-co-operators to defend themselves when prosecuted, and this of course re-acted on their own heads during the stress of the volunteer movement in 1921-22, and facilitated the work of executive officers of Government at a time of great pressure.

116. **Boycott of Schools.**—The effect of the boycott of Government educational institutions is shown in the Quinquennial Report of the progress of education in India in 1917-1922, published by the Bureau of Education, from which the following is taken:—

"NON-CO-OPERATION MOVEMENT."

"(a) *Its beginnings.*—It is not within the scope of an educational report to consider the political origins of the non-co-operation movement. It did not at first make any direct attack upon the schools, though attendance at political meetings, enrolment as volunteers and other similar activities served to distract the attention of students from their studies and to impede discipline. It was only after the meeting of the Indian National Congress held in Nagpur in December 1920 that the campaign was launched which succeeded in crippling some schools beyond hope of recovery, in disorganising the work of others for six months or a year and in ruining the careers of many promising scholars. At the Nagpur meeting resolutions were passed declaring a boycott of all schools recognised by Government. This started a movement which spread in successive waves over the whole of India. In no province did it maintain its maximum force for more than a few months, so that some provinces were already recovering from the shock while in others the disturbance was at its height. Its progress is marked by a rapid local decline in a attendance at schools and colleges and by the occurrence of school strikes and other signs of indiscipline."

"(b) *Its appeal* —Originally forming, as it did, part of a campaign which aimed at paralysing the administration, it was purely destructive in character. It was an appeal to the student community to break away from the control of Government, and Government control is represented to students by the authorities who direct their studies. A large number of students who responded to the appeal did so under the impression that they were thereby in some obscure way serving their country. The power of the appeal was strengthened by a very genuine discontent with a course of education which appeared to lead to nothing but the acquisition of the degree, an honour no longer worth the money spent in obtaining it. The political appeal was thus supported by the economic. Finally it must be remembered that the appeal was made to most inflammable material. 'The drabness and joylessness of student life in Bengal has been a matter for frequent comment. The Calcutta University Commission Report has perhaps said the last word in describing the conditions of this life. Poverty, the cram-drudgery of his studies, the dreary surroundings in which a student too often finds himself housed, make him ' moody, depressed and absorbed in himself and his prospects. ' He needs therefore more than other students of the same age, recreation and diversion. It is not surprising, therefore, if in moments of despondency, he falls a victim to uncontrollable excitement sometimes of the most serious and violent nature.' Thus the appeal of the agitators, ostensibly to the noblest instincts of the student, his love of country and eagerness for sacrifice, couched in terms that suggested glowing ideas of 'national' service, found its response in that natural craving for excitement in the adolescent, which in other countries would have found vent in college 'rags,' in sport, in a hundred and one ways made impossible to the student in Bengal by his circumstances.'

"All classes of students have been affected; and among those who responded to pressure are those whom colleges could least afford to lose as well as those whose departure caused no regret. There was something in the movement that appealed to most diverse types of mind. The call to 'national' service and self-sacrifice found a quick response among the best, unintelligible to those who do not realize the emotional background of student life and the absence of a strong sense of humour. While older men have been seeing visions the young men are dreaming dreams. Imagination has been fired and a spiritual 'uplift' initiated. Something that had long been wanting in our college life had been supplied. To another class of temperament the situation presented possibilities of romance and adventure that irradiated a colourless existence. Picketing and processions were as irresistible to such minds as a bump-supper and a 'rag' to Oxford under-graduates. Others became for the first time conscious that they were wasting time over a kind of education not suited to their needs and leading them at its best to an office stool. It is greatly to the credit of the staff that these feelings, so natural in themselves but affording such excellent material for unscrupulous agitators, found expression comparatively seldom in violent or offensive action and that judgment was so often suspended and scope left for reflection. Credit is also due to parents, as has specially been recorded in the Punjab report. Though other reports refer gloomily to the decay of parental authority it is clear that the losses would have been far greater had not many parents, in the teeth of local ridicule and opposition, brought great pressure to bear on their sons."

"(c) *The effect of attendance.*—It is of course impossible to say how many students were actually withdrawn from schools or colleges as a result of the non-co-operation movement since a variety of other factors, chief among which was the high cost of living also affected the attendance in the years following the war. The following statement give some indication of the losses:—

Year.	Arts Colleges.		Secondary Schools.						Primary Schools.	
							Total.			
	Institutions.	Scholars.	High Schools.	Scholars.	Middle Schools.	Scholars.	Institutions.	Scholars.	Institutions.	Scholars.
1919-20 . .	150	52,482	2,113	632,032	6,595	649,778	8,708	1,281,810	155,844	6,133,521
1920-21 . .	160	48,170	2,184	600,583	6,739	653,942	8,923	1,254,525	159,345	6,327,973
1921-22 . .	167	45,933	2,248	594,910	6,739	644,614	8,987	1,239,524	160,072	6,310,451

Province.	National Schools and Colleges in 1921-22.		Approximate effect of "Non-co-operation" on certain recognised institutions up to March 1921.			Remarks.
	Institutions.	Scholars.	Scholars.	Withdrawn from institutions.	Returned.	
Madras	92*	5,072*	1,71,111	820	†	
Bombay	189	17,100	42,416	2 350	239	
Bengal	190	14,819	1,03.107	11,157	No information.	
United Provinces	137*	8,476*	49,171	2,626	789	
Punjab	69	8,046	1,11,078	1,309	481	
Burma	92	16,218	36,875	13,031	747	
Bihar and Orissa	442	17,330	23,190	1.826	†	
Central Provinces	86*	6,338*	71,759	1,824	454	
Assam	38	1,908	12,186‡	1,139	356	
North-West Frontier Province.	4*	120*	41,342	*Nil*	...	
Minor Administrations	10	1,255	45,508	571	70	

*Opened till 31st July 1921.

†There was a general tendency to return.

‡Till January 1921.

" (*d*) *National Institutions*.—I have so far dealt with the destructive side of the movement. It was not, however, long before the parents of the absenting scholars demanded some form of education to take the place of that which their sons had foregone. The year 1921 saw the outcrop of a large number of 'national' institutions, ranging from a Muhammadan University at Aligarh to the municipal primary schools at Surat. Some of these institutions were new, but many of them had been recognised schools and were 'nationalised' by their managing committees, sometimes at the instance of the scholars themselves. The Municipality of Surat, for example, 'nationalised' all its schools. The Government of Bombay was forced ultimately to suspend the operations of this body and to appoint a committee of management. A recent account says:—

" There are in the town about 8,000 or 9,000 school-going children and the managing committee claims that the number of its pupils has risen from 1,700 to about 4,000 children, with a daily average attendance of 3,000. The non-co-operationists put their figure at 7,500 with a daily attendance of 5,500. . . . . . On their own showing the

> non-co-operationists have succeeded only in dividing the school-children of the city into rival camps on a merely political basis. The section brought under their own wing is detached from the state-aided schools with the amiable motive of teaching the children to rebel against constituted authority. Whether they are taught anything of value is a subject on which no outside authority has any opportunity to pronounce; and it would be utterly inconsistent with the theories underlying national education to bring the matter to the test of any Government or university examination'."

" (e) *The meaning of " nationalisation."*—The first step in the 'nationalisation' of a school was the repudiation of Government grants and recognition. But the act of "nationalisation" was also held to signify some alteration in the character of the school. It is no exaggeration to say that, provided that the new schools did not interfere with the work and the discipline of existing institutions, Directors and others interested in education would have welcomed what purported to be the inauguration of a new educational experiment. Any such hopes were doomed to disappointment. The new schools, if they showed any distinctive features at all, showed none that were worthy of imitation. The two elements of ' national education,' on which the acknowledged leader of the non-co-operation movement, Mahatma Gandhi, had laid great stress, were the use of the *charkha* or spinning wheel and the encouragement of the vernacular. Spinning wheels were at first provided in many of the national schools, but an elementary knowledge of child nature is sufficient to explain their early disuse. Apart from the supreme dullness of this particular form of manual exercise, it has no educative value at all comparable with that possessed by other forms of hand and eye training; its disappearance from the curriculum is no matter for regret. The economic value of the *charkha* may be great, its educational value is negligible. There is little evidence that the vernacular was any more extensively used in the national schools than it is under the present regulations in recognised institutions. There is, on the other hand, clear evidence that many of the national schools gained a brief popularity by commencing the study of English at an earlier stage than is permitted by departmental regulations. In some of the institutions for older students, such for example as the National University at Aligarh, politics entered largely into the programme of studies. Apart from this, the curricula of the national institutions differed very little from those prescribed by the Education Department. The teachers were all products of the recognised system and were only qualified to teach what they had learnt. Too often they were not even qualified to do this and the discipline of the new schools was notoriously lax. The best of the national schools have now sought and regained recognition and the number remaining must be a small fraction of those which are shown in the preceding table.

" It would be tedious to follow the development of the movement from province to province, but the following account from Bengal may be taken as typical of its course."

" (*f*) *In Bengal.*—' As a result of the Khilafat agitation in August and September 1920 a strike took place in October at the Calcutta Madrasah. The backwash of this strike was felt at the Chittagong Madrasah, but it seems that the Mussalman element in the movement seeing the lack of support at the time from Hindu sources, realised the disastrous effect of such a sectional upheaval, and in consequence, shrank from going to extremes. After the students' conference at Nagpur a sudden demand arose from the students of many colleges in Calcutta that the institutions should be nationalised. The students of the Central and Bangabasi colleges led the way. Excitement and intimidation were rife in certain areas of Calcutta, and largely as a precautionary measure the colleges of Calcutta with the exception of the Bengal Engineering College, the Medical College, the post-graduate classes and the Law College, were closed. This closure was criticised at the time as pusillanimous for it seemed clear that the demands as formulated were the demands of a small, very vocal, and highly organised minority, which, as in similar circumstances universally, was for a time able to impose its will upon an unorganised majority. It is significant in this connection that Presidency College, surrounded as it was by hostile pickets and crowds and subjected to constant endeavour to sap its loyalty, stood firm. In the end and in consonance with the action of other Calcutta colleges, Presidency College was closed. As a result, the loyal elements were no longer subjected to constant indignity and insidious argument, and the dispersal of students, whether well or ill-affected, to their homes brought them into contact with the moderating influence of age and experience. Further the hottest heads were given ample leisure to realise that the golden age promised them as a result of 'national' education was but a fantasy, since the net-work of *charkha*-spinning *plus* Urdu or Hindi teaching institutions refused to materialise, charm the agitator never so wisely.'

' The picketting of colleges and schools was carried to such a length that the entrance to the examination hall was blocked against the ingress of the law candidates by rows of supine students. Only the most determined of examinees ventured to cross this barricade.

' Outside Calcutta the acuteness of the situation seemed to vary directly in proportion to the distance of an institution from the capital. Thus at Rajshahi the work was only temporarily suspended, while at Dacca the students, though subjected to great pressure, resisted stoutly and the college was never completely closed. The net loss of the colleges appears to have been over 27 per cent. of the students who normally would have been promoted from the first and third to the second and fourth year classes, respectively. A curious feature is that the admission to the science departments of the colleges and post-graduate classes showed an increase in 1921. This seems to support the assertion frequently made that the desertion was due in part, not to aversion from the system as a Government or Government-aided system, but to a growing and frequently expressed idea that the purely literary side of education has been overdone and that, as many of the students stated the case, it is 'science or nothing.'

'The movement hardly affected the primary and middle schools at all but there was a fall of 23 per cent, approximately, *i.e.*, of 45,000 students, in the attendance at high schools. 'Girls' schools have as yet little significance in the life of the people, and this obscurity has been of service to them in saving them from sharing, except in very minor degrees, in the attacks made on those for boys.'

'There was a recrudescence of the movement in the winter of 1921-22 in the shape of a much more barefaced and cynical attempt to use the students and the school-boys as political tools. The activities of the non-co-operationists were directed towards a complete 'hold-up' of normal city life on certain days. Their methods were the employment of so-called 'volunteers' for the picketting of cloth and liquor shops and for the holding up of traffic, and the organisation of illegal processions for the purpose of courting arrest. As evidence of that movement, so far as it concerned students, was entirely divorced from educational considerations, may be adduced the fact that in the cases of strikes in Calcutta colleges, there was no accompanying demand for nationalisation; the reason given was generally that the strike was a protest against the action of Government or against the arrest of some particular leader. While it is admitted that the movement may have given rise to a more constructively critical attitude towards the present system of education yet its evil disciplinary effects are patent. In the end 'political agitation seems to have tailed off into teaching bad manners to school boys'."

"(*g*) *The lessons of the Non-co-operation Movement.*—This episode in the history of Indian education is closed. It has not been without its valuable lessons to the educationist. It has brought to light evidence of a genuine dissatisfaction with the processes of education in India. It was due to the politicians that the attack was directed against the system of educational administration, and because the system, though capable of improvement, is on the whole suited to the country the attack failed. But strength was added to the attack by underlying discontent with the character of the education provided under this system. For this discontent, it would appear, in the subsequent pages that there is some justification. 'It is probable that the large bulk of the students suddenly realised, to their intense pain and disappointment, that much of their education is ill-suited to their practical needs. While the professor was lecturing to them on the annals of the Holy Roman Empire, their thoughts were inevitably and irresistibly turned to the great liberal and national movements of the nineteenth century. In economics they desired to study the application of general principles to the problems of their own country instead of to those of distant lands. Students, both at school and at college, began to wonder whether they were being trained for life and for service or for mere success in the examinations, for it was the ideals of service that were uppermost in their minds.'

"In short the educational organisation of India emerged triumphantly from the ordeal, but the crisis has left behind the conviction that our educational aims need re-statement. If the function of education is the adaptation of the future citizen to his environment, then the content of education must change in harmony with changes in that environment. The political and economic conditions of India have been undergoing change and the national school movement can at least claim that it lent strength to the advocates of educational reform."

In 'Indian Education in 1922-23' also published by the Bureau of Education, it is mentioned that there was a marked recovery from the effect of the Non-co-operation Movement on the attendance at schools and colleges in British India, and the following figures are given :—

Year.	Arts Colleges.		Secondary Schools.						Primary Schools.	
			High Schools.		Middle Schools.		Total.			
	Institutions.	Scholars.	Institutions.	Scholars.	Institutions.	Scholars.	Institutions.	Scholars.	Institutions.	Scholars.
1922 . . .	170	47,632	2,246	595,402	6,731	643,839	8,977	1,239,241	159,889	6,304,457
1923 . . .	174	52,639	2,312	632,943	6,732	698,462	9,044	1,331,405	162,015	6,600,116

117. **The Temperance Campaign.**—The Temperance Campaign, which was one of the features of Non-co-operation activity all over India, had ostensibly the excellent motive of reducing the consumption of intoxicating liquors and in this garb the movement was placed before the public. It was launched at a time of economic stress and this undoubtedly bore no little part in the success which it attained. It is certain that real object was to reduce the Government revenues, and the campaign actually had the effect of increasing the manufacture of illicit liquor in many places. During the financial year 1921-22, in which Non-co-operation activity was at its height, the Excise Administration Reports of most provinces show that it had considerable effect in reducing excise revenue, and in the Punjab, Bihar

and Orissa and Bombay this reduction was respectively thirty-three, ten and six lakhs of rupees. The methods whereby this result was attained were principally the so-called "peaceful" picketting and the boycott of vendors and excise officials. This picketing, like all phases of the Non-co-operation boycott, was often forcible and although the greatest punishment which the followers of Non-co-operation were supposed to impose on vendors was social ostracism, yet, not infrequently the latter were assaulted, and their shops were sometimes looted and burnt. The campaign, therefore, not only resulted in an increase of offences under the Excise and Opium Laws, but also under the Indian Penal Code.

The Provincial Excise Administration Reports for the year 1922-23 show that the gradual disappearance of the anti-excise agitation resulted in the reversion of excise affairs to their normal state.

118. **Boycott of titles.**—The boycott of titles was never treated very seriously and those honoured were not the type of persons to be carried away by Non-Co-operation agitation. An exceedingly limited number of title-holders abandoned the honours conferred on them, and those who did, had often some private motive for adopting this course. For example, a Police Inspector who resigned in 1921, ostensibly on account of Non-co-operation but actually to take up a post in business, at the same time refused to receive the King's Police Medal, probably because he thought this act would add to his popularity in his new walk of life.

119. **The Boycott of Legislative Bodies.**—The boycott of the Legislative Assembly and the Provincial Councils by Non-co-operators was effective during the elections in 1920-21, in so far that followers of the Congress creed generally, neither stood for election nor voted. By the time the next elections took place in 1923-24, the Swaraj Party had abandoned the boycott of Legislative bodies and thereby, as already shown, had killed orthodox Non-co-operation.

PART II.

A History of the Khilafat Movement.

CHAPTER I.

Pre-war Pan-Islamic Agitation in India, 1911-1914.

1. **The spread of pan-Islamism to India.**—A contributor to the Calcutta *Guardian* in 1924 traced the Indian Khilafat Movement *via* pan-Islamism to the Russo-Turkish War of 1876-78. In support of this contention he quoted the following extract from a writer on that subject, who said:—" The Islamic World was aroused to the fact that the area of Islamic independence was steadily narrowing, and the Quranic theory that Islam should dominate over every other religion was giving way to the contrary system. It was felt that the only Muslim power which could deal with those of Europe as an equal was Turkey; and pan-Islamism everywhere inculcated the doctrine that Turkey should be strengthened and supported. The Sultan was urged to advance through Persia into India and make common cause with the Sudanese Mehdi, and restore Egypt to an Islamic Sovereign. Abdul Hamid was far too astute a statesman to listen to such counsels; but he sent propagandists to preach the doctrine of the Khilafat and these found a hearing, especially in India."

2. **The Turkish Italian War.**—The propagandists sent at that time to preach in India may have had a hearing, but pan-Islamism in this country did not become a live force until it was stimulated by events in 1911. In the autumn of that year war was declared between Italy and Turkey and shortly afterwards Persia was partially occupied, in the north by Russia and in the south by the British. These events resulted in Muhammadan unrest in Northern India regarding which Mr. Petrie, who was then Assistant Director of the Intelligence Bureau, made enquiries in the Punjab. His Report written in February 1912 showed that the belief, held up to that time by Muhammadans in India, that the British Government was a safe custodian of Islamic interests, was rapidly evaporating; and further that a rumour was gaining credence to the effect that the Christian Powers had set themselves of deliberate purpose to encompass the ruin of Islam, with which object Great Britain had entered into a secret alliance with Italy with respect to the latter's attack on Turkey. He pointed out that the belief in this rumour had been strengthened by the re-Partition of Bengal at the end of 1911, which was viewed with dismay by Bengali-Muhammadans, and, since the Partition of 1905 had been announced as " a settled fact ", its annulment was regarded as a breach of faith on the part of Government. In the course of his Report, Mr. Petrie indicated that Zafar Ali Khan, the editor of the *Zamindar* of Lahore, and Muhammad Ali, the editor of the

Comrade of Calcutta, were among the most probable leaders of any Muhammadan agitation which might occur in India; and he summed up the situation as follows:—" The sympathy of all Indian Muhammadans with Turkey especially, which is the custodian of the sacred places of Islam, is still very real and must continue to influence the political out-look of the illiterate and partially educated for some time to come. The Muhammadan is always a potential fanatic and once that fanaticism is aroused, it may go to great lengths. It is peculiarly easy to confuse in the Muslim mind the issues of religion and politics, and it may be assumed that whenever Britain's political relations with Muslim countries admit of representation as hostility to the Islamic religion, there will be no lack of persons, just as at present, to impart the sinister twist calculated to inflame the latent fanatic. On such occasions it is doubtful if the Muslim leaders, who are ordinarily recognised as such, could do anything towards " holding " the more restive sections of their community; at present many of them have admitted they could not. The formation of the Muslim League has imparted a degree of solidarity to Muslim sentiment such as it has not before known, and Muhammadans have before their eyes the object-lessons of the Reformed Councils and the annulment of the partition to bear testimony to the solid success of agitation among the Hindus. If at any time Government is called upon to act in marked opposition to the clearly expressed wishes of the Muslim community, that community may voice its disagreement in no uncertain fashion. The older and wiser heads fear even at the present time the formation of a hot-headed Nationalist party which will be but little amenable to their control or influence, and the present agitation is certainly well-calculated to lay the foundations of such a body. There is no need to dwell upon the many undesirable effects which might result from such a step, but it admits of no doubt that a Nationalist Muslim Party of hot-headed young zealots might, either by itself, or in conjunction with Hindu patriots, be productive of no little mischief. The Hindus would welcome any such development, as they are in a deplorable state of physical weakness, and they themselves clearly realise this. Many Hindu papers have abounded in expressions of somewhat fulsome sympathy for Muhammadans in Turkey and elsewhere, and the motives have, in many cases, been only too apparent. I do not regard the eventuality I have endeavoured to describe as at all alarmist or visionary. A consideration of the present agitation points to such a step as by no means a remote possibility, and the taking of that step would be, I should say, the most dangerous turn which pan-Islamism in India is for the present capable of taking."

In July 1912 he wrote an addendum in which the following passages occur:—" The most serious result of the influences that have been at work is the general unsettling of Muhammadan confidence in the British Government, and the deep-seated mistrust that has been aroused of the purity and uprightness of its intentions towards Islam. The cry of the impending destruction of Islam by Christianity has moved many to whom questions of ordinary politics could make no appeal, and it is unfortunate that circumstances should have so combined as to make it possible for an improbable tale to receive a very wide degree of credence. The general acceptance of this rumour must have the result of bringing together both those who are imbued with a blind fanatical hatred of Christianity as well as those more sober-minded persons who are actuated by no other motive than the instinct of self-defence in the cause of their traditional religion."

* * * * *

"The belief that the British Government is no longer a safe custodian of Islamic interests is gaining ground in more enlightened quarters, and with the spread of that belief there arises the problem how best Muhammadans can protect those special interests which they believe the present Government has set itself either weakly or treacherously to betray. In what direction the Muhammadan politicians may turn it is hardly yet possible to say, though a union with the Hindu Congress party seems a probable solution." * * *

* * * * *

"At the moment many of the barriers to a Hindu-Muhammadan union have thus been thrown down, and the modern Muhammadan is too fully cognisant of the success of Hindu methods of agitation not to appreciate the advantages of such an alliance. But the Muhammadan is less quiescent and much quicker to action than the Hindu, and it is quite possible that events in Turkey or elsewhere might occur to rouse Muslim feeling to immediate action, independently of the matured policy of their leading politicians. Such action would probably take the shape of local outbreaks, such as the recent Beadon Square affair of Calcutta, though they would, no doubt, be on a more serious scale. At any rate the whole situation is such as to call for very close and intelligent study and for very careful observation."

In the light of subsequent events his forecast of the probable result of trouble with Turkey has proved prophetic.

3. **Turkish trouble with Balkan States.**—The tribulations of Turkey did not end with the termination of the Italian-Turkish War, for she was then involved in hostilities in the Balkans, which dragged on throughout 1912. This served to maintain Muhammadan unrest in India, and extremists did not hesitate to identify the whole of Europe with the Balkan States. Thus we find Abul Kalam Azad, early in 1913, advocating the boycott of European goods, both in his paper—the *Al Hilal*—and on the platform, and in Calcutta some extremist Hindus took part in these boycott meetings.

In March 1913 a *fatwa* was published in the *Aligarh Institute Gazette* in which it was urged that Muhammadans, being brothers of the oppressed Turks, should curse those who, seeing oppression, wished to help the oppressors, and that no opportunity should be lost to impair the strength of the enemies of Turkey. It was specially added that the British were not exempt from the application of this *fatwa*. In Lucknow Maulvi Wahid-ud-Din Salim in his paper, the *Muslim Gazette*, deprecated open expressions of loyalty on the part of Muhammadans. He stated that the Quranic injunction to obey God and government only applied to Muslim rulers.

A feature of the annual session of the Muslim league, which was held in March, was an appeal made by the president to start a United India League, open to all classes and creeds, with a view to the evolution of a common Indian nationality. The League also condemned mischievous attempts to widen the breach between Hindus and Muhammadans.

4. **The Anjuman-i-Khuddam-i-Kaaba.**—In the month of April a scheme was published by Mr. Mushir Husain Kidwai of Gudia, Barabanki, United Provinces, for the formation of a society called the Anjuman-i-Khuddam-i-Kaaba ', which has been fully described in a note, dated 20th February 1914, prepared by Mr. Isemonger of the Punjab Police. Briefly this society aimed at maintaining the honour and safety of the Kaaba and the defence of the Holy Places from non-Muslim aggression, to ensure which, the members were at all times to be ready to sacrifice their lives and property. This organisation was supported by the Ali Brothers—Muhammad and Shaukat—and by Abul Kalam Azad and Abdul Bari, all of whom were subsequently to take a very active part in the Khilafat Movement.

5. **The Indian Medical Mission to Turkey.**—In the previous year, practical effect had been given to the sympathy of Indian Muhammadans for Turkey during the Balkan War, by the despatch of an All-India Medical Mission under Dr. Ansari which reached Constantinople at the end of December 1912. During their sojourn in Turkey, the members of the Mission came into contact with leading Turkish politicians and statesmen, such as Enver Bey, and with the well-known Egyptian nationalist—Sheikh Abdul Aziz Shahwesh. One of the members of the Mission, who visited Cairo in February 1913, spoke bitterly of English rule in India, characterising it as undurable. Zafar Ali Khan visited Turkey early in 1913 and he with some members of the Mission, took an active part in furthering a Turkish proposal to provide a colony in Anatolia for Muslim refugees.

This scheme, in which Sheikh Abdul Aziz Shahwesh was interested, was supported by the *Comrade* (which had transferred its headquarters to Delhi at the end of 1912) in a series of articles contributed by Abdul Rahman Siddiqi, who was General Manager of the Mission. The *Comrade* also urged the purchase by Indians of Turkish Bonds.

Dr. Ansari and Zafar Ali Khan returned to India about the middle of 1913 and the former, in a speech to the students of the M. A. O College, Aligarh, on the 12th of July, assured his audience that the spirit of the Turkish Nation was not dead and asserted that the most important result of the Medical Mission was the fusion of a union between Turkey and India.

6. **The Cawnpore Mosque incident.**—The re-occupation of Adrianople by the Turks in the summer of 1913 slightly improved the situation in India, but this was more than countered by a serious riot which occurred at Cawnpore on the 3rd of August. In that city a hostile demonstration took place as the result of the removal of a platform adjoining a Mosque. The Police were stoned and were forced to fire on, and charge the mob, and several rioters were killed. The scene of disturbance was visited by Muslim leaders, including Muhammad Ali, who used the incident to foment agitation against Government. Khwaja Hasan Nizami of Delhi issued an inflammatory pamphlet which was eventually proscribed, and a leaflet was found stating that India was no longer *Dar-ul-Aram*—a land of peace—but was *Dar-ul-Harab*, where it was the duty of the Faithful to slay infidels.

The situation became so serious that His Highness the Nawab of Rampur convened a meeting at Delhi on the 1st of October, which was attended by a number of representative Muhammadans from Northern India, " to consider remedial measures to relieve the present tension of feeling among Muhammadans and to assure Government of the genuine loyalty of the community to the British Throne." The meeting, however, proved to be abortive and the situation was not eased until His Excellency the Viceroy visited Cawnpore and sanctioned the re-construction of a platform at the place of dispute.

Muhammad Ali, after this incident, went to Europe, visiting Cairo *en route* where he is reported to have stated that England would not rule for long in India and that Germany was the coming power. He also is alleged to have said that Muhammadans in India were preparing to subscribe the cost of a dreadnought as a contribution to the approaching struggle for freedom.

7. **Muslim League Session, Agra, 1913.**—Towards the end of 1913, the All-India Muslim League held a session at Agra at which the presence of His Highness the Aga Khan, the President of the League, exercised a moderating influence In his speech, Sir Ibrahim Rahimtollah, who was President of the Agra Session, stated that no country could remain for ever under foreign rule however beneficial that rule might be, and added, " India is our motherland, our proud heritage, and must in the end be handed over to us by our guardians " Eventually the League emerged with an announcement that henceforth its goal would be self-government in India. At this session a resolution was passed suggesting the organisation of a body of voluntary workers similar to the ' Servants of India Society '—a society founded in 1905 by Mr. Gokhale with the object of obtaining Dominion Self-Government for India.

8. **Pro-Turkish agitation.**—During 1913 the security of Zafar Ali Khan's newspaper—the *Zemindar*—had been enhanced, but it continued its objectionable campaign, with the result that its security had to be confiscated at the beginning of 1914. This action on the part of Government served as a cause for agitation, the result of

which was apparent in the following incident. Another Lahore paper, the *Paisa Akhbar*, which had criticised the *Zemindar*, received an anonymous communication from Peshawar conveying a threat of vengeance on behalf of the *Zemindar*. Three days afterwards—at the end of January—the premises of the *Paisa Akhbar* in Lahore were burnt down.

In the middle of 1914 the London Branch of the All-India Muslim League addressed a letter to the Secretary for Foreign Affairs regarding the expulsion of Muhammadans from the provinces ceded to Greece. It characterised this act as "one of the saddest lapses from the standards of European civilisation". The letter expressed a desire that Indian Muslims should resume their normal feeling of amity towards the western world, and redirect their energies into channels of internal development, but added that unless the condition of affairs which existed in Macedonia improved, it would be well nigh impossible to allay the excitement and bitterness which prevailed in India.

At about the same time attempts were made to revive agitation with respect to the Cawnpore Mosque affair and Muhammadans who had taken part in the compromise were urged, in a pamphlet issued from Bareilly, to admit their error and to explain to Government that no portion of a mosque could be demolished and replaced as had been done at Cawnpore. Early in July 1914, a trifling incident in a bioscope film, which had been shown at Karachi during the previous month, was utilised to inflame the minds of Muhammadans against Government. The picture was denounced as an insult to the Prophet, and the *Comrade* pretended to believe that it was a manifestation of a deeplaid plot engineered by Christian missionaries to bring disgrace upon Islam.

9. **Activities of the Khuddam-i-Kaaba Society.**—Some time previously, the Khuddam-i-Kaaba Society had sent out a number of preachers to enrol members and to lecture on the objects of the Anjuman. The emissaries exhibited no desire to be either scrupulous or truthful, and one of them was reported to have stated in the Lahore District, that the sacred places of Islam were in danger and that infidels were threatening to capture and demolish them. A journal of the Society was published at Delhi and the first issue, which included the rules, stated that the membership was over nine thousand. Shaukat Ali, as Secretary of the Anjuman, visited Bombay in June and there stimulated an agitation against certain proposed regulations relating to pilgrims performing the Haj. At about the same time his brother, Muhammad Ali, in a speech delivered at Delhi, stated that the Anjuman did not want members who were afraid of the Police and that the community would be loyal to Government provided that such loyalty did not involve disloyalty to their own religion. He added that the objects of the Anjuman were to revive the zeal which had led to the conquest of Egypt, Spain and Persia.

10. **Visits to India of suspicious Turks.**—During 1914, India received several suspicious visitors from Turkey. The first of these

were Kemal Umar Bey and Adnan Bey who, as representatives of the Turkish Red Crescent Society, came to India in February ostensibly for the purpose of conveying the thanks of the Turkish Government to Indian Muhammadans for their assistance during the Balkan War. They visited Bombay, Delhi, Lahore, Patna and Calcutta, and while they were careful to avoid politics themselves, their presence gave occasion for a number of inflammatory speeches. While in India they were joined by S. M. Tewfik, a Turk who was the editor of a Persian paper in Constantinople, and who (as will appear later) corresponded with well known pan-Islamists in India. These delegates were followed by two Turkish visitors named Muhammad Samey Bey, formerly private Secretary to the Wali of Basra, and Lieutenant Mustafa Sadek of the Turkish Army, who arrived at Karachi early in July and paid a flying visit to Bombay, Delhi and Lahore. At Bombay they met the Turkish Vice-Consul and Shaukat Ali, and during their tour in India they conveyed the impression that they were in the confidence of the Young Turk Party and that their visit to India had been undertaken with the expressed intention of cementing the relationship between the pan-Islamic Party in India and the Young Turk Party in Constantinople. At Delhi they associated with Dr. Ansari and the Ali Brothers and were entertained by the members of the Anjuman-i-Khuddam-i-Kaaba.

Another party of three Turks with two servants arrived at Bombay from Smyrna on the 9th of August and reached Peshawar on the 5th September with the expressed intention of crossing the Frontier, telling the Police that they were on their way to Chinese Turkestan *via* Kashgar. The conduct of these individuals excited suspicion, which was subsequently confirmed by information received from Egypt to the effect that one of them, who gave his name as Mustafa Samey, was otherwise known as Haji Samey Bey and had been sent to India by the Committee of Union and Progress (a Turkish Society which formed the nucleus of the Young Turk Party) to stir up Indian Muslims. Samey Bey's brother, Ashraf Bey, had been sent on a similar mission to Egypt, where he had been arrested. In addition to the suspected Turkish emissaries mentioned above, there were indications that Turkey was endeavouring to spread pro-Turk and pan-Islamic ideas in India through its press. A weekly Turkish paper, the *Jihan-i-Islam*, published in Arabic, Turkish and Urdu and edited by an Indian Muhammadan, found its way in considerable numbers into India before the War, and the avowed object of this periodical was to promote intercourse between Muhammadans and to encourage Indians to trade with Muslim countries

11. **The outbreak of the War.**—When the war between Servia and Austria broke out, Muhammadan sympathies were entirely on the side of Austria on account of the recent hostilities between Servia and Turkey, and when Russia and Germany subsequently joined the conflict, Muhammadan feeling was in favour of Germany owing to the memory of the Russo-Turkisn War. However, when Britain

entered the arena, Muhammadan sympathy appeared to have veered round to her side, and endeavours were made to organise a Red Crescent Mission composed of Muhammadan volunteers to assist British troops. Shaukat Ali, even, was reported to be favourably inclined to sending volunteers from Aligarh. The situation at that time was summed up by the Director, Central Intelligence, in the middle of August 1914, as follows:—

"The position generally taken up by the nationalist press is that Indians are loyal because they aspire to self-government within the British Empire. Muhammadans, however, have of recent years been inclined to rank England as an enemy and Germany as a friend of Islam. The attitude of the Muhammadan press is, therefore, the more important at the present juncture, and it is satisfactory to find that most of the Muhammadan papers give expression to the loyalty of the community they represent. A noteworthy and somewhat surprising example is the *Zamindar* of Lahore, the tone of which since the outbreak of the war has been unexceptionable. The staff of the *Zamindar* has subscribed Rs. 205 to the Prince of Wales Fund. There are, however, one or two departures from the general attitude. Thus the issue of the *Comrade*, dated 12th August, contains a good deal of pernicious writing on the subject of the war. While expressing a lukewarm loyalty to the British Government, the writer makes no concealment of the fact that his real sympathies are with Germany. 'Frankly, we have not been impressed by Sir Edward Grey's apologia about the war against Germany.............. Again, we do not like England fighting on the side of Russia. We hold no brief for Germany, but it seems to us that, if there is any combatant who is defending the cause of civilisation in this struggle, it is the Germans fighting the great Slav menace to the liberties and institutions of civilised Europe. It is difficult to withhold our admiration or the cool courage and resolve which the Kaiser and his people are showing in the hour of their heaviest trial............The Triple Alliance is dead through the desertion of Italy, and one cannot but despise this perfidious power who has broken her truth so lightheartedly' The writer joins in the demand that the rulers of India should allow the people to train themselves for the defence of the country and the Empire. After enumerating in nine distinct clauses of one portentous sentence the main grievances of Muhammadans against the British Government, he states that all these considerations are outweighed by the one supreme consideration that the tutelage of England is necessary to India in her present stage of national and communal growth. The

> Muhammadan community will, therefore, remain loyal to England ' whether she crushes the naval power of Germany and becomes a dictator to Europe, or the last ship of her mighty Armada sinks in the North Sea and her last soldier falls down and dies round Liege or London '. It may be doubted whether the declaration of loyalty is meant to impress the reader so much as the enumeration of grievances. ' If ', concludes the writer, ' we cannot hastily command in others an enthusiasm for this war which we ourselves do not feel, let us once and for all assure the Government that so far as we and those within the orbit of our influence are concerned they can sleep in peace '. The articles of the *Comrade* from which these quotations are made may be taken to represent fairly accurately the views of the Indian Pan-Islamist "

12. **Extremists become objectionable.**—At a meeting in Delhi early in September 1914, Maulvi Abdul Majid, a well known preacher of the Anjuman-i-Khuddam-i-Kaaba, pointed out that Indian Muhammadans were well aware of the treatment meted out to Muslims by Christians during the Tripoli War, and he mentioned the Crusades in Palestine and the wounding of the Prophet by Christians. He urged that the present crisis was an excellent opportunity for Muhammadans to better their condition by uniting in defence of the Kaaba with which object they should subscribe freely to the funds of the Anjuman. In the same month the intention of the Turks to participate in the War was directly evident from letters written by S. M. Tewfik Bey (already mentioned) to leading pan-Islamists in India, saying that Turkey intended to join Germany and Austria and urging Indian Muslims to subscribe hand-somely to the Ottoman Red Crescent Society. A circular on the same subject signed by Kemal Umar Bey and Adnan Bey, whose visit to India has already been mentioned, also came to light.

At this time the attitude of Muhammad Ali's paper—the *Comrade*—became very objectionable. He sneered at any loyal effusion which appeared, and frankly expressed his own admiration of the Germans in a leading article entitled " The Choice of the Turks " in which he set forth the grievances which Turkey had against each of the Allies. Zafar Ali Khan, the editor of the *Zemindar* did not lag behind, and at the end of September he made an objectionable speech at Lahore, in consequence of which he was ordered to reside in his village and to refrain from taking any part in journalism or politics. Muhammad Ali of course criticised strongly this curtailment of the liberties of his confrère.

13. **Turkey enters the War.**—In spite of these expressions of disloyalty by certain agitators it seemed clear, when war was declared with Turkey on the 1st November 1914, that the Turks were disappointed with the lack of support from India. It appeared that the

Turkish delegates who had visited India earlier in the year had gained the impression that leading Muslims in India actively sympathised with them, but as nothing immediately materialised from this sympathy, efforts were made to stimulate it to action. In November leaflets which had been distributed to pilgrims in Mecca found their way to India. They stated that the Allies were the enemies of Islam and any one who helped them was an infidel. The Cawnpore mosque case and the Karachi bioscope incident were mentioned and the English were accused of robbing Muhammadans, pulling down their mosques and insulting their Prophet. In the same month, a newspaper published in Kabul, named the *Siraj-ul-Akhbar* which was read by leading pan-Islamists in India, became very objectionable and described India as *Dar-ul-Harab*.

In December, news reached India that the Sultan had declared *jehad* and Turkish papers, which arrived during that month, published five *fatwas* signed by the Sheikh-ul-Islam containing the declaration.

CHAPTER II

Muhammadan Agitation during the War. 1915–1918.

14. **The Sheikh-ul-Islam declares Jehad.**—Early in January 1915 the proclamation of *jehad* by the Sheikh-ul-Islam at Mecca and Jeddah was confirmed by pilgrims returning from the *haj* who reported that about 700 of their fellows had remained behind in order to fight for the Faith. These were led by two members of the Anjuman-i-Khuddam-i-Kaaba named Atta Muhammad and Abdul Wahid Aba, one of whom subsequently returned and was interned, while the other visited various countries in Europe where he took part in revolutionary activities. In the same month, Abul Kalam Azad, the editor of the *Al Hilal*, made a very objectionable speech at Lahore in which he stated that Muslims owed their duty to God alone and that no earthly power could claim allegiance from them. At the same time he refrained from declaring the policy of the Anjuman-i-Khuddam-i-Kaaba with respect to *jehad*, though it was obvious that its members were not prepared lightly to disregard the proclamation of the Sultan. At the end of 1914, Muhammad Ali had produced a new paper in Delhi named the *Hamdard*, and it was reported that the question of *jehad* in India and its incumbency upon Muhammadans was discussed in the office of that organ by several Muhammadans, including Shaukat Ali, who expressed the view that India was *Dar-ul-Harab*.

15. **The bulk of Muhammadan opinion loyal.**—It will have been noticed that up to this period agitation was confined to self-declared extremists and that the bulk of Muhammadan opinion, while undoubtedly disturbed by the Turkish entry into the War, had not come to any definite conclusion as to the religious significance of the fact. This was exemplified by a *fatwa* drawn up by Maulvi Abdul Haq of Calcutta and Delhi. This *fatwa* was signed by a number of leading Ulemas and declared that the war with Turkey was political and not religious. Abdul Bari of Lucknow, the Secretary of the Anjuman-i-Khuddam-i-Kaaba, was one of the few notable Maulvis who opposed this *fatwa* which, unfortunately, lost much of its value by a foolish statement by Abdul Haq to the effect that it had been inspired by Government.

16. **The first fruits of agitation during the War.**—Early in February, a leaflet was distributed broadcast in Delhi which enquired why Muslims should remain loyal to a government which demanded every sacrifice without any return, and concluded by appealing to the Hindus and Muhammadans to forget their differences and, for the sake of their honour, self-respect and country,. to unite in opposition to the tyrant. Continuous propaganda of this nature was bound to produce some result, and the first victims were a section of the Muhammadan students in various colleges in Lahore who abandoned

their studies and crossed the Frontier on the grounds that India was *Dar-ul-Harab*. This incident is of some importance as these students subsequently took an active part in the Silk Letter Conspiracy, which will be described later.

17. **Internment of the Ali Brothers.**—At about this time, certain mosques in Calcutta were utilised to spread pro-Turkish feeling and special prayers were offered in them for the Sultan's victory. The campaign against Government carried on by the Ali Brothers resulted in their internment in May 1915 within the limits of the Delhi Province, and they were forbidden to attend public meetings. Their internment caused a good deal of excitement and an agitation ensued with the object of forcing Government to cancel it. The Government action resulted in the closing down of the *Hamdard*, and the *Al Hilal* also ceased publication at about the same time.

18. **Turco-German Conspiracy.**—In the middle of 1915, information was received of Turco-German schemes to incite Indian Muhammadans against the British Government, in order to cause trouble in India and thus to embarrass England in the War. The notorious Egyptian pan-Islamist, Abdul Aziz Shahwesh, was specially appointed by the Committee of Union and Progress to put into execution these anti-British schemes; and among those on whom the Committee relied for assistance may be mentioned the names of Zafar Ali Khan of Lahore, Muhammad Ali of Delhi and Imam Uddin of Calcutta.

19. **Muslim League meet at Bombay, X'mas 1915.**—In the latter part of 1915, the question of holding a session (which had been suspended during the previous year) of the All-India Muslim League was discussed. It was eventually decided, in spite of much local opposition from a large and influential section of Muhammadans in Bombay, to hold a meeting of the League in that town during X'mas week of 1915. The opposition chiefly came from the Sunnis who emphasised that it was perfectly useless to worry the British Government for concessions while war was being waged and that, though Sunni Muhammadans were bound by deep sentimental ties to the person of the Khalifa, their best course was to remain quiet until peace was declared and then to submit their claim for recognition by the British Government. Their opponents, led by Mr. Jinnah, on the other hand, were equally determined to force a meeting of the League upon Bombay in order to come to some mutual understanding with the Hindus on the subject of self-government. Mr. Mazhar-ul-Haq presided over the meeting, but as both he and Mr. Jinnah were disliked by orthodox Muhammadans on account of their affectation of the European mode of living, dissension arose and the meeting eventually broke up. On New Year's day 1916, however, an adjourned meeting of the League was held at the Taj Mahal Hotel, at which local Sunnis were conspicuous by their absence, and at which the Raja of Mahmudabad was elected president of the All-India Muslim League in succession to His Highness the Aga Khan (who had resigned), while Wazir Hassan was elected Honorary Secretary.

20. **The Punjab Branch of the League divided.**—At this time considerable internal friction existed in the Punjab branch of the Muslim League, of which the younger and more extreme spirits were dissatisfied with the policy of their Secretary, Mr. (now Sir) Mian Muhammad Shafi. His opponents were strengthened by the support of Wazir Hassan and Mazhar-ul-Haq whose displeasure Mr. Shafi had incurred by his determined opposition to the meeting of the League at Bombay. They saw in him an obstacle to the joint League and Congress policy of political education, and it was argued that, as the term of office under the constitution was limited to three years the fact that there had been no election of office-bearers for four years, automatically treminated the existence of the League. Therefore, a meeting to reconstitute the provincial League was held in Lahore, shortly after the Bombay meeting, while Mr. Shafi also summoned a meeting of the old league at which he was re-appointed Secretary and Sir Behram Khan Mozari was elected President. This resulted in two Provincial branches of the Muslim League in the Punjab, and, for the time being, the weight of public opinion appeared to be on the side of the old branch and Mr. Shafi.

21. **The Silk Letter Conspiracy.**—It is now necessary to give some account of what is known as the Silk Letter Conspiracy, and this can best be taken from the Sedition (Rowlatt) Committee's Report, published in 1918, which described it as follows:—

> "In August 1916 the plot known to Government as the Silk Letter case was discovered. This was a project hatched in India with the object of destroying British rule by means of an attack on the North-West Frontier, supplemented by a Muhammadan rising in this country. For the purpose of instigating and executing this plan a certain Maulvi Obeidulla crossed the North-West Frontier early in August 1915 with three companions, Abdulla, Fateh Muhammad and Muhammad Ali. Obeidulla is a converted Sikh and had been trained as a Maulvi in the Muslim religious school at Deoband in the Saharanpur district of the United Provinces. There he infected some of the staff and students with his own militant and anti-British ideas, and the principal person whom he influenced was Maulana Mahmud Hassan, who had long been head Maulvi in the school. Obeidulla wished to spread over India a pan-Islamic and anti-British movement through the agency of Maulvis trained in the famous Deoband school. But his plans were thwarted by the Manager and Committee, who dismissed him and some of his chief associates. There is evidence too that he got into trouble over some accounts. Maulana Mahmud Hassan, however, remained and continued to receive visits from Obeidulla. Secret meetings were held at the Maulana's house and it was reported

that men from the Frontier had been received there. On September 18th, 1915, Mahmud Hassan, with a certain Muhammad Mian and other friends, followed Obeidulla's example by leaving India, not however for the North, but for the Hedjaz tract of Arabia.

Before departing, Obeidulla had started a school in Delhi, and had put two books into circulation preaching militant fanaticism to Indian Muhammadans and impressing on them the supreme duty of *jehad*. The common object of this man and his friends, including the Maulana, was to promote a great Muslim attack on India which should synchronise with a Muslim rebellion. We shall see how each endeavoured to accomplish his purpose.

Obeidulla and his friends first visited the Hindustani fanatics and afterwards proceeded to Kabul. There he met the members of a Turco-German Mission with whom he fraternised and after some time he was joined by his Deoband friend, Maulvi Muhammad Mian Ansari. This man had accompanied Maulana Mahmud Hassan to Arabia and returned in 1916 with a declaration of *jehad* received by the Maulana from the hand of Ghalib Pasha, then Turkish Military Governor of the Hedjaz. While on his way, Muhammad Mian distributed copies of this document, known as the " Ghalib-nama ", both in India and among the frontier tribes. Obeidulla and his fellow-conspirators had devised a scheme for the provisional government of India after the overthrow of British power. A certain Mahendra Pratap was to be President. This man is a Hindu of good family and eccentric character, who, at the end of 1914, was granted a passport to travel in Italy, Switzerland and France. He had gone straight to Geneva, had there met the notorious Hardayal and had been by Hardayal introduced to the German Consul. He had then proceeded to Berlin and had thence been despatched on a special mission, having apparently impressed the Germans with an exaggerated idea of his importance.

Obeidulla himself was to be Minister of India, and Barkatulla, a friend of Krishnavarma's and a member of the American *Ghadr* party, who had also travelled to Kabul *via* Berlin, was to be Prime Minister. Son of a servant of the Bhopal State, he had visited England, America and Japan. He had been appointed Professor of Hindustani at Tokio. He had there edited a bitter anti-British paper called " *The Islamic fraternity* ", which was suppressed by the Japanese authorities. He had later been dismissed from his appointment and had then joined his *Ghadr* friends in America.

The Germans of the Mission, failing to achieve their object, left Afghanistan early in 1916; but the Indians remained, and the ' Provisional Government ' despatched letters to both the Governor of Russian Turkestan and the then Czar of Russia inviting Russia to throw over her alliance with Great Britain and assist in the overthrow of British rule in India. These were signed by Mahendra Pratap and subsequently fell into British hands. The letter to the Czar was on a gold plate, a photograph of which has been shown to us.

The Provisional Government ' also proposed to form an alliance with the Turkish Government, and in order to accomplish this object Obeidulla addressed a letter to his old friend, Maulana Mahmad Hassan. This, together with another letter dated the 8th *Ramzan* (9th July 1916), written by Muhammad Mian Ansari, he forwarded under a covering note addressed to Sheikh Abdur Rahim of Hyderabad, Sind, a person who has since absconded. Sheikh Abdur Rahim was requested in the note to send on the enclosures by hand of some reliable *hadji* (pilgrim) to Mahmud Hassan at Mecca, or even to convey them himself if no trustworthy messenger were obtainable. We have ourselves seen the letters to Mahmud Hassan which came into British hands. They are neatly and clearly written on yellow silk. Muhammad Mian's letter mentioned the previous arrival of German and Turkish missions, the return of the Germans, the staying on of the Turks, " but without work ", the runaway students, the circulation of the " Ghalibnama ", the " Provisional Government ", and the projected formation of an " Army of God " This army was to draw recruits from India and to bring about an alliance among Islàmic rulers. Mahmud Hassan was to convey all these particulars to the Ottoman Government. Obeidulla's letter contained a tabular statement of the " Army of God ". Its headquarters were to be at Medina, and Mahmud Hassan himself was to be general-in-chief. Secondary headquarters under local generals were to be established at Constantinople, Teheran and Kabul. The general at Kabul would be Obeidulla himself. The table contains the names of three patrons, 12 field marshals, and many other high military officers. Of the Lahore students, one was to be a major-general, one a colonel, and six lieutenant-colonels. Most of the persons designated for these high commands cannot have been consulted as to their appointments. But the whole information conveyed by the silk letters has rendered certain precautions advisable, and these have been taken.

In December 1916 Maulana Mahmud Hassan and four of his companions fell into British hands. They are now prisoners of war interned in a British possession. Ghalib Pasha, the signer of the " Ghalibnama ", is also a prisoner of war and has admitted signing a paper put before him by the Mahmud Hassan party. A translation of its prominent passages runs as follows:—

'The Muhammadans in Asia, Europe and Africa adorned themselves with all sorts of arms and rushed to join the *jehad* in the path of God. Thanks to Almighty God that the Turkish Army and the Mujahidin have overcome the enemies of Islam . . . . Oh Muslims, therefore attack the tyrannical Christian government under whose bondage you are . . . . Hasten to put all your efforts, with strong resolution, to strangle the enemy to death and show your hatred and enmity for them. It may also be known to you that Maulvi Mahmud Hassan Effendi (formerly at the Deoband Madrassa, India) came to us and sought our counsel. We agreed with him in this respect and gave him necessary instructions. You should trust him if he comes to you and help him with men, money and whatever he requires.'

The facts narrated in this chapter establish clearly the anxiety of some Muhammadan fanatics to provide first sedition and then rebellion in India. For the purpose of accomplishing their objects they seek to co-operate with the enemies of Britain. Their methods of waging war range from subterranean intrigue and propaganda to open defection. Sometimes they send recruits or collect and remit money. Sometimes they go themselves. Always they preach sedition. Against their designs the loyalty of the general Muslim community and the effective power of the Government are the only safeguards."

* * * * * *

22. **Abul Kalam Azad externed and Hasrat Mohani interned.**— In March 1916, Abul Kalam Azad in delivering a lecture on slavery at his school, the *Dar-ul-Irshad*, stated that the Quran forbade Muhammadans to remain in subjection, and that since a country like India which had once been under Muhammadan rule should never be relinquished, it was incumbent on them to strive to regain their lawful control. Shortly afterwards, the Government of Bengal, on account of his activities in that province, externed Abul Kalam Azad and since similar orders had been passed against him by the Governments of the Punjab and United Provinces, he took up his residence in Ranchi in April 1916. Fazl-ul-Hassan Hasrat Mohani, the well-known agitator of Aligarh, was interned by

the United Provinces Government at Lalitpur in the Jhansi District at about the same time, as it was learnt that he intended to go to Kabul whence both he and Abul Kalam Azad were reported to have received communications from Barkatullah of the 'Provisional Government of India'. Hasrat Mohani was subsequently sentenced to two years' imprisonment for failing to comply with the internment orders.

23. **The Sharif of Mecca declares independence.**—During this year the Arab revolt occurred resulting in the declaration of independence by the Sharif of Mecca, and his seizure of Mecca, Jeddah and Taif, which came to public knowledge in India in June 1916. This seizure of the holy places of course fundamentally affected the whole question of the Turkish Khalifate and a report prepared at the time in the Central Intelligence Bureau as to how it was received in India, reads as follows:—

> 'The official communiqué announcing the declaration of independence by the Sharif of Mecca and the seizure of Mecca, Jeddah and Taif by the Sharif's forces was made public on June 23rd. The news was at first received with silence both by the Muhammadan press and by their public bodies. The great mass of the Muhammadan public had not had time to realise the news and the educated classes throughout India were for a time either incredulous or too bewildered by its unexpectedness and its overwhelming importance to the Muhammadan world to express any ready comment. Many frankly disbelieved the news, others thought the incident had been grossly exaggerated and expected that the Turks would soon adjust matters in the Hedjaz, as incipient risings in Yemen and Asir had before been settled; others again suggested it was an ingenious trick by which the Turks hoped to relieve scarcity in Syria and Arabia by misleading England into shipping food-stuffs to the supposed enemies of Turkey. Some, even at this early stage, jumped to the conclusion that Great Britain had instigated, or intrigued with the Arabs to this end. In the meanwhile some of the English-owned newspapers had published historical or critical articles, developing the vexed question of the Khalifate with reference to the seizure of the Holy Places and emphasising the permanence of the Sharif's step.
>
> It is probable that these early articles first brought home to the educated class a realization of the far-reaching consequences of the Sharif's action. One of them in particular, published in the Calcutta *Statesman* of the

> 25th June, which said in addition that "Muhammadans generally were delighted with the news", seems to have stung the pan-Islamic sections into action. Maulana Abdul Bari of Lucknow, as President of the *Anjuman-i-Khuddam-i-Kaaba*, sent a strongly worded telegram to His Excellency the Viceroy expressing the "consternation and painful anxiety" caused to Mussalmans by the fear that the rising would "convert their most sacred places into fields of slaughter and carnage". The telegram added that "the impudent besieger of the tomb of the Holy Prophet and his sympathisers will stand for ever condemned in the eyes of the Muslim world as enemies of Islam" At the same time, *i.e.*, on June 26th, an emergency meeting of the Council of the All-India Muslim League at Lucknow under the presidency of the Raja of Mahmudabad adopted the following resolution:—'The Council of the All-India Muslim League places on record its abhorrence of the action of the Arab rebels headed by the Sharif of Mecca, whose outrageous conduct may place in jeopardy the safety and sanctity of the Holy Places of Islam in the Hedjaz and Mesopotamia and condemns them and their sympathisers as enemies of Islam'. This was followed in quick succession on June 27th by a public meeting in Lucknow at which the resolution of the League meeting was repeated and another passed disclaiming the announcement of the *Statesman* that Indian Muhammadans welcomed the revolt."

The agitation which was the outcome of this news was originated by the leading lights of the Muslim League and the Anjuman-i-Khuddam-i-Kaaba, and the Lucknow meeting mentioned above, which was attended by about 300 persons, was the only important result attained by their efforts. The effect of the news on the North-West Frontier Province was reported to be bad, and the supporters of the Muslim League in Calcutta and Bombay did not hesitate to express their belief that the Arab revolt was the result of British intrigue. The bulk of Muslim opinion in India at this time, however, exhibited no great excitement and although in some quarters sympathy for the Sharif's action was apparent on the grounds that it was the natural outcome of years of Turkish misgovernment, yet on the whole the general feeling seems to have been one of depression and fear lest the safety of the Holy Places should be jeopardised, and of condemnation of the Sharif for bringing them into danger

The *Mujahidin*, or Hindustani Fanatics in Independent Territory, claimed the revolt to be the final sign of British determination to overthrow Islam, and busied themselves in using the incident as a lever to stir up trouble on the Frontier, with which object they sent out *maulvis* on propaganda tours. In the middle of July, the Kabul newspaper—the *Seraj-ul-Akhbar*—which has already been referred to, condemned the Sharif of Mecca as a traitor to his sovereign and to his religion.

24. **The Lucknow Pact.**—In his book "India in the Years 1917-18" Professor Rushbrook Williams wrote:—

> "In the course of the year 1915, a definite rapprochement had taken place between some of the leaders of advanced Hindu and of advanced Muhammadan opinion. The Muslim League, which had until recently stood mainly for the protection of Muhammadan interests against anticipated Hindu ascendancy, had gradually become dominated by those members of the "young" Muslim party, who upheld the new ideal of self-government for India. As a consequence of this, the Muslim League probably became less representative of conservative Muhammadan opinion in India; for the Muhammadan community, educationally less advanced than the Hindus, seems at present also less attracted by Nationalist ideals, and less patient of political, as distinct from religious leadership, by any party of advance."

This rapprochement bore fruit at a meeting of the Congress at Lucknow during X'mas week 1916 in the shape of the Hindu-Muhammadan Pact (the terms of which had been settled at a joint meeting of the All-India Congress Committee with the Committee of the All-India Muslim League) which was an agreement to give Muhammadan minorities in certain provinces enhanced representation in Legislatures and other elective bodies at the expense of the Muhammadan majorities in Bengal and the Punjab. It was apparent, however, that this entente did not find support among those Hindus who placed their religion before politics, and it was condemned at a meeting of the All-India Hindu Sabha which was held at Lucknow at the same time.

The All-India Muslim League also held a meeting at Lucknow during X'mas week 1916 under the leadership of Wazir Hassan, the Raja of Mahmudabad, Mazhar-ul-Haq and Mr. Jinnah. The League at this period had become little more than an adjunct to the Congress. It disaffiliated the old Punjab Provincial Branch of the League of which, it will be remembered, Mr. Mian Muhammad Shafi was President and which incidentally was then the only section on revolt against the current policy of the main body.

25. **The Fall of Baghdad.**—During March 1917, the fall of Baghdad became known to Muhammadans in India and this created a feeling of deep depression among the less intelligent classes, though this appeared to be due not so much to sympathy with Turkey as to

genuine religious grief at the thought of one of the Holy Places of Islam falling into the hands of infidels.

Shortly afterwards it was learnt that a *jehad* leaflet was being distributed by the Amir of the Hindustani Fanatics. It was addressed to the " Muslim warriors who are under the yoke of the British, French and Russians " and it attempted to prove that Muhammadans who had fought for the Allies were infidels, while those who fought for the Central Powers were " doing *jehad* in the way of God." The leaflet went on to urge the former to mutiny, to assassinate their oppressors and to declare their independence under the leadership of the Ottoman Empire. It purported to be signed by eight members of the Muslim Ulema Association, each of whom represented a different country, and it was believed to have emanated from Berlin. About the same time it became apparent that the Hindustani Fanatics were receiving considerable monetary support from Wahabis in Bengal.

26. **Friction in the Muslim League.**—The Council of the All-India Muslim League met at Lucknow on the 7th of May, and the proceedings showed that there was much friction among the members. The Council appointed sub-committees in the various presidencies to carry on propaganda in connection with the promotion of " the Home Rule for India " scheme, but the work of these sub-committees was handicapped by the internal dissension in the main body. This dissension resulted in a steady loss of influence by the League, which incurred considerable adverse criticism in the pan-Islamic press. This criticism chiefly took the shape of declarations that the League was inactive, and practically moribund, and that it had abandoned its policy to the tender mercies of the Hindu Congressmen and Home Rulers. The bulk of this criticism, in which Hasrat Mohani took an active part, was directed against Wazir Hassan and Mazhar-ul-Haq. Shortly afterwards Wazir tendered his resignation of the Secretaryship of the League ostensibly on the ground of failing health and pressure of private work, but his resignation was not immediately accepted.

During the first half of 1917 it became very apparent from the tone of the Indian Press that the agreement arrived at between the leaders of extremist Muhammadan and extremist Hindu opinion did not find a counterpart among the two communities generally. Some of the Hindu organs blamed their leaders for consenting to confer so generous a representation upon Muhammadan: but their attitude was far less strongly marked than that of the conservative Muhammadan press which continued to voice distrust of the intention of the Hindus and denied that the Muhammadan political leaders, in assenting to the Lucknow compromise, had any claim to represent Muhammadan opinion throughout the country at large. Doubts were also thrown on the power of the Indian National Congress to commit Hindus in general to such liberal recognition of Muhammadan claims, while the Muslim League was accused of betraying the interests of Islam into the hands of the Hindus who would subordinate these interests to their Home Rule Movement.

27. **Hindu Muslim Riots.**—This inter-communal friction resulted in very serious riots between Hindus and Muhammadans in September 1917 in several places in Bihar and in the United Provinces, and in the course of these disturbances Muhammadan villages in Bihar were attacked and looted and a number of the inmates were killed. These incidents further embittered the relationship between Hindus and Muhammadans throughout India, and the Muhammadan Press was loud in its denunciation of the Hindu rioters; while the opponents of the Hindu-Muslim Pact claimed that their fears as to the treatment which Muslims might expect at Hindu hands, had been confirmed. These fears found expression at the meeting of the All-India Muslim League, which assembled in Calcutta in X'mas week 1917, in a demand by some of those present, that the representation of the Muhammadan community in the Councils, as contemplated in the Hindu-Muslim Pact, should be increased; and a disposition to attack speakers, who favoured the Hindu-Muslim entente, was evident.

28. **Meeting of the Muslim League, Calcutta, December 1917.**—This meeting of the League was presided over by the Raja of Mahmudabad who had drawn up some notes for his presidential speech, which he had handed to Mr. Jinnah to elaborate. Mr. Jinnah passed them on to Mr. Horniman, editor of the *Bombay Chronicle*, who drafted a speech, instinct with the spirit of Islam, which contained references to the Khilafat in terms very objectionable to Government. The President received the speech just before the meeting and he refused to read it, but delivered an extemporary address in Urdu, in which, however, he made equally objectionable remarks The Raja of Mahmudabad only presided at this meeting in the absence of Muhammad Ali who had been elected president, and a feature of this session of the League was the concern shown for the Ali Brothers, whose internment had caused a considerable amount of agitation during the year. A Calcutta Muhammadan in the course of his speech threatened Government that if the Ali Brothers were not released, the whole Muhammadan community would renounce the honours and resign the posts conferred on them by Government.

29. **Further Hindu-Muslim trouble.**—Hindu-Muhammadan friction continued during 1918 and this for a time engaged the attention of Muhammadan public opinion to the exclusion of the anti-British agitation, protagonists of which, however, did not cease to make efforts to stir up trouble with respect to the War. Early in the year an anonymous leaflet appeared in Delhi, urging Muhammadans to engage in *jehad* and drink the cup of martyrdom. In February, at a meeting of Muhammadans in Calcutta, two or three speakers used violent language in advocating the adoption of passive resistance in connection with their demands for the release of the interned Muslims. Any hope that these agitators had of getting a hearing was extinguished about March by further inter-communal rioting, resulting in

serious bloodshed in Bihar and at Kartarpur and Shahbad in the United Provinces.

30. **The "Indian Daily News" incident.**—In the middle of the year, however, agitation was stimulated by an unhappy phrase used by the *Indian Daily News*—a Calcutta paper— in describing a Muhammadan municipal employee in Paris, which was claimed by Muhammadans as an insult to the Prophet. Indignation meetings were held in various parts of the country at which violent speeches were made and Government were threatened that unless the editor of the offending newspaper was punished, Muhammadans would consider the declaration of *jehad*. The *Indian Daily News* published an apology stating that it had reproduced the article from a contemporary (*The Catholic Herald*) and that it had absolutely no intention of offending the religious susceptibilities of Muhammadans. In spite of this the excitement became so intense that the Government of Bengal found it necessary to prohibit meetings. In the meantime, however, a circular letter had been issued from Calcutta to Muhammadans all over India, signed by a number of Maulvis and inviting the recipients to attend meetings at Calcutta for the purpose of discussing Muhammadan grievances. Several editors of extremist papers responded to this invitation and stimulated local excitement until they were externed by the Government of Bengal under the Defence of India Act. At the same time Muhammadan papers published garbled accounts of incidents which had occurred in various parts of India and which offended, either in reality or in imagination, the Muslim faith—and religious feeling in Calcutta ran very high.

31. **The Calcutta Riots.**—In the beginning of September a deputation of Muhammadans was received by H. E. the Governor of Bengal who, for obvious reasons, was unable to accede to their request to permit a meeting. In the meantime a crowd of some 500 Muhammadans proceeded towards Government House and when they were stopped by the Police, serious rioting ensued which spread to other parts of Calcutta and continued for two days necessitating the use of fire-arms to restore order. An indication of the strained Hindu-Muslim relations during these riots was attacks on Marwaris, some of whom were beaten to death by Muhammadans.

Muslim feeling with respect to internal affairs, in the absence of further inflammatory incidents, abated, and by the time the War terminated in November 1918 in the complete surrender of Turkey, Muhammadans were in a position to take an interest in external matters and showed great concern as to what would be the ultimate fate of the Ottoman Empire and the Khilafate.

32. **Muslim League Session, Delhi, December 1918.**—The 11th annual session of the All-India Muslim League was held at Delhi on the 30th and 31st December 1918, and it is interesting to note that several Ulemas were present. Dr. Ansari was Chairman of the Reception Committee and he delivered a speech (giving his views on

the Sharif's revolt and its effect on the Khilafate) which had particular weight since he had first-hand knowledge of Turkey. "During the course of the present war", said Dr. Ansari, "actuated by personal ambitions and selfish interests, Sharif Husain raised the standard of revolt against the unquestioned Khalifa of Islam, whom he himself had recognised as such. By doing so he not only disregarded a rule of political morality, but, according to Muslim belief and religious teaching, broke an explicit and clear commandment of God and the Prophet." He then quoted several texts from the Quran, which contain a definite inducement to the murder of the Sharif such as, "if anyone attempts to divide the unity of my people, kill him with the sword, whosoever he may be." He went on to assert that the Sultans of Turkey had discharged the duties of Khalifa and protector of the Holy Places to the entire satisfaction of the Muslim world and that the present Sultan was the only Muhammadan who could possibly be capable of successfully combating the intrigues and secret machinations of non-Muslim governments. He proceeded to define the limits of the Holy Places and quoted passages from the sacred traditions of Islam to prove that the whole of Arabia, Palestine and Mesopotamia was included in the Jazirat-ul-Arab from which all non-Muslim influence must be removed. Appealing to the principle of self-determination, he demanded that the integrity and independence of existing Muslim States should be maintained intact and that the Arabs of North Africa and the Tartars and Turks of Central Asia should be allowed to choose their own form of government. Self-determination is no doubt a useful principle but it hardly seems to cover the claim of the All-India Muslim League to decide that the Arabs or the Armenians should continue to be ruled by Turkey. The remainder of the speech dealt with internal affairs and need not be discussed in detail. One passage from the opening paragraph of this section may be quoted:—"Our sympathies with the Turks are well known and patent. The Mussalmans, however, exercised admirable self-control over their feelings and, in spite of innumerable provocations, proved successful under the severest tests. And if the anxieties and agonies of the war were not sufficient, nearer home, in India, we were being subjected to a treatment which no self-respecting people would have tolerated. Had it not been that our rulers were engaged in a struggle of life and death, the Mussalmans would have taken such constitutional measures as would have compelled attention." The whole proceedings of the League meeting indicated that the Muhammadan agitators considered that the cessation of hostilities had absolved them from the necessity of exercising any restraint.

The Presidential address of Mr. Fazl-ul-Haq consisted of a long account of the evil effects of British rule in India, such as might have been delivered at any Congress meeting. It contained only a few passing references to Turkey and the Khilafat and coming after Dr. Ansari's violent appeal to religious fanaticism, fell absolutely flat. The first day's proceedings closed with the passing of a few formal resolutions, moved from the chair. On the 31st the proceedings began with a resolution welcoming the Ulemas. Speaking on behalf of the Ulemas, Maulvi Kifayetullah repudiated the charge that they considered that religion and politics were two separate things. No doubt they had left politics to the League in the past, but when the call went out, they were only too glad to join the political body. After reading a resolution passed at a meeting of Maulvis at the Fatehpuri Mosque in Delhi, he said that Government had promised to respect the Holy Places and should keep their promise by evacuating Jerusalem and Najaf. If they failed to do so, he would not answer for the loyalty of Indian Muhammadans.

The next resolution was about the Calcutta riots. In supporting it, Dr. Saifuddin Kitchlew of Amritsar made an objectionable speech in which he said that if the Germans had fired on hospitals and hospital ships, it was because the wounded men in these hospitals and ships had been fighting against them, but the Government in Calcutta had allowed the wanton killing of inoffensive and unarmed Muhammadans.

Maulana Abdul Bari of Lucknow was the most important speaker on the resolution asking for the evacuation of the Holy Places. He began by taking exception to the Union Jack having been used in decorating the hall, saying that although it was the flag of Britain, it contained the emblem of the cross, which Muhammadans could not respect. In his prepared speech he discussed the question whether India is *dar-ul-Islam* or *dar-ul-harab*, and stated that in *dar-ul-Islam* there must be complete religious liberty. If a Muslim country is attacked, the inhabitants of *dar-ul-Islam* are bound to go to its assistance. It is not clear whether the Maulana completed his syllogism by stating that because Indian Muhammadans were not permitted to go to the assistance of Turkey, therefore India is *dar-ul-harab*. He quoted a saying from the Prophet, " Remove the Jew, the Christian and the idolator from the Holy Places at all cost," and urged Indian Muhammadans to continue their efforts to secure the evacuation of the Holy Places by non-Muslims. As regards the Khilafate, he said that the Sultan of Turkey was the only rightful Khalifa and it was the duty of every Muhammadan to help him to maintain his position. The Sharif of Mecca was a rebel and could not possibly become Khalifa.

Abdul Majid Khwaja of Aligarh who practised as a barrister at Bankipur, moved an amendment adding a clause to the effect that the occupation of the Holy Places was likely to shake the loyalty of the Muhammadans, who were bound by their religion to guard the Holy Places at any sacrifice. The President said that that had been made clear in the speeches and need not be inserted in the resolution. He asked the mover to withdraw the resolution. Abdul Majid refused to do so unless Abdul Bari asked him, whereupon Abdul Bari got up in great excitement and declared that he would do more than what the amendment said; with one word of his mouth and one stroke of his pen he would shake the world, but as the duty was his, he would choose his own time. On this the mover withdrew his amendment and the resolution was passed with acclamation. The remaining resolutions elicited a number of speeches of a more or less objectionable character, but none of these deserves specific mention. Only two of the resolutions need be noticed, *viz.*, one requesting the British representatives at the Peace Conference to see that the " fullest consideration is paid to the requirements of Islamic Law with regard to the full and independent control by the Sultan of Turkey, Khalifa of the Prophet, over the Holy Places and over the Jazirat-ul-Arab as delimitated in Muslim books "; and one authorizing the Council of League to send a deputation to England at an early date. A clause was added to the latter to the effect that Hasrat Mohani (who, after serving a term of imprisonment for sedition, had continued his objectionable activities, necessitating his internment from which he had just been released) should go to England at once to prepare the way for the deputation. As usual, the demands of the Congress were echoed by the Muslim League, but the interest of the meeting lay not in its extremism on internal political questions, but in its display of pan-Islamic enthusiasm. In the Muslim League, as in the Congress the moderates had lost all control, and this was evidenced by the resignation of the Raja of Mahmudabad and Wazir Hassan, respectively President and Secretary of the League.

33. **Ajmal Khan's Speech as Chairman of the Congress Reception Committee.**—Hakim Ajmal Khan was Chairman of the Reception Committee of the session of the Indian National Congress which assembled at Delhi at the same time, and in his speech he laid emphasis on Hindu-Muslim unity and also urged for a greater spirit of co-operation between Indians and officials: which is interesting in the light of his subsequent conduct during the Non-co-operation Movement. After referring to the War and India's services, he dwelt on the question of the Khilafate as follows:—

> " Closely connected with the War and its results is the question of Muslim Holy Places, the Khilafate and Muslim States. I think it necessary to give expression to Muslim feeling on these questions, from this platform, for, I feel that no assembly which claims to represent the whole of India can ignore questions so profoundly affecting 70 millions of her population. To show the vital relations of these questions with Indian politics and the safety of the Empire, I cannot do better than quote the acknowledged and revered leader of the country, Mahatma Gandhi, to whom I take this public opportunity to offer the grateful thanks of my co-religionists for his sincere and brotherly sympathy in their troubles and for his brave and outspoken championship of their cause. Need I assure him that my co-religionists fully and cordially reciprocate the brotherly feeling expressed by him? In this mutual sympathy and

good-will lies the secret of true unity. In his letter to the Viceroy, dated Delhi, the 27th April 1918, Mahatma Gandhi writes:—

> Lastly I would like to request His Majesty's Ministers to give definite assurances about Muhammadan States. I am sure you know that every Muhammadan is deeply interested in them. As a Hindu I cannot be indifferent to their cause. Their sorrows must be our sorrows. In the most scrupulous regard for the rights of these States and to the Muslim sentiment as to the places of worship and in your just and timely treatment of Indian claim to Home Rule lies the safety of the Empire.'

No better exposition of the case could be made. Mussalmans in India occupied a peculiarly difficult and delicate position during this war, and it does not need my statement to show with what commendable restraint they conducted themselves. The Government was engaged in a war with their brothers in faith and most painful and provoking news about their Holy Places incessantly poured in. They were not difficient in courage to give expression to their feelings during the continuance of the war but they preferred to wait till after the great conflict was over. . . . The safety and independence of the Holy Places is another question which touches Mussalmans deeply. These places are sanctified by the pious memories of their great prophets and sacred injunctions of their Holy Book, and are in fact a very considerable phenomenon in their social, political and religious life. Their present condition is causing them great anxiety and profound pain. They want to see them in truly independent Muslim hands and I urge upon the Government the recognition of their most cherished and deepseated religious sentiment. Closely associated with this is the question of Khilafate. It is a purely religious question, the decision of which rests entirely with Mussalmans. It is a part and parcel of the Muslim faith and no kind of outside interference with its settlement will be tolerated by the Mussalmans. If all the powers of the world combine to force a Khalifa on Mussalmans, the humblest of them will not follow him. If anyone can have a right to choose a new religion for Mussalmans he can also appoint a Khalifa for them. It is not for me to point out that when the meanest nationalities and the smallest countries are being given the fullest liberty in temporal matters it will be highly detrimental to the great principles of true statesmanship which are the very basis of every civilised and good government, if Mussalmans are made to feel that it is proposed to interfere with their religious questions."

CHAPTER III.

The Khilafat Movement takes shape and is utilized by Gandhi, 1919–1920.

34. **The causes of the comparative calm during the War.**—The Delhi session of the Muslim League is of considerable importance in relation to the subsequent Khilafat movement. It has been shown already that the outbreak of war between Great Britain and Turkey did not immediately stimulate pan-Islamism in India as much as might have been expected. To account for this there is no doubt something in what Dr. Ansari said, to the effect that had their rulers not been engaged in a struggle of life and death, Muslims would have taken measures to compel attention; though it is probable this finer feeling was not sensed by extremists of his own type. Another factor which contributed towards the apparent peaceful atmosphere during this period was the Defence of India Act and other War Regulations, which had been used to curb the activities of some of the leading pan-Islamic agitators and which served as a constant threat to deter others from following their example. Also while the war was being waged, the ultimate outcome was problematical, and even when a Turkish defeat was assured, a feeling which existed among Indian Muhammadans that Great Britain would be more sympathetic in its attitude towards the Turks than the other Allied Powers, acted against anti-Government agitation. Finally during the latter years of the war, the attention of Muhammadans was diverted by their dissensions with Hindus.

35. **The delay in settling the Turkish Peace Terms increases Muhammadan anxiety.**—When war ended in the complete surrender of Turkey leaving the determination of the fate of the Khilafat entirely in non-Muslim hands, and removing all hope of an honourable Turkish Peace, Muhammadan opinion at once commenced to harden in India. As Professor Rushbrook Williams says in "India in 1919":—"Had it been possible to declare the Turkish peace terms early in the year 1919, it is probable that this feeling would, if confronted with established facts, never have grown to its present dimensions. But the statements appearing in various journals in Europe as to the punishment which Turkey's rash acts were likely to bring upon herself made advanced Muhammadan opinion in India fear that their views were not sufficiently regarded by the British Government and the Allies. As it was with the educated classes in the matter of constitutional aspirations, so was it with the advanced Muhammadans in the matter of pro-Turkish sentiment: there was a most unfortunate, and quite groundless feeling that loyalty, during the war might very well count for nothing after the danger to the Commonwealth had passed away."

In consequence the year 1919 saw a steadily increasing pan-Islamic agitation in India regarding the ultimate fate of the Khilafate. This subject was the main topic of the Muslim press and engaged Muhammadan attention to the exclusion of all other matters.

36. **Abdul Bari inspires a Fatwa.**—Soon after the Delhi meeting of the League, Maulvi Abdul Bari of Lucknow, endeavoured to secure *fatwas* on the subject of the Khilafate and the Holy Places from a number of Ulemas; his object being to obtain an authoritative pronouncement from Muhammadan religious leaders in support of the views expressed by Dr. Ansari in his Delhi address. The particular points on which he wanted a ruling in his favour were:—

(1) It was the duty of the Muhammadans to appoint a Khalifa

(2) The fact that the Sultan of Turkey did not belong to the Quresh was no bar to his being the Khalifa and he had been recognised as such since the Qureshi rival was neither influential nor powerful. The Sharif of Mecca, a Qureshi, claimed to be Khalifa but it was lawful for the non-Qureshi Khalifa to oppose him, especially since the former was supported by infidels.

(3) The late Sultan of Turkey was Khalifa; and the Muhammadans were bound to obey the successor of the Khalifa (Sultan) whose duty it was to turn out the rebel Sharif from Mecca and Medina. The temporary expulsion of the Sultan under circumstances which were beyond his control, viz., that he was ousted by the infidels (English) and the Sharif, was no bar to his title of Khalifa. It was, therefore, incumbent on Muhammadans to assist the Sultan to retake the Holy Places.

(4) Arabia comes under the definition of "Islamic country" and includes Syria and Mesopotamia (where Arabic is spoken). This being so, Muhammadans all over the world were bound to aid the Sultan of Turkey to recover them.

He ultimately succeeded in getting a *fatwa* in his favour from some Ulemas, a copy of which he sent to H. E. the Viceroy.

37. **The proposed deputation to England, and extremist views as expressed by the Ali Brothers.**—The Council of the All-India Muslim League assembled in March at Lucknow and elected 35 members, including Hasrat Mohani, Dr. M. A. Ansari, Yakub Hasan and Muhammad Ali, to proceed to England in pursuance of the Delhi resolution to send a deputation to that country.

A good idea of the views at this period of the Extreme Section of Indian Mussalman opinion on the Khalifat problem will be gathered from the following extracts from a letter which the Ali Brothers wrote to H. E. the Viceroy at the end of April 1919:—

"Muslim loyalty and support had so often been assured to Government in our generation, and even Muslim contentment was so often unduly taken for granted that other communities had with some justice made our attitude towards Government almost a matter of reproach. It was strange return for all this loyalty and support that without any effective protest and often with the concurrence of His Majesty's Government blow after blow was aimed at the temporal power of Islam . . . . Government could not have been unaware of the sorrow and sufferings that all this entailed to the Mussalmans of India. No section of the community remained unaffected or unmoved. Princes in their palaces and peasants in their huts alike passed anxious days and sleepless nights . . . It was not, however, the fear of losing political dominance that troubled Mussalmans most. The spiritual force of Islam does not depend on political supremacy and far the most vital tradition of our faith is the humble beginnings of Islam in the midst of hostile elements of extraordinary potency and malice and the ceaseless persecution of our Prophet during the greater part of his Prophetic career. . . . What the cruel occurrences in Tripoli and the Balkans, at Holy Meshad and Tabriz had led Mussalmans to apprehend was, that the temporal power of Islam might be so weakened that it might become liable to suffer, without adequate power to prevent, the curtailment of its spiritual influence through the pressure of the temporal power of rival creeds. The Muslim Press of India did everything in its power to warn the Government against the disastrous consequences of the policy it seemed bent on pursuing, and no method was left untried of impressing Great Britain that if she desired to retain the goodwill of the Mussalmans, she must be a friend and keep the Khalifate on her side and deal more fairly with Muslim Kingdom and countries such as Persia, Afghanistan and Morocco. But not one of these warnings was heeded. The result was inevitable and when war was declared between Great Britain and Turkey some sort of an apologia as well as an assurance was felt to be needed. Accordingly *on the 2nd November 1914*, on the authority of His Majesty's Government, the Viceroy gave a most solemn pledge 'in regard to the Holy Places of Arabia including the Holy Shrines of Mesopotamia and the port of Jeddah in order that there may be no misunderstandings on the part of His Majesty's most loyal Muslim subjects as to the attitude of His Majesty's Government in this war.' This pledge was to the effect that these Holy Places and Jeddah will be immune from attack or molestation by the British Naval and Military Force . . . . As for Mesopotamia, the land of the Holy Shrines, a perusal of the Mesopotamian Commission's report makes it abundantly clear that an attack which had been provided for a month before the declaration of war, was already in progress when the pledge of immunity was being given. With the varying fortunes of the war the desire of an advance on Baghdad varied in intensity. But the disastrous result of the Gallipoli campaign, made His Majesty's Government utterly regardless of their solemn assurances. On the 21st October 1915, less than a year after the pledge of 2nd November 1914, we find the Secretary of State for India telegraphing to the Viceroy as follows:—

> At present moment . . . . our position and prospects in Galliopli are most uncertain . . . Arabs are wavering and will probably join the Turks unless we can offer them great inducement . . . It is suggested that we should occupy Baghdad giving assurances to Arab leaders that we favour creation of Arab State, independent of Turk.'

When these assurances were being contemplated, it seems the great need of a striking success in the East had driven out all recollections of the solemn assurances that had been given to His Majesty's most loyal Muslim subjects. As the sequel has only too plainly proved Holy Najaf, Karbela, Kazmain and Samarra remained no more immune from attack or molestation than did Baghdad and today all are under British occupation and control. *What is still more intolerable Indian Mussalmans including Rulers of States and their subjects and civilians as well as soldiers, have been required to assist in the prosecution of a war against the Khalifate and given no option to stop further assistance when the Khalifa declared a jehad* . . . We have now only to define the more particularly Muslim demands though we are happy in the belief that they are no longer exclusively urged by the Mussalmans of India, but have received from our fellow-countrymen of other creeds also, a firm pledge of support even unto death. These demands are as follows:—

(1) There should never be any attempt to interfere by pressure or persuasion in the free choice, by the Mussalmans, of the Khalifa of their Prophet.

(2) No Mussalman, whether a soldier or a civilian, should be asked to assist in any manner whatsoever in the prosecution of a war or of any other hostile design against the Khalif, when he has declared a *jehad* in the exercise of the functions of the Khalifate, and such assistance has become *haram* thereafter according to the law of Islam, and any Mussalman undergoing at present any form of punishment for their refusal to render such assistance should be given complete amnesty.

(3) No part of the territories included in the expression Jazirat-ul-Arab as defined by the Muslim religious authorities should be directly or indirectly occupied, or subjected to any form of non-Muslim control, but must remain as heretofore *under independent Muslim occupation and control* as required by the testamentary injunctions of the Holy Prophet.

(4) There should be no attempt to remove, whether directly or indirectly, from the independent, indivisible and inalienable sovereignty of the Khalifa, who is the recognised Servant of the Holy Places and Warden of the Holy Shrines, any portion of the territories in which such Holy Places and Shrines are situated, including the territories in which are situated the three sacred Harems of Mecca, Medina and Jerusalem and the Holy Shrines in Najaf Karbella, Baghdad, Kazmain, Samarra, Constantinople and Konieh; and *such territories should forthwith be evacuated by the forces of His Majesty and of the Allied and Association Governments and restored to the Khalifa, the Sultan of the Ottoman Empire.*

(5) Nor should there be any such attempt to dismember and parcel out even among Muslim Governments or in any other manner weaken the Khalifa's Empire with the object of weakening the temporal power of Islam.

(6) His Majesty's Government should restore to the Khalifa the Villayet of Egypt and should make determined efforts to induce other powers also to restore similarly such other territories like Bosnia, Herzegovina and Tripoli, as they have forcibly been taken from him, and similar justice should be done in the case of other Muslim territories like those of Algiers, Tunis, Morocco, the Caucasus and the Khanates and Kingdoms of Central Asia.

(7) No Mussalman should in any manner be deprived of his liberty or otherwise punished, molested or disquieted by reason of his expressing and promoting sympathy with his brother Mussalmans in any part of the world, or maintaining and strengthening the allegiance of all Mussalmans to the Khalifa of the Holy Prophet; and all persons thus dealt with should be forthwith set at liberty and all newspapers suppressed for a like reason should be permitted a free publication.

We now urge on Your Excellency's Government the extreme necessity of an early satisfaction of these legitimate demands of the Indian Mussalman . . . . We desire to declare that we shall wait for a reasonable time for an indication of a change for the better in the Government's attitude and if no convincing proof is given of such a change at an early date, and Muslim claims continue to receive the same disdainful treatment, it will be our duty to ask for our Passports and to recommend the same grave and extremely painful step to our co-religionists so that they and we could migrate to some other land where to be a believing Mussalman and an ardent patriot is not considered a crime."

38. **Hostilities with Afghanistan.**—In the latter part of February 1919, an event had occurred which proved to be of great importance to India. This was the assassination of Habib Ullah Khan, Amir of Afghanistan, who had always been friendly disposed towards the British. His successor, Amir Amanullah Khan, however, had no such amicable feelings and immediately began to commit various aggressive acts which soon led to war. At the end of April, his Foreign Minister sent confidential instructions to the Afghan Envoy at Simla in which it was suggested that endeavours should be made to obtain the allegiance of both Hindus and Muhammadans to the Amir; in return for which Afghanistan would assist them in their struggle for independence. The Envoy was directed to make enquiries from the British Government regarding the inhuman law, *i.e.*, the Rowlatt Act, which formed the basis of Gandhi's original *Satyagraha* campaign. The Envoy was further instructed to insert exciting articles in the Indian newspapers and to "speedily carry out any work which you think desirable to further the views of His Majesty which are known to you." He was also advised to get in touch with certain anti-British elements across the Border and to gain the favour of Hindus and endeavour to remove Hindu-Muslim ill-feeling. With this letter was enclosed another from one of the Silk Letter Conspirators to the address of Shah Abul Kher—an influential divine of Delhi (since deceased)—in which it was indicated that the Amir had decided to proclaim *jehad* and that the assistance of the recipient was required. Hostilities broke out between Great Britain and Afghanistan on the 9th of May and terminated about six weeks later when the Amir asked for an armistice.

In May Abdul Bari circulated an inflammatory leaflet, and a very lengthy *jehad* pamphlet came to light in the United Provinces. In this numerous quotations were made from the Quran, and the sayings of the Prophet were utilised to show the necessity of undertaking a religious war at that juncture. In the same month the Ali Brothers commenced to disobey the orders interning them under the Defence of India Act. Their objectionable activities at Chindwara, where they were domiciled, soon compelled Government to confine them in jail under Regulation III of 1818.

39. **The effect in India of the Afghan War.**—A reference to the history of the Non-co-operation movement will show that it was at about this period that Gandhi's *Satyagraha* campaign had led to serious disturbances in the Punjab,* originating at Delhi where a riot† took place in connection with the observance of a fast ordained by him. Gandhi admitted that the Afghan War had caused him to think seriously as to his programme for the future and that the unrest on the North-West Frontier had a bearing on his plans for the fast, but, in view of insistent demands from all quarters, he had decided that the fast should be observed—with the result mentioned above.

---

*Part I, paragraph 9.
†Part I, paragraph 7

In fairness to Dr. Ansari it must be recorded that he recommended, at this time, loyalty to Government during the Afghan War and that Hakim Ajmal Khan joined him in thanking the Delhi officials for their considerate handling of the riots.

In spite of the attitude of these leaders, however, the Afghan trouble and the Punjab disturbances had the effect of hardening extremist Muhammadan feeling, especially in the United Provinces, against Government. Gandhi was not slow to seize this opportunity to close the Hindu-Muslim breach, and, on the 9th of May, while addressing a meeting of Muhammadans at Bombay, he dwelt at length on the paramount necessity of Hindu-Muslim unity.

40. **Propaganda in London.**—At about the same time a pamphlet, written by Mushir Hussain Kidwai, entitled "The Future of the Moslem Empire", was published by the Central Islamic Society, London, in which certain proposals were made for the future constitution of the Ottoman Empire. The following is an extract from this pamphlet:—"The disintegration of Turkey—the Last Muslim Empire—will be a direct challenge to Islam. It will mean that the Muslims are to be made homeless, like the Jews. But the Muslim nation is so constituted that it cannot exist like the Jews. It is bound to enter into a deadly struggle with all those forces which would tend to bring it to that position and the struggle will be all the worse for being hidden. Muhammad (peace be upon him) did not allow himself to be crucified. He took the sword against the world of enemies who sought to exterminate his religion and his people. No League of Nations can be superior to the command of God, and it is the command of God to Muslims to safeguard Islam even with the last drop of their blood. If England takes any part in the disintegration of the last Empire she will be taking the position of the enemy of Islam. It will be England which will have to bear the brunt of the defensive attack of Islam before long. At present Muslims may be powerless. They might even be hypnotised or deceived. But one day they will awaken, and a cry of revenge will go out against the enemy of Islam. Before this, Russia was considered to be the chief enemy of Islam. She was hated by the whole Muslim world. Is England prepared to take up the position of Czarist Russia in the East? The cry of befriending Islam, of befriending the Arabs and Syrians cannot deceive any sensible Muslim. All this ostentatious sympathy for Arabs and Syrians is neither for the good of these people nor for the good of Islam. The actuating motive is to smash up the solidity of Islam and to secure more lands for exploitation by the so-called Christian. The Mussalmans of India know all that."

41. **Proposal to send a deputation to H. E. the Viceroy.**—In the middle of May 1919, Mr. Yakub Hassan of Madras who, incidentally, had married a Turkish lady, left for England having received authority in writing from Bombay Muhammadans to speak on their behalf with respect to the Khilafat question. This authority had been signed by

Mr. Muhammad Jan Muhammad Chotani (a wealthy merchant, often known as seth Chotani) as president of a mass meeting of Muhammadans which had taken place on the 19th of March. Shortly afterwards M. M. Chotani urged the pressing necessity of sending a deputation to H. E. the Viceroy to represent to His Excellency the religious views and sentiments of the Mussalmans of India with regard to (1) the guardianship of the Holy Places, (2) the Khilafate, and (3) the threatened dismemberment of the Turkish Empire. He was supposed to have been supported in this proposal by His Highness the Aga Khan.

Possibly owing to the repressive action taken in the Punjab combined with the enervating effect of the hot weather and the fast of *Ramzan*, there is little to record regarding the middle of 1919. The disturbances, however, did not tend to allay excitement, so the fire kindled by the agitation continued to glow.

42. **Hindu-Muhammadan relations.**—It has been shown already that Hindu-Muslim friction decreased at the end of 1918 and progress towards amity continued during the following year. The effect of this was summed up by the Director, Intelligence Bureau, in September 1919 as follows:—"In March last an understanding was arranged between Mr. M. K. Gandhi and Moulana Abdul Bari to the effect that the Hindu politicians would espouse the cause of Turkey and the Muhammadans would refrain from slaughtering kine. Whilst the Hindu politicians have kept their word and Mr. Gandhi and his fellow-workers have done much to excite Muhammadans in the matter of the ultimate fate of the Turkish Empire, the Muhammadans have not refrained from killing kine both for food and for sacrifice. Maulana Abdul Bari has doubtless tried his best to bring round his co-religionists to his views, but his success has not been at all great or even fair. As an intelligent and fair-minded Muhammadan explained to me the other day the slaughter of kine among Muhammadans is determined by economic considerations. Nothing then Maulana Bari can say will in this matter carry much weight with Muhammadans who as a rule are poor. It may be added that the Hindu-Muhammadan combination of the kind effected by Messrs. Gandhi and Abdul Bari is dominated by a most mischievous anti-British spirit."

The *Bakr Id* which took place in September passed without any disturbance, and Abdul Bari wired to Gandhi that in order to remove all causes of friction between the two communities, no cow sacrifices would take place in the Firanghi Mahal, Lucknow. A similar attempt to secure abstinence from cow sacrifice in Delhi, failed. In Bihar, however, which had been the scene of serious inter-communal rioting in the past, the freedom from disorder was not due to good feelings between the two communities, and from all over the Province petitions were received by the authorities from both communities indicative of strained relations. It was reported that in several districts police work was almost paralysed by the amount of time which officers had to spend in taking precautions to avoid communal riots.

43. **Rumours regarding the Turkish Peace Terms.**—Rumours regarding the Turkish Peace Terms, published during 1919, threatening the dismemberment of the Turkish Empire and the maintenance of non-Muslim influence over the rulers of the Holy Places, was a signal for an outburst of Muhammadan feeling, about September, which found expression in the Press and on the platform.

In October, the Indian pan-Islamist and revolutionary, Maulvi Barkatullah—who has been mentioned already—produced a pamphlet endeavouring to reconcile the divergent principles of Islam and Bolshevism. He appealed to Muhammadans to respond to the divine call of liberty, equality and fraternity sent forth by Lenin and the Soviet and stated that the Soviet considered that Constantinople should remain Muslim and that treaties for the division of the Ottoman Empire should be burnt. Muhammadans were urged not to recoil from Russia but to shun the savage wolves of Europe.

At no time, however, was there any serious indication of Bolshevism carrying much weight with Muslim opinion in India.

44. **Muslim Conference, September 1919.**—On the 21st September, a Muslim Conference was held at Lucknow which was remarkable for the note of despair which ran throughout the proceedings, due to the belief that nothing could save the Ottoman Empire owing to the strong anti-Turkish feeling prevalent in most European countries. Up to this point, in spite of frequent expressions of anti-Turkish opinions in the English press, many Muhammadans in India realised that their Government was sympathetically disposed towards the Khilafat question, but subsequently this view became obscured in consequence of the continuous propaganda directed against it. This propaganda came chiefly from their own extremist leaders, but Gandhi and his satellites were not slow to use the feelings excited both by the Khilafat question and the Punjab disturbances to further their own Home Rule campaign—for which the hatred of the British Government by the masses was essential.

45. **Formation of the Central Khilafat Committee.**—Provincial Khilafat Committees had commenced to spring up. The first of these of which Mohammed Jan Mohammed Chotani was President, was constituted in the Bombay Presidency. At a meeting on the 11th of November, it changed its title to the 'Central Khilafat Committee of India, Bombay'. The aims and objects of this organisation were defined as follows:—

(1) To secure for Turkey a just and honourable peace.

(2) To secure the fulfilment of the pledges given by the Right Honourable Mr. Lloyd George in his speech of the 5th January 1918 and to preserve the integrity of the Turkish Empire.

(3) With a view to securing the above objects to memorialise the British Ministers, H. E. the Viceroy and, if necessary, the President of the United States of America.

At about the same time, the Delhi Khilafat Committee of which Ajmal Khan was President, decided to convene an all-India Khilafat Conference which was held at Delhi on the 23rd and 24th of November.

46. **Khilafat Conference, Delhi, November 1919.**—It was presided over, on the 23rd of November by Mr. Fazl-ul-Haq of Calcutta, who delivered a lengthy address which was not free from mis-statements and malicious accusations against the British Government and virulent abuse of other European Powers. The attendance, however, was neither large nor representative, the majority of the delegates coming from the United Provinces, Delhi, Rajputana and Sind. The consensus of opinion was undoubtedly strongly anti-British, but there were differences as to the most effective means of propaganda. Resolutions were passed to boycott the peace celebrations, to boycott British goods, to send a deputation to England and, if necessary, to America and to refuse to co-operate with the Government unless the Khilafat and the Holy Places were treated in accordance with Muslim desires. A sub-committee was appointed consisting of Syed Hussain, Fazl-ul-Haq, Abdul Bari, Ajmal Khan and others to examine the question of Non-co-operation further and to propose effective action.

These resolutions are of particular interest as they indicate the commencement of Gandhi influence over the Khilafat leaders and the movement in general. He attended the meeting on the 23rd and presided over it on the 24th. The meeting was also attended by Swami Shradhanand, a leader of the Arya Samaj, who was one of the most prominent Hindus in assisting Gandhi to bring about the Hindu-Muslim entente,—which he was afterwards to do so much to destroy by means of his Shuddhi Movement.

47. **The Islamic Information Bureau, London.**—This meeting was one of the first indications of the intention of Muslim extremists in India to take definite action regarding the Khilafat question, and there is little doubt that their programme was inspired to some extent by the activities of an Islamic Information Bureau in England. This Bureau was run by Pickthal, Ispahani and Kidwai and, by the end of 1919, was producing a weekly journal called "The Muslim Outlook." It also published a considerable amount of miscellaneous pro-Turkish literature which endeavoured to keep before the public exaggerated accounts of the atrocities committed by the Greeks in Smyrna and to cause apprehension by declaring that the Muslim world was in a state of frenzy owing to the threatened dismemberment of the Ottoman Empire. The Bureau had, of course, been in close touch with leading agitators in India, including Yakub Hassan of Madras, who, when he reached England, joined its staff.

48. **The Reforms.**—The end of 1919 saw the introduction of the Reforms Act and the amnesty to political prisoners resulting in the release of, among others, the Ali Brothers and Dr. Kitchlew, who had been confined in connection with the Punjab disturbances. In view of the fact that advanced Hindu and Muhammadan politicians had associated for some time past in the demand for Home Rule, the grant of the Reforms, which was a long step towards their goal, should have eased the situation. Actually it was largely counter-balanced by the resulting freedom of firebrands of the Ali Brothers' type, whose first act on release was to attend the meetings of the Congress* and Muslim League at Amritsar in X'mas week, 1919, where they quickly indicated that they had no feelings of gratitude towards Government

49. **Muslim League Session, Amritsar, December 1919.**—Hakim Ajmal Khan was president of this session of the All-India Muslim League and Dr. Kitchlew was president of the Reception Committee. The Ali Brothers were, of course, among the principal speakers and Shaukat Ali reiterated his Anjuman-i-Khuddam-i-Kaaba vow to the effect that he would sacrifice his life and property to protect the Kaaba. He declared that Indian Muslims had degraded themselves by becoming the disciples of expediency and renouncing their religion, and he yearned to go to the Turks and die in their country. He claimed that during an enquiry into the grounds for interning him under the Defence Act, he had openly stated that if *jehad* was proclaimed by the Khalifa, no Muhammadan could refuse to obey the summons. He finished by asking the audience whether they wished to remain British subjects or Muslims, and if the former, he would sever his connection with them and seek martyrdom. Shaukat Ali shed tears in the course of his speech, and that of his brother, Muhammad Ali, which followed, was almost equally emotional. Muhammad Ali claimed that they were subjects of God and not of Great Britain and he exhorted the audience to defend the honour of God's house even at the sacrifice of their lives and those of their mothers. He declared that they could only obtain true release when they had shed their blood in the cause of Islam.

The extent to which Muslim extremists had, by this time, come under the influence of Gandhi is apparent from the fact that a resolution was passed prohibiting the slaughter of cows on the occasion of the *Bakr Id*. Among the other resolutions passed, was one expressing gratitude to His Majesty the King for the spirit in which the Royal Proclamation had been issued and promising to accord to His Royal Highness the Prince of Wales a hearty welcome. In this resolution also the hand of Gandhi is seen, for at the same time, he was carrying a similar motion through the Congress in spite of considerable opposition; and the fact that the resolution did not incur serious opposition in this session of the Muslim League was clearly due to Gandhi's

*Part I, paragraph 12.

influence on the extremists. Some of the other resolutions dealt with the action taken to quell the Punjab disturbances, and one of these demanded "the vindication of justice and the reputation of the British for fairness in connection with the shocking disclosures made by General Dyer in his evidence before the Disorders Enquiry Committee." While speaking on one of these resolutions, Abul Kasim of Bengal described Jallianwalla Bagh as worse than the Black Hole of Calcutta and stated his conviction that the Hunter Committee had been appointed to whitewash the officers of Government.

A resolution was passed expressing the deep resentment felt by Indian Muhammadans at the disregard shown by the British Government to the repeated representations made by them, through their representatives in England and India, in connection with the question of the Khilafat and Jazirat-ul-Arab. It stated that the Muhammadans in India would be justified in carrying on all the possible methods of constitutional agitation. In addition to this resolution, an amendment proposed by Hasrat Mohani to add the words "including the boycott of the Indian Army if it is likely to be used outside India for Imperial and anti-Islamic purposes" was also passed. This amendment was of importance as the Ali Brothers afterwards endeavoured to give effect to it by attempting to tamper with the loyalty of Indian troops.

A resolution to the effect that all the Muhammadans of the world regarded Sultan Wahid Uddin of Turkey as the recognised Khalifa of Islam was passed unanimously after Abul Kasim had explained that officials were endeavouring to persuade Muhammadans that the Sultan of Turkey was not their Khalifa.

50. **Provincial Khalifat Conference, Sind, January 1920.**—The proceedings of the Muslim League at Amritsar showed how far the League had come under the control of extremists. Immediately afterwards it was followed by a Sind Provincial Khilafat Conference at Hyderabad, on the 4th and 5th January 1920, which was remarkable for the vehemence of the speeches made, in the course of which the Delhi proposals to boycott foreign goods and to join forces with the Home Rulers were raised. Most of the time of this conference was taken up in denouncing the "intrigues of those infidels" who had criticised the acceptance of the Sultan of Turkey as the Khalifa of Islam; and it was resolved that if Government failed to take suitable action against them, Muhammadans would have to deal with them according to the tenets of their religion. One speaker declared that the British were the bitterest enemies of Islam and that if the decision with respect to Turkey was not satisfactory, Muhammadans would be compelled to obey the Quran and declare *jehad*. Another declared that the British atrocities at Amritsar showed him that it was better to die than to leave the Holy Places of Mesopotamia in the hands of *kafirs*. A Maulvi of Larkhana named Haji Ahmed said that he could not understand why

the Ulemas were delaying the declaration of *jehad* and reiterated the statement that Great Britain was Islam's worst enemy. This Khilafat Conference was followed by numerous others, all over India, of the same type.

51. **Muhammadan Deputation waits on H. E. the Viceroy.**—On the 19th of January 1920, a Muhammadan deputation waited on H. E. the Viceroy to place before him their views on the Khilafat question and to ask for his sympathetic assistance not only in conveying those views to the Peace Conference at Paris, but also in facilitating the despatch to England of a deputation. The deputation to the Viceroy consisted of about 35 persons and among them were included the Ali Brothers, Hakim Ajmal Khan, Dr. Ansari, Abdul Bari, Seth Chotani, Abul Kalam Azad, Hasrat Mohani, Dr. Kitchlew and also Gandhi and Swami Shradhanand. This deputation which, it will be remembered, had been suggested nearly a year before by Chotani, had materialized as a result of a cable from H. H. the Aga Khan to the effect that the fate of Turkey would be decided during the following month.

52. **Abdul Bari's Speech, Calcutta, February 1920.**—At the end of February 1920, a Khilafat Conference was held in Calcutta which is noteworthy only on account of an extremely violent speech delivered by Abdul Bari. Having excited the feelings of his audience by references to the woes of the Khilafate, he urged them to die for their religion and pointed out that even though Indian Muhammadans had no firearms, they could well make use of bricks, and that if each Muhammadan in India were to throw a handful of dust, they would bury their enemies in India. A note of this speech, which was loudly applauded by the Muhammadans who heard it, is given in Appendix E.

53. **The Delegation to Europe.**—In February 1920, the Delegation to Europe which had formed the subject of resolutions at several Muhammadan meetings during the preceding year, actually sailed. It consisted of Muhammad Ali, Syed Hussain, editor of the *Independent* (Allahabad), Said Sulaiman Nadvi and Abul Kasim, who followed later. The Delegation, however, found that it could make no headway with the British Government, and, on the 17th of March it was informed by Mr. Lloyd George that Turkey could not be treated on principles different from those applied to other countries, and that though she would be allowed to exercise temporal sway over Turkish lands, she could not be permitted to retain lands which were not Turkish. The Delegation also approached Mr. Asquith and representatives of the Labour Party from whom also it received little consolation.

While in Europe, the Delegation, in May 1920, addressed a lengthy appeal to the Khalifa urging him to stand forth as the "Champion of the Faith." This appeal as republished in the *Comrade* in November 1924, with the *Comrade's* comments thereon, is given at Appendix F.

54. **Intensive Propaganda and its effects.**—The receipt of the news in India of the lack of success of this Delegation, coupled with numerous Press telegrams which appeared at about the same time foretelling drastic treatment for Turkey, greatly strengthened the position of Khilafat propagandists in India, and the effect of their agitation became more and more extensive.

In February, Shaukat Ali was elected Secretary of the Central Khilafat Committee and he subsequently undertook a series of propaganda tours throughout India in the course of which he visited practically all places of importance in the Northern Provinces, but it is interesting to note that he avoided the Native States. His speeches during this period were extremely bitter.

In spite of the agitation, the bulk of Muslim opinion in India at the beginning of 1920 was still reasonable and it is quite clear that the more moderate element, though very depressed, fully realised that the Khilafate was more a sentimental than a religious matter. Moreover, orthodox Muhammadans frankly disliked the anti-cow-killing resolution of the Muslim League at Amritsar, which they had no intention of obeying and which they regarded was an admission of subordination to Hindu political aims.

The delay in the ratification of the Peace Treaty, which was largely due to the refusal of America to accept the mandates allotted to her, coupled with the intensive propaganda which was undertaken by extremist leaders during this period, however, had the effect of thrusting the roots of the agitation deeper and deeper into the minds of illiterate and ill-educated Muhammadans in India, with the result that during the year of 1920, the Khilafat Movement became a steadily increasing danger to the peace of the country.

55. **Near Eastern Intrigue.**—During the early part of 1920 much pan-Islamic intrigue centred round Mustapha Kemal Pasha, the leader of the Turkish Nationalists, who was then consolidating his position in Asia Minor. This intrigue spread to Egypt, Russia, Persia and along the North-West Frontier of India, and the knowledge of its existence undoubtedly strengthened the confidence of such Indian Khilafat agitators as were involved. Anonymous leaflets appeared, one of which described the Muhammadan troops who had fought against Turkey as guilty of heinous sin, for they had assisted in destroying the Khilafate and desecrating the Holy Places. Another asserted that *jehad* had been proclaimed and that Enver Pasha (the leader of the Young Turk Party) was co-operating with the Bolsheviks with a view to the invasion of India; and urged Muhammadans to murder the British.

56. **All-India Khilafat Conference, Bombay, February 1920.**—An All-India Khilafat Conference assembled at Bombay in the middle of

February under the Presidency of Mr. G. M. Bhurgri of Hyderabad Sind. Among the questions considered were (*a*) the boycott of British goods and withdrawal of co-operation with Government, (*b*) service of Muhammadans in the Army and (*c*) the evacuation of Jazirat-ul-Arab. In the discussions on these subjects, the mention of *jehad* was frequent and the extremists appeared to be in the ascendancy, but a decision was ultimately postponed, at the instance of the President, pending the receipt of definite information as to the result of the deputation sent to Europe.

57. **Gandhi's Manifesto, March 1920.**—Gandhi, as already shown, had fully realised the value for his own purposes of the excitement caused by the Khilafat question and he lost no opportunity to stimulate it. In a manifesto dated the 10th of March with respect to it he wrote as follows:—"Now a word as to what may be done if the demands are not granted. The barbarous method is warfare, open or secret. This must be ruled out if only because it is impracticable If I could but persuade everyone that it is always bad, we should gain all lawful ends much quicker. The power that an individual or a nation forswearing violence generates is a power that is irresistible. But my argument to-day against violence is based upon pure expedience, *i.e.*, its utter futility. Non-co-operation is therefore the only remedy left open to us. It is the cleanest remedy as it is most effective, when it is absolutely free from all violence. It becomes a duty when co-operation means degradation or humiliation or an injury to one's cherished religious sentiment. England cannot accept a meek submission by us to an unjust usurpation of rights which to Mussalmans means a matter of life and death. We may therefore begin at the top as also the bottom. Those who are holding offices of honour or emolument ought to give them up. Those who belong to the menial services under Government should do likewise. Non-co-operation does not apply to service under private individuals. I cannot approve of the threat of ostracism against those who do not adopt the remedy of Non-co-operation. It is only a voluntary withdrawal which is effective. For voluntary withdrawal alone is a test of popular feeling and dissatisfaction. Advice to the soldiers to refuse to serve is premature. It is the last, not the first step. We should be entitled to take that step when the Viceroy, the Secretary of State and Premier leave us. Moreover, every step withdrawing co-operation has to be taken with the greatest deliberation. We must proceed slowly so as to ensure retention of self-control under the fiercest heat."

The 19th of March was fixed for an all-India protest against the dismemberment of Turkey in a manifesto signed by Abdul Bari, Abul Kalam Azad, Shaukat Ali and Mushir Husain Kidwai, who had returned to India in February. The very inflammatory propaganda to which the mass of Muhammadans had been subjected was sufficient to make the observance of the date a success. Gandhi was largely responsible for the organisation of this Mourning Day ' and, as already indicated, his proposal to cease to co-operate with Government had been considered in extremist Muhammadan circles and had begun to crystallize into (*a*) resignation of title-holders and members of Council, (*b*) resignation of members of the civil services and Government employees, (*c*) resignation of sepoys in the Army and (*d*) refusal to pay land revenue.

58. **Khilafat Conference, Cawnpore, March 1920.**—The *hartal* on the 19th of March was followed in April by a National Week in connection with which the Khilafat question was kept in the forefront. On the 4th and 5th of that month, under the auspices of the United Provinces Ulemas Association, a Khilafat Conference was held at Cawnpore. The Provincial C. I. D. described the resolutions as a distinct defence of those passed at Calcutta in that they confirmed Abdul Bari's Calcutta speech, ordained the publication of his *fatwa*, prescribed the forcible prevention of the arrest of the Khilafat workers, decided to boycott the coming elections and made use of the formula 'complete Independence of British rule'

During a meeting of the Subjects Committee of this Conference with Abdul Bari in the chair, the question was considered whether *jehad* was compulsory, and if compulsory what definite steps were to be taken. The speeches on this subject left no doubt as to the consensus of individual opinion, but the Committee as a whole appear to have burked the main issue, for, while resolving to send students to preach *jehad* in the mofussil, it declined to send them to learn bomb-making in Bengal. Abdul Bari appears to have feared that he had overstepped the bounds of decency at this meeting, for he hurriedly left Cawnpore and subsequently issued a proclamation from Lucknow advocating patience, the adoption of the advice of wise and experienced politicians and the gradual withdrawal of co-operation; Government employees meanwhile remaining in service. This Khilafat Conference was the occasion of several large public meetings at Cawnpore, at one of which an excited mob of 6,000 Muhammadans unanimously swore by raising their hands, to act as directed by the leaders. At this period agitation appears to have been more fruitful in the United Provinces than elsewhere, but very violent speeches were at the same time made in Bengal.

59. **The Afghan Peace Delegation.**—A fresh complication arose in the latter part of April owing to the arrival in Mussoorie of the Afghan Peace Delegation. At the end of April a Khilafat Workers' Conference met at Delhi where again the speeches were very violent. At one made at this time it was stated that the members of the Afghan Mission had engaged in political discussion with local Muhammadans in the Jumma Masjid at Musoorie, in the course of which, the head of the Mission, Mahmood Tarzi, had declared that their chief object was to secure just and honourable peace terms for Turkey. References were also made to a speech of Amir Aman Ullah in which he had said that he was ready to die for the integrity of the Khilafate and

to offer an asylum to any Indian whom religion might drive from India. This speech was published in full in a Delhi vernacular paper, and certainly tended to stimulate the excitement of United Provinces Muhammadans who took this to be a promise on the part of the Amir of Kabul to raise the banner of Islam. A Cawnpore Muhammadan association changed its name to 'Anjuman-i-Khuddam-i-Khilafate,' and its members proceeded to learn drill. At this time endeavours were made to prevent recruits joining the Army, and police constables were refused admission into mosques, while the Muhammadan public was advised not to institute cases in British courts.

A Shahjahanpur Khilafat Conference deprecated a *fatwa* issued by the *Sheikh-ul-Islam* condemning the Turkish Nationalists, and at Jhansi, the title of 'Naib-ul-Khalifa' was conferred on the Amir of Afghanistan, while pan-Islamic newspapers reproduced statements from a Kabul paper to the effect that the Amir was supporting the Khilafat agitation.

60. **Central Khilafat Committee Meetings, Bombay, April and May 1920.**—The Central Khilafat Committee met at Bombay on the 11th of April and resolutions were passed relative to further deputations to Europe and Mesopotamia and confining action for the time being to propaganda.

It was decided that when further action should become necessary it should take the form of withdrawal from co-operation with the Government, step by step, in the order shown in the following plan which was drawn up by a Special Committee of which Gandhi was the principal member:—

(1) All titles and honours to be relinquished.

(2) Resignations by members of Councils.

(3) Private servants to give up their posts.

(4) Resignations of subordinate Government servants including the Police.

(5) Resignations of superior Government servants.

(6) Withdrawal of Mussalmans from the Army.

(7) Refusal to pay taxes.

On the 12th of May, the Central Khilafat Committee again met. In the interim, news reached India foreshadowing the Turkish Peace Terms which were rumoured to be very drastic, and *jehad, hijrat* and Non-co-operation had been freely discussed. The C. K. C., therefore, took a step further and appointed a sub-committee consisting of Chotani, Shaukat Ali, Abul Kalam Azad, A. H. S. Khatri and Muhammad Ali of Dharair to work out a scheme for the initiation of Non-co-operation. This caused the more moderate members of the C. K. C. to resign. A conference held at the Kalandhar fair passed a resolution urging the Ulemas to issue a *fatwa* ordering the severence of relations with Government and calling upon the people to obey it.

61. **Khilafat Conference, Sind, May 1920.**—The Sind Khilafat Conference was held at Jacobabad on May 2nd and was the occasion for most fanatical and excited speeches which so played on the feelings of the audience that many interruptions were made by men who declared themselves ready to become *ghazis*, to make *hijrat*, to renounce their titles and privileges and to refuse to pay land revenue. The usual attempts were made to put severe pressure on those refusing to join the agitation. The English as a race came in for denunciation, and the statement, first made in the United Provinces or Bihar, that many English goods imported into India were made of the fat of cows and pigs was repeated here. It is not necessary to analyse the speeches which were only differentiated from other Khilafat oratory by the degree of their violence but the *fatwa* issued by the Conference over the signature of 16 *pirs*, *maulvis* and prominent Muslims was so obnoxious and dangerous that it must be mentioned. It was to the effect that as in the sacred places infidels had killed pigs and had walked with booted feet, smoking cigarettes and drunk with liquor, it was incumbent upon every Muhammadan to renounce his title, etc., otherwise the fire of hell would burn him.

62. **The Turkish Peace Terms, May 1920.**—The Terms of Turkish Peace emanating from the Conference at San Remo were published in India on the 15th May and further excited the Muslims. The terms were vigorously criticised and great Britain was freely attacked for being a party to them. In Bengal, Fazl-ul-Haq predicted that the next ten years would bring about the fall of the English and the emancipation of Islam through Afghanistan backed by Bolshevik Russia.

At the Oudh Khilafat Conference, which met at Fyzabad under the Presidency of Kidwai in the same month, the speeches were very objectionable and reference was made to assisting foreign invaders and welcoming Bolshevism. Shaukat Ali described Non-co-operation as a declaration of independence, and Hasrat Mohani stated that if the Prince of Wales did not abandon his proposed visit to India, *hartals* would be arranged at every place which he visited. The Conference appealed to the Ruling Chiefs, especially to the Nizam, to take up the agitation and to give full liberty to their subjects, and it condemned the Nawab of Rampur for his repressive action and the Oudh representatives in the Imperial and Provincial Councils for their inactivity.

63. **Kidwai protests against the moderation of the C. K. C.**—The rather moderate attitude regarding the Peace Terms taken up at this time by the Central Khilafat Committee at Bombay, called forth a letter of protest from Kidwai to Chotani. From a translation of this the following extracts have been taken:—" If the Central Khilafat Committee does not work with more readiness and with more regard for public opinion and public expectations from it, then undoubtedly there will spring up another class which will be more ready and responsive to public desires and I myself would have no excuse

against joining it. The people who get afraid of even ordinary proposals give the irresponsible English help, and self-seeking persons an opportunity to separate themselves and form a separate body. Personally I do not wish to conceal that the Central Khilafat Committee does not take steps in the direction of practical work with the same readiness as it ought. This leads to an increase of general complaints. It is also giving selfish people and people desirous of getting a name and fame for themselves, an opportunity to come forward. As much pressure should at this time be put on the British Ministers as is possible, by means of resolutions and by showing readiness for practical measures. But it should at the same time be carefully borne in mind that no mischief or disturbances of any kind whatsoever occurs at this time. In fact no violent act should be committed now. This is the time merely for preparations to take practical measures. But this is also not the time to lose heart or to show cowardice. Harshness in proposals does not matter. On the other hand it is essential otherwise group after group of Muhammadans will get out of hand. It is also extremely important that there should be no proposal on which we are not ready to act. At present the Muhammadans are ready to act upon the most serious proposals, *i.e.*, even to sacrifice their lives. The sole effort at this time should be that practical work should not be of any inciting nature. In the same way I say that the two last clauses of the Non-co-operation scheme should on no account whatsoever be taken out of the programme. I also say that on no account whatsoever should action be begun on them at this time. At this time we solely desire to put pressure, and pressure in sufficient degree, on the British Ministers so that it may be impressed upon them that the Turkish Empire would be ruined only when the British Empire at least is also ruined if the whole world is not upset. After producing such an impression the British Ministers should be given an opportunity so that they may be able to give some concessions after the reply of delegates of Turkey. Therefore it should also be so arranged that only such persons be put in the forefront the acceptance of whose requests is not considered by British as derogatory to her greatness or nugatory to her power."

64. **C. K. C. Manifesto, May 1920.**—This letter may have stimulated the C. K. C. for, at the end of May it issued the following Manifesto:—

"As a crisis of the first magnitude is being reached on the question of the Khilafate, it is necessary even at the risk of repetition, to state its terms and to define the means to be adopted for seeking redress.

" The Muslim claim is:—

(1) European Turkey to be left as it was at the time of the war, specially where the Muslim population was preponderant, with such guarantees as may be necessary for the fair treatment of non-Muslim races.

(2) The retention of Turkish suzerainty over Jazirat-ul-Arab with self-Government for the Arabs if they so desire. Jazirat-ul-Arab includes:—Hedjaz, Yaman, Nejd, Iraq, Palestine and Syria. The Muslim religious authorities define the Jazirat-ul-Arab as a country bounded by the Mediterranean, the Red Sea, the Indian Ocean, the Persian Gulf, the Euphrates and the Tigris.

(3) The Khalifa's control of Holy Places of Islam, *viz.*, the three sacred Harams, namely, Mecca, Medina and Jerusalem, and the Holy Shrines, namely, Najaf, Karbala, Smarra, Kazmain and Baghdad.

" This claim is supported by President Wilson's declaration and the Pledges of Mr. Lloyd George and Lord Hardinge. It is supported by Islamic scriptures and is therefore a religious question with the Mussalmans, and as Hindus desire to show their brotherly feeling towards their Muslim fellow-countrymen by co-operating with them, it is also a question of such magnitude as to overshadow all other questions. On the political side, again, the Indians have a right to examine the justice or otherwise of all measures that may be contemplated for determination of countries subjugated with the help of Indian men and money, for instance Mesopotamia. We believe that if the Turkish question is not settled to the satisfaction of Mussalmans, more men and money will be required from India to keep order in Muslim countries, which will materially retard the progressve development of our own.

" There is no question of compromise in this matter of life and death with millions of Mussalmans. We still hope that justice will be done, but if unfortunately the issue is decided against us, there is no rest for India till the wrong is redressed. We shall not count the cost in order to secure a just solution and we hold that in making His Majesty's Ministers fulfil their promises, we shall have served the Empire of which we claim to be members. We have studied the Peace Terms and we consider that they are direct violation of the pledges referred to and in no way calculated to satisfy the requirements of justice or of Islamic law.

" The remedy that lies before the Hindus and Mussalmans is simple. The least we can do is not to help the Government if it supports the wrong. We must therefore advise the country to withdraw co-operation from the Government and continue to do so until justice is done. But we have no desire to take hasty steps which may result in violence or unnecessary embarrassment to the Government.

" We wish to state in the most emphatic terms that in the joint Hindu Muslim scheme of action there is at no stage of it any idea of doing violence secretly or openly. We recognise that the pressure must be peaceful and moral. We must evoke a sympathy by suffering. We wish to cultivate a world opinion in favour of our cause by inviting suffering on ourselves. Violence can only retard the process of enlightenment. We therefore propose to resort to non-co-operation in the following stages for the time being:—

(1) Surrender of honorary titles and offices and stopping of all voluntary financial support.

(2) Surrender of Civil employments under Government.

(3) We reserve our opinion as to the other stages suggested and approved by the Central Khilafat Committee.

(4) The methods we wish to adopt for the purpose of securing the acceptance by those concerned are of the foregoing programme and open agitation in the press and on the platform, to individual canvassing. We shall neither use nor tolerate any force being exercised; we shall depend upon argument and social pressure to bring about non-co-operation. Definite steps to be taken will be advised from time to time. It is hoped that no one will take initiative without consultation with the authority of the Joint Committee.

"No departure from policy will be taken without joint deliberation. It has been stated that the Hindus have serious misgivings about the ultimate aim. The Mussalman signatories therefore desire to state that they have no other aim than to serve their religion and the country of their birth. In serving their religion they wish to keep the Khilafate intact. They certainly desire the Muhammadan powers all the world over to prosper for the common good of humanity. But they do not desire to oust England and introduce a Muhammadan or any other power to rule over India. They wish to realise the highest national aspirations in association with the British but they would certainly seek to end the British connection if it hampers India's advance or if it puts an affront upon cherished religious sentiments.

"At the same time it should be remembered that India's loyalty in terms of the proclamation of 1858 is conditional upon absolute protection of all religions flourishing within the British Empire.

" The Mussalmans of India will fight to the last man in resisting any Mussalman power that may have designs upon India. They wish to respect to the full the religious sentiments of the Hindus and they expect them to respect in an equal measure those of the Mussalmans. The latter have realised by bitter experience that too often have the bureaucracy played the one against the other. Disputes and differences we shall have. It should be our duty to settle them all by mutual discussion or arbitration. The Mussalmans desire to state further that, whilst they do not accept the view that boycott of British goods is not a lawful political weapon, out of consideration for some of their Hindu friends, they have abandoned the boycott propaganda. They, however, realize that the country has become impoverished and enslaved by reason of having abandoned Swadeshi. We shall, therefore, by every means at our disposal restore Swadeshi to its original status, and we advise all to encourage home manufactures, even though it may be at some inconvenience and sacrifice, and to encourage hand-weaving and hand-spinning and all other cottage industries so as to be independent, so far as possible, even of all foreign machinery.

"Our attention has also been drawn to the unrest permeating in the student world. We desire to state that students ought not to take active part in the agitation, save in so far as it is necessary from the religious standpoint. In no case should they harbour thoughts of violence.

"Finally, the Mussalmans desire to observe that whilst they expect full success through the peaceful method of non-co-operation, they realize that either through Hindu apathy or disunion amongst Mussalman ranks, non-co-operation may fail to achieve the end. In that case and no other the Mussalmans reserve to themselves the right to take such other and further steps as may be enjoined upon them by their religion for the purpose of securing a satisfactory solution of the Khilafat question.

"The framers of this manifesto invite all who wish to help the movement and who wish to avoid violence and guide it through proper and healthy channels, to sign this and give such support as they are capable of giving. We expect that the course of action we have outlined is not only in the interest of the faith of millions of Muslim subjects of the Empire, but also in the interest of the Empire itself, to which we have shown our active loyalty times without number."

65. **Agitation in the Punjab.**—The excitement stimulated in the United Provinces by the Oudh Khilafat Conference rapidly extended to the Punjab and extreme violence of speech and large appreciative audiences were the feature of a campaign of intensive propaganda carried through several districts of that Province during May. Maulvi Ataullah of Amritsar was the chief agitator and was assisted by others, including Kitchlew. The trickery of the "white monkeys" and the necessity of frustrating it, was their theme, and, in developing it, they gave much attention to the Army, practically inciting soldiers to mutiny. Zafar Ali Khan of Lahore assisted this agitation by publishing violently worded articles in the *Zemindar*. During this period frequent reports were received of the formation of Muhammadan secret societies, and there is no doubt that these were contemplated freely, but little appears to have materialised.

66. **Meetings of Leaders, Allahabad, June 1920.**—At the beginning of June 1920, a Khilafat Conference met at Allahabad and this was followed by a meeting of the leaders of all parties.* The proceedings of the Khilafat Conference show that the Muhammadans were prepared at that time to go a good deal further than the Hindus, and

*Part I, paragraph 14.

Ulemas were asked for a ruling as to the *hijrat* and Non-co-operation. A meeting of Ulemas, which assembled at the same time, declared that the *hijrat* was optional, but apparently postponed a decision on the question of Non-co-operation which was dealt with in the *Mutafiqa Fatwa* which came into being in the following November. At the meeting of the all-India leaders, opposition on the part of Hindus, excluding Gandhi, to the more extreme measures of the Non-co-operation programme was apparent, but ultimately the four stages of Non-co-operation, previously discussed, were accepted. These were (1) resignation of titles and honorary posts, (2) resignation of posts in the civil services of Government (the Police being excluded), (3) resignation of service in the Police and Army, and (4) refusal to pay taxes.

During June and July 1920, the general agitation decreased considerably and it is difficult to account for this otherwise than by the inability of its promoters to maintain it at boiling point for a lengthy period, especially during the Ramzan and hot weather. It may to some extent have been due to reports which appeared in the Indian Press at about this time, indicating a revival of optimism among the members of the Khilafat Delegation in Europe. Their optimism was based on what they believed to be a more favourable attitude on the part of France and Italy towards the Near Eastern questions. The Delegation consequently concentrated on these two countries, and, while in France, it seems to have endeavoured to arouse a sentiment as much anti-British as pro-Turk.

The principal leaders in India, however, did not relax their efforts in spite of their apparent lack of success, and Muhammad Akram Khan, in the course of a *hartal* notice which appeared in the *Navayuga* in Calcutta on the 26th of June, announced that nobody should lend money to Government nor enlist as a soldier of the Government. nor should anybody go to Basra, Mesopotamia or other places to do the work of soldiers and sailors. To realise the significance of this pronouncement it must be remembered that Bengal furnishes a very large number of *lascars* to the mercantile service. In Lahore, Abul Kalam Azad made some very inflammatory speeches, exhorting his co-religionists to rise against Government and to free Islam from the shame and humiliation to which it had been subjected by Great Britain.

67. **The Muhajirin.**—The Khilafat agitation had one striking effect in the middle of 1920, namely, the *hijrat* movement, which was the migration of a number of Muhammadans from India on the ground that it was *Dar-ul-Harab*. This movement, while undoubtedly stimulated by the Amir's speech offering an asylum to Indian Muhammadans, was the direct result of Khilafat propaganda. It first started in Sind whence it spread to the North-West Frontier Province where it produced an extraordinary effect. About twenty thousand persons after selling their land, goods and chattels for next to nothing, marched through the Khyber into Afghanistan, apparently imagining that having got there, they would be maintained at the expense of the

Amir for the rest of their natural lives. This maintenance, however, was not forthcoming, and in consequence the penniless emigrants ultimately struggled back to India where Government did what it could to re-establish them.

68. **Ultimatum to H. E. the Viceroy, 22nd June 1920.**—On 22nd June 1920, a memorial signed by a very large number of Mussalman leaders and Ulemas was sent by M. K. Gandhi on behalf of the Central Khilafat Committee to H. E. the Viceroy, requesting him to urge upon the British Cabinet the vital necessity of revising the Turkish Peace Terms and holding out the threat that if their suggestions were not adopted they would withdraw co-operation from the Government with effect from 1st August 1920

69. **Association of Gandhi with Muslim leaders.**—During July, Gandhi toured in the Punjab in company with Shaukat Ali and Kitchlew, in the course of which the Muhammadan agitators made violent speeches at Amritsar and Lahore. Gandhi, at the latter place, expressed himself opposed to the *hijrat* movement which he characterised as a great mistake as it decreased the number of their effective workers. At the same time frequent discussions were held among these leaders themselves on the Non-co-operation programme and the best means of carrying it out, and there is no doubt that a good deal of friction existed between them on the question of method, though they were unanimous as to the object—which was the destruction of British influence in the East.

70. **Khilafat and N. C. O. agitation approximate.**—Towards the end of July agitation increased, but from this point the Khilafat question became more and more merged in Non-co-operation, and consequently this revival of the agitation can be attributed to Gandhi's Non-co-operation programme rather than to the Khilafat question, though of course, the leading Khilafatists took a very active part in it. The following notice which was circulated at about this time by the Central Khilafat Committee is indicative of the transfer of their interests from external to internal matters:—

> "Brethren, Hindus and Muhammadans of our country are hereby informed that the time is at hand when we should look to our own interests so that our country prosper; and with our combined efforts we may get our lawful rights successfully; and therefore you should fill up the following declaration and send it to the officer in charge of the Central Khilafat Committee:—
>
> DECLARATION.
>
> I hereby declare that from this day I will never use foreign goods except Swadeshi goods and also always try to draw the attention of my countrymen to the above declaration.
>
> Signature............................
>
> Date...............................

71. **Khilafat Conference, Sind, July 1920.**—A Khilafat Conference was held at Sind from the 23rd to 25th July which was attended by about ten thousand people who were treated to seditious speeches of the worst kind, inciting them to *jehad*. The meeting was attended by Gandhi and Shaukat Ali and samples of their speeches are given below:—

Shaukat Ali said that the way to stop the Khilafat agitation was not opposition and putting Gandhi, Pir Jhandewalla, Jan Mahomed Junejo, Abdul Bari and others in fear of sending them to the gallows, but by conceding the demands of Khilafatists. Mussalmans should sacrifice trade, commerce, children for the commandments of the Prophet and God. The British would not have won the war if the Khilafate had been taken up earlier. If the demands were not granted they should say openly that neither the British were their rulers nor they their subjects. They had only two courses open, *hijrat* and *jehad*. Jan Mahomed Junejo had been honoured as Nawab by Afridis, 25,000 of whom had received the *Muhajirin*. If any are weak let them perform *hij at* and if not, proclaim *jehad*. Let two or five lakhs leave India and the rest take up *jehad*. Non-co-operation is also a part of *jehad*. *Jehad* is undertaken to decrease the strength of the enemy and to increase their own.

In his opinion to kill or be killed in the service of God was martyrdom. It was a sin for Muslims to help the enemies of Islam who were also the enemies of Hindus on account of the Jallianwalla Bagh. He was prepared to die in the cause of the truth and hundreds of the audience should go to jail and the gallows and be shot.

Gandhi advised "23 crores of Hindus to help 7 crores of Moslems" as the latter's religion was in danger. Union between them should exist. No physical assistance or power would help but soul power. They should live faithful to a Government only when religion is not endangered. Government had more physical power and a heavier sword. They must not assist a tyrannical Government.

He advocated Non-co-operation and explained it. He knew Muslims would be violent and use the sword, but General Dyer had proved he could be more violent and use a heavier sword. He advocated unconditional sacrifice when Government with guns and aeroplanes would be helpless. The Secretary of State had said that he, (Gandhi) had become mad and would not have the freedom he had last year, but he had not felt free. The Khilafat and Punjab disturbances made him feel in prison. He preferred to die for Mussalmans and if he was sent to the gallows, they should congratulate him. He urged his audience to use no violence and not to resist but follow Non-co-operation which was to begin on August 1st, or if too weak to follow Non-co-operation to do *hijrat*.

In connection with this Conference, an Indian official reported that he had gathered that the object of the *hijrat* movement was to train the *Muhajirin* in the cult of Bolshevism, in Afghanistan for a time and then to bring them back to India to sow the seed of discord.

72. **The Murder of Mr. Willoughby.—At** about the same time reports from Bengal indicated that the local agitators were beginning to fear that the excitement which they had aroused was getting beyond their control, and employees of the Ichapore Rifle Factory spread many exciting rumours alleging the disorganization of the British Government. From some other parts of India instances occurred of sepoys in the Army fraternising with well known agitators. A tragic result of the agitation was the murder of Mr. Willoughby, Deputy Commissioner of Kheri in Oudh, by fanatical Muhammadans who admitted that the act was the result of the propaganda to which they had been subjected.

73. **Press Propaganda.**—In addition to the platform campaign the Press had been exceedingly active, and a number of Muhammadan extremist papers had sprung up all over India. These expressed ideas very little less objectionable than those of the extremist leaders, and it is clear that they were only deterred from out-Heroding Herod by the fear of prosecution. It is probable that the action of the Punjab Government in demanding security from the *Zemindar* under the Press Act at about this period, had a wholesome effect. The editor of this paper, Zafar Ali Khan, had made several particularly objectionable speeches in the middle of 1920. One of these, made on the 14th of August before an audience of 30,000, is summarized in the Punjab History of Non-co-operation as follows:—"He said that the time was come to rebuild the ruined house of Islam. It was time also for the advent of the Mehdi. They should fulfil the programme of non-co-operation and the Government would perish. He referred to the dropping of bombs in Mecca and the outraging of virgin Turkish girls; the Turkish treaty was a scrap of paper; they should now perform *hijrat*—not all, but wealthy persons, doctors, engineers and *mistris*, especially the young and strong—and collect money for the purpose. He then declared General Dyer to be a *yazid** and a bastard. If they failed in non-co-operation, they were all *kafirs* themselves. He said further the face of an Indian soldier killed at Baghdad had been turned into that of a pig, and they should never join the army."

He was prosecuted under Section 124-A and 153-A, I. P. C. and sentenced to 5 years' transportation.

74. **Special Session of the Congress, Calcutta, September 1920.**— Shortly afterwards a special session of the Congress was held at Calcutta in September which resulted in the triumph of Gandhi and the acceptance of his Non-co-operation programme. By this time the leading Khilafat agitators were feeding out of Gandhi's hand and he—knowing that the Hindu-Muhammadan entente was essential to the

*The Khalifa in whose reign Hussan was martyred.

†Part I, paragraph 15.

success of his programme—took care to retain their allegiance. In consequence the disaffected Muhammadans, by reason of their fanaticism, were probably at this period stronger supporters of Gandhi than were his fellow Hindus. They were certainly more vigorous in their language and the following extract of a speech made by Shaukat Ali at Shahjahanpur on the 16th October is typical of Khilafat propaganda at the end of 1920:—"Tell every Muhammadan clearly that it is his religious duty to avoid being recruited for the Army. Do not give a single soldier that he may behead his brother with his own hands * * * * * * The Turks are being oppressed; Egypt and Palestine are being occupied and efforts are being made to occupy Persia and Afghanistan. Why is all this being done? It is done simply to deprive the neighbourhood of India of even the faintest tinge of freedom * * * *. To-day Indian armies are being sent to enslave our independent brothers; to-morrow their armies will be brought to smash our heads; and then we will be able to do nothing. * * * * There is one course more for Mussalmans, and it is this—that you should use the same force against your opponent which he used against you. It is called *jehad*, *i.e.*, the *jehad* which the Mahatmaji has preached to you. We believe that we will be able to use sword against sword and that God will give us the power."

75. **The Mutafiqa Fatwa.**—In November, a meeting of the Jamiat-ul-Ulema was held at Delhi at which it was decided to declare that Government service, including service in the Army, was *haram*. The proceedings of the meeting were, however, not published and it was not until the following year that the *Mutafiqa Fatwa* (as this decision was called) came to prominent notice. The original *fatwa* was given in the form of a catechism and a translation is given as Appendix G, but various abbreviated editions appeared in print, in 1921, and the following is a paraphrase of one of them:—

(1) It is unlawful to be members of Government Councils.
(2) It is unlawful to do pleadership in Government Courts.
(3) It is unlawful to get education in Government Schools or Colleges aided by Government.
(4) It is unlawful to keep honorary magistracy and other honorary ranks and the titles given by Government.
(5) All the Government services from which Government receives help are forbidden (*haram*). Specially serving in Army and Police is a serious sin as they are in duty bound to shoot their brothers and God says in honourable Quran Surra Mirraj, "whoever will intentionally slaughter any Muhammadan will be punished in hell for ever," and Prophet has said, "whoever lifted weapon against Muhammadan would cease to be a Muhammadan." This verdict contains seals of Maulana Abul Kalam Azad, M. Mufti Muhammad Kifayat Ullah of Delhi, Maulvi

Azad Subhani of Cawnpore, Maulvi Muhammad Daud of Ghazni, Maulvi Abdul Bari of Lucknow, Maulvi Sana Ullah of Amritsar, Maulvi Azizul Rahman Mufti, Deoband School, and other great learned men of India, Delhi. The same is announced by Mahatma Gandhi and other distinguished Hindu and Muhammadan leaders of India.

76. **The Elections, 1920.**—The latter part of the year saw political activities centred on the elections for which the Non-co-operation agitation had been unable to prevent an adequate supply of candidates. Therefore the efforts of the supporters of that policy were concentrated on persuading electors to refrain from voting. At about the same time Muhammad Ali, who had returned to India in October 1920, established a National Muslim University at Aligarh which had the effect of taking away a number of students from the Aligarh College. At this time the Hindu University of Benares received the personal attention of Gandhi, who endeavoured to persuade the students to leave, but in this, however, he was opposed by Pandit Madan Mohan Malaviya who had great influence there and warned the students against the danger of abandoning their studies. The activities of the students of the National Muslim University will be dealt with elsewhere.

77. **The Nagpur Meeting, December 1920.**—In Christmas Week 1920, the All-India Muslim League and an All-India Khilafat Conference were held at Nagpur. With the addition of emphasis on the Turkish and Khilafat wrongs, the general attitude of the All-India Muslim League was similar to that of the Congress.* A significant fact, however, was the passing of a resolution asking the Amir of Afghanistan to refrain from making any treaty with England as it would be used by the English to strengthen their hold on India.

---

*Part I, paragraph 19.

CHAPTER IV.

Intensive Agitation and its Results, 1921.

78. **Proposed Khilafat Deputation to Afghanistan.**—In 1920, Shaukat Ali had addressed the Afghan Envoy on the subject of sending to Afghanistan a Khilafat Deputation regarding the sufferings of the *Muhajirin*, of whom large numbers had returned, while the condition of those who remained was reported to be far from enviable. Early in 1921, two of their leaders who were in Kabul, urged Shaukat Ali to expedite the despatch of the Khilafat Delegation and suggested that Muhammad Ali also should visit Kabul. The despatch of the Delegation was opposed by Government and the project fell through.

79. **Khilafat Conference, Lucknow, February 1921.**—The question of Swaraj was brought into prominence at a Khilafat Conference, held at Lucknow at the end of February, which was presided over by Maulana Muhammad Ali. An influential Maulvi, named Abdul Majid, of Budaun, proposed a resolution to secure Swaraj for India. Mr. Gandhi also delivered a speech explaining the meaning of Swaraj, and while dwelling on the position of various communities in India he said that he had joined the Khilafat Movement to help the Muhammadans, for, to him their success meant Swaraj The Conference also considered the draft constitution of the Central Khilafat Committee and passed the following, among other, resolutions; (1) expressing confidence in the Sultan of Turkey and requesting him to acknowledge and encourage Mustapha Kemal Pasha's Party; (2) thanking the Amir of Kabul for having agreed to receive the deputation of Indian Muslims in connection with the *Muhajirin* and condemning the refusal of the Government to permit the deputation to proceed; (3) asking the Oudh representatives of the Khilafat Movement to make Non-co-operation a success and to collect funds.

In the course of his speech, Muhammad Ali said, "I declare to-day that the Indian Army is the army of Mahatma Gandhi; the Indian Police is the police of Mahatma Gandhi; every man is on the side of Gandhi, nay, on the side of religion and country. The aspect of affairs is now quite changed. I see that God hath already issued his commandments."

80. **The only sign of dissent.**—The only Muhammadan organisation which at this time desired or dared to assert itself in the opposite direction was the Bengal Muhammadan Association which published a declaration that it would preach the advantages and benefits of loyal co-operation "to save the Muslim community from the foolish and nauseating movement of Mr. Gandhi".

81. **The general lines of agitation.**—Although the question of Swaraj was prominent on Khilafat platforms, yet, at the beginning

of 1921, the Provincial Khilafat Committees concentrated their attention mainly on the Turkish question. The Khilafat Committee in Sind, at a meeting held at Karachi on the 21st of February, declared that no settlement would be acceptable if inconsistent with the Islamic law regarding the Khilafate and allied matters, including Jazirat-ul-Arab. Some of the prominent agitators began to pay attention to the Army and, at Bhiwani in the Punjab, at a meeting held in February, Abul Kalam Azad, referring to the position of Muhammadans in Government service, said that a Muhammadan ceased to be such if he fought against Muhammadans and even if he offered lakhs of prayers and observed lakhs of fasts, he would earn perdition. The agitation also touched upon other grounds, and at Ajmere, on the occasion of the Urs (an annual Fair at the local shrine which is regarded as being particularly holy) a Khilafat Conference was held on the 13th and 14th of March at which one of the most prominent features was an attack on Native States. No less than seven resolutions were passed which struck a note of warning to Indian Chiefs, and the agitators hoped that the seed of discontent would be disseminated by the large number of pilgrims present from surrounding States.

The Conference re-affirmed Non-co-operation and expressed confidence in the work of Kemal Pasha and allegiance to the throne of the Sultan of Turkey. A Hindu speaker was reported to have moved a resolution requesting the Amir of Afghanistan not to enter into a treaty with the British Government and to take into consideration the feelings of the people in India. The Conference was attended, among others, by Muhammad Ali, Abul Kalam Azad, Abdul Majid and Abdul Bari.

82. **Further Khilafat Conferences.**—In the same month (March) a number of Khilafat Conferences were held in the United Provinces and in Bengal. At Bareilly on the 24th—26th of March a meeting of the Jamiat-ul-Ulema took place at which the President—Abul Kalam Azad—reiterated that enlistment in the Army was illegal according to the Shariat. He announced that the Jamiat-ul-Ulema had given a *fatwa* to this effect and that the Ulemas would punish the opponents of Non-co-operation through the Dar-ul-Qaza (House of Justice). Resolutions were passed that arbitration courts should be established and that the complete independence of India was necessary for the integrity of the Islamic Shariat. Some of the Maulvis present at this meeting were, however, reported to be opposed to an alliance with Hindus.

The Anjuman-i-Ulema-i-Bangala held a largely attended session at Rangpur on the 28th and 29th of March under the presidentship of ex-detenu Maulana Husain Ahmed Nadwi, and resolutions were passed supporting Non-co-operation and requesting the Amir of Afghanistan to protect the safety of the Holy Places and to help India to obtain Swaraj.

In the same month Abdul Kalam Azad wrote an article in the form of a *fatwa* on Non-co-operation and national education which dealt with the religious and political aspect of the Khilafat question, and its circulation was reported to have had considerable influence on political thought in certain circles in Sind. In the N.-W. F. P. as a result of the activities of the Bannu Khilafat Committee, Shariat tribunals were established in a few places and a national school was started at Utmanzai. A session of the Majlis-ul-Ulema, Trichinopoly, was held at Erode in the Madras Presidency, on the 2nd and 3rd of April, which, in the absence of Abdul Bari, was presided over by his nephew Kutubuddin of Lucknow. Other meetings were also held by Ulemas who had proceeded to Erode after their visit to Ajmere and resolutions were passed re-affirming non-violent Non-co-operation, recommending the collection of funds for Turkey and condemning the atrocities in Smyrna.

83. **Muhammad Ali frightens his Hindu Friends.**—A very violent speech was delivered by Muhammad Ali in Madras in which he openly stated that he would assist an army invading India from Afghanistan, provided that the invaders came to free the country and withdrew after accomplishing their task. His speech created considerable apprehension among Hindus and particular endeavours were subsequently made by prominent Hindu and Muhammadan Non-co-operation leaders to allay these fears.* Mr. Gandhi defined his own attitude in *Young India* as follows: "I would, in a sense, certainly assist the Amir of Afghanistan if he waged war against the British Government; that is to say, I would openly tell my countrymen that it would be a crime to help the government, which has lost the confidence of the nation to remain in power. On the other hand, I would not ask India to raise levies for the Amir."

84. **Khilafat Conference, Meerut, April 1921.**—An All-India Khilafat Conference assembled at Meerut on the 7th and 10th of April with the expressed object of defining Muhammadan policy. It was reported that some of the Ulemas present, to the embarrassment of the leading agitators, seriously objected to Hindu-Muslim unity and demanded its scope to be defined according to the Shariat. Among others, the following resolutions were passed, (1) condemning the invasion of Anatolia by the Greeks, which was said to have been undertaken at the instigation of the Allies, particularly Great Britain; (2) binding Mussalmans to adhere to Non-co-operation until Swaraj was obtained and requesting them to join the Congress; (3) urging the enlistment of one crore of Muhammadans and five crores of Hindus as members of the Khilafat and Congress organisations; (4) condemning the refusal of Government to allow the deputation to proceed to Afghanistan.

85. **Session of the Jamiat-ul-Ulema, Moradabad, April 1921.**—A special session of the Jamiat-ul-Ulema was held at Moradabad on

*Part I, paragraph 28.

the 10th and 11th of April under the presidentship of Maulana Sulaiman Nadwi to consider the situation arising out of the "unsatisfactory" reply given by the British Prime Minister to the Indian Khilafat Deputation. In a speech delivered on this occasion, Shaukat Ali declared that as long as the Holy Places were in the hands of enemies, particularly the British, it was *haram* for Muhammadans to sit at ease. Muhammad Ali also made a very objectionable speech in which he referred to the maintenance of white soldiers who could not live without beef, and attributed to their existence in India the responsibility for cow-killing.

86. **Border conspiracy.**—Information was received that the Khilafat Committees in Bannu, Kohat and Thal in the N. W. F. P., were corresponding with hostile elements in Khost. It was learnt that R. A. Zakriya, 'Minister of Communications' of the 'Provisional Government of India', had written a cipher letter at the end of 1920 to Shaukat Ali from Herat. The writer said that he was proceeding to Russia in company with Abdul Haq, Minister Plenipotentiary of Bokhara, and that on his way to Herat he had seen Djemal Pasha who had told him about the "promises made between us". The letter concluded with the following words, "Pray God we prove equal to the great responsibility we took up voluntarily. Please send Khilafat Delegation soon" Subsequently in July 1921, certain Afridis addressed the Central Khilafat Committee expressing their sympathy with Indian Mussalmans and adding that, as there was a famine in their country, the Committee might help them.

87. **The alleged bombardment of the shrines at Najaf.**—In April the agitation derived further strength from the report of the alleged bombardment of the shrines at Najaf. It was referred to at a largely attended meeting which was held at Lucknow on the 15th of that month at which reference was also made to the Premier's description of the War as a Crusade. An All-India Shia Conference, which was held at the same place shortly afterwards, resolved to send a deputation to Najaf to enquire into the allegation.

At this time moderate Muhammadan opinion in Bengal again attempted to assert itself and some Muhammadan Members of the Bengal Legislative Council decided to form an association with the following, among other, objects:—(*a*) to make the Reforms a success, (*b*) to work for the realisation of full and responsible government within the British Empire by constitutional means and legitimate methods.

88. **The Second Khilafat Deputation.**—The Second Khilafat deputation consisting of Seth Chotani, Hasan Imam, Dr. Ansari and Qazi Abdul Ghaffar which had left for Europe in February, returned to India in May. Dr. Ansari submitted a report to the Central Khilafat Committee regarding the work of this delegation in England. The report was not made public but in a statement to the Press, Dr. Ansari declared that the gravity of the situation in India was fully realised

by the Secretary of State and partially by the Prime Minister. He advised redoubled efforts and suggested the despatch of competent men, including at least one Hindu, to Europe to remain in touch with the situation there, as well as with Near Eastern affairs.

89. **Action against the Ali Brothers considered.**—During the first half of 1921, one or other of the Ali Brothers had been touring India in company with Gandhi and their violent speeches had aroused considerable unrest, with the result that it was resolved to prosecute them. However, after an interview between H. E. the Viceroy and Mr. Gandhi, the Ali Brothers issued a statement to the effect that they had never intended to incite violence and expressed regret for the unnecessary heat of some of the passages in their speeches. They also publicly gave assurance that so long as they were associated with the Non-co-operation Movement they would not directly or indirectly advocate violence or "create an atmosphere of preparedness for violence" From this declaration, however, they soon recanted and at the Gujrat Khilafat Conference held at Broach on the 2nd of June, Muhammad Ali attempted to explain that his so-called apology was in reality an expression of regret to some of his friends and that he owed no apology to Government.

90. **Kemal Pasha gains the sympathy of Indian Moslem.**—In the course of a statement published in the newspapers in June by Abul Kalam Azad and Abdul Bari to the effect that they considered non-violent Non-co-operation a useful weapon, they said that the hopes of Muhammadans rested with the Turkish Nationalists and that if England departed from her attitude of neutrality regarding the situation in Anatolia, she would be immediately "in a state of war with Islam". This transference of the hopes of Muhammadans to the Turkish Nationalists was due to the fact that this party had consolidated its position in Asia Minor under Kemal Pasha and had set up an independent government at Angora. The views of Abul Kalam Azad and Abdul Bari were endorsed at a Khilafat Conference held at Bihar on the 14th and 15th of June, under the presidentship of Abdul Majid of Budaun, at which a resolution was passed that the Government of Angora was the only remaining Muhammadan power and on it the fate of the whole Muslim world and the protection of the Khilafate depended. On the 19th of June a District Khilafat Conference was held in the Belgaum District of the Bombay Presidency which was attended by the Ali Brothers and at which it was resolved that an Indian Republic should be declared in consultation with the Indian National Congress, if Great Britain, directly or through the Greeks, fought the Turkish Government of Angora.

91. **Proposed appointment of Provincial Amir-i-Shariat.**—A conference of Ulemas assembled at Patna on the 15th of June. The main feature of the Conference was a decision (*a*) to establish Dar-ul-Qaza courts in all districts of Bihar and Orissa; (*b*) to appoint district Amirs; (*c*) to select an Amir-i-Shariat or provincial leader. Abul

Kalam Azad was believed to have been the originator of this scheme and there was reason to believe that he hoped that similar organisations would be established in other provinces in India and that he himself would eventually secure the chief appointment of Sheikh-ul-Hind. Shah Badr-ud-Din was elected Amir-i-Shariat, but opposition to the plan soon appeared and other provinces did not follow the example of Bihar and Orissa. The opposition came from the Ali Brothers and Abdul Bari who were probably jealous of Abdul Kalam Azad's growing influence, and Abdul Bari wrote a letter to the press in which he said that it was open to Abul Kalam Azad to perform *hijrat* and to join the Chamarkhand party of Hindustani Fanatics if he desired to further his project. At a meeting of the Jamiat-ul-Ulema held some months later, it was agreed that the Amir of Afghanistan and the Angora Government should be asked to nominate persons approved by them for the office of Amir-ul-Hind; while an alternative proposal was made to appoint only provincial Amirs and to leave the all-India office vacant.

92. **Conference of Ulemas, Karachi, July 1921.**—At a meeting of Ulemas at Karachi on the 10th of July the question of *jehad* was discussed, and the argument proceeded on the line that as Indian Mussalmans were not in a position to undertake *jehad*, they should continue to work the Non-co-operation programme. At the same time and place an important All-India Khilafat Conference was held which was presided over by Muhammad Ali, at which the following resolutions were passed:—

"1. This meeting of the All-India Khilafat Conference respectfully professes its most devout allegiance to the Khilafat-ul-Muslimin Amirul Mominin Sultan Wadhi Uddin Mohamed, successor of the Holy Prophet, and assures His Imperial Majesty that the Indian Muslims would spare no sacrifice in upholding the integrity and prestige of the Khilafate and in liberating the Muslim territories especially Jazirat-ul-Arab from non-Muslim control. This meeting further expects that the Khilafat-ul-Muslimin will fully appreciate and value the meritorious efforts of Ghazi Mustafa Kemal Pasha and his comrades in their noble struggle for the preservation of the Islamic interest.

2. This meeting places on record its heartfelt sorrow and grief on the sad demise of Raisulmuhajirin, Jan Mohamed Junejo and, while recognising his self-less services in the cause of his religion and country, prays Allah to keep his soul in peace.

3. This meeting views with appreciation and gratitude the valueable services of the devotees of religion and country who gave practical proof of their strength of faith in the path of truth and righteousness and endured with fortitude and

courage sufferings and hardships inflicted on them by the repressive action of the authorities. In this connection this meeting reiterates its sense of appreciation of the way in which their Sindhi brethren are undergoing self-imposed travails in prison and congratulates them on their facing them bravely and courageously.

4. This meeting emphatically declares that the demands of the Indian Muslims regarding the integrity of the Khilafate, preservation of the sanctity of Jazirat-ul-Arab and the Holy Places of Islam, formulated in accordance with the commandments of Shariat, are still the same as stated hereto before and that until those demands are entirely satisfied the Indian Muslims would not rest themselves nor would they permit the enemies of Islam and the Khilafate to rest. In order to make the matter further clear this meeting declares that the Indian Muslims would under no circumstances tolerate non-Muslim control or domination of any type over any part of Jazirat-ul-Arab, whether Palestine, Mesopotamia or Syria and that the British and the French Government shall have to evacuate the said territories without further delay after which the Turks and the Arabs would under the guidance of the Amirul Mominin Khalifa of the Holy Prophet and in consultation with the Muslims of the whole world, adopt suitable measures regarding the future administration of those Holy regions without the least intervention of any foreign power whatsoever. That Thrace and Smyrna shall remain integral parts of the Turkish Empire as before the war and no control or domination thereover whether by Greece or any other power would be tolerated by the Indian Muslims. Further this meeting is of opinion that the restrictions regarding the Military, Naval and Aerial forces or Fiscal, Judicial or any other administrative functions contemplated to be imposed on the Turkish Government by the Allies, which tend to reduce the power and lower the prestige of the Khilafate and the Ottoman Empire would not be tolerated by the Mussalmans.

5. In view of the fact that Mesopotamia is among the Holy Places and is the burial place of the members of the family of the Holy Prophet, Imams and Saints of Islam, being a part of Jazirat-ul-Arab, the domination by the non-Muslims over it or their colonization therein without owing allegiance to the Islamic power is strictly forbidden by Shariat. Such domicile besides being a flagrant breach of the commandments of Shariat * * * will thereby afford them occasion to give vent to their long standing enmity against Mussalmans just as they did against the Holy Places and the Khilafate during the last war and at the time of the

Russian invasion of Armenia when they armed themselves and joined the enemies of the Khilafate. In view of these religious and political considerations, this meeting declares that it is the duty of every Mussalman to strive for the supremacy of the word of Allah in this Holy Land so that no nation hostile to Mussalmans may be so domiciled.

6. This Conference directs the Central Khilafat Committee to send from time to time its representatives to other Muslim countries, whenever feasible and necessary, with a view to establish and maintain fraternal brotherhood with Mussalmans of other countries and to remove their sufferings and hardships and to promote other Islamic interests.

7. This meeting offers hearty congratulations to Ghazi Mustafa Kemal Pasha and the Government of Angora on their brilliant victories and heroic efforts for the preservation of the Islamic Empire and prays the Almighty that they may similarly succeed as early as possible in expelling the Allied forces from every corner of the Turkish territories. This meeting further emphatically declares that in the present circumstances the Holy Shariat forbids every Mussalman to serve or enlist himself in the British Army or to raise recruits for it, that it is incumbent on all Muslims in general and all Ulemas in particular to carry this religious commandment to every Muslim soldier in the British Indian Army. This meeting further declares that in case the British Government directly or indirectly, secretly or openly, resumes hostilities against the Government of Angora, the Indian Muslims will be compelled in co-operation with the Congress to resort to civil disobedience and at the next session of the Congress at Ahmedabad to declare India's independence and the establishment of an Indian Republic.

8. This meeting directs all Khilafat Committees to take satisfactory steps in their jurisdictions for the prevention of the use of liquor and in co-operation with the Congress Committees, and congratulates all workers and volunteers of those places where the use of liquor is almost stopped.

9. This meeting earnestly invites the attention of all Indian Muslims in general, and Provincial and District Khilafat Committees in particular, to immediately enrol one crore of Khilafat members as already decided, and collect 40 lakhs of rupees through sale of Khilafat receipts for aid of sufferers from Smyrna and *Muhajirin* and other national requirements and thereby to give practical proof of their Islamic zeal and brotherhood.

10. This meeting earnestly requests all revered Pirs and Zemindars of Sind to redouble their efforts and energies in the Khilafat

cause and hopes that the Pirs would recommend the same course to their disciples and followers.

11. This meeting places on record its indignation at the repression exercised by the Government of the North-West Frontier Province, against Khilafat workers particularly by threatening them with imprisonment and securities* in Hazara, imprisoning Khilafat workers of Peshawar, disallowing freedom of speech and action in Kohat district, destroying harvests in some parts of Bannu district, killing innocent people, devastating their houses, imprisoning Khilafat workers, interning or expelling students of the National Muslim University, Aligarh, from the province and congratulates Khilafat workers of that province on their patience, perseverance and fortitude.

12. This meeting congratulates Sardar Sardul Singh Cavessiur† on the strength of character and spirit of sacrifice in discharge of his national duties, and while protesting against the cruel repression and high-handedness of the Punjab Government in suppressing communal and political awakening among the Sikhs, expresses the heartfelt sympathy with their Sikh brethren in their struggle.

13. This Conference earnestly requests all Indians in general, and Muslims in particular, to make it incumbent upon themselves to use handspun and handwoven cloth exclusively and to reserve the use of Indian machine-made cloth for their poor brethren and to offer all stock of foreign cloth for Muslim sufferers of Smyrna. This meeting further expects that people will manifest the same zeal and energy in this direction as was shown by them in collections for the Swaraj Fund. It also invites Indian sisters to revive the old art of spinning and thereby to remove poverty from India."

These resolutions have been reproduced *in extenso* in order to show the steps which, at that time, the Khilafat agitators were prepared to take to gain their ends. The resolutions are also of interest in view of the fact that the principal organisers of this meeting were subsequently prosecuted, as will be shown later. During this conference Shaukat Ali is reported to have said that he could easily spend a lakh of rupees on propaganda in the Army and that work in this direction had succeeded beyond expectation although it had been conducted without any systematic programme, under the guidance of himself, Dr. Kitchlew, Abul Kalam Azad, Abdul Majid. Sanaullah of Amritsar and Muhammad Ali of Lahore. An Army Propaganda Committee was apparently formed at this time which resolved to place five thousand rupees at the disposal of Ulemas, and one thousand rupees at the disposal of other persons for work among sepoys.

---

* Presumably under the preventive sections of the C. P. C.

† Part I, paragraph 33.

93. **Khilafat Non-co-operation Committee.**—In the same month (July) a Non-co-operation Committee appointed by the Central Khilafat Committee submitted a report signed by Gandhi, Kitchlew, Shaukat Ali and Ahmed Saddiq Khattri saying that, so far as Non-co-operation was concerned, it was obvious that every further step should be determined by the condition of the people of India, while the question of civil disobedience should be decided by the All-India Congress Committee. In the report of this Committee the following occurred :—

> " We hold that it is high time that a soldier refrained in a higher measure than he has hitherto done, from joining the Army. We consider it to be the duty of all Indian soldiers to refuse to assist the British Government should it require them to fight against the Turks. The Muslim Ulemas should exert themselves to the fullest extent to bring home to the Muslim soldiery the Commandments of Islamic Law They and all Non-co-operators should now lay stress upon the opinion expressed by the Working Committee of the Congress Committee with regard to the duty of Indian soldiers, in the event of re-opening of hostilities against the Turks."

94. **Propaganda among the Army and Police.**—At about this time a *fatwa* was distributed in leaflet form which declared service in the Army and Police to be *haram* and an enquiry showed that the *Mutafiqa fatwa** of the Ulemas of India, formulated in November 1920 by the Jamiat-ul-Ulema Conference at Delhi, was being enforced. The leaflet *fatwa* which had been distributed to many units in the Indian Army was proscribed by several Local Governments and the office of the Jamiat-ul-Ulema was searched in August and over 800 copies of the *fatwa* were seized. In spite of these steps the *fatwa* in various forms was widely circulated, and it was reported that forty students of the National University, Aligarh, had been ordered to go to the Punjab and N. W. F. P. for propaganda among the troops.

95. **Shaukat Ali's Speeches.**—As examples of Khilafat propaganda at this period, the following extracts from speeches made by Shaukat Ali are quoted :—

Delhi, 15th July, 1921.—To a party of Indian soldiers who were proceeding on leave he said, " We have all to take our revenge from the English. Swords, guns, bullets, whatever you get from them should be used against them and not in destroying our Indian brothers. If you act thus you will be saved from great sin. Many of our brothers have been deported and many are still in chains. The only punishment that remains is death. We are all ready to meet death in expelling the English from India. Do you see Mahatma Gandhi, the Sardar of the country? Go and pay your homage to him."

---

*Paragraph 75.

Hyderabad (Sind), 23rd July, 1921.—In the course of his Presidential Address at a Khilafat Conference, he said, " The King and his ministers have treated with hostility this demand (Muslim demand) in spite of solemn pledges, although we have lavishly wasted humility and submissiveness. Our clear duty now is emphatically to declare that neither the King is our King nor we are his subjects. This is no ingenious invention but a clearly defined divine command * * * There are two courses now open to us, *Hijrat* or *Jehad.* Those who cannot suffer tyrannies and persecution entailed by the firmness for faith and conscience may well adopt *hijrat* as an instrument of saving Islam." Speaking on *jehad,* he said, " I do not think Non-co-operation is excluded from this programme. I declare on high theological authority that it is a form of *jehad* and is to be employed in minimising the power and effectives of our enemy. Anything proceeding from the Muslims tending to strengthen Government's power is to be withdrawn and withheld. * * * I want to announce in unequivocal terms that to kill or be killed in God's path is never dangerous * * * I also treat with indifference what form of death I may suffer for the Khilafate because God is enough for me. Rise you all in token of your fearlessness (all stood). My last word is remain faithful to your demonstration of fearlessness and keep sobriety as your guiding principle. Let none entertain any idea of violence or bloodshed against Englishmen for it would tarnish our past reputation."

96. **The Moplah Rebellion.**—The Moplah rebellion broke out in August after Khilafat agitators, including Abul Kalam Azad and Hakim Ajmal Khan, had been making violent speeches in that area. At the time the Madras C. I. D. reported that the revolt was the first fruit of the Khilafat agitation and that ever since the Majlis-ul-Ulema Conference at Erode in April, the feelings of the Moplahs had been steadily growing with respect to the Khilafate, while the non-violent Non-co-operation movement was receding more and more into the background. A Khilafat Ulema Conference had been held at Pannani about the middle of July at which the highly exciting speeches, followed by clear suggestions for the proclamation of a republic in the event of a hostile British attitude towards Angora, provided the requisite torch to the inflammatory and fanatical Moplahs. It is unnecessary to describe at length this revolt in the course of which numerous atrocities were committed and which necessitated punitive measures, extending over several months, before it was quelled. The rising was in response to the repeated calls for *jehad* made by Muslim agitators and though these calls were usually qualified by appeals for non-violence the contradiction in terms was beyond the comprehension of the Moplahs who resorted to the only form of *jehad* which they could understand. The principal feature of this rebellion was its religious aspect and the forcible conversion of Hindus to Islam in complete disregard of the much-vaunted Hindu-Muhammadan unity. To show the nature of the propaganda to which the

Moplahs were subjected at this period, the following extracts from a speech of one of their leaders is given:—

"We have extorted Swaraj from the white men and what we have secured we are not going to give up so easily. * * * We shall give Hindus the option of death or Islam. We have the example of the Holy Prophet that it is a good act to kill for God's work. * * * The Jews and Christians, as believers in a revealed book, may be tolerated, but the idolatrous Hindus can only be allowed to live in a Muslim State on sufferance. * * * Success of our cause is certain * * Ali Musaliar* of Tirurangadi was told in a dream by Mampratti Thangal that the time for establishing the Khilafat has come. * * * Ali Musaliar also told us that God would show us some signs and portents to indicate the time when we were to begin the great fight for Khilafat. Just before the outbreak did you see anything peculiar in the moon? Did you see in it (i) green, (ii) red, (iii) blue, (iv) black, and (v) white? (The crowd after consultation, 'Yes, we all saw, we all saw'). All this shows that God is with you. In all our Muslim States there will be no expensive litigation. We do not want Vakils. For a paper which is worth a quarter anna the Government is taking from us 150 and 200 rupees. This injustice must go. * * * In our new State there shall be no private property. No one should have more than what he actually wants. * * * * We do not want the present system of police. We have already organised our police, 16 men per village. They have agreed to serve at the rate of four annas per day. The total expenditure under this head is only Rs. 4 per day. We have destroyed the Taluka offices and looted the treasury for very good reasons. The money in the treasury is our own. * * * We do not want such expensive buildings for the carrying of our simple every-day routine work * * All the costly buildings and expensive machinery of administration which the Sirkar has invented are a delusion and a snare. All this system must go and nothing but complete destruction will answer our purpose The whole administration and system of punishment require drastic change. Everything is provided in the Quran and nothing but Quranic law shall be tolerated in the new Muslim State we have established. Don't be afraid of defeat. The Englishman has no army. He had only 1,500 soldiers and two bombs. These bombs have been stolen. As for the soldiers he has troubles in Madras, Trichinopoly and Bombay and the

*An agitator of North Malabar.

> whole Islamic world will be up in arms immediately * * * The white men cannot starve us. We have plenty of paddy just harvested. We shall rush at him (white man) and capture his guns. So do not be dispirited. The Swaraj we have won, we are not going to give up. One thing more. You know it is said in our books that when Mecca and Medina are held by non-Muslims, it is the time to fight for the Khilafate and after this fight which will bring victory to us there will be no non-Muslim in this world."

During the suppression of the rebellion a most unfortunate catastropy occurred resulting in the suffocation of a number of Moplah prisoners in an ill-ventilated railway waggon, in which they were being transported from the disturbed area. Needless to say this calamity was made the most of by agitators who insinuated that it was due less to accident than to design.

97. **Efforts to help the Turks against the Greeks.**—In September, Muhammadan politicians attempted to initiate a movement for the collection of funds for the purchase of war material for Angora, and Mr. Chotani cabled from London to the Central Khilafat Committee that, as the Allied Council in Paris had decided that private parties might supply arms to both Turks and Greeks, Indian Muhammadans should take the opportunity to support the former. Incidentally, he mentioned that the decision of the Allied Council was obviously a mere subterfuge to explain the continuance of British assistance to the Greeks. The Bengal Provincial Khilafat Committee took the matter up and endeavoured to carry into effect a scheme for the formation and despatch of a volunteer corps to Angora, and the Bihar Provincial Khilafat Committee also attempted to rouse enthusiasm over the same subject.

98. **The Ali Brothers convicted.**—In the same month, the Ali Brothers, Dr. Kitchlew and four others were arrested and prosecuted in connection with the Karachi Conference on various charges of sedition, conspiracy and tampering with the loyalty of troops, and the more important of the accused (including those named) were convicted at Karachi and were each sentenced to two years' rigorous imprisonment.

Gandhi seized the occasion as opportune for the issue of an appeal to Mussalmans in India which is reproduced at Appendix H. After eulogising the Ali Brothers for their steadfastness and patriotism, the appeal exhorted Muslims to follow their example and to be prepared to suffer even unto " the final consummation on the gallows—if need be "

99. **Meetings of the C. K. C. and Jamiat-ul- ulema, Delhi, September 1921.**—Meetings of the Central Khilafat Committee and the Jamiat-ul-Ulema were held in Delhi on the 21st and 22nd September.

At the meeting of the Central Khilafat Committee, the arrest of the Ali Brothers, the proscription of the Ulemas *fatwa* and assistance to Angora were the chief topics of discussion. With regard to the first two points, fiery speeches were made demanding the immediate adoption of civil disobedience as the only possible course left open to Muhammadans in the face of the insult to their religion. The extremist section were eventually persuaded to agree to a postponement on the ground that the adoption of civil disobedience by only one section of the community was bound to fail and they must wait until they had obtained the support of the Hindus, which entailed a decision of the Indian National Congress. Considerable friction occurred before this decision was reached, and Hakim Ajmal Khan explained that Gandhi, " the recognised leader of all Indians ", considered that the time was not yet ripe for civil disobedience. The meeting then decided to collect funds for the purchase of munitions destined for Turkey, and to re-affirm, on all possible occasions, the Karachi resolutions, for which the leaders had been arrested.

At the meeting of the Jamiat-ul-Ulema resolutions were passed congratulating the Ali Brothers and other leaders on their arrest and urging that every possible effort should be made to publish and circulate the Ulemas *fatwa* by public and private sale of printed copies, by circulating hand-written copies, and by all other conceivable means; ignoring the Government order regarding its proscription. It also resolved to dissuade Muhammadans from joining the Army and to persuade those already in it to resign.

100. **C. K. C. Meeting, Bombay, October 1921.**—A meeting of the Central Khilafat Committee was held at Bombay on the 9th and 10th of October at which it was resolved that a crore of rupees should be collected and made over to Angora as a gift. At the same time it was reported that Abul Kalam Azad had stated that the subject of propaganda in the Army had been discussed at Gandhi's residence where it was decided that the time had not come to call out the sepoys (who would not be paid from Khilafat funds if they resigned), and consequently action should be confined to the repetition of the Karachi resolutions. At this period Khilafat activity was flourishing and at Bombay bonfires were made of European cloth, and the boycott of the visit of H. R. H. the Prince of Wales was freely discussed. This boycott led to serious rioting in Bombay when His Royal Highness arrived there the following month.

101. **Provincial Khilafat Committee Meeting, Agra, October 1921.**—Abul Kalam Azad, when presiding over a meeting of the United Provinces Khilafat Committee at Agra on the 25th and 26th of October, said that Hindu-Muslim unity was not only a political necessity but also a religious injunction of the Quran. The following were among the resolutions passed:—

(1) That the Government of India was not the true representative of the people and its policy had always been to enslave India and not to defend its frontier.

(2) That a free India would be in no danger from neighbouring or other independent States and therefore the meeting was not in favour of any treaties repugnant to the interests of the country.

(3) That negotiations with neighbouring powers by the Government of India were meant to improve the latter's position and the meeting hoped that neighbouring powers would not conclude further treaties with the British and assured Muslim Powers that after the attainment of Swaraj, the foreign policy of India would naturally be to safeguard the religious rights of Islam.

(4) That Muhammadans should boycott the visit of the Prince of Wales.

(5) That foreign cloth should be boycotted.

(6) That the Central Khilafat Committee should engage in propaganda outside India and inform the world of the high-handedness of the British Government in religious matters.

102. **Jamiat-ul-Ulema Conference, Lahore, November 1921.**—Abul Kalam Azad also presided over the Jamiat-ul-Ulema-i-Hind Conference at Lahore on the 18th-20th of November and the following were among the resolutions passed by the Subjects Committee:

(1) Confirming the resolution passed at Delhi on the 21st of September relative to the proscription of the *fatwa* of the Ulema-i-Hind and inviting all Muslims to perform their duties and to propagate and proclaim this commandment of the Shariat;

(2) Declaring that the efforts to liberate India from the domination and aggression of the present Government fell within the scope of religious duties, and that it was essential that Muslims should be at perfect liberty and completely independent with respect to their religious life and that no force or power should be a hinderance or restraint in the declaration and propagation of Islamic commandments, either social or penal;

(3) Acknowledging that Muslims can and will achieve liberty and freedom in conjunction with different Indian communities subject to the provisions of the Islamic law and religion;

(4) Declaring that service in the Police and the Army of the British Government was *haram* since the Army was and could be employed in the destruction of Islamic governments, in the murder of Muslims and in the suppression of the rights and privileges of humanity and justice;

(5) Recommending the appointment of a deputation which would travel throughout India to propagate the ideals of the Khilafate and Islam, to collect funds for Kemal Pasha and to appoint *Dar-ul-Quzas*.

103. **Jamiat-ul-Ulema Meeting, Budaun, December 1921.**—The Jamiat-ul-Ulema assembled again at Budaun on the 10th and 11th of December and confidential information was received to the effect that this meeting had been convened by Abdul Majid with the object of consolidating the position of Muhammadans in the event of a Hindu combine against them after the attainment of Swaraj. He therefore wished to arrange for the appointment of an Amir-i-Shariat, who would possess quasi-Papal powers and would be at the head of the Indian Maulvis but would be governed by a definite constitution. The number of Maulvis who attended this meeting was, however, insufficient to appoint an Amir-i-Shariat, and the Conference confined itself to appeals for funds in aid of Angora and to urging the election of Qazis in every district and the establishment of subordinate courts in villages.

The Karachi resolution was reiterated at an Ulema's conference held at Raipur on the 20th and 21st December at which copies of the *Mutafiqa fatwa* were distributed and appeals made for subscription to the Angora Fund.

104. **All-India Khilafat Conference Ahmedabad, X'mas 1921.**—The resolutions passed at an All-India Khilafat Conference and at a session of the All-India Muslim League at Ahmedabad during X'mas week were very similar. Hakim Ajmal Khan of Delhi was president of the Khilafat Conference while the ex-convict Fazl-ul-Hassan Hasrat Mohani presided over the meeting of the Muslim League. The Subjects Committee of the former passed a resolution to declare " independence without foreign control ", but a somewhat similar resolution was thrown out by the Subjects Committee of the Muslim League, while the resolution was also ruled out of order at the Khilafat Conference by the President. For this act Hakim Ajmal Khan was subjected to such bitter criticism that he left the Pandal.

At this Conference the most important resolutions passed were the following:—

(*a*) " As the British Government is not prepared to do justice over the Khilafat and Jazirat-ul-Arab questions in spite of all efforts of Indians that are humanly possible, but on the other hand is carrying on its intrigues in order to destroy the prestige of the Khilafate, and whereas the repression under cover of so-called law and justice is growing more day by day and the peaceful Volunteer Corps have been declared unlawful in order to stop the Khilafat movement by unlawful means, and whereas the best representatives of the nation and even the respected Ulemas are being imprisoned and public and private meetings are forcibly stopped and whereas the question of religious freedom has no respect in the eye of the Government as is apparent from the Karachi resolution and practical experience shows that the method of demanding and safeguarding rights adopted by the Khilafat Committee is right and it is necessary to go further under the present circumstances, this Conference, therefore, calls upon all the Muslims of and above the age of 18 to forthwith join the Khilafat Volunteer Corps and to carry on the proposed duties pertaining to religion and country conjointly with the National Volunteer Corps and prepare themselves for going to jail and to suffer other punishments.

(*b*) " For the success of the Khilafat cause and to obtain Swaraj and justice for the Punjab the Central Khilafat Committee will issue instructions from time to time regarding civil disobedience. Instructions to hold public and private meetings in contravention of orders prohibiting them should be issued to begin civil disobedience simultaneously if the Provincial or Central Khilafat Committees are satisfied that there will be no likelihood of breach of peace."

Resolutions were also passed urging Muhammadans to collect funds for Angora, congratulating the Ali Brothers on their imprisonment and Kemal Pasha on his successes, and expressing allegiance to the Khalifa.

In speeches made at this meeting Muhammadans were called upon to prepare to resort to civil disobedience in conjunction with the Congress, and united action with the Congress had very strong supporters in Hakim Ajmal Khan and Dr. Ansari.

105. **Hasrat Mohani's Presidential Speech.**—In his presidential address to the Muslim League, Hasrat Mohani admitted that the League had done nothing independently as a Muslim political organisation for some years, as the attention of the Mussalmans had been devoted to the Khilafat question which had been taken up by the Central Khilafat Committee. He suggested a change in the constitution of the League to permit the enrolment and election of members on the lines of the Congress in order to make the institution more representative and efficient in the future. Should a new compact between the League and the Congress come into existence the latter should not arrive at an understanding regarding Swaraj so long as the Khilafat question remained unsettled. Without complete independence the Khilafat question could not be settled. In case of complete independence the apprehensions that the Hindu majority will predominate or that the Mussalmans will join a foreign Muslim invader will disappear by having a republic on the lines of the United States of America. The majority of Mussalmans in the Punjab, Bengal and Assam will equalise the majority of Hindus in Madras, U. P. and Bombay. He dwelt at length on the necessity of declaring independence and urged the audience to ask Mahatma Gandhi, who was present there, to do this with effect from 1st January 1922.

As regards non-violence he said that should Martial Law be declared there would be only two alternatives left, either to give up the programme or to face bullets. In the latter event violence was the natural and religious course to adopt in self-defence and they would have to resort to guerilla warfare.

As regards the Khilafat question he said Mussalmans would not be satisfied until the Turks had regained Smyrna and Thrace, the freedom of the Straits, complete control of Constantinople and finances, the suzerainty of the Khalifa over the Jazirat-ul-Arab comprising Mesopotamia, Palestine and Syria and the right to maintain an Army. The British mandate with respect to Muslim countries should be withdrawn and the inhabitants should be left free to do anything they like as regards their future connection with Turkey.

It was at the session of the All-India National Congress, which was held at the same time and place, that the volunteer pledge was altered so as to set a time-limit on the policy of non-violence.* Gandhi explained that it was entirely in deference to the wishes of Shaukat Ali that the pledge was changed so as to make volunteers declare their belief " that as India is circumstanced, non-violence alone can help "

A chronological account of the chief activities of the Khilafat agitators during 1921 has been given above and it is now necessary to consider the effects of their efforts. There can be little doubt that but for Gandhi's advocacy of peaceful methods, outbreaks of violence by fanatical Muhammadans would have been much more common than they were, for the Khilafat leaders themselves were by no means peacefully inclined. As it was, several instances of violence occurred as the result of Khilafat agitation, by far the most serious being, of course, the Moplah rebellion which has been dealt with already.

For the rest it is exceedingly difficult to distinguish at this period between the fruits of the Non-co-operation and Khilafat agitations, and since the common effect of these has been the subject of Chapter III of the History of the Non-co-operation Movement, it is necessary here to touch only upon the direct results of the Khilafat Movement.

106. **National University, Aligarh.**—In pursuance of the scheme of Non-co-operation the Ali Brothers tried, in January 1920, to induce the Trustees of the Muhammadan Anglo-Oriental College, Aligarh, to give up the Government grant-in-aid and to sever connection with Government. Failing in this, a rival institution, called the National Muslim University, was set up near the old College with the object of weaning away students from the latter. Hakim Ajmal Khan of Delhi and Haji Musa Khan of Aligarh were elected President and Secretary respectively of a Foundation Committee, and Ulemas were appointed to prepare a new curriculum, with theology as a compulsory subject. Muhammad Ali was appointed to be the first Principal, but as his attention was chiefly devoted to carrying on the Khilafat agitation, he relinquished this post and was replaced by Abdul Majid Khawaja, Barrister-at-Law, Aligarh Towards the end of 1920, it

*Part I, paragraph 54.

was reported that English games were considered *haram* and that the students (who numbered about 130) were drilling regularly. Students from the National University attended the Nagpur Congress in December 1920, and, early in the following year, it was learnt that some of them were in communication with Indians in the Harbiya College in Kabul. It was reported that students were being sent out for propaganda purposes and those coming from the North-West Frontier Province had been selected to go to Afghanistan—there to get into touch with the different anti-British elements. By the middle of May, students had been distributed for propaganda in the various provinces in India in the following numbers:—22 to the Punjab, 17 to Bombay, 16 to the N.-W. F. Provinces, 14 to the United Provinces, 11 to Oudh, 7 each to Bihar, Madras, Central Provinces and Sind, and 1 to Delhi.

In July it was announced that the University would affiliate National Schools in every province in India.

In October there were only 62 students in the University and the Principal pressed the Central Khilafat Committee for financial aid. He stated that in accordance with Gandhi's proposal, a factory for hand-spinning and weaving had been started in the University and that cheap *khaddar* would shortly be available for sale. He also said that 200 students were engaged in propaganda work, and he concluded by remarking that the College was in debt to the extent of Rs. 6,000.

107. **Collection of Funds.**—It is difficult to arrive at an accurate estimate of the funds collected and utilised for Khilafat agitation. From some records of the Central Khilafat Committee seized in a search in November it appeared that a balance of five lakhs of rupees was in hand, but it was believed that the method of keeping the accounts left much to be desired. There had been numerous complaints of misappropriation of funds and, as an interesting example of the way these complaints were met, the following extract from a Central Khilafat Committee leaflet published in June is cited:—

> "Some people complain that their contributions never reach Smyrna, but from the religious point of view the donor has done his duty as soon as he has made his contribution, and he will acquire merit with God whether the money reaches its proper destination or not."

Contributions were also received from Muhammadans in various parts of the world such as South Africa and Madagascar, and one donation from Johannesburg amounted to £1,700. According to a press report H. E. H. the Nizam of Hyderabad also contributed towards the Smyrna Fund, and it is believed that at the instance of Hakim Ajmal Khan of Delhi some other Ruling Princes also subscribed on condition that their names were not published. Early in the year, Mr. Chotani had issued an appeal for £50,000 for relief of distress in Smyrna, and £10,000 were reported to have been sent during March and April. In June the Central Khilafat Committee had sent £8,000 for relief of distress in Turkey, and in the following month the

" Tribune " stated that in all £25,000 and 5,000 blankets had been sent from India for Turkish relief.

Various methods were devised to collect funds from the masses and one of the most pernicious of these was the issue of Khilafat notes of various denominations which purported to be repayable when Swaraj was attained. These notes and others like them were freely used by unscrupulous persons to swindle the ignorant.

108. **Khilafat Volunteers.**—The call for Khilafat volunteers met with considerable response during 1921 and a regular volunteer corps was formed in the United Provinces early in that year, followed by similar organisations in other parts of the country. It is impossible to give any accurate figures as to the number of these volunteers, but 5,000 at one time were said to have existed in the United Provinces where recruitment seems to have been more successful than elsewhere. The volunteers recruited were almost invariably low-class individuals who, in several places, were equipped with uniforms. On occasions they were drilled and they were in evidence with drawn swords at meetings in Saharanpur. Proposals were also made to recruit volunteers for Angora to fight for Kemal Pasha's Army, and in September some 25 were enrolled for this purpose at Dacca, in Eastern Bengal, and were drilled regularly.

Ostensibly Khilafat volunteers were warned to be non-violent, but these warnings were often qualified with references to the success of violent revolution in other countries. For example, in April, Muhammad Ali, while addressing the Madras Presidency Volunteer Corps, after urging the necessity of passive methods, referred to the success achieved by the Irish people in their struggle for independence which, he said, was due to the splendid organisation of the Irish Volunteer Corps. Shortly afterwards a very large crowd of Khilafatists obstructed the Police search of the Khilafat Committee Office in Madras with the result that the search had to be postponed, and subsequently was conducted under the protection of armed police. At the end of the year Muhammadan volunteers in Madras were apparently aspiring to usurp the functions of the Police, for it was proposed to divide the City into areas, similar to Police divisions, each with its own staff of volunteers.

As mentioned in Part I, Chapter III, volunteer associations and political meetings were declared illegal in most parts of India during the latter part of 1921, and these orders were frequently disobeyed both by the Non-co-operators and the Khilafatists. The latter also often evaded the law by raising political issues at mosques or at meetings ostensibly assembled for religious purposes.

Demonstrations by Khilafat volunteers led to violence in many parts of the country, but it is difficult generally to distinguish between their activities and responsibilities and those of the Non-co-operation volunteers. It is sufficient to say that during the year 1921 the

Khilafat and the Non-co-operation Movements reached their zeniths and the volunteer organisations of both flourished.

109. **The Muhammadan masses affected.**—In many parts of India the masses were deeply effected, with the result that they constantly came into conflict with the authorities. Moderate Muhammadan opinion, while refusing to be entirely carried away by the agitation, undoubtedly felt deeply the troubles of the Khalifa and, in an article written from Paris on the 8th of November, His Highness the Aga Khan, whose loyalty is unquestioned, wrote as follows:—

> "I urge that the least possible basis of a permanent settlement is to restore to Turkey immediately and fully her sovereign rights in Anatolia and Asia Minor. The next imperative necessity is that the Turks should receive back their capital of Constantinople. A matter of even greater importance and interest to all Muhammadans of all sects is that the Sultan Khalifa should be freed from the scarcely veiled bondage in which he is detained. The Turks must be given the opportunity of developing a free national State. This is the only possible solution of the problem. The dangers in the East will not be removed until the Turkish question is settled on the lines I have indicated and I would add that the unrest among the Mussalmans of India is likely to continue until justice is done."

CHAPTER V

The Agitation continues until Kemal Pasha deposes the Khalifa, 1922.

110. **Agitation flourishes.**—The year 1922 opened with Non-co-operation and Khilafat agitation flourishing all over India, and in many places both organisations were recruiting volunteers rapidly with the expressed intention of disobeying the orders promulgated by Local Governments declaring volunteer associations illegal. In addition, preparations were being made at several places, particularly at Bardoli, to indulge in mass civil disobedience, and the immediate resort to this was only postponed in order to see the outcome of the negotiations between political leaders and Government at the proposed Round Table Conference.*

111. **Manifesto regarding the Turkish Peace Terms.**—In addition to the enrolment of numerous volunteers, Muhammadans were being induced to become Khilafat members. Propagandists throughout the country were busy impressing upon them the necessity of a very strenuous effort in order to weight the scales in favour of Turkey, in the event of a re-adjustment of the control of lands in the Turkish sphere of influence consequent on the successful war being waged by Kemal Pasha against the Greeks in Asia Minor. Early in the year, a lengthy manifesto was published over the signatures of Chotani, Ajmal Khan, Ansari, Syed Mahmud and A. H. S. Khatri which summed up the terms which the signatories thought that the Allies were likely to force upon Turkey and defined the Muhammadan attitude as follows:—

> "It is now the duty of Indian Muslims to make their voices heard and to warn the Powers that only the complete acceptance of the Khilafat demands by the Nations of Europe will satisfy the Islamic people of Europe, Asia and Africa. Let not English, French, Italian or Greek statesmen imagine that they can deceive the world of Islam again as they have deceived us so often before. If they desire a peace of friendship with the world of Islam they must express their desire by genuine actions and not by mere high-sounding professions. For we fear that the spirit of exploitation of land-hunger, which in the last fifty years has moved Europe to despoil the Turkish Empire by open or secret means, by unjust wars of aggression or covert intrigues and secret agreements is not yet dead. We fear that England's change of heart is bred only of expediency. We fear that under cover of a sudden friendship for Turkey, England will seek to retain her hold over the Holy Places of the Faith hoping

*Part I, paragraphs 52 and 53.

that a display of generosity towards the Turks in the matter of the homelands of the Turkish nation will induce them and all the Islamic peoples to acquiesce in this. If such indeed is England's hope let her speedily be undeceived. The world of Islam has grown wise in adversity. We are no longer easily duped by specious pretences. Turkey and the Khalifa of Islam have too often been betrayed by European Powers for us to trust in their good faith to-day. Only by genuine actions can Europe again win the friendship of the Islamic world. The settlement with Turkey must include the release of the Jazirat-ul-Arab from all suggestion of control by a non-Muslim Power and the Khalifa's authority over the administrations of the Holy Places must be recognised. It must include the complete independence of the Khalifa in his own capital. It must include the granting to the Muslims of Syria, of Palestine, of Iraq, and of Egypt the common right of determination. No other statement will bring peace. These are the only terms on which Islam can with self-respect admit the Powers to friendship. If these terms are refused to-day they will be offered to-morrow, since Truth must prevail, and the Federation of the Islamic peoples of the world grows stronger every day. Let the recent speech of His Majesty the Amir of Afghanistan warn the Powers of Europe that in sympathy Islam is one and undivided as it is in the Faith. Muslims demand only freedom for Islam—freedom to develop the civilisation and the culture we know to be true and beautiful. This freedom is our God-given right and we can be content with nothing less. Islamic civilisation cannot develop and thrive if it is in bondage, even if the bonds are called Mandates.

"To the Muslims of India we workers then in the Khilafat cause, appeal that they show an unshaken front. Our Hindu brothers are with us in our struggle. Their numbers give us confidence in our strength and they are our brothers in all truth for the Holy Quran teaches that the friends of the Faith are our brothers. In all mankind it is only enemies of the Faith who are not brothers to true Muslims. Our Hindu brothers are doubly so for they love our country as we do, the country is their's as well as our's to love. And they suffer with us and for us in the common cause Indians have made to win freedom by non-violent Non-co-operation. Together we will win Swaraj—a Swaraj that will enable us to secure justice for Islam. Our enemies seek daily to divide us but let us not fear their intrigues. We have given final proof of our brotherhood in that the Muslims have loyally accepted the dictatorship of that great saint and thinker—Mahatma Gandhi—in our struggle for freedom. Hence forth Hindu-Muslim unity will prevail. We Muslims are called the Army of the Faithful the world over. At this crisis in the history of Islam let us merit the description. Let us remain the Faithful in thought, word and deed, faithful to our cause, to our country, to the leader we have chosen—Mahatma Gandhi. Though the Powers of Europe may seek to deceive us again in the matter of the Khilafat claims, let us have no doubt but that truth will prevail. Making our voice heard and our demands known, let us work loyally for freedom and Swaraj through non-violent Non-co-operation. Let us above all remain the Army of the Faithful, India's Muslims have achieved and suffered a great deal for the Faith. Perhaps they believe their suffering has been in vain. But the truth is that through suffering they have grown stronger far than formerly. And much more remains to be done—much more must be suffered—before we win complete victory—complete freedom for Islam and India. The immediate work before us is that we must—

(1) Collect fifty lakhs for the Angora Fund.

(2) Be prepared to fill the gaols of British India when our Dictator Mahatma Gandhi bids us.

(3) Preserve non-violence at all costs because success depends on this.

(4) Preserve inviolate the sacred spirit of Hindu-Muslim unity.

(5) And last but not least follow Mahatma Gandhi unflinchingly."

112. **Efforts to maintain enthusiasm.**—On these lines the agitation continued, and strenuous efforts were made to collect subscriptions for the Angora Fund in the course of which very objectionable speeches were made by agitators all over the country. The Allies were frequently falsely accused of having desecrated the Holy Places, and although H. E. the Viceroy and the Secretary of State for India sympathised with, and endeavoured to alleviate Muslim anxiety, yet they were not exempted from the objectionable criticism levelled at the British Government generally. Every word and action of a British official was misinterpreted and misrepresented, and the most outrageous allegations were made against Government servants. During this period Bi Amma, the mother of the Ali Brothers, came to notice, and it became fashionable to invite her to preside over Muhammadan meetings. At about the same time, according to the *Paisa Akhbar* of Lahore, placards

bearing the words, "Service in the Police and the Army is *haram*" were tied to the collars of stray dogs in that city. The proscribed *fatwa*, or copies differing from it but little, were discovered in various places and strenuous efforts were made to tamper with the military and the Police. The Police being scattered about all over the country, in isolated places, were, of course, very exposed to attack and, in a few instances, officers and men succumbed and tendered their resignations.

113. **Central Khilafat Committee meet at Bombay, January 1922.**—A meeting of the Central Khilafat Committee was held at Bombay on the 12th and 13th of January at which the following office-bearers for 1922 were elected:—

President and Treasurer—Seth Chotani.

Vice-Presidents—Hakim Ajmal Khan and Abul Kalam Azad.

Maulana Shaukat Ali, Mr. Yakub Khan and Dr. Kitchlew were re-elected Honorary Secretaries, but as they were in jail, Mr. Khatri, Dr. Ansari and Dr. Syed Mahmud were elected as additional Honorary Secretaries. A working committee consisting of the following members in addition to Mahatma Gandhi was formed:—

Maulana Hasrat Mohani, Maulana Abdul Majid of Budaun, Maulana Syed Sulaiman Nadvi, Maulana Azad Subhani and Seth Haji Abdullah Haroon.

The following resolutions were adopted:—

(1) "In view of the present situation, the working committee in addition to powers already vested in it regarding the supervision and management, is empowered to exercise in urgent cases all powers that are exercised by the Central Khilafat Committee in accordance with its constitution; and decisions of the Working Committee shall hold good until they are amended or altered by the Central Khilafat Committee. But by virtue of this resolution Working Committee shall not be entitled to change the aims and objects or means thereof of the Central Khilafat Committee or to make any settlement regarding the Khilafate, Jazirat-ul-Arab and the Holy Places of Islam without the sanction of the Central Khilafat Committee.

(2) This Committee, while expressing deep sympathy and Islamic brotherhood for their brethren of Egypt in their struggle for complete independence, declares that having regard to the principles put forward by European Powers, particularly England, before the world during the war, the inhabitants of Egypt are perfectly justified in their struggle for complete independence of their country; and that the British occupation of Egypt is the result

of the same unjust and aggressive policy as has been adopted by the British Government towards other Islamic countries. Further in view of the fact that Egypt is specially connected with the Middle East, complete preservation of Khilafate, Jazirat-ul-Arab and the Holy Places of Islam is impossible unless Egypt is free from non-Muslim control or influence and comes under full control of the people of Egypt. This Committee assures their brethren of Egypt that the Mussalmans of India fully sympathise within them in their struggle for complete independence.

114. **Abul Kalam Azad's views on the truce.**—In the following month, Abul Kalam Azad was convicted for making seditious speeches in Calcutta and was sentenced to a year's rigorous imprisonment. The *Amrita Bazar Patrika* at about the same time published a statement purporting to have been made by him, giving his views on the "terms of truce," the concluding portion of which reads as follows:—

"As regards the truce I am of opinion that unless the following terms are agreed upon no truce is possible:—

(1) Khilafat demands should be fulfilled by the Imperial Government or at least guaranteed. They are four in number:—

(a) English mandate and domination over Mesopotamia should cease to exist in the real sense, and should be left completely to the people themselves.

(b) Palestine also to be left to the Christians, Jews and Muslims of that territory who may settle terms of independence with the Turks.

(c) All restrictions should be removed from the Ottoman Government and its capital—Constantinople.

(d) Turkish rule should be recognised over Thrace, Smyrna and the whole of Asia Minor which the Turks have taken back and are still fighting for with the help of their sword.

(2) All the Khilafat and Swaraj prisoners should be unconditionally released.

(3) All the repressive laws introduced during the last two years should be abolished.

(4) A conference should sit to discuss Swaraj."

115 **Enthusiasm maintained.**—At this period excitement was particularly intense in the Presidencies of Madras, where it had probably

been stimulated by the Moplah rising, and Bombay, where Bardoli was being prepared for civil disobedience, while the rest of India was subjected to the most pernicious propaganda which was particularly virulent in Bengal. The most outrageous statements were made regarding the alleged desecration of the Holy Places, and the British were painted as a people without morals of any kind. Orders under section 144 C. P. C. served on agitators were ignored and the people were frequently urged to withhold the chaukidari tax. Agitators throughout India generally had very little regard for the truth, but in Bengal they appear to have had none at all, and the note of dissent to Non-co-operation which had in the past been sounded by moderate Muhammadans in that Province was completely stilled. The only vocal opposition to Non-co-operation on the part of Muhammadans came from Peshawar, where, in the middle of February, a meeting of the Anjuman-i-Ahmadia condemned it as being diametrically opposed to the Quran which insisted on loyalty to the government established by the law of the land.

116. **Funds.**—The immediate object of most of the meetings held at this period was the collection of funds with which to assist the Turks in Asia Minor. On the 1st of February the *Bombay Chronicle* published a statement of accounts of the Central Khilafat Committee, purporting to have been audited, which showed that the total receipts from all sources during the year 1920 amounted to Rs. 6,43,766-1-4 and the total expenditure under various heads to Rs. 4,73,688-5-8, leaving a balance of Rs. 1,70,077-11-8. During 1921, the total receipts were shown as amounting to Rs. 20,99,789-4-5 and the balance of the 31st of December 1921 as Rs. 9,28,480-3-2. The accounts also showed that Rs. 5,34,857-13-10 and Rs. 3,75,231-3-9 had been remitted to Smyrna and Angora respectively.

117. **The Bardoli Resolution February 1922.**—The agitation was everywhere flourishing when the massacre of the Police occurred at Chauri Chaura in February 1922. As a result of this outrage Gandhi, at Bardoli, decided to postpone mass civil disobedience.*

The Bardoli resolution, by taking the sting out of the Non-co-operation agitation, had of course an immediate effect on the Khilafat Movement which, as already shown, was dependent to a very great extent on Congress support. As was natural the leading Muhammadan extremists had been far less impressed by Gandhi's non-violent programme than were his co-religionists, and they had accepted it merely in order to attain the Hindu support which they considered was essential to the success of their agitation. When Gandhi and his Congress followers withdrew from their forward programme, their Muhammadan allies were extremely disappointed and almost immediately signs of Hindu-Muslim friction appeared, for the Muhammadan public began to realise that they had been utilised merely to further the Hindu aim

---

*Part I, paragraph 73 *et seq.*

of Swaraj for India,* and that their own grievances, including the Khilafat question, had been pushed into the background. This feeling was shared by their leaders, who, however, realised the necessity of concealing it in order to maintain at least a semblance of the much-desired Hindu-Muslim unity.

118. **All-India Khilafat Conference, Delhi, February 1922.**—The All-India Khilafat Conference which assembled at Delhi on the 25th and 26th of February 1922 under the presidency of Chotani, was faced with this situation and they attempted to solve the difficulty by passing the following resolutions:—

(1) To continue non-violent Non-co-operation which is the only right means in India for the attainment of Khilafat demands.

(2) To enlist volunteers and revise their lists, and to recruit one lakh of members for Khilafat purposes in three months.

(3) To advise Muhammadans to work under the Congress organisations in all matters concerning the politics of the country, and to fix the following lines of action for itself, so that resolutions such as that of Bardoli should have no effect on the Khilafat movement and also there should remain no danger of a split between Congress and Khilafat workers—thus keeping Hindu-Muhammadan unity intact:—

(i) Collection of Angora Fund.

(ii) Enlistment of Khilafat members.

(iii) Boycott of British goods.

(iv) To establish relations with the Muhammadans of other countries and to try to unite them.

(v) If possible, to revive *hijrat* after consulting Mustafa Kemal Pasha and after proper organisation and a full consideration of facilities and difficulties.

The leading Muhammadan extremists endeavoured to maintain the agitation and as an example of their propaganda at this time the following extract from the *Bombay Chronicle* dated the 4th of March regarding the subsidies paid by the British to the King of the Hedjaz and the Sultan of Nejd is quoted:—

"India's Muslims have no two opinions about the King of Hedjaz for certain obvious reasons and do not hold this gentleman in very great respect or esteem. The information that he has been receiving a salary of £25,000 will not enhance the Sharif's reputation nor will it bolster up the fiction of independent Muslim control of the Holy Places. India's Muslims are now virtually assured that the Sharif has virtually sold the independence of

*In the Punjab, at this time, a common joke wa that Swaraj meant Swah (ashes) for the Muhammadans and Raj for the Hin s

Muslim control over the Sacred Shrines for a total payment of £1,200,000. To the Christian capitalist's view the price is doubtless a high one. To the Muslim view it is ridiculously low to tempt a Muslim. All the wealth in the world could not buy the independence of Islam (of which independence Islamic control over Sacred Shrines is a symbol) from a good Muslim. The King of the Hedjaz to-day is no more independent than a Muslim Nawab in India."

119. **Ulemas Conference, Ajmere, March 1922.**—On the 5th of March an Ulemas Conference assembled at Ajmere at which Abdul Bari made a violent speech which excited the audience, but the resolutions passed by the Conference were in favour of non-violence and supported the resolutions passed by the meeting of the All-India Congress Committee at Delhi confirming the Bardoli resolution. Subsequently it was reported that Gandhi had visited Ajmere with the object of censuring Abdul Bari for his speech, the effect of which the latter then watered down by issuing the following manifesto which was reproduced in the *Tribune* on the 12th of March:—

"I had agreed with Mahatma Gandhi that until I become hopeless of the success of the non-violent Non-co-operation movement, I would not do anything against it openly or secretly. Proceedings of the Bardoli and Delhi meetings had depressed me and I said so in my speeches. I have now met Gandhiji and he has fully satisfied me that further efforts on our part can make the movement a success. Under these circumstances it is the duty of the public strictly to abstain from violence in every shape or form. I am determined to continue preaching non-violence, so long as I am convinced of success of the pacific movement, as I have already made it quite clear in my speeches."

Another example of the nature of the propaganda then employed by Khilafat agitators is given in the following extract of a speech made by a Wahabi at Dinajpur in Bengal in which he said:—

"The people of India are being treated like bullocks by the English and are being laid with yokes on their shoulders. Now, if the yoke be thrown off and a rush made at the white-skin dogs, they would be done for. Even pricking with needles by thirty crores of Hindus and Muhammadans would make it impossible for the British to stay in India, so I would advise the people of India to wake up."

120. **Effects of the Bardoli resolutions on the Khilafat Movement.**—Although there was no immediate cessation of the efforts of Khilafat agitators subsequent to the Bardoli resolutions, yet the reaction which

had taken place in the Non-co-operation campaign had the effect of damping enthusiasm for the Khilafat cause. In spite of efforts to suppress it, indications of Hindu-Muslim friction were increasingly visible, and the *Civil and Military Gazette* in the middle of March published a telegram received from Calcutta, purporting to set out Hasrat Mohani's grievances against Mr. Gandhi. It enquired why Gandhi himself had not been arrested, and claimed that, although the proportion of Hindus to Muhammadans in India was four to one, yet ninety-five per cent. of those who had gone to jail in connection with the agitation were Muhammadans. Hasrat Mohani afterwards repudiated this statement and his confrères endeavoured to ease the situation, but they were torn between the desire to denounce Gandhi for letting them down and the anxiety to retain Hindu support. A letter published in the *Leader* in the middle of March by Kidwai is quoted as showing how they expressed themselves:—

> "It is a great pity that most of the Indian Muslims notwithstanding their remarkable after-war sacrifice and enthusiasm for the cause, have yet failed to understand the full import of the Khilafat question. The key to the question is that it is an international question first and foremost, and, being, Islamic, can in no case be confined within the Himalayan boundaries. It cannot be surprising if Mr. Gandhi and other Hindu leaders fail to understand the international significance of Islam, but it seems that many Muslim followers of Mr. Gandhi have also lost sight of the special characteristic of Islam and closed their eyes to the ever-changing European influences which, and which alone, have thrust this question upon us and which we can never ignore.

> "It is the duty of the Indian Muslims to have a well-organised and powerful delegation of statesmen in Europe to watch all the European moves against Islam and the Khilafate. It was fortunate that the greatest living statesman of India was in Europe and I say once more from personal knowledge that the Aga Khan has done more for the Turkish cause than any other Indian Muslim. The Angora Turks and the Constantinople Turks both recognise this fact. But the Indian Muslims as a body have failed to strengthen the hands of His Highness and now it so happens that he also is in India although continuing his most valuable services to the cause. Now the Khilafat question has once more come to a head. The Foreign Minister for Angora as well as Izzat Pasha from Constantinople have come to France, Indian Muslims should lose no time in sending at least four men as their representatives. These four men should be H. H. the Aga Khan, Seth Chotani, Mr. Moazam Ali as the Secretary and Mr. Jinnah as the spokesman of the delegation.

Even if the delegation can serve no other purpose it can act as a liaison between the Turks and the Indians and between the two parties of the Turks themselves. It so happens that the Palestine delegation is also in Europe and needs help and advice from Indian Muslims.

"I cannot but help reminding Mr. Gandhi that his programme of removing untouchability or picketing liquor shops or boycotting Councils and Universities or even of wearing nothing but khaddar cannot have the slightest effect on the Khilafat question. The idea of converting all Indian Muslims to Jainist beliefs may be a very good method of solving the Khilafat question for India, but fortunately for Islam it is not practicable.

"As an old Indian 'Nationalist' of the 'extreme' wing I can say this without being misunderstood that the most urgent question for India to-day is the Khilafat question. That is the *danger point* and Hindus and Muslims should both unitedly attend to the solution of that question first and when a calm atmosphere is obtained Indians of different shades of political and religious views should meet in a conference to draw up a constructive and definite scheme for Swaraj.

"If the goal of Indians is really what was put forward by the Ahmedabad Congress then it should be attained by constitutional methods."

121. **Manifesto by Ajmal Khan and Ansari.**—The *Bombay Chronicle* dated the 20th March published a manifesto issued by Hakim Ajmal Khan and Dr. Ansari mentioning the demands of the Indian Mussalmans, which fell under the following heads:—

(1) The Turkish portion of the Ottoman Empire, comprising Thrace, with Adrianople, Constantinople and the whole of Anatolia, including Smyrna, should be restored to Turkey, with full sovereign rights without any financial, economic, military or naval control, and without the capitulations.

(2) The Arabic-speaking portions of the Ottoman Empire comprising Palestine, Syria, Mesopotamia and Hedjaz, should be given full independence without any non-Muslim control, provided that the suzerainty of the Sultan is maintained over the Holy Places of Islam.

The message stated that these demands represented the irreducible minimum, based on the religious commandments of Islam:—

"The Government of India have only aimed at a partial fulfilment of our demands. It must, therefore, be made clear that we will go on with our efforts unabated, until we have achieved the irreducible minimum. But let us hope that the justice of our cause may still convince the British representatives of the righteousness of our claims as it has already done in the case of France and Italy."

122. **The views of the C. K. C.**—The *Bombay Chronicle* dated the 21st March published the following statement issued by the Central Khilafat Committee of India:—

"While endorsing fully the statement issued by our brothers Hakim Ajmal Khan and Dr. Ansari regarding the irreducible minimum of Indian Muslims' demands in respect of the Khilafate, we would briefly emphasise the following considerations:—

(1) The independence of the region known as the Jazirat-ul-Arab must be complete without the least semblance of suspicion of non-Muslim control. Thus mandates, protectorates, and garrisons to guard non-Muslim interests are ruled out. Nor must the Muslim rulers of this territory be in receipt of subsidies in any shape or form if these entail territorial or other obligations to the payers of the subsidies, which obligations conflict with a State's complete independence. Further, the independent Muslim authorities in this region must acknowledge the Sultan-Khalifa as their temporal and spiritual overlord, as is obligatory on all Muslim rulers.

(2) Thrace and Smyrna, being homelands of the Turkish people, must be restored unconditionally to the Turks. No species or semblance of financial, territorial or military control by the Allies or any single non-Turk Power can be acquiesced in by Indian Muslims. Turkey must be an *independent* nation and not another Egypt.

(3) It follows from the above that the Straits must remain a Turkish region and independent. Without this the Sultan-Khalifa cannot be considered an independent sovereign and his people cannot remain secure from fear of attack.

(4) Constantinople and Adrianople must be evacuated before the Turks are asked to sign a new peace treaty. Any treaty signed while troops garrison these towns must be suspected by Muslims, since Muslim suspicions are now growing that Britain desires to retain permanently her commanding and ruling position in Constantinople the Straits Area, Irak, etc."

These statements of the conditions required to satisfy Indian Muslims and such agitation as occurred at this period were called forth by the necessity of keeping up the pressure during the Near East Conference which assembled at Paris in March 1922, where the revision of the Turkish peace terms, in the light of the result of the hostilities between Kemal Pasha and the Greeks, came up for discussion.

123. **Post Bardoli Activities.**—After the Bardoli resolutions there was very little volunteer activity, but it had not entirely ceased. For example, at Ludhiana Muhammadan volunteers re-introduced the picketing of liquor shops and Muhammadan volunteers were very active on the 6th of March in Peshawar on the occasion of the visit to that city by H. R. H. the Prince of Wales. By vigorous picketing they managed to effect a complete *hartal* and prospective spectators were driven away, aggressive insults were offered to military and civil pensioners and several acts of hooliganism occurred. Both in Peshawar and Kohat at about this time brothels were also picketted and intending visitors were rigidly excluded.

Apart from these manifestations, however, Indian Muhammadans awaited the result of the Near East Conference, and extremist leaders began to fear that their agitation would die out if Kemal Pasha accepted the proposals made to him. This fear was apparent in a joint letter issued at this time by the Secretaries of the Bengal Provincial Congress and Khilafat Committees to their subordinate bodies, from which the following is quoted:—

> "We wish to make it abundantly clear that Khilafate is unattainable without Swaraj and that Swaraj without Khilafate would be weak, inglorious and transient. We wish to point out that the problem of the Khilafate cannot be solved without the deliverance of the Jazirat-ul-Arab from non-Muslim control and if Mustapha Kemal is compelled to accept a treaty which abandons Jazirat-ul-Arab, our struggle for religious freedom will still continue and Khilafate can then alone be saved by the attainment of Swaraj."

124. **Central Khilafat Working Committee meet—Bombay, March 1922.**—The Central Khilafat Working Committee met at Bombay on the 26th and 27th of March 1922, under the presidency of Chotani, and Maulana Abdul Majid was elected vice-president of the Central Khilafat Committee in the place of Abdul Kalam Azad,* while Mr. Moazzam Ali was appointed Secretary *vice* Dr. Mahmud who had also been arrested. The following resolutions were passed:—

(1) Eulogising the services of Mr. Gandhi and congratulating the people of India on the perfect peace and order preserved after Mr. Gandhi's arrest, and expressing gratification "that this atmosphere of perfect calmness clearly shows that the whole country has not only carried out Mahatmaji's wishes, but has also brought nearer the goal of success by acting upon the programme of non-violence."

*In jail, *vide* paragraph 114.

(2) Appreciating the valuable services of Dr. Mahmud, congratulating him on his arrest and emphatically declaring that in spite of the arrest and incarceration of five secretaries of the Central Khilafat Committee, one after another, the "Committee and the Indian Mussalmans are fully determined to continue their struggle with accelerated speed for the honour and integrity of the Khilafate and the Jazirat-ul-Arab."

(3) "This meeting considers the circumstances which have compelled Mr. Montagu to resign, owing to his having openly helped the Khilafat cause, as a clear proof of the hostile attitude of the British Cabinet towards the Khilafate and emphatically declares that not only the British Cabinet has utterly disregarded the solemn deliberate pledges made to the Indian Mussalmans during the war regarding the Khilafate and the Holy Places of Islam, but also the attitude of the Prime Minister and the statement of Lord Curzon have proved that the British Cabinet is not prepared to pay any heed with the least sense of justice and fair play, even to those imperfect demands of the Indian Mussalmans regarding the Khilafate and the Holy Places which have been placed by the Government of India and Mr. Montagu, and therefore, the British Cabinet is solely responsible for any disastrous consequences that are likely to arise * * * "

(4) "Khilafat Committees and Khilafat workers should carry out the constructive programme of Non-co-operation vigorously so that the following items of the programme be complete by the 31st May 1922, and the hands of the Central Khilafat Committee be strengthened to advance the steps and adopt further measures for the success of the movement:—

(*a*) To enlist at least one crore of Khilafat members and organise Khilafat Committees in all the towns and villages throughout the country.

(*b*) To preach and popularise the use of Khaddar and boycott of all foreign cloth.

(*c*) To revise and organise Khilafat Volunteers Corps so that only those people may be enrolled as volunteers who believe in the programme of non-violent Non-co-operation in word and deed and follow the principles of Shariat in practice.

(*d*) To introduce religious and national education independent of Government control.

(*e*) To induce the Mussalmans to settle their litigation in accordance with the commandments of Shariat and to make arrangements for that.

(*f*) For the success of the Khilafat cause to devise all legitimate means for promoting unity among Hindus, Sikhs, Parsees and other nationalities of India for the attainment of Swaraj.

(*g*) All Provincial Khilafat Committees should be instructed to send in their weekly or monthly reports regularly on the above to the Central Khilafat Office, Bombay."

125. **The Near East Conference.**—In spite of the efforts of their leaders, the mass of Indian Muhammadans declined to respond to agitation until they had heard the result of the Near East Conference. As already indicated, it was the fixed determination of extremist leaders of all denominations to endeavour to maintain the agitation irrespective of any concessions which might be granted to the Turks. When therefore the result of the Conference was published, although it greatly mitigated the Turkish Peace Terms ratified at Sevres, it was at once denounced as inadequate. The Central Khilafat Committee protested against the clauses of the Near East proposals as being at direct variance with Muslim religious aspirations, with the British Premier's pledge to Indian Muslims, and with the promise made by the Allies during the War. The same attitude was taken up by the Congress leaders, and the *Hindu* on the 31st of March published the following summary:—

"(1) The demilitarization of the Straits zone threatens the national security of Turkey leaving her open to attack by any future enemy.

(2) Gallipoli and Thrace including Adrianople are predominantly Muslim in population and ownership of soil, and Greece has no vestige of claim to consideration as regards the possession of this territory. In the case of Gallipoli its assignment to the Greeks, which is absolutely inadmissible and incompatible with benevolent designs towards Turkey is regarded by all Muslims as a direct menace to the safety of the Turkish capital and the seat of Khilafate and a seed of future wars. The City of Adrianople possesses many Muslim shrines held in great veneration by Muslims all over the world and Greece has no claim to its possession. Historically the city is Turkish and is moreover, a frontier city, the possession of which by the Greeks will allow them to threaten the security of Constantinople and the Turkish Empire, similarly in the case of Smyrna the semi-internationalisation of this port and city threatens the safety of the whole of Turkish Asia Minor. Muslims cannot allow the possibility of the tragedy of bombardment of Alexandria being repeated in Smyrna. The internationalisation of Smyrna and the assignment of Adrianople to Greece can only be regarded as needlessly affording opportunities for further successful aggression against Turkey on the part

of her enemies. Smyrna is a Muslim City, there are many Islamic associations and shrines here also, while the special regime provided for the port by the Near East Conference proposals fetters Turkish independence in the matter of the control of customs and trade passing through the greatest mart in Asia Minor and one of the cheap ports of the Ottoman Empire. The internationalisation of Smyrna would gratuitously sow the seed of future invasion of Asia Minor and endanger the safety of Turkey in Asia and the Ottoman State.

(3) The suggested ratification of the capitulations imposed by the Sevres Treaty cripples and enslaves Turkey financially and conflicts with the conception of Turkey as an Independent State.

(4) The specific restoration of the legal rights of the Khilafate of Muslims over the Holy Places, pledged by England to the Muslim world, is ignored. Religious obligations compel Muslims to insist on this point.

(5) The freedom of Jazirat-ul-Arab, namely, Syria, Irak, Mesopotamia, Palestine and Arabia from non-Muslim domination and control is likewise not provided for in accordance with England's pledges to the Islamic world. This is a religious obligation on which there can be no compromise.

(6) Proposals referred to in items, 1, 2, 3 and 4 above are in direct variance with the British Premier's historic pledge of January 1918 given to the Muslims of India and the world regarding complete independence of Turkish homelands.

Thus the demilitarization of the Straits zone constitutes a standing menace to the Turkish capital and nation . * * * * "

Inspite of the efforts of the leaders, however, India remained comparatively peaceful at this period as was usual during the fast in the month of Ramzan which coincided with May, in 1922.

126. **Working Body of the C. K. C. meet at Bombay, May 1922.**— In May 1922, Hasrat Mohani was arrested and again convicted for sedition, and was sentenced to two years' rigorous imprisonment for violent speeches made at the time of the Ahmedabad Congress.*

The Working Body of the Central Khilafat Committee met at Bombay on the 14th of May and elected Pandit Motilal Nehru as a member in the place of Hasrat Mohani, and resolved to deduct ten per cent. from all subscriptions collected for Angora and Smyrna to meet Khilafat expenses in India. Mr. Chotani, as president of the Central Khilafat Committee, issued a statement to the press saying that the Muslims of India viewed with alarm what appeared to be

*Part I, paragraph 54.

an attempt on the part of the British Cabinet and Government to prejudice the Near East settlement in favour of the Greeks. He added that in order to secure a real enquiry tending to a reconciliation between the East and West, the Imperial Government should—

(1) Authorise immediately the publication of the report of the Inter-Allied Commission of Inquiry into Greek atrocities in Smyrna.

(2) Set the deep suspicion of the Muslims at rest by a convincing refutation of the charges of phil-hellenism brought against it by Mr. Montagu.

(3) Appoint Muslim delegates in equal number with the Christian representations on the Commission of Inquiry.

(4) Appoint a delegate or delegates chosen by the Central Khilafat Committee to represent the Indian public (not the Government of India) at the Inquiry.

(5) Give definite pledges to the Kemalists and to the world of Islam that the Inquiry is not made with the purpose of spying out the Kemalists' strength and position.

(6) Extend the scope of the Inquiry as demanded by France and members of the British Parliament to include atrocities committed by the Greeks on Muslims in Turkish territory.

(7) Forbid the negotiation by Greeks of a loan in Britain until the Inquiry is concluded and further, until a Near East settlement has been arrived at and agreed to by the Turks and the Greeks.

He went on to say that only on these conditions being fulfilled would Muslims cease to suspect the British Government of assisting the Greeks in their criminal designs on Muslim territory, life and property, and he added that if the British Government were disposed to do justice to Turkey and to conciliate Islam they should first reveal the truth about the Grecian outrages in Asia Minor before proceeding to enquire into allegations against the Turks. At this time allegations and counter-allegations of atrocities in the war area in the Near East were common and in May the Council of the All-India Muslim League protested against an announcement made by Mr. Chamberlain in Parliament, regarding a change of attitude towards Angora in consequence of the massacre and deportation of Greeks. The Council expressed alarm at the propaganda surreptitiously carried on in the interests of Greece and warned Government that the encouragement of this propaganda would be detrimental to the interests of the Empire of which Muhammadans form such a large proportion. The Council also accused Government of deliberately suppressing the publication of official reports regarding atrocities by the Greeks in Asia Minor and added that if the British Government continued to proceed in this suicidal policy a joint special session of the Muslim League and Khilafat Conference should be held to consider the situation.

127. **Joint Committee Meeting, Lucknow, June 1922.**—In the middle of 1922 the question of the revival of civil disobedience was prominent in extremist circles and this led to the appointment of the Civil Disobedience Enquiry Committee.* A joint meeting of the Working Committees of the Jamiat-ul-Ulema and the Central Khilafat Committee was held in Lucknow on the 5th of June at which the following resolutions were passed:—

(1) That a general meeting of the Congress, Khilafat and the Jamiat-ul-Ulema should determine the question of the right of private defence of personal honour and faith in the light of the principle of non-violence, as a retaliatory measure in the event of attack by Government on religion, life and honour of individuals working for the national cause.

(2) That a Committee be appointed, which, with a view to the boycott of British goods and British business, should report as to what British goods should be boycotted in addition to piece-goods, and what means could be adopted to injure British trade and business.

(3) This Committee should also consider the question of effective boycott of British manufacture and British capitalism in other eastern countries besides India.

(4) This Committee should also consider the question of establishing trade and economic relations with eastern countries.

(5) The joint meeting of the Working Committees of the Jamiat-ul-Ulema and the Khilafat expressed its opinion about the question of Swaraj that, in view of the real benefit and in obedience to the opinion of the country and nation, it is essential that it should be defined in one manner only, *i.e.* complete independence, and recommended to the Indian National Congress to consider it in this light and to fix complete independence as the real meaning of Swaraj as soon as possible.

(6) That the question of high prices of foodstuffs be considered and measures be adopted to reduce the prices.

At about the same time Mr. V. J. Patel was elected as a member of the Central Khilafat Committee *vice* Gandhi who had been arrested and convicted in March.†

128. **C. K. C. meet at Lucknow, June 1922.**—The Central Khilafat Committee met at Lucknow on the 7th, 8th and 9th of June and the question of retaliation to acts of oppression on the part of Government were considered. The majority of the members present appeared to be in favour of permitting retaliation in all cases, but ultimately it was decided, in view of the religious intricacies involved, to appoint

*Part I, paragraph 89.
†Part I, paragraph 83.

a committee of 12 persons including Ulemas to report on the following question:—

> "As the question of determining the point where non-violence should end and violence begin, is of grave importance and most intricate, it is, therefore, necessary that a committee of the following persons be appointed to report on this matter in view of the religious injunctions, conditions in the country, and the Khilafat programme."

The personnel of this committee was:—

1. Maulvi Kifayatullah, President, Jamiat-ul-Ulema.
2. Maulvi Abdul Qadir, Vice-President, Jamiat-ul-Ulema.
3. Maulana Abdul Majid.
4. Maulana Sulaiman Nadvi.
5. Maulana Salamatullah.
6. Maulana Azad Subhani.
7. Hakim Ajmal Khan.
8. Dr. Ansari.
9. Tassadduk Ahmad Khan Sherwani.
10. Maulvi Abdul Qadir of Kasur.
11. Pandit Motilal Nehru.
12. Maulana Habeeb-ur-Rahman of Deoband.

The question of civil disobedience was also discussed and it was clear that the majority were in favour of adopting this step irrespective of the decision of the Congress on the subject. However, after Ajmal Khan had pointed out that Muslims alone would not be able to carry on the "war", the following resolution moved by Abdul Majid was passed:—

> "Whereas our demands regarding the Khilafate, as well as other national demands have not been conceded until now and the attitude of the British Cabinets towards the Khilafat question has consistently been hostile and further, whereas divers kinds of pression and oppression are being practiced to suppress and kill the movement for achieving the aforesaid object, especially at a time when on our part we have absolutely abstained from having recourse to any kind of aggressive activity and as a consequence the country appears to be inclined to resort to some effective plan of action, therefore in view of the popular inclination of the country the Committee is of opinion that civil disobedience at least is unavoidably necessary.

For this purpose, therefore, the Committee desires all the provincial Khilafat Committees to put forth their utmost efforts to complete the Khilafat constructive programme by 15th of August 1922 when the Central Khilafat Committee will after considering the situation decide upon civil disobedience.

This meeting further resolves that a number of persons to be selected by the Working Committee should tour the country with the Congress deputation and submit their report of enquiry on or before the aforesaid date."

The Committee went on to issue a number of instructions to Provincial workers as to how to carry on the Khilafat Movement.

At the conclusion of the proceedings the following resolution was passed:—

"In 1920 the Khilafat deputation requested the British Cabinet and the British public to send an enquiry committee to enquire into the atrocities committed in Anatolia, but the British Cabinet returned no reply to it. To-day the British Cabinet is showing great activity in bringing about the appointment of such a committee to enquire into Turkish atrocities which clearly shows its bad intention and interested propaganda. This committee places its condemnation of the tactics of British Cabinet on record."

In June Mr. Chotani as President of the Central Khilafat Committee nominated the following Muhammadans to co-operate with and accompany the Congress Civil Disobedience Enquiry Committee and to submit a report to the Central Khilafat Committee:—

(1) Maulana Abdul Majid of Budaun, Vice-President, Central Khilafat Committee.

(2) Maulana Syed Sulaiman Nadvi, Member of the Khilafat Working Committee.

(3) Maulana Abdul Qadir Sahib of Kasur, Member, Khilafat Working Committee.

(4) Tassaduq Ahmed Khan Sherwani of Aligarh.

(5) Moazzam Ali, Secretary, Central Khilafat Committee, and

(6) Zahoor Ahmed, in charge of propaganda and publicity.

129. **Indications of Hindu-Moslem friction.**—In addition to indications of Hindu-Muslim friction which has already been referred to there was at this period, *i.e.*, the middle of 1922, considerable dissension within Khilafat organisations themselves, due chiefly to allegations of misappropriation of funds. Also a good deal of discussion occurred with respect to the attitude which the Khilafat Committee should maintain towards the Congress and the fear was frequently expressed that the former organisation was subordinating itself

to the latter. This matter came up frequently and the discussion it caused was manifested in the repeated quarrels which occurred at this period over the question of cow killing.

In the middle of June a letter written by Abdul Bari of Lucknow to Chotani in Bombay came to light confidentially. Extracts of this letter are given below:—

> "I consider it very necessary to tell you certain things * * * The goal before us is to give protection to the Turks and there are only two ways of doing this. Firstly, we should compel those who help the Greeks, to give up giving help by changing their opinion or by force, and secondly to give so much strength to Mustapha Kemal that he may defeat the Greeks and their supporters. I understand that Muslims of India have not got the power to strengthen the hands of Angora. A small amount is not enough to give them sufficient strength. * * * If money we are sending to the Turks were utilised for our requirements (in India) it would give us sufficient strength to be of some use to the Turks. * * * By means of Non-co-operation we cannot prevent the Allies from giving help to the Greeks. * * * So far no impression has been created on the Allies. * * * As far as I can make out the Non-co-operation movement is dying down. Many people think the same thing. The Non-co-operation movement may be allowed to go on as it will be of some use in future, but there is this fear also that civil disobedience may develop into a suicidal policy and that Non-co-operation may become a theory only as has happened before now. Under these circumstances if the Turks got support by the co-operation of the co-operators and non-co-operators I do not see any harm. * * * An opportunity has arisen to bring round the Sharif of Mecca and the Amir Feisul. Their relations with the Turks should be made pleasant * * I have exchanged views with the Sharif on this subject and I hope to bring about a settlement."

The writer then pointed out that while weakness in the Khilafat organisation would be harmful to the Khilafat cause, yet the aloofness of the Muslims from the Congress would be even more harmful.

> "Hindus will succeed in attaining Swaraj and that Swaraj will not be in any way beneficial to us. Malaviya by his cleverness is usurping the position (of Gandhi) but Muslims have no faith in him nor can they have as they had in Gandhi * * * Let us see whether we have still to cling to this movement (non-violent Non-co-operation) or some other way is found out of the difficulty. In my opinion it would be far more

beneficial if the Muslims improve their own status, Indian Muslims in India, Arabs in Arabia, Afghans in Afghanistan and Turks in Turkey. They should then unite. For the present whatever concessions could be obtained for the Turks they should be obtained, but we should not ruin ourselves for their sake. The condition of the Arabs should be improved so that the Arabian peninsular may remain safe from foreign aggression."

The letter concluded:—

"After the imprisonment of Muhammad Ali *khadi* was put on, after the arrest of Gandhi *charkha* was used and after the arrest of Fazal Hussain (Hasrat Mohani) use of mill-made cloth was given up. Such courses will bring no result."

130. **Sind Khilafat Conference, July 1922.**—A Khilafat Conference was held in Sind on the 7th of July at which Marmaduke Pickthall presided. He said:—"When I remember what it was two years ago, at the time when the terms of the iniquitous Treaty of Sevres were first announced it seems to me that a miracle has been wrought in our favour in these two years. When I left England in September 1920, public opinion was strongly anti-Turkish. * * * Think of the situation then and of the situation as it is to-day * * * To-day, in England there is a great volume of public opinion favourable to the Turkish claims. A considerable section of the press is on our side, thanks—let us give thanks where thanks are due—thanks very largely to the efforts of Mr. Montagu as representative in England of the Government of India." * * * * The speaker then said that Italy, though a little jealous of France, in her Angora Treaty had definitely adopted a pro-Muslim policy. In Germany, Austria and Hungary there was strong pro-Turkish sentiment and Russia was in close alliance with Angora * * "I do not want you in India to think, because the little ruling clique in England sides with Greece for its own unmentionable reasons, England as a nation sides with Greece. It is quite the opposite and the ruling clique are perfectly aware that the position has changed since 1919 and that they can no longer do as they like in the Near East without the risk of angering their own electors * * * Now let us turn to the situation in India. I know there are some people who think it wrong for Muslims to accept the leadership of a Hindu. But I think that a Hindu saint who lives upon the higher plane is a better guide for Muslims than a Muslim sinner who lives upon the lower plane, for upon the higher plane here is but one law for Muslim, Hindu, Christian, Jew or any man and that law is the divine law revealed in the *Quran-esh-Sharif*."

131. **C. K. C. and Jamiat-ul-Ulema meet at Bombay, July 1922.**—On the 18th of July the Central Khilafat Committee met at Bombay and an acrimonious discussion ensued as to whether the Angora Fund

could be utilised for any purpose other than Angora. Ultimately, on it being pointed out that the balance in the Angora and Smyrna Funds was then about sixteen lakhs of rupees, while the balance in the Khilafat was only a few thousands, it was decided to transfer one lakh from the Angora Fund to the Khilafat and to send ten lakhs to Angora.

A meeting of the Jamiat-ul-Ulema was held in Bombay on the 26th of July at which it was resolved to ask the Central Khilafat Committee not to side too strongly with the anti-cow-killers and not to go to the length of rescuing cows brought for sacrifice, as this would be interference with religion.

132. **Further indication of Hindu-Moslem Friction.**—Although the Jamiat-ul-Ulema confined itself to recommendations for leniency as to cow killing, individual Muhammadan extremists were less restrained. In August Bashir Ahmed Khan, the President of the Anjuman-i-Islamia at Gurdaspur in an open letter to Ajmal Khan, definitely stated that the Hindus were the bitterest enemies of Turkey and accused them of having waited for centuries for the destruction of Islam in India. He went on to point out how they had managed to overthrow the ascendancy of Muslims in this country by occupying almost exclusively all posts in the public services, commerce, railways and municipal administrations, and he voiced his belief that they had no regard for the terms of the Lucknow Pact. He added that the agitation up to this stage had merely had the effect of increasing robbery and dacoity and stated that in his opinion the idea of Muhammadans combining with Hindus in order to start civil disobedience against the existing Government was fatuous. At about the same time Mushir Hassan Kidwai, writing to Chotani, said, "In the heads of our brothers no other thing except *charkha* comes. May the curse of God be on this *charkha* and the question of untouchables." Writing to Dr. Ansari, he said, " If such coldness is shown towards the Khilafate I will shortly raise a standard of revolt against the Khilafat Committee and the Congress. Even if the Hindus do not stand by us we would not give up the Khilafate. * * * If in future any Khilafat work is to be done a conference may be held or the services of the Muslim League or Jamiat-ul-Ulema-i-Hind may be utilised. For the attainment of Swaraj, National Education and political concessions, the Muslims should work with Hindus in the Congress, etc."

133. **Agitation temporarily revives.**—The lack of response to the agitation was the cause of this despondency among the leaders During the middle of 1922, the numerous pernicious speeches made by propagandists (of whom not the least active was Bi Amma, the mother of the Ali Brothers) had had little result and it was not until about September of that year that the excitement was rekindled. This moreover is not attributable to internal propaganda, but to strained elations between Great Britain and the Angora Government. During

September and October, Kemal Pasha was clinching his victory over the Greeks and his success brought into prominence the question of the continued occupation of Constantinople by the Allies. In this matter Great Britain took up a stronger line than did either France or Italy and for some little time her relations with the Angora Government were in a critical condition. The news of Kemal Pasha's success coupled with Turco-British friction to some extent revived Muslim enthusiasm for the Khilafat cause and numerous meetings were held throughout the country at which these matters were discussed. The agitation at this period, however, never approached the heights it had reached in the preceding year.

At about the same time Chotani was the subject of considerable criticism for his administration of the Angora Fund, and allegations, that he had diverted some of it to his own personal account, were lent colour by the fact that about 17 lakhs were in hand at the end of July which he had failed to remit to Angora. Abdul Bari wrote to him urging him to remit the money in order to allay public anxiety and added that the lack of confidence in their leaders was the only thing which prevented Muhammadans, whose feelings were running high, from subscribing further funds. One manifestation of the excitement at this period was the revival of the proposal to despatch an Angora Legion from India to assist Kemal Pasha, but, beyond protestations from various directions of willingness to serve, little materialised.

The possibility of war between Britain and Turkey revived the interest in the *Mutafiqa Fatwa*, and, Muhammad Sajjad, *vice Amir-i-Shariat*, Bihar, who for some time past had been a very active anti-British propagandist, wrote to Chotani urging its amplification. He pointed out that the *Mutafiqa Fatwa* of the Jamiat-ul-Ulema confined itself to general terms and he pressed for a fresh *fatwa* on the following lines to be promulgated and distributed among the troops:—

(1) The lives, properties and honour of Muslims are sacred and to harm them in any way is a great sin and all the more so if it is done in the service of infidels and Christians.

(2) To kill a Muslim intentionally is a sin which is equal to *Kufr* (infidelism) and the killer will be consigned to hell for ever.

(3) It is *haram* (forbidden) to kill a non-Muslim without sufficient reason and, therefore, to kill, injure or dishonour brother Indians, though they may be non-Muslims, is also *haram*.

(4) Service, under the present circumstances, in all the Indian Army is *haram* and therefore all those who are in the Army should give up service or firmly refuse to oppose and kill Muslims and Hindus.

(5) A Muslim soldier who may be killed for disobeying such orders will be *Shahid* (martyr) and will gain eternal bliss.

(6) Hindus should also issue similar injunctions in accordance with their religion.

(7) All monies advanced to Government on loan should be immediately withdrawn.

By the middle of October the settlement of the Near East question had considerably eased the situation, but it was at once apparent that the Khilafat agitators were determined to carry on their agitation regardless of any reasonable steps which were taken to propitiate them.

134. **C. K. C. meet at Delhi, October 1922.**—A meeting of the Central Khilafat Committee was held at Delhi on the 17th to the 19th October at which it was apparent that the feeling against Chotani* ran exceedingly high, and further excitement was caused by the circulation among the delegates of a poster printed in Bombay accusing Khatri of using Khilafat funds for the purposes of satisfying his unnatural passions. At this meeting the subjects of the more important resolutions were as follows:—

(1) Presentation of a sword of honour and two aeroplanes to Kemal Pasha.

(2) The internationalisation of the Straits is detrimental to the freedom of the Khilafate.

(3) Despatch of a deputation to the Hedjaz to study the present situation in Arabia.

(4) Proposal to send an Indian Khilafat Deputation headed by Hakim Ajmal Khan to the coming Near East Conference.

(5) Proposal to invite representations of all Muslim countries in the world to the forthcoming All-India Khilafat Conference at Gaya in December.

The meeting further resolved that the united struggle of Muslims of the world was to continue until Mesopotamia, Palestine, Hedjaz, Yemen and Syria are completely free, and it described the treaty concluded with the "so-called Government of Iraq" as absolutely unacceptable to Indian Muslims on the ground that Mesopotamia would not be free from British interference. The Committee went on to declare that they would continue their efforts until they had succeeded in removing this non-Muslim interference from the Holy Places.

135. **Kemal Pasha deposes the Khalifa.**—In spite of this resolution, the rekindled flame diminished with the successful conclusion of Kemal Pasha's hostilities with the Greeks, and it was quenched

---

*During the following year it was finally established that Chotani had diverted Angora Funds to his own use, and he handed over to the C. K. C. two Saw Mills valued at 18 lakhs as compensation. From the trouble the C. K. C. experienced in disposing of them, the valuation appears to have been fictitious.

very shortly afterwards by the deposition of the Sultan of Turkey, and abolition of the Khilafate in November 1922, by the Turkish Nationalist Party headed by Kemal Pasha.

Since the maintenance of the temporal power of the Khalifa was one of the main objects of the Khilafat agitation, this action, by a purely Muslim agency, completely took the wind out of the sails of the agitators. Of course, the cognate question remained, *i.e.*, the freedom of the Holy Places from foreign influence and control, and an effort was made by the leaders to carry on the movement on this ground: but up to date this agitation has been confined to the irreconcilable extremists.

The bulk of Indian Muhammadans, who place their religion before politics, have not yet recovered from the act of the viper whom they cherished in their bosoms and who rewarded them by removing their spiritual head. Their attention has, therefore, been mainly concentrated on the purely religious aspect of the situation and endeavours were made to hold a conference of representatives of all Muslim nations to consider the question of the Khilafate and the re-appointment of a Khalifa. As yet, however, there are no indications of this conference materializing.

136. **The end of the Khilafat Movement.**—Spasmodic efforts to secure Muslim control of the Holy Places continued in 1923 and 1924, but little resulted beyond the despatch of a delegation to the Hedjaz at the end of the latter year. The Delegation did not get beyond Jeddah owing to the hostilities which had then commenced between the Government of the Hedjaz and Ibn Saud, and it seems to have confined itself mainly to delivering the following statement of the " Aims of the Indian Khilafat Committee " to the Government of the Hedjaz:—

1. To set up a lawful (*i.e.*, in accordance with Shariat Law) republican government in the Hedjaz which shall be independent internally and whose foreign policy shall be such as to satisfy the Muslim world and meet its views in regard to the complete and absolute independence of the country—an independence free from foreign influence, whether open or concealed.

2. To call a Muslim Conference for the formation of this republic, in which there shall participate delegates from admittedly independent-minded Muslim societies in Muslim lands which are under domination, and representatives of the independent Muslim Governments, and delegates of the Hedjaz.

3. Neither the Sharif nor his family to have any connection whatsoever with this assembly or in any matter affecting the centralisation (*sic*) of the Hedjaz.

4. To bring about general unity and religious brotherhood between the Arab rulers as the commands of Islam dictate, so that no room may be left for foreign greed, that the way may not be opened for strife to enter the country, that the shedding of innocent blood may be stopped, and that the Arabs may appear in perfect unity before the world and with united force against the enemy.

5. Mecca to be the seat of the Conference, if circumstances permit.

6. The Sultan of Nejd and the Imam Yahya to be entrusted with the task of assembling the delegates of the Arab Muslim rulers for the proposed Conference.

7. To fix as early a date as possible for the Conference (it should be) before the expiry of the coming pilgrim season. The invitations to the Muslim World to be issued by Ibn Saud and the Imam Yahya and the Hedjaz people.

8. Until the Conference has come to a final decision about the Hedjaz and the form of its government, the Hedjaz territories to be governed temporarily by elected delegates of the people under the overlordship of Ibn Saud.

Apart from this delegation, such Muhammadan agitation as was apparent subsequent to the deposition of the Khalifa, was confined almost entirely to internal affairs. The Shuddhi and Sanghathan Movements and the increasing importance of the Hindu Mahasabha caused Indian Muslims to consider their position *vis à vis* the Hindus. This resulted in the initiation of the Tabligh and Tanzim Movements, the objects of which are to gain converts to Islam and to prevent conversion from that religion. These organisations are mainly confined to Northern India and have not yet attained any great dimensions, but they serve to absorb such Muhammadan energy as exists, to the almost total exclusion of the Khilafat Movement.

APPENDIX A.

(*Vide* preface.)

History of the Non-Co-operation and Khilafat Movements in Burma.

So far as the Government of India* mean by the Non-co-operation movement, the movement which has extended to all the Provinces of India, is inseparably connected with the name of Gandhi, and has had a central India directorate, it may be said at once that that movement, as also the Khilafat movement, has had no independent history in Burma. Both movements have had their followers here, and their supporters have organized *hartals*, and volunteers and public meetings of protest to commemorate and show sympathy with events in India. But these supporters have without exception been Indians: their efforts have contributed an insignificant appanage to the two movements in India: they have had among them no leader who has counted in either movement, or who has been of more than purely local influence. Their history is a pale and purely imitative reflection of the history of the movements in India; its details in themselves are of no interest. They have, however, had this importance that they have provided patterns for the Burman movement proper to follow, and that their leaders have stimulated and advised the leaders of that movement.

Burma is predominantly a Buddhist country: the woes of Islam make no appeal to it, and the Hindu doctrines on which much of Gandhi's propaganda has been based are not understood. Burman leaders may occasionally pay lip-worship to Gandhi or the Ali Brothers, but it is generally only done in Indian company, or else from a desire to link themselves up in name with movements which are making a noise in the world. Owing to the paucity of original political ideas among the Burman leaders, the extremist movement in Burma has largely followed the lines of the Non-co-operation movement in India. To some extent it has been aided by the dislike of government as such which belongs to the traditions of the people and is crystallised in the Buddhist doctrine which includes "Government" among the "five evils." This may explain why the movement has "caught on" with the mass of the people. On the other hand the absence of a large unemployed *intelligentia*, and the fact that almost any young man of ability can still find a career in Government service or in one of the professions has prevented the movement from obtaining any men of real ability for its leaders.

The non-co-operation movement may be said to have started in Burma in 1920, and to have had its origin in the resentment which certain political leaders felt or professed to feel against the proposal, first made by Sir Reginald Craddock's Government in 1918, to give Burma a reformed constitution which was considered to be less advanced than the constitution given to India, and also in the opposition which was organised for political purposes against the scheme for the constitution of a University in Rangoon.

The stormy petrel of Burmese politics then, as before and since, was the Arakanese monk U Oktama, who has always been in active communication with Indian extremist politicians. And in its earlier manifestations the movement owed much to the encouragement received from Bernard Houghton, I.C.S. (retired), who was and still is a regular contributor to the Burmese political press

In October 1920 Swami Shardha Nand came to Burma in connection, ostensibly with the Arya Samaj movement. Political leaders in Burma were at the time of his visit in a decidedly susceptible state, and it is fairly certain that the tales which this Swami had to tell of the progress of the Non-Co-operation movement in India fell on fertile soil. His visit coincided moreover with a period of industrial unrest which was marked by a series of strikes. And just

---

* This history was written at the request of the Government of India.

at this time the Rangoon Tramway Company put up its fares to the annoyance of the public, and a boycott was organised, which proved entirely and unexpectedly successful and forced the Company to lower its fares. The success of this boycott was probably largely responsible for the prominence which the boycott as a political weapon has since attained in the political history of the Province.

At a conference of branches of the Young Men's Buddhist Association and kindred associations held at Prome at the end of October 1920 it was decided that Burmans should not take part in the forthcoming elections for the Indian Council of State and the Legislative Assembly " in view of the electoral rules not being acceptable to the Burmese people and on account of the delay in granting reforms to Burma."

As the result of this resolution a bitter campaign was waged against Maung Po Bye, a retired Extra Assistant Commissioner, who had refused to withdraw his candidature for the Council of State.

At the beginning of December 1920 the College students and the boys of certain schools in Rangoon went on strike. Their action was undoubtedly to a large extent the result of Swami Shardha Nand's visit and exhortations, though nominally it was directed against the policy embodied in the University Bill. The strikers' cry was for a system of " National Education."

This strike had not been in progress for a week when Colonel Wedgwood paid a five-days' visit to Burma, and while ostensibly dissociating himself from the Non-co-operation movement, actually by the faintness of his discouragement of the movement and by his insinuations against the good faith of Government succeeded in adding much fuel to the flames. About this time, too, the Indian extremists were carrying all before them at the meeting of the Congress at Nagpur. At the end of December the General Council of the Y.M.B.A. resolved—

(1) to remove Maung Po Bye from the Association;

(2) to support the students' boycott movement; and

(3) to open " National Schools."

In January 1921 the boycott of individuals was pursued with great bitterness, the chief sufferers being Maung Maung Sin of Mandalay, who had been elected to the Legislative Assembly, and Maung Po Sein, the well known actor, who had refused to give free performances for the benefit of school boys on strike.

About this time an attempt was made to discourage the purchase of foreign goods, and the large European Department Stores of Rangoon felt the effect, though this particular movement was short-lived.

In February 1921 it became known that there was a likelihood of Burma being granted the same measure of political reform as had been granted to India, and political Burma was split into two camps—those in favour of accepting dyarchy, and those in favour of standing out for complete Home Rule: a section of the latter led by U Oktama advocated " complete independence." From this time onwards there was a continuous struggle between the dyarchists and the Home-Rulers for the control of the Y.M.B.A. and more particularly of its funds.

In March 1921 Oktama was arrested for sedition, and his trial, which was very protracted, brought into the field a number of other monk-politicians who threw their weight on to the side of the extremists.

Oktama was convicted at the beginning of July and at a meeting of the Exectutive Council of the G.C.B.A. (General Council of Burmese Associations, which had succeeded to the political activities of the Y.M.B.A.), resolutions were passed to the effect that as a protest against the conviction of Oktama a campaign of Non-co-operation should be inaugurated, British goods and institutions should be boycotted, and the Whyte Committee (the Committee which was to report to the Secretary of State on the details of the measure of dyarchy to be granted to Burma), should also be boycotted. On the 14th and 16th August 1921 a full meeting of the G.C.B.A., attended by a thousand delegates, was held, when it was resolved, though not without much discussion and some opposition, that a Sub-Committee should be appointed to consider and suggest the various stages of the Non-co-operation programme, whether Non-co-operation should be adopted or not and if adopted to what extent, and that, as a first step; foreign (excluding Indian) cloth should be boycotted and every one should refrain from liquor. Consideration of the proposal to boycott the Whyte Committee was deferred.

About this time the formation of village associations (*athins*) became very marked. Nominally temperance and the prevention of the slaughter of cattle were their objects, but it was foreseen that they would eventually be used for political purposes.

September 1921 was marked by considerable activity in the formation of associations of monks, and the Burmese Press discussed with gusto and enthusiasm the prospects of boycotts of all sorts.

At a meeting of the G.C.B.A. held on 24th and 25th September 1921 the boycott of the Whyte Committee was definitely resolved. A proposal to boycott the visit of His Royal Highness the Prince of Wales was discussed but a decision deferred.

On the 21st October 1921 the G.C.B.A. held a Conference at Mandalay which was attended by about 8,000 people and the extremists carried every thing before them. It was decided to boycott British goods, the Whyte Committee and all persons taking part in the reception to the Prince of Wales and "to adopt non-co-operation as far as possible where it does not effect the speedy attainment of Home Rule." The words "within the Empire" were deleted from this last resolution. A resolution to boycott dyarchy was defeated, but only because the conference did not desire to commit itself to a definite course of action, one section being in favour of contesting the seats and then abstaining from attending the Council. At this conference a retired Deputy Inspector of Schools announced amid loud applause his intention of surrendering his A.T.M. (a Burmese decoration). This is almost the only case in which a decoration has been surrendered, and the retired Deputy Inspector has long since repented his precipitancy.

In November 1921 the Whyte Committee held its sittings, which were picketed. No Burmese politicians, excepting one or two staunch loyalists, gave evidence before the Committee.

Towards the end of the month the boycott raged with increasing intensity, persons participating in preparations for the Prince's visit being specially selected as victims. Early in December seven leading agitators were interned under the Defence of India Rules, in view of the growing intensity of the agitation to secure a complete boycott of the visit and the likelihood of such agitation leading to violence, and other preventive action was taken. These measures produced a marked effect and even led to the G.C.B.A. (in the enforced absence of the more extreme of their leaders) opening negotiations as to the conditions on which the G.C.B.A. would be prepared to take part in the reception to the Prince—which negotiations, however, broke down. The Prince came to Burma at the beginning of January 1922 and although the efforts of the boycotters resulted in His Royal Highness being given a far less warm and popular welcome than would otherwise have been the case, his reception was far more cordial than it was in India and no untoward incident of any sort marred his visit.

About this time proceedings were instituted under section 124A against a *mofussil* pleader who had advocated non-payment of revenue. Proceedings were subsequently withdrawn on receipt of an apology.

There was a marked lull after the Prince s visit, the comparative success of which had done much to discourage the extremists and to hearten the moderates.

The introduction of the Anti-Boycott Bill in the Legislative Council excited far less opposition than might have been expected. Extremist propaganda continued, the monks, as usual, being particularly violent. But the G.C.B.A. was quiescent, probably because of dissensions among the leaders as to the policy to be adopted towards the constitutional reforms, the details of which were announced at the end of May.

On the 17th and 18th June 1922 a momentous meeting of the G.C.B.A. was held. Chit Hlaing then and still the titular leader of the extremists, who has, however, a penchant for going to ground when important decisions have to be taken, was unavoidably prevented from attending, and the chair was taken by U Ba Si, a moderate. On the first day a resolution was passed that affiliated members should take no part in the forthcoming elections for the new District Councils and Circle Boards which were about to be brought into being under the Rural Self-Government Act, 1921. This resulted in the resignation, announced on the second day, of eight members of the Executive Council (including the Hon'ble U Maung Gyee and the Hon'ble U Pu, now Ministers, U Ba Pe, M.L.C., now Deputy President of the Legislative Council, and Dr. Ba Yin, M.L.C., until recently President of the Corporation of Rangoon).

This was followed by the issue of a manifesto by 21 of the leading Burmese politicians strongly opposing the decision taken at this meeting.

A further meeting of the G.C.B.A. was held on the 15th and 16th July which was attended by U Oktama, recently released from jail, who delivered a long address (written probably by one of his Indian friends), strongly opposing the acceptance of dyarchy. The question of boycotting the Legislative Council was debated at great length, and at the conclusion of the discussion the chairman (U. Ba Si), ignoring previous resolutions and amendments, proposed as a compromise that as many seats as possible should be captured, but that the question of participation or non-participation in the proceedings of the Council should be deferred until next meeting, and declared the motion carried. This decision was hotly challenged and the proceedings terminated in some disorder.

The "21" as the moderate party has since been popularly known, now began to make strenuous efforts in private to consolidate their position, and at a meeting of the Executive Council of the G.C.B.A. passed a resolution in favour of standing for election to the Council. Leadership of the extremists on the other hand, passed more and more into the hands of the younger monks who were conducting an active propaganda in the districts.

On the 26th and 27th August 1922 a meeting of the G.C.B.A. attended by about 3,000 persons, of whom 1,000 were monks was held under the auspices of Chit Hlaing, Maung Pu (of Tharrawaddy) and Tun Aung Gyaw—the three titular leaders of the Hlaing-Pu-Gyaw or extremist party. U Oktama dominated the meeting, and a resolution to boycott the Legislative Council was carried without opposition.

Endeavours were then made to effect a reconciliation through the medium of some of the older and more moderate monks, but the extremists were in no mood for compromise. The premises of the G.C.B.A. were picketed by crowds of young monks.

The "21" then convened a meeting of the G.C.B.A. on the 30th September. The meeting was attended chiefly by moderates. The proceedings lasted for three days. A motion to boycott the Legislative Council was defeated and resolutions were passed advocating entrance into the reformed Council "and agitation therein, in accordance with the mandates of the G.C.B.A. so long and as far as the speedy attainment of Home Rule is not prejudiced thereby," and the appointment of a Standing Committee of the G.C.B.A. to be known as the Reformed Committee, and to consist of twenty members for the purpose of (*a*) choosing and nominating candidates for the Reformed Council, (*b*) planning and conducting the electioneering campaign and (*c*) laying down rules to regulate the conduct of G.C.B.A. members in the reformed Legislative Council. Another resolution was passed giving full support to persons who had secured seats on the new District Councils and Circle Boards.

The next meeting was the Annual Conference of the G.C.B.A. held on the 9th, 10th and 11th November under the auspices of the Hlaing-Pu-Gyaw party. The conference was attended by five or six thousand people and presided over by Chit Hlaing. The venerable Beme *Sayadaw* of Mandalay, President of the all Burma Sangha Sametgyis (Associations of monks) pledged the priesthood to support the Hlaing-Pu-Gyaw party. A vote of censure was passed on the "21" for illegally retaining the Association's furniture, account books, etc. Resolutions were passed that associations affiliated to the G.C.B.A. should form arbitration courts and committees to try civil suits and non-congnizable criminal cases, and that a sub-committee should be appointed at the next meeting of the G.C.B.A. for the encouragement of cotton weaving and spinning in every household. (It may be mentioned here that these arbitration courts and the doctrine of salvation through hand spinning have never "caught on" in Burma. In 1921 and 1922 a few political enthusiasts wore home-spun coats, but the Burman has far too keen an interest in dress for its own sake to take to *khaddar* and probably not a single Burman has ever discarded his picturesque *gaung baung* for a Gandhi cap).

On the motion of Maung Pu (of Tharrawaddy) a motion was passed for the appointment of a committee to find ways and means for the *Wunthanu athins* (Nationalist societies) to hasten the grant of Home Rule by the boycott of foreign goods, the boycott of the dyarchical Council (*i.e.*, District Councils) and Circle Boards, and by means of National Education.

The elections were held in the latter part of November and the "21" secured 28 out of 79 elected members. The Hlaing-Pu-Gyaw party stood entirely aloof and in some areas conducted a campaign of boycotting. There was, however, no actual intimidation.

With the introduction of the reforms, the installation of the "21" party as the official opposition and the acceptance of office by two of its members, that party became definitely pledged to a policy of co-operation. And in this course they received the support of the great majority of the *Intelligentsia* of the country. They had got as full a measure of reform as they had hoped to get and a little bit over. The Hlaing-Pu-Gyaw party, on the other hand, could count on the support of the large majority of the village folk, who were lured by dreams of the restoration of the Burmese dynasty and the abolition of taxation, and with whom the names of U Oktama, Chit Hlaing and even Maung Pu (of Tharrawaddy) had a glamour which none of the "21" leaders had succeeded in attaining. The party, therefore, now set themselves to consolidate their position in the districts and to organize Non-co-operation in the villages, and to this end their campaign became directed very largely against the authority of the Village Headman. Gradually there sprung up in the more advanced districts a net-work of village *Wunthanu athins* with a definite anti-headman bias. Simultaneously the younger monks established local branches of the *Sangha Sametgyi*. And in spite of the Anti-boycott Act, social and religious boycotts continued to make things unpleasant for the supporters not only of Government but also of the "21." About May 1923 *Bu athins* began to spring up in the Henzada District and elsewhere, the object of which was definitely to refuse co-operation in any form with Government.

Meanwhile the split between the "21" and the Hlaing-Pu-Gyaw party widened as the result of the compromise effected by Government with the "21" over the National Schools, which had come into being after the school and college boycott of 1920-21 and had hitherto stood outside the Government educational system.

In August 1923 the *Bu athins* of the Henzada District had to be declared unlawful under the Indian Criminal Law (Amendment) Act, 1908, in spite of which similar associations continued to be formed in other districts.

Meanwhile there were signs of an approaching split in the Hlaing-Pu-Gyaw party, owing partly to the large demands made on the party's funds by Maung Pu (of Tharrawaddy). In November 1923 meetings of the Hlaing-Pu-Gyaw party were held at Mandalay, Pagan and Pakokku, and a campaign was inaugurated to prevent His Excellency the Viceroy visiting the pagodas at Pagan. About this time Chit Hlaing began to arrogate to himself the trappings and symbols of royalty. Generally speaking, the party lost ground during the year, and how completely the Non-co-operation movement had died out in the towns was shewn by the whole-hearted way in which the people of Rangoon and Mandalay turned out to enjoy the various shows which were held in honour of the Viceroy's visit.

It may be noted that Oktama had left Burma for a trip to Europe in June 1923, whence he did not return until January 1924. On his return he inaugurated a more active propaganda.

In April an attempt was made by the G.C.B.A. adherents of the Henzada District to effect a reconciliation between the "21" and the Hlaing-Pu-Gyaw party. A conference was held at Henzada, but it was boycotted by the Hlaing-Pu-Gyaw people and the only result was the emergence of a new centre party known as the '8' under Maung Kyaw Yan, the Deputy Inspector of Schools, who had given up his A.T.M. in October 1921. This party received the backing of a number of respected senior clerics, but has remained without influence on the political situation. As a counterblast to this Henzada Conference, the Hlaing-Pu-Gyaw organised a conference of their own at Paungde in May 1924 which was attended by 30,000 people including about 2,000 monks. The most important part of the proceedings was the discussion on a proposal that if dyarchy were not withdrawn, payment of *Thathameda* (house-hold tax levied in Upper Burma) and of capitation-tax (poll tax levied in Lower Burma) should be refused. This was opposed by Maung Pu (of Tharrawaddy) on the ground that the time was not yet ripe for it, whereupon he was roundly attacked by Oktama. Eventually a resolution was passed to the effect that "if the already tax-ridden people adopt non-payment of taxes, consequent on the refusal of Government to withdraw all fresh taxes and to abolish the *Thathameda* and capitation taxes as promised," Government would be responsible. This resolution was in the nature of a compromise. The speeches delivered by Oktama, Chit Hlaing and others displayed, however, an uncompromising hostility to Government, and considerable excitement prevailed, and immediately after the Paungde conference Oktama and Chit Hlaing proceeded on a lecturing tour in the Mergui and Tavoy Districts. For many months local meetings of the party had been held all over the districts at which resolutions advocating a boycott of foreign goods (a resolution to which no practical effect was attempted to be given), or denouncing marriages between Burmese women and foreigners were passed. Boycotting was prevalent in many districts, and in April it was noted that the situation in the Mergui District would want watching. In the Toungoo District Non-co-operation took the form of setting up a *Wunthanu* bazaar in opposition to the Municipal Bazaar.

In June 1924 there was a movement in the Delta districts to refuse to pay taxes to village headmen, whose business it is to collect them, and who receive commission for so doing, and in the same month the Anti-Boycott Act had to be extended to the Tavoy District.

In July there was a recrudescence of boycotting in the Pegu Division and it was noted that everywhere the formation of societies was having the effect of introducing dissension and bitterness among the agricultural population; in Mergui Town payment of capitation tax was refused on political grounds.

In August the holding of meetings in Mandalay by the all-Burma Union, an offshoot of the '8' party, led to a counter-demonstration by the Hlaing-Pu-Gyaw party, which was attended by Oktama and in which Tun Aung Gyaw, Treasurer of the party, played a prominent part A procession of the latter party came into conflict with the police with the result that one monk was killed and two wounded, and two policemen were killed and fifty injured.

During this month the movement for the non-payment of taxes spread to four districts. Vigorous efforts were also made by the Hlaing-Pu-Gyaw party to force villagers to form village societies by threats of causing local priests to be withdrawn unless such societies were formed. The monks in fact were taking an increasingly prominent part in the boycott movement. Much capital was made out of the Mandalay *fracas* by the younger and more excitable party of monks.

By September the number of districts affected by the movement for non-payment of taxes was seven. Companies of Military Police were despatched partly to overawe the villagers and partly to protect law-abiding citizens. Numerous outrages were being committed against persons who paid their taxes or who purchased the property of revenue defaulters when offered for sale. Crops were burnt, cattle maimed and in one or two cases headmen were murdered.

In October U Oktama was sentenced to three years' rigorous imprisonment for sedition. An indignation meeting chiefly attended by monks which was held at Fytche Square had to be dispersed by force and a day or two later an American Missionary and his wife who were walking past a monastery were brutally assaulted by monks.

Meanwhile, however, the non-payment of taxes movement was checked and the certainty that it must fail led the G.C.B.A. publicly to disavow connection with it.

Since October there has been a distinct *détente* in the situation. Oktama is in jail for sedition; Tun Aung Gyaw is in the Mandalay Jail being tried for his share in the Mandalay *fracas* and Chit Hlaing is lying very low avoiding appearance in Court to answer a charge under section 188, Indian Penal Code. The Non-co-operation movement is now almost wholly in the hands of the monks. Maung Pu of Tharrawaddy, influenced doubtless by the success of the Council-Entry party in India, by the thought of the elections to the Legislative Council to be held next October and perhaps of the selection of himself as a Minister should the Hlaing-Pu-Gyaw party sweep the polls, is shewing obvious signs of a desire to effect a *rapprochement* with Government. It remains to be seen, however, whether he will be able to carry any appreciable portion of the party with him.

The non-payment of taxes movement is not yet dead but it is in its death-throes, and there seems to be little danger of a revival in the near future. The Non-co-operation movement is at a lower ebb than at any time since 1920. On the other hand, five years' persistent vilification from the press and from the platform has undoubtedly poisoned the minds of the people against the Government. The younger monks are still irreconcilable (and likely always to remain so) and it would be rash to say that the Non-co-operation movement was more than merely scotched.

APPENDIX B.

(*Vide* Part I, paragraph 14.)

[*Letter from Mr. M. K. Gandhi to His Excellency the Viceroy (pages 197—200 of publication entitled "Young India" by Babu Rajendra Prasad.)*]

YOUR EXCELLENCY,

As one who has enjoyed a certain measure of Your Excellency's confidence, and as one who claims to be a devoted well-wisher of the British Empire, I owe it to Your Excellency, and through Your Excellency to His Majesty's Ministers, to explain my connection with and my conduct in the Khilafat Question.

At the very earliest stage of the war, even whilst I was in London organising the Indian Volunteer Ambulance Corps, I began to interest myself in the Khilafat question. I perceived how deeply moved the little Mussalman World in London was when Turkey decided to throw in her lot with Germany. On my arrival in India in January of 1915 I found the same anxiousness and earnestness among the Mussalmans, with whom I came in contact. Their anxiety became intense when the information about the Secret Treaties leaked out. Distrust of British intentions filled their minds and despair took possession of them. Even at that moment I advised my Mussalman friends not to give way to despair, but they express their fear and their hopes in a disciplined manner. It will be admitted that the whole of Mussalman India has behaved in a singularly restrained manner during the past five years, and that the leaders have been able to keep the turbulent sections of their community under complete control. The peace terms and Your Excellency's defence of them have given the Mussalmans of India a shock from which it will be difficult for them to recover. The terms violate ministerial pledges and utterly disregard Mussalman sentiment. I consider that, as a staunch Hindu wishing to live on terms of the closest friendship with my Mussalman countrymen, I should be an unworthy son of India if I did not stand by them in their hour of trial. In my humble opinion, their cause is just. They claim that Turkey must not be *punished* if their sentiment is to be respected. Muslim soldiers did not fight to inflict punishment on their own Khalifa or to deprive him of his territories. The Mussalman attitude has been consistent throughout these five years.

My duty to the Empire to which I owe my loyalty requires me to resist the cruel violence that has been done to the Mussalman sentiment. So far as I am aware, Mussalmans and Hindus have as a whole lost faith in British justice and honour. The report of the Majority of the Hunter Committee, Your Excellency's despatch thereon and Mr. Montagu's reply have only aggravated the distrust.

In these circumstances the only course open to one like me is either in despair to sever all connection with British rule or, if I still retained faith in the inherent superiority of the British constitution to all others at present in vogue, to adopt such means as will rectify the wrong done, and thus restore confidence. I have not lost faith in such superiority and I am not without hope that somehow or other justice will yet be rendered if we show the requisite capacity for suffering. Indeed, my conception of that constitution is that it helps only those who are ready to help themselves. I do not believe that it protects the weak. It gives free scope to the strong to maintain their strength and develop it. The weak under it go to the wall.

It is, then, because I believe in the British constitution that I have advised my Mussalman friends to withdraw their support from Their Excellency's Government, and the Hindus to join them, should the peace terms not be revised in accordance with the solemn pledges of Ministers and the Muslim sentiment.

Three courses were open to the Mahomedans in order to mark their emphatic disapproval of the utter injustice to which His Majesty's Ministers have become party, if they have not actually been the prime perpetrators of it.

They are :—

(1) To resort to violence.

(2) To advise emigration on a wholesale scale.

(3) Not to be party of the injustice by ceasing to co-operate with the Government.

Your Excellency must be aware that there was a time when the boldest, though the most thoughtless, among the Mussalmans favoured violence, and the *Hijrat* (emigration) has not yet ceased to be the battle-cry. I venture to claim that I have succeeded by patient reasoning in weaning the party of violence from its ways. I confess that I did not--I did not attempt to—succeed in weaning them from violence on moral grounds, but, purely on utilitarian grounds. The result, for the time being at any rate, has however been to stop violence. The school of *Hijrat* has received a check, if it has not stopped its activity entirely. I hold that no repression could have prevented a violent eruption, if the people had not presented to them a form of direct action involving considerable sacrifice and ensuring success if such direct action was largely taken up by the public. Non-co-operation was the only dignified and constitutional form of such direct action. For it is the right recognised from time immemorial of the subject to refuse to assist a ruler who misrules.

At the same time I admit that non-co-operation practised by the mass of people is attended with grave risks. But in a crisis such as has overtaken the Mussalman of India, no step that is unattended with large risks can possibly bring about the desired change. Not to run some risks now will be to court much greater risks if not virtual destruction of Law and Order.

But there is yet an escape from Non-co-operation. The Mussalman representation has requested Your Excellency to lead the agitation yourself, as did your distinguished predecessor at the time of the South African trouble. If you cannot see your way to do so, and Non-co-operation becomes a dire necessity, I hope that Your Excellency will give those who have accepted my advice and myself the credit for being actuated by nothing less than a stern sense of duty.

I have the honour to remain,

Your Excellency's faithful servant,

(Signed) M. K. GANDHI.

Laburnum Road, Gamdevi,
Bombay, 22nd June 1920.

APPENDIX C.

(*Vide* Part I, paragraph 16.)

Non-co-operation Instructions.

The All-India Congress Committee, after considering the report of the Sub-Committee appointed at Calcutta on 9th September to draft instructions to carry out the resolution of the Congress on Non-co-operation resolved to issue the following :—

Instructions to carry out the Resolution.

(*a*) *Boycott of Titles.*—Workers in every town, taluka and district should compile a list of such holders of titles and honorary offices, and a small deputation of the leading non-co-operationists should wait upon such holders, and, with all respect and humility, urge upon the necessity of surrendering their titles and honorary offices for the good of the country. No undue pressure of any kind whatsoever should be exercised, violence of language should be scrupulously avoided, and lists of those who have not surrendered their titles and offices should be furnished to the provincial headquarters for publication. Those who have already surrendered their titles and honorary offices will be expected to induce others to do likewise. Those who hold such titles and offices and who have voted for non-co-operation are naturally expected immediately to surrender their titles and offices, mentioning the purpose, *viz.*, the resolution of the Congress.

(*b*) *Boycott of Government Functions.*—(1) Deputations and public meetings to ask Durbaris to have their names removed from the list. (2) Deputations and public meetings to be organised on the occasion of a leave, Durbar or such other function in order to urge upon persons likely to attend them, the necessity of abandoning the idea for the good of the country. (3) When any function is being organised by Government, a local body, an association, or any private individual, in honour of an officer of Government, similar steps should be taken to induce people not to attend such a function. Deputation and public meetings should also be organised to request local bodies, associations or private individuals not to give any address to any officer of Government, or hold or organise any function in his honour.

(*c*) *Boycott of Schools and Colleges aided or controlled by the Government.*—We advise gradual withdrawal of boys and girls from schools and colleges and earnest attempts to establish National Institutions. Meanwhile reliance should be placed upon private education and where even that is not available or possible for want of means, boys should be apprenticed to patriotic merchants or artizans. Vigorous propaganda should be organised and carried on amongst the parents, schoolmasters and schoolboys who are over the age of 18 years. Canvassing should go on for volunteer teachers, and where parents and schools other than those under direct Government control agree, those schools should give immediate notice to the Government dispensing with all control or aid by way of inspection or otherwise. They should be conducted as national schools with such modifications in the training as local circumstances may require. If men of education take interest in this movement of truly nationalising our education, local committees of inspection and guidance may be formed ultimately resulting in provincial or district universities. Lists of parents who have withdrawn their children, or boys who have themselves withdrawn, and of schoolmasters who have resigned, and list of local schools established, as also of volunteer teachers, should be sent to the provincial headquarters and should be published.

N.B.—By a "National Institution" is meant any educational institution that does not receive any aid from Government, is not in any way controlled of inspected by Government and is not affiliated to any University established by Government.

(*d*) *Boycott of Law Courts*.—Those lawyers who suspend practice and who require to be supported, should be supported by the nation, either by utilising their services for national schools, or in connection with private arbitration or for propaganda work. A deputation such as has been suggested for holders of titles, etc., should also wait upon lawyers and ascertain their wishes. Lists of lawyers in each town or district should be prepared marking out those who may suspend their practice and forwarded to the provincial headquarters for publication.

Lawyers should help in inducing parties not only to refer future disputes to arbitration but also to withdraw cases now pending in the British Courts, and submit them to the National Arbitration Courts.

District Committees should make lists of lawyers and other prominent citizens commanding public confidence who are to preside over Arbitration Courts.

As there is at present no machinery to enforce the orders of Arbitration Courts, some kind of social boycott should be imposed on parties who fail to carry out such orders.

It has been pointed out that certain lawyers who are ready and willing to suspend their practice immediately, are not in a position to do so completely at a moment's notice, as they have already entered into engagements from which, as honourable men, they cannot withdraw without consent of their clients. In these cases the lawyers will be expected to attend only to such engagements and to make every endeavour to cease to practise completely at the earliest possible date.

(*e*) **Boycott of Councils*.—The boycott of Councils being of immediate importance, it requires the greatest concentration of energy to make it as complete as possible. Candidates who have already come forward should be approached by deputations requesting them to withdraw their candidature and electors should be approached to sign the following form :—

> " In view and in virtue of the resolution of the Special Session of the National Congress and the All-India Moslem League we, being voters in the . . . electoral district of . . . for election to the Reformed Councils, hereby place on record our desire that we do not wish to be represented at the Provincial Legislative Council (or the Legislative Assembly or the Council of State), and hereby inform all candidates for election that if they seek election in spite of our wishes to the contrary, they will not represent us. We do hereby declare further that we do not desire to be represented on any legislative bodies until full Swaraj is established, which alone can make impossible the repetition of the Punjab atrocities and breach of solemn pledges as in the matter of the Khilafat."

Lists of those who have withdrawn their candidature and those who persist should be forwarded to the provincial headquarters. Greatest care should be taken to put the pros and cons before the voters prior to asking to sign the abovementioned form which should be translated in the vernacular of the district concerned.

(*f*) **Recruiting of Labour for Mesopotamia*.—Propaganda should be carried on by workers among those who are likely to offer themselves for such services placing before them the true situation, and then letting them make their choice.

(*g*) *Boycott of Foreign Goods*.—Every non-co-operator is in duty bound to simplify his or her wants and dispense with all luxuries that are depended on the use of foreign articles.

* A reference to the resolutions passed at the Congress will show that (*e*) and (*f*) have been alternated.

(*h*) *Swadeshi.*—We attach great importance to Swadeshi in the form of revival of hand-spinning and hand-weaving and distribution of cloth so manufactured. Thousands of workers need special training for this work. Ladies of high station especially should be induced to take up hand-spinning and to use only such cloth as can be woven out of hand-spun yarn. Classes should be formed in every street. Spinning-wheels can be manufactured by any ordinary carpenter. Those taking up this branch of work should communicate with the manager of Satyagrah Ashram, Sabarmati, near Ahmedabad.

(*i*) *Swaraj Fund.*—It is very necessary that a National Fund should be established for the purpose of carrying into effect the Congress resolution. Funds will be required for propaganda work, for encouraging Swadeshi, for establishing national schools, and for supporting lawyers who have suspended their practice and are unable to support themselves. Provincial Congress Committees with the help of district and other organisations should therefore make every endeavour to collect funds and submit monthly reports of receipts and expenditure to the All-India Congress Committee.

(*j*) *Volunteer Corps.*—Provincial, District and Town organisations should form volunteer corps for the purpose of disciplining the people and maintaining order.

(*k*) *Finally* we should advise that where there is a sufficient number of workers a batch should specialise in order to make one particular item successful. Where the workers are not sufficient, precedence should be given to the boycott of the Councils because results must be shown in this item of non-co-operation before the middle of December next.

APPENDIX D.

(*Vide* Part I, paragraph 95.)

OUTLINE SCHEME OF SWARAJ.

Note.

In some public statements made by me in October and November, 1922, and again in my Presidential Address at the Gaya Congress, on 26th December, 1922, I drew the attention of the public to the need for stating the fundamental principles and formulating the broad outlines of a Scheme of Self-government which should form the basis of Indian Swaraj.

Subsequently, the new party (known as the Congress-Khilafat Swaraj Party) which has been formed within the Congress, in consequence of division of opinion over the question of contesting elections for the official Councils, desired me to outline such a scheme, in conjunction with other friends, who also had been pressing the matter on the attention of the Indian People for some time past, and were co-opted for the Drafting Committee.

The Outline now placed before the public is the result. It was placed before a meeting of leading members of the new party, at Bombay, on 29th January, 1923. There was no time to discuss it properly. Many of the members present (from almost all the larger Congress Provinces) expressed a general approval; others reserved opinion. But it was unanimously agreed that the draft should be placed before the Indian People, through the Press, and suggestions and criticisms invited.

It was also unanimously agreed that the Outline represents the Ideal which should be kept in view, as one to be gradually worked up to, and that a certain number of intermediate and progressive steps have to intervene, but which must all definitely, unmistakeably, steadily and progressively help to change the present regime so as to realise that ideal at no distant date.

CHITTA RANJAN DAS.

BOMBAY,

30th January 1923.

NOTE—It is requested that all suggestions and criticisms may be sent, in envelopes marked on the face with the words, "Swaraj Scheme", to the address of Pandit Motilal Nehru, Ananda Bhawan, Allahabad.

OUTLINE SCHEME OF SWARAJ.

CHAPTER I.—ESSENTIAL PRINCIPLES.

The principles which guide this outline are those which have been honoured in India from time immemorial, and have been re-iterated in the Presidential Address of the Gaya Congress, in December, 1922, thus;

"To form a scheme of government, regard must be had

(1) to the formation of local centres more or less on the lines of the ancient village system of India;

(2) the growth of larger and larger groups out of the integration of these village centres;

(3) the unifying state should be the result of similar growth;

(4) the village centres and the larger groups must be practically autonomous;

(5) the residuary power of control must remain in the Central Government, but the exercise of such power should be exceptional, and for that purpose, proper safeguards should be provided, so that the practical autonomy of the local centres may be maintained, and at the same time, the growth of the central government into a really unifying state may be possible. The ordinary work of such Central Government should be mainly advisory."

Briefly, *a maximum of local autonomy*, carried on mainly with advice and co-ordination from, and only *a minimum of control by, higher centres*, which will have some special functions besides.

To this should be added that *every possible care should be taken to ensure that the people's elected representatives*, who will constitute the Chief Authority for each grade of centre, local and higher, with power to make laws and rules, *shall be*, not self-seekers, but *seekers of the public welfare.*

CHAPTER II.—ADMINISTRATIVE DIVISIONS.

(a) *Local Centres.*

1. The foundation of the whole administration should be in Local Centres (*grama*), small but practically autonomous.

2. A Local Centre should ordinarily consist of a number of villages of which the population should total about ten thousand souls.

(b) *Town Centres.*

3. Towns (*nagar*), should form separate entities, and might, as necessary, be sub-divided into wards or quarters, of about the same population limits as the rural Local Centres.

(c) *District Centres.*

4. Rural and urban Local Centres should be integrated into larger groups or District Centres (*zila*) with populations of from five to twenty lakhs.

(d) *Provinces.*

5. District Centres should be integrated into Provincial Organisations.

6. Provinces (*sooba*) should be demarcated on the linguistic basis. Any which are considered too large may be divided into smaller ones.

(e) *All-India Organisation.*

7. The Provincial Organisations should be integrated into and be co-ordinated by an All-India (Bharata-varsha or Hindustan) Organisation according to population.

8. Subject to these general principles, each Province should draw up its own scheme of administrative divisions to suit provincial variations.

CHAPTER III.—ADMINISTRATIVE FUNCTIONS.

Functions should be as below :

A. (*i*) Provision for appropriate *Education* of all educable children and youth of both sexes (*Shiksha* or *Talim*).

(*ii*) *Provision for Recreation* (*vinoda* or *dil-batsagi*) *e.g.*, Public Gardens, Parks, Museums, Playing-grounds, Libraries, Reading Rooms, Art-galleries, Popular Lectures, Recitations, Processions, Pageants, Religious Festivals* (Katha,

* As regards "Places of Public Worship, for the various Creeds", see Appendix, Note to Chapter III.

Yatra, Kala-kshepam, Kirtana, Ram-lila, Krishna-lila, Maulud, Christmas and Easter celebrations, *etc.*) refining, elevating and instructive Dramas, Cinema and Magic Lantern Shows, Games and Sports, *etc.*

B. Provision for *Protection* (*Raksha* or *Hifazat*), by means of

(*i*) Police and Local Militia and Regular Military Forces;

(*ii*) Justice and Settlement of Disputes, through Arbitration Courts or Panchayats in the narrower sense, and Registration of Deeds;

(*iii*) Appropriate Medical Help and Sanitation.

C. Provision for *Economic and Industrial Welfare* (*Jivika* or *Maash*), by promotion of

(*i*) Agriculture (*Krishi* or *Zira-at*);

(*ii*) Cattle-breeding (*Go-raksha* or *Taraqqi-maweshi*), *i.e.*, increase and preservation of domestic animals of all kinds, for purposes of milk, wool, plough, transport, *etc.*;

(*iii*) Other Productive Industries relating to Mines, Forests, Fisheries, Salt, Sericulture, Arboriculture, etc., (*Akara-karma* or *Madaniyat*, etc.);

(*iv*) Arts and Crafts and Manufactures of all kinds (*Shilpa* or *Sanaat-hirfat*);

(*v*) Trade and Commerce (*Vanijya* or *Tijarat*); and

(*vi*) By promotion and regulation of the various means which subserve the above, *e.g.*, Railways, Post and Telegraph, Shipping, Roads, Waterways, Canals, Bridges, Ferries, Presses, Public Buildings, Monuments, Rest-Houses, Currency, Measures of Flood and Famine Relief, Rates and Taxes, Tariff and Customs, Surveys of various kinds (Geographical, Geological, Botanical, Meteorological, Statistical, Archæological, etc.), Friendly Relations with other States, etc.

D. The above provisions would be made

(*i*) by means of laws and rules which would be framed by the different grades of Panchayats, and would have force within the domains of their respective makers, the enactments of the lower grades of Councils being made with advice from and co-ordination by the higher when needed;

(*ii*) by appointment of executive officials (who would be wholly responsible to the Councils appointing them) to carry out the laws and rules; and

(*iii*) by supervision of their work.

CHAPTER IV.—PANCHAYATS AND ALLOCATION OF FUNCTIONS.

A. Local Centres or Communes and Local Panchayats.

(*a*) For each rural or urban Local Centre or Commune there should be one Local Panchayat of twenty-one periodically elected members.

(*b*) This Panchayat should be in charge of the different functional departments mentioned above, so far as the Commune affords scope for them, and should carry on the work by means of sub-committees.

(*c*) Under *Education*,

(*i*) they would maintain local Schools, giving elementary cultural and vocational-technical instruction, and

(*ii*) would provide for suitable Recreation.

(*d*) Under Protection,

(*i*) they would appoint their own *Chaukidars* (Watchmen), and would form Local Militia out of such chaukidars and other able-bodied men, and would provide for their proper training;

(*ii*) they would arrange for Arbitration Courts (the members of which would be separately elected), which would deal with simple civil (including what are now known as rent and revenue, *divani* and *mal* or *artha-vivada*) and criminal (*faujdari* or *parushya-vivada*) cases;

(*iii*) they would also maintain an adequate Hospital (*chikitsalaya* or *shafakhana*) and Medical Staff which would provide treatment free and be responsible for the proper Sanitation of the Commune.

(*e*) Under *Economical and Industrial Ministration*, the Local Panchayat would be responsible to its Electorate primarily, on the one hand, and to the higher Panchayats, on the other, secondarily,

(*i*) to see that arable lands are properly tilled, and village commons, playing-grounds, pasture-lands, groves, orchards, *etc.*, are properly maintained, and a sufficiency of necessaries, specially corn, cotton, and cattle, (or other forms of food, clothing, and accessories, in specially circumstanced tracts), for the use of the Commune, is always available within their jurisdiction;

(*ii*) that co-operative organisations, in the shape of Stores, Banks, *etc.*, are maintained in the needed numbers;

(*iii*) that wells, tanks, *tals*, canals, and all means of supply of good water for drinking and other domestic purposes, and for irrigation, and all roads, *etc.*. within their Commune, are properly maintained;

(*iv*). that production of surplus corn, cotton, cattle, and other necessaries as well as comforts, and of mineral and other products and means of increasing the wealth of the locality is encouraged, cottage-industries promoted, and arrangements made for commercial dealing with this produce in such a manner as to avoid competitive waste.

B. Intermediate Centres or Districts and District Panchayats.

(*a*) The District Panchayat should be constituted by each Local Panchayat (or group of Local Panchayats) periodically choosing one member, who may or may not be one of them; provided that the total number of members should not exceed one hundred; and provided also that at least two-fifths of them should be residents of towns.

(*b*) They would form sub-committees among themselves on the lines before mentioned.

(*c*) The District Panchayat would generally *advise* and *not control* the Local Panchayat, in respect of all functions. Special provision would be made for such control as may be occasionally or absolutely necessary.

(*d*)—(*i*) Under *Education*, the District Panchayat should maintain one or more higher educational institutions (like colleges and high schools) as may be necessary, which will give cultural as well as technical instruction.

(*ii*) They would also provide *Recreation*, arranging for the more expensive items which may not be within the means of the Local Panchayats.

(*e*) Under *Protection*, they would

(*i*) co-ordinate, the Local Police;

(*ii*) arrange to maintain some special Reserve or District Police;

(*iii*) organise and co-ordinate the Local Militia, so that they might discharge the functions of a disciplined Army; and

(*iv*) maintain one or more larger Hospitals and supply medical and sanitary advice to their Communes.

(*f*) Under *Economic and Industrial Ministration*, the District Panchayat would

(*i*) co-ordinate the Local Banks and Stores and other local economic and industrial and commercial enterprises; and

(*ii*) organise or promote such independent enterprises.

C. Town Centres and Town Panchayats.

(*a*) Aggregations of dwellings containing ten thousand or more inhabitants should be regarded as towns.

(*b*) Towns should be organised in the same way, generally, as the rural Local Centres; and the same general principles should be applied to their functioning as to the rural Local Centres, as far as practicable, but regard must be had to the special variations, the economic and other circumstances.

(*c*) For the purposes of the integration of the District Centres and the election of the District Panchayats, the rural and the urban Local Centres should be counted side by side as component units; and the headquarters or the seat of the District Panchayats would ordinarily be the largest town of the district.

(*d*) For the purpose of unifying the administration of each town as a single whole, the Town Members of the District Councils, together with such other members as may be specially elected by the Ward-Panchayats, in the proportion of two per ward, should form a Town Panchayat (like the present Municipal Boards), which would be intermediate between the urban Local (*i.e.*, Ward) Panchayats and the District Panchayat, and would discharge as many of the functions of the District Council, towards the whole Town, as may be conveniently possible.

D. Provinces and Provincial Panchayats.

(*a*) The Provincial Panchayats should consist of members elected by the District Panchayats in the proportion of one for every two lakhs of the population; provided that the total number shall not fall below twenty-one, nor exceed one hundred; and provided also that at least half the number should be urban residents. They may or may not be members of the District Panchayats.

(*b*) The Provincial Panchayats would advise the District Panchayats and co-ordinate them and their work, using residuary powers of control under proper safeguards.

(*c*) Its special work would be,

(*i*) to maintain advanced Educational Institutions (in the nature of Vidyapithas, Dar-ul-ilums, "Seats of Learning," "Centres of Knowledge," Universities) which would give expert cultural and technical training and promote research;

(*ii*) to maintain special Police and Military Forces, for the guarding of Frontiers, Sea-boards, *etc.*;

(*iii*) to make provision for Justice in special cases;

(*iv*) to administer Provincial Railways, Water-works, Canals, Roads, *etc.*

E. The India Panchayat.

(*a*) The All-India Panchayat should consist of members elected by the Provincial Panchayats in the proportion of one for every thirty lakhs of population, but Provinces which may have a total population of less than thirty lakhs would send one representative. At least three-fifths of the members should be urban.

(*b*) The functions of the India Panchayat would be similar to those of the Provincial Panchayat, *mutatis mutandis;* a special one would be to deal with neighbouring States (including Indian States) and Foreign Countries.

(*c*) The India Panchayat should create a Consulting Senate, consisting of eminent men and women of thought and special knowledge, belonging to all parts of India, who would be elected by the India Panchayat, from time to time, without restriction of members, and who would be asked for advice on any subject, as needed, by the India Panchayat or the Provincial Panchayats.

(*d*) The language of the India Panchayat should be Hindustani, while the Provinces would use their mother-tongues.

F. Special Provision for Filling up Vacancies.

Generally, if a member of a lower Council is elected to a higher, his place may be filled up by a new election by the same electorate.

CHAPTER V.—THE QUALIFICATIONS OF THE CHOOSERS AND THE CHOSEN.

1. Every individual of either sex, who has resided in India for at least seven years, and is at least twenty-five years of age if a man, and twenty-one years if a woman, should be entitled to elect to the Local Panchayat.

2. The members of the Local Panchayats should elect to the District Panchayat.

3. The members of the District Panchayat should elect to the Provincial Panchayat.

4. The members of the Provincial Panchayat should elect to the India Panchayat.

5. The members of all four grades of Panchayats should be permanent residents of the country, preferably of the particular centre, and should be chosen irrespective of their creed, caste, class, color, race, or sex, but subject to adjustment, where unavoidably necessary, for purposes of creedal or communal representation.

6. Such representatives should ordinarily be not less than forty years of age; should have done some good work in any walk of life; should, if rural, be at least literate, and, if urban, should possess higher educational qualifications, and, in the case of rural and urban members of the Provincial and India Councils, should have corresponding higher and superior educational qualifications or equivalent expert experience; should have retired from competitive business or other professional life of bread-winning or money-making, and be able to support themselves on their own savings, or be assured of all necessaries and personal requirements by their families or friends; should give practically all their time to national work, and should do so without any cash remuneration. But their travelling and other *ex-officio* expenses, which might be necessary to enable them to discharge their public duties, should be met from State funds, and their status as Members of Panchayat should be regarded as having greater honor attached to it than any salaried office, so that they would receive precedence at public functions.

7. The members of each Panchayat should possess, between them, experience of all the main departments of the communal life which they have to administer.

8. No one should offer himself, or canvass for himself, as a candidate for election; but, if requested by electors, he might publicly signify his consent to accept the burden of office, if elected.

CHAPTER VI.—SEPARATION OF FUNCTIONS.

1. Throughout the whole administration, Legislative, Judicial, and Executive functions shall be kept separate from one another.

CHAPTER VII.—FINANCE.

1. The revenues needed to meet necessary expenditure should be raised by the Local Panchayats by means of taxation, with advice from the upper Panchayats.

2. State factories might be opened as necessary, with a view to prevent waste by individual competition, over-production, bad production, *etc.*, to cheapen commodities, and to reduce taxation, but not so as to create monopolies and stifle private enterprise.

3. Where practicable, Local and District Councils should make such improvements in the locality as might result in addition to the communal income, *e.g.*, public wells, tanks, canals, roads, groves of timber and fruit trees, *etc.*, and thereby lead to reduction of taxation.

4. Contributions would be made by the Local Panchayats to make up the revenues of the District Panchayats; by them to the Provincial; and by the Provincial to the India Panchayat.

5. Special taxation might be imposed by the Provincial and India Panchayats.

CHAPTER VIII.—PROPRIETORSHIP.

1. Private property would be recognised and maintained and the growth of individual wealth, both movable and immovable, would be permitted, but so as not to encroach on or make impossible or impracticable the growth of public possessions as well; and the owner of individual wealth, who spends it on pious works, *i.e.*, works of public utility, as requested by a Panchayat, would receive special marks of honor.

APPENDIX.

NOTE TO CHAPTER I.

Fundamental Principles.

(*a*) Excessive centralization, and the concentration of all power in the hands of a bureaucratic clique, mindful of its own prestige and emoluments, careless of the public weal, walling itself off more and more thickly from touch with public opinion, in fact arrogant and disdainful towards the public, regarding itself as public-*master* rather than public-*servant*—this is the bane, in consequence of which the public servant waxes and the public wanes, more and more, every day, in India. Genuine decentralization of administration, substantial distribution of power, and real responsibility of the public servants to the People's trusted representatives—this is the only remedy. Hence the formulation of practical local autonomy as a fundamental principle.

(*b*) The failure to secure *ethical* fitness, the philanthropic and humanitarian out-look upon life, in the elected legislators,—in consequence of which failure, the laws made by them are not wise and just, but partial to special class interests, and promote an excessive inequality and therefore widespread discontent and conflicts of all kinds and degrees—this is the disastrous and all-vitiating defect of western system of Swaraj, the cause of all their internal ferments and their external wars, of the enslavement of Labour by Capital, of the many by the few, within each State, and of the ruthless exploitation of weaker nations without. This failure must be strenuously guarded against in our scheme. Hence the formulation of the second fundamental principle.

NOTE TO CHAPTER II.

Administrative Divisions.

This scheme of administrative divisions is in accord with the time-honoured traditions of the country. The agricultural village and the village community were, are, and ought to continue to be, the natural basis of our special type of culture and civilisation, and of all wise administration in a country ninety per cent. of the population of which is rural. Most writers and thinkers about India are agreed in this. In the most ancient days, of which accounts are available, the socio-politico-economical divisions were the village, the group of ten villages, the group of ten tens or a hundred, the group of ten such or a thousand—grama, janapada, pranta, vishaya, mandala, and so on. In medieval times and the days of the Moghals, the arrangement was much the same—mauza, tappa, pargana. zila, sooba, etc. It is the same to-day in the Indian States and in the territories under British occupation. The names of the divisions and sub-divisions differ in the different provinces. No radical change can be made in this principle of groupings and integration. But for the purposes of the electoral principle, which worked sub-consciously in the old days of the panchayat and the village community, and has to work consciously and deliberately now, a population basis is suggested for the initial groups, and also for the next intermediate groups, though with greater elasticity. For the third grade, linguistic basis is the most natural and has been already recognized by the Congress. The fourth and the final grade is governed by many considerations, geographical, political, economical, cultural, etc.; for fixing the outermost boundaries of this whole, no single principle suffices.

The single village cannot well be accepted to-day as the initial unit of administration. The population of the five hundred thousand villages of British-occupied India varies from a few dozens to a few thousands. Therefore, in the interests of a convenient uniformity, a population basis of approximately ten thousand is suggested. This will give about three to four thousand electors for the Local Panchayat (dealt with in a subsequent chapter)—not too large a number for such common consciousness and general acquaintance, by reputation or directly, as is needed for electoral purposes. For the whole of India, the proportion of women over twenty-one is, roundly, about sixty-five millions out of one hundred and fifty; and of men over twenty-five, also about sixty-five millions, but out of one hundred and sixty.

The treatment of towns as separate entities is suggested for obvious reasons. The difference between the conditions of the two, town and country-village, *pura* and *jana-pada*, *shahar* and *dehat*, has been recognized in all times and climes. The one represents (by no means exclusively, but only by predominant feature) the *intellectual power* (*budhi*, *aql*) of the People; the other, their *vital power* (*prana*, *jan*). They are *inter*-dependent. *Both* are necessary for a full civilized life for the People as a whole. But the modern western plutocratic and bureaucratic centralizing tendency causes the town to grow *excessively* and absorb the vitality of the country inordinately. This excess needs to be checked, and *a just balance between the two* to be restored, in order to prevent disastrous devitalization of the soul and the body of the vast agricultural population, and the consequent crashing down, before long, of the whole much too top-heavy organism.

This balance will be restored by emphasizing the *separate autonomy* of the village groups and the towns—the needed co-ordination and mutual support being secured by the advice, and, where absolutely necessary, the control, of the Provincial Authority. The need of this separateness is recognized even under the British regime by the distinction between Municipal Boards and District Boards, though, of course, in that regime, the local '*self*-government' of the Boards is carried on under the strict '*other*-government' of the district officials.

The reason for fixing more elastic population-limits for the District and Town Groups is this. In the Punjab, the population of the existing twenty-nine districts varies from five lakhs to ten lakhs, and gives an average of about seven lakhs. The twenty-six districts of Bombay vary between three and twelve lakhs, and give an average of eight. The average for Bengal is sixteen; the largest population, not only in Bengal, but the whole of India, being that of Mymensingh, *i.e.*, forty-five lakhs. The average for Madras is also sixteen. Also for Behar. That for the U. P., ten. Some of the larger districts, *f.i.*, Mymensingh with forty-five lakhs, Vizagapatam and Gorakhpur with thirty-two each, Dacca and Darbhanga with thirty each, Muzaffarpur and Midnapore with twenty-eight each, are too bulky for convenience of autonomous administration. Even the men of the British regime have been thinking of dividing some of them into two or three districts each. The capital towns have eleven or twelve lakhs. The lower limit for towns may be regarded as ten thousand. The Census officials of the present regime have defined the town as every continuous collection of houses inhabited by not less than five thousand persons. Ten thousand is suggested in the text, later on, in view of the fact that that figure has been suggested for the rural Local Centre also. In British-occupied India, there are about twelve hundred 'towns' or villages, with a population between five and ten thousand, or a total of about eighty lakhs. In view of such facts, elastic limits, of five to twenty lakhs, have been suggested for the District. For purposes of symmetry, the figure might have been fixed at ten lakhs uniformly. It is the actual average for the two hundred and seventy-five districts of British-occupied India. But the centre of a district has, ordinarily, to be a fair-sized town. And in tracts where towns are few and far between, large agricultural areas and populations have to be grouped around and with them. Natural boundaries, rivers, forests, ranges of hills, etc., also make for variation of area and population.

Note to Chapter III.

Functions.

Western writers divide the functions of government into (*i*) Constituent or Protective, and (*ii*) Ministrant or Promotive. The former are what may be called negative mainly, (*a*) the prevention of crimes and breaches of peace. and (*b*) adjustment of wrongs; in other words, preventive and curative, or police-military and judicial. The others are positive and constructive, the active promotion of the welfare of the community.

The *laisser faire* school of socio-political thought, looking at the mischievous consequences of over-interference by the State, *i.e.*, the Bureaucracy, would confine the duties of government to the former only; and would give to the individuals, regarded as units, who compose the Public or People, full liberty to work out their own destiny in their own ways, in competition with each other, so far as positive welfare or 'success in life'—whatever that might mean—is concerned. This is the school of Individualism. Another school, looking at the immense waste of energy and life, which results from unregulated competition, and at the exploitation of the less cunning and less able 'many' by the more cunning and strong 'few', (so that the evils of bureaucracy re-appear as the evils of plutocracy) and also realising that widespread and substantial and lasting 'success in life' depends more upon 'mutual aid' and co-operation and communal organization, than upon individual enterprise, recommend State-regulation and the free exercise of promotive functions by the State in new ways which will obviate the evils resulting from bureaucracy.' This school of thought is generally known as that of Socialism; but by differences of views as to the ways, becomes divided into many, known as Collectivism, Communism, Anarchism, State-socialism, Guild-socialism, etc.

As usual, the truth is in the golden mean, and error in the extremes. The best course is the middle course. Our Swaraj must maintain a balance between Individualism and Socialism (*swartha*, and *parartha*); must reconcile the two. For *both* are *necessary* to full civilized life, even as the pronouns 'I' and 'We'. The needed reconciliation will be effected by maximising local elective autonomy and minimizing centralization.

As to the preventive and curative functions, Police-Military and Justice, there is no dispute. Also as regards Medicative and Sanitative, which may be regarded partly as protective and partly as promotive, Sanitation being preventive of disease and promotive of health, and Medication being curative of ills.

But a certain amount of "promotive" work must also be done by the various grades of Centres. This work may be grouped under two main heads, the promotion (*i*) of right Education, the very foundation, of all communal welfare, (and therefore placed here before even Protection) and (*ii*) of Economic and Industrial Well being. Education will include Recreation also, as being indirect education in a popular and elastic and almost more effective form.

It is the duty of the elders of the family (*i*) to protect the younger generation, (*ii*) to amuse and educate them, (*iii*) to settle them in life, to put them in the way of earning a livelihood. The duty, the right, the function, of the elders of the villages, of the districts, of the provinces of the country as a great whole, is *none other*. All the functions of government are either these, or subsidiary to these.

A word may be specially added here on the subject of Recreation. The object of measures under this head would be two-fold; (*i*) to provide such *refined entertainment*, for young and old alike as will give healthy *relaxation*, as well as healthy *tone*, and also *indirect* yet very useful education, to the mind and body of all sections of the public, in leisure hours; and (*ii*) at the same time to *displace the evil recreations* of drink and drugs and other social vices and harmful indulgences. It should be borne in mind that *some* recreations human beings will have; and where healthy ones are not easily available, evil ones *will* be resorted to.

The desirability should be considered here, of putting provision for "Places of public worship for the various creed" among the duties of the Panchayat, under the head of Education and Recreation, and putting it even in the forefront. The Worship of the Infinite, (a more indubitable fact than the Finite, is Re-creation, creation anew of the soul and the finer elements of the body, nourishment for the inmost heart, in a very real sense). That the Elders of the Commune should have the duty of making this provision duly (and separately only to the extent unavoidably necessary, and with at least one place where members of *all* and *any* creed might join occasionally in a Common Prayer worded so as to be acceptable to all)—this would conduce to the liberalisation of all the creeds concerned and thence to the Religious Peace which is indispensable for India's and the world's progress.

Note to Chapter IV.

Panchayats and Allocation of Functions.

The placing of the head-quarters of the District Panchayat in the largest town of the district will make the co-ordination of the administration of the town and the country easy. And it is in accordance with natural tendency. The danger that the town may begin to dominate the country, is guarded against by the provision that the country members of the District Panchayat should be in the majority.

The proportion of the two classes of members is made equal in the Provincial Panchayat, and reversed in the India Panchayat, because the upper bodies have to deal more and more with technical and non-agricultural affairs.

The Essential Change.

"*Advisory* and not *mandatory*—excepting in rare cases"—this is the essence of the change needed in the administration. The change is one of *spirit*. The details of the official executive machinery may remain much as they are now; but if the executive, the judicial, and the legislative powers are separated, and the 'legislators' (in the broad sense) who compose the Panchayats, of all grades, are elected, and the higher Panchayats ordinarily *advise* and not *command* the lower Panchayats, and the executive officials are really responsible to the Panchayats, then, it is expected, the evils of the present regime will be cured. For the autocracy and the Bureaucracy will be replaced by what may be called an aristo-demo-cracy. Aristocracy, because the panchayats will be composed of the *best* and most trusted and honoured of the people; demo-cracy because the people will *choose them*. The members of the Panchayats would not exercise any executive powers directly, either in their individual or their corporate capacity, but would only make laws or rules or pass resolutions. These would be carried out by the Executive. And the Executive, or at least the chief officials thereof, would be appointed and, if necessary, dismissed or otherwise punished, by the Panchayats. In some cases the executive official may be an elected one. He too would be subject to the supervision of the Panchayats. The control of the Panchayat-Legislative would thus be exercised over the Executive by means of this power of appointment, dismissal, or advancement. The Judiciary would be mostly elective also, subject to approval by the Panchayat-Legislative.

This separation of powers would minimise the temptations to, and opportunities of, corruption for all, and would make Executive (and also the Judiciary) *responsible* to the People, in the persons of their Elect, which responsibility is the one great desideratum to-day.

It will be remembered that Mr. Gokhale suggested and endeavoured that Advisory Committees should be formed in each district, to advise the district officer in all important matters. Of course, the Bureaucracy declined, on the ground that it would interfere with the individual responsibility of the district office. When they said 'responsibility', they, of course, mean ir-responsibility; for when was the district officer responsible, and to whom? If he was or is responsible at all, it was and is only to the Bureaucratic Clique. If Mr. Gokhale could have agreed, as was suggested in some quarters, that the Advisory Committee should be nominated by the district officer himself, then, indeed, there would have been no difficulty in the acceptance of his suggestion. Only, then, each district officer would have had a standing Darbar of so many courtiers, the nawab-ic arrangement would have been completed, and the People would have been worse off than before.

What is needed is that the Advisory Committee should be a Panchayat made up of the Elders of the People, which will not *interfere* with the pretended and non-existent responsibility of the executive official, but will make it *real* and *enforce* it.

Measures are outlined later on, for further safeguarding and ensuring, as far as is humanly possible, the uprightness of the members of the Panchayats themselves; for such safeguarding is the very heart of the whole scheme.

It should be noted that, though option is given, the presumption is that the majority of the members of the higher Panchayats will be chosen from among the members of the lower, who will be all directly elected by the People. Constant and sympathetic touch and unity of spirit and of work will thus be maintained throughout, and the People will, for all practical purposes, directly elect to all the Panchayats, Local, Intermediate, and Central, even though, technically, the election to the latter will be by a process of distillation through electoral colleges. The latter process has some advantages, which too will be secured by this method. The immense worry and trouble and expense of holding huge elections, by millions upon millions of voters over and over again, for a handful of seats, would be all saved. And in the Local Panchayats, with their small area and population, and through them, in the upper ones, the elected and the electors will be in constant touch with each other, public opinion will carry its full weight and receive its full due, influencing the members of the Local Panchayats and through them those of the upper ones effectively.

It is very desirable that there should be a certain number of persons who should belong to all grades of Panchayats. They will serve as the personal linking medium and would bind together all parts of India continuously and effectively, and at the same time keep all the centres in real touch with each other. And this would be one important measure for guarding against the possibility (which is always present in federations of practically autonomous areas and communities) of their falling apart, under the influence of false provincialisms and insularities and other such causes, (which are very liable to be fostered by the linguistic demarcation), and so weakening the whole. Another measure is connected with finance, in the shape of some special All-India taxation; and a third, with the use of a common language by the All-India Panchayat. Both are mentioned in their proper places.

In this way, the virtuous (and not the vicious) circle of (not to use the harsh word 'government', but) administration of the affairs of the People, for the People, by the Peoples (Trusted and Chosen Elders) will be wholesomely completed. Human affairs should be administered by those who know human nature in mind and body; a People's affairs should be administered by those who are its Elect and are in constant and sympathetic touch with, and therefore know, the People and their requirements of body and mind.

It will be seen that, under the scheme, the District Councils will be fairly large in point of numbers. A district of the maximum population of twenty lakhs, will have a Panchayat of one hundred members; whereas the provinces which are largest in population (at present) will have no more in their Provincial Panchayats. As the bulk of the administrative work will be disposed of by the Local and the District Councils, when they are really autonomous, very large numbers for the upper Councils are unnecessary from the standpoint of disposal and distribution of work between and by sub-committees. Very large numbers are also otherwise undesirable in deliberative bodies. The personnel may be changed at short intervals, by framing rules in that behalf. It may be observed here that these sub-committees properly framed and used, would correspond to heads of guilds, and would secure to the communal administration, the advantages, on a higher level, of the village-community as well as the city-guilds-system.

NOTE TO CHAPTER V.

Qualifications of Choosers and Chosen.

With regard to the ages suggested for Electors, the idea is that only those who are mature in body and mind, and have had some experience of life, and specially of family responsibility, should be entrusted with the duty of choosing those who would rule their affairs. The ages suggested would ordinarily give these requisites in India. It seems that in England the difference is reversed, twenty-one is fixed for men and thirty for women.. Perhaps it was thought that at the earlier age, women would be too busy with family cares and work inside the home, to be able to take much interest in the work outside. In India women are as mature in body and mind at twenty-one as men at twenty-five; and these different ages, if fixed as suggested, would generally enable husband and wife to go to the poll together.

As regards the qualifications of the elected it has been said at the outset that the conditions for election should be such as would make it humanly probable that the electors may be seekers of public weal and not self-seekers. The qualifications mentioned in the Outline Scheme are as "the outward symbols of the inward grace". They are such as ordinarily go with the wise and self-denying and philanthropic nature. The reasons for suggesting them may be mentioned in greater detail as below.

(*a*) Legislators should be permanent residents of the country for which they are to legislate; but their creed, caste, class, colour, race, or sex should not, as such, be regarded either as a qualification or as a disqualification. Without permanent residence in the country. sympathetic understanding is not possible; while taking account of creed, caste, *etc.*, in the elections, imports into the resulting legislature the vicious spirit of conflicting interests and party-politics in place of the virtuous spirit of each caring for all. But if, because, at present, there is much creed and caste and class jealousy existent in the country, it should seem necessary that some exceptions should be made, there is provision for communal representation. It is to be trusted, however, that once the scheme begins to work, the whole atmosphere will change so that these jealousies will disappear, and it will be realised by all that civic well-being is independent of creeds and sectarian beliefs, as has been realised in Japan.

(*b*) At forty, persons have well passed middle age and usually have children of their own and thus experience of the household life. This will make reasonably probable that the legislator possesses intimate knowledge of human nature in its more common and important aspects, knows what responsibility for the well-being of others means, and has sober and mature judgment. But he should have also retired from all competitive bread-winning or money-making and should be living on his past earnings or on a 'pension' So, he would feel financially independent; his outlook upon life, his attitude towards his fellow-beings, would have changed from that of selfish taking to that of unselfish giving; and he would have all the leisure needed for his public duties.

It may be that many persons are not able to retire from their business or profession at forty. But we do not want many. Exceptions will be able to. And we want exceptionally selfless men for this essential and highest kind of public work. Twenty-one persons in ten thousand are not too many to expect. If the country cannot provide even so much self-denial, it may as well give up all attempts at Swaraj. But the country *has* been showing capacity for self-denial; and there is no need to be doubtful. Moreover, if few people are in a position to give up business or profession at forty, many *can*, and *ought to*, at forty-five or fifty, with considerable benefit to the whole moral tone of them-selves and their community. And if the Panchayat members are fifty years or more, there is no harm done, but rather more mature wisdom and experience secured. After all, even under the current managements, the deliberative and legislative and guiding assemblies of most nations and communities are composed of grey-haired persons. A younger and physically more vigorous and active age is wanted in the executive offices, where action is required more than thought. It has to be remembered that the old *have been young*, and *know* what the young know; but the young *have not* been old, and *do not know* what the old know; though it is devoutly to be prayed that they may all become very very old and learn all that the old know, except the pains of old age! It may be that many persons tend to become mentally inactive also, after fifty-five or sixty. But between forty-five and fifty-five is, ordinarily, a very good age for the kind of deliberative and legislative work we have in view here. And there are cases, though rare, in which the mind is thoroughly capable and active, and the body healthy, right up to seventy or more. But it may be worth while to fix a maximum age-limit also, say sixty or sixty-five as the minimum is forty.

Provision may also be made for exceptions. It may be that these high age-limits will sometimes exclude really brilliant younger men. Our conception of the legislator requires not *brilliance* but *wisdom*. Brilliance comes and goes, and plays false, and proves tinsel, and makes messes, but wisdom lingers. Wisdom is matured knowledge *plus* philanthropy, patriarchal benevolence. Brilliance may well wait and mature into a softer, steadier, soberer light and do its duty so much the better *after* attaining the forty years. If it is substantial, it will not get extinguished by waiting a few years. Yet, for cases in which the work of the Panchayat concerned is likely to suffer if any particular person is shut out because of the age-limit, provision may be made for exceptions, as said.

(c) We want another qualification in our Panchayat member. He should have done outstandingly good work in *some* walk of life—whether literary, scientific, educational, priestly, medical, artistic, *etc.*, or administrative, official, military, etc., or commercial, agricultural, industrial, financial, *etc.*, or as a labourer and manual worker; and he should have done this and at the same time acquired a reputation for uprightness and honest dealing and sympathy for fellow-creatures. An aged agriculturist who has tilled his few acres successfully, has raised up a good family, is respected and trusted in his own and neighbouring villages, and can express his views clearly, is a wise village-elder, in short, may be a more useful member of a legislature which has to deal with vast agricultural interests like those of India, even though he may be only just able to sign his name, than many brilliant speakers or writers with only a college education that has little touch of reality.

(*d*) Another desirable condition is that the legislator should not receive any cash remuneration for his work from the public funds. Such cash payment, while perfectly right and even necessary in other fields of work, taints the peculiar fiduciary status of the *legislator*, who should stand in the position of Trustee and Elder to the people. He should therefore meet all his *personal* expenses himself. But, of course, all his *ex-officio* expenses must be met out of public funds. This would invest the legislator with the venerable dignity which naturally belongs to such an Elder. Trust, honour, reverence—these are the proper, the only, and the natural price of patriarchal benevolence and caring; and they usually *are* paid, where the generous instincts and traditions of the community have not been perverted. Also, the giving and receiving of such honour—a reward greater than power and wealth and amusements, for it can be enjoyed not only in life, but also after the death of the physical body, which the others cannot be—is a great nourishment to the heart of both giver and receiver, and is a continuous inducement to benevolent work on the part of the latter (*when it is not mixed up with and corrupted by power and wealth*), and a powerful check against temptations to corruption. The natural corollary of this is that in all public functions, the unsalaried legislator should have rank and precedence above all salaried office-bearers as well as persons engaged in competitive money-earning professions.

It will be readily seen that the idea underlying this condition is that which has been discussed and emphasised before, the idea of spiritualising politics by changing the whole culture and civilization of society from its present *mercenary* to a *missionary* basis, even as the work of the elders in a family is done for the youngers, not for mercenary motives, but of 'missionary' benevolence. The right instinct is already there; it has only to be revived. Many western countries do not, or until recently did not, give any salary to their legislators. Aldermen are not paid. Nor are justices of the peace. The theory about the *honorarium* of the barrister is the same. But the prevailing mammonism of western civilization has corrupted the whole moral atmosphere of human life and penetrated into and vitiated even the most sacred domestic and fiduciary relations. If this atmosphere cannot be purified by the introduction of the missionary and patriarchal spirit in the Panchayats, the Legislators and the Courts of Arbitration, then there is no hope of true Swaraj.

(*e*) It goes without saying that, grade after grade, each Panchayat should have, in its personnel, members possessing between them, all the knowledge and experience needed for dealing with all the different kinds of work which the panchayat as a whole has to attend to. For making rules for, and dealing with, each main department of work, the Panchayat will have to form a sub-committee out of its own members; and it is obvious that these should have special knowledge of that kind of work.

(*f*) Another important point is this : there should be no 'standing' offering of, or canvassing for, himself by any one, as a candidate for election. The idea of self-display and *seeking* election is wholly incongruous with the spirit of philanthropic public service. Favours are sought, not burdens. The conception here should be, not that the electors confer a favour or honor on the elected, but that they place a heavy burden of public work on him; and it is therefore, they who are to be placed under obligation, and should request the electee, instead of being requested by him. *Seeking* election for oneself has an inevitable savour of selfishness of some sort or other, about it, which is quite inconsistent with our ideal of the legislator. Of course there will always be possibilities of abuse. But the point to be considered is whether they will be *less* or *greater* than under the current systems, under which the gross abuses of "electioneering", are as much a by-word as commercial and financial "profiteering" and bureaucratic "domineering." And it has also to be remembered that the mere *public acceptance and declaration of the principles* and ideas here suggested will change for the better, the whole tone and atmosphere of politics.

It may be objected that we may make a rule that there must be no canvassing, *etc.*, but—will not persons surreptitiously get others to nominate and canvass for them? The reply is that obviously we do not profess to be able to abolish all evil. Whoever or Whatever made the Universe has not succeeded in doing so.

Human beings can obviously not do better. Indeed, some people think and believe that if evil *were* abolished, *good* would disappear automatically also. But what human beings ought to and can do is, to try to minimise the evil and maximise the good, in a given time, place and circumstance. We profess only to make suggestions towards this. No doubt, there will be room for underhand doings. But the *other* conditions which we propose must not be overlooked. They will blunt the edge of the temptations to such doings. Thus, legislators will not be entrusted with executive powers, as they are to-day, in the capacity of Ministers or Executive Councillors, *etc.* Judicial powers will also be separated off from the other two. And the re-formed public opinion will make a different atmosphere altogether. The general recognition of the non-mercenary principle; and of the principle of the division of the rewards of extra honor, and special official powers, and extra wealth, and more amusements, *etc.*, in correspondence with the division of labour and functions and the difference of the main kinds of temperaments and capacities, the condition that legislators should not be engaged in any money-making business, which will naturally keep the public eye alertly and wakefully upon his purity—all this will make the election some thing to be accepted only from a sense of duty, as a burden for which the only (but great) recompense is honor, rather than to be eagerly sought for as a means of easy selfish joys.

Note to Chapter VI.

Separation of Functions.

That Judicial functions should be separated off from Executive functions is admitted even by the Bureaucracy in profession; though they are avoiding, might and main, the carrying out of their profession into practice. But it is not equally generally recognised that the Legislative function should also be separated off from the other two. Even more radically dangerous than the combination of Judicial and Executive, is the combination of Legislative and Executive. If the Executive-Judge will always *decide* in favour of himself, or of his class or clique, the Executive-Legislator will *make laws* in favour of himself or of his class or clique—a far more radical danger, mischief at the very root.

In the ancient Indian scheme, the man of thought was the Legislator, and the man of action was the Executor of his law. Such a pioneer of reform in India as Raja Ram Mohan Roy has expressed an opinion that the downfall of India began when the Rajas usurped the power of making laws from the Pandits. The ancient *Smritis* are all composed by Rishis, not by Rajas. The Islamic tradition is similar, too. Therefore no legislator should have direct executive power; but the Legislature should supervise and control the Executive which should be responsible in every way to the Legislature. This is the very essence of responsible government and self-government as conceived here. Where the chief Executive and the chief Legislative are practically identical, and the members of the former are substantially or heavily salaried as in England, true responsibility ceases, manœuvres and intrigues of party politics become rampant, and legislation cannot be disinterested. In other places the opposite error is observable, *viz.*, that if the Legislative is separated from the Executive, the latter is free of control by the former.

Note to Chapter VII.

Finance.

These provisions will reverse the present order of things, secure financial autonomy, and provide a safeguard against the disastrous extravagance and top-heaviness which are the consequences of excessive centralisation, have plunged western countries in hopeless indebtedness and bankruptcy, and are ruining India also.

NOTE TO CHAPTER VIII.

Proprietorship.

Two opposite tendencies are patent in politics and economics, as throughout human and other nature, in all the aspects and manifestations thereof. The current names for them are Individualism and Socialism. Other names for them are egoism and altruism, the separative 'I' and the communal 'We', mutual struggle or struggle for existence and mutual aid or alliance for existence, competition and co-operation. To endeavour to suppress either, and retain the other only, is a fatal error, due to ignorance of the very elements of human nature, or to blinding arrogance and greed for power and wealth. Bureaucracy and all other 'cracies', as also the many current schemes of collectivism—one of which is being tried in Russia under the name of Bolshevism—are always committing this disastrous error of one-sided and lop-sided excess and exaggeration, and therefore are always committing suicide while causing grievous disturbance and injury to the People. Russian Bolshevism, after a vain endeavour to abolish private property, in the course of which widespread misery of the most awful character has been caused, seems now to have decided to recognise private property, as was inevitable. Safety lies in recognising both these indefeasible and unabolishable aspects of human nature, and in trying to reconcile them wisely. The growth of the sense of separate *Individuality*, the growth of egoistic intelligence, of the institution of monogamous marriage and the sentiments connected with it, of the definition of the family life, of the sense of private property, of the customs of inheritance, of the incentive to productive efforts of an ever more complicated order—all these are inter-connected, interdependent, flourish or decay together. At the same time, by that paradox of antimonial duality or ambivalence which is the very nature of the universe, their flourishing is possible only in the setting of a Society. Society and Individual, "We" and "I", are interdependent yet opposed. The reconciliation must be found in a National Organisation of Society, such as will give due play to the instincts, or forces of individualistic competition, (*droh-atmaka-vibhuti*) as well as socialist co-operation (*sambhuya-samutthana, sangh-atmaka sambhuti*). Refinement of life is not possible without accumulation of wealth; and that is not possible without some play of Individualism (*vyashti-buddhi, bheda-buddhi, swartha, khud-gharazi, khudi*) the sense of private, exclusive, separate possession. But the excess of individualism leads to class-wars and disruption of communities and (when the spirit of Individualism puts on the mask and the larger form of Nationalism) to world-ruining wars, like the recent or indeed still continuing European War; and so it defeats its own ends and commits suicide. To guard against this excess to set due limits to private accumulations, to ensure even the refinement against degenerating into vulgar loudness, to bring about an equitable distribution of necessaries and comforts—this is the work of the spirit of Socialism (*Samashiti-buddhi, abheda buddhi, parartha, aql-i-jamaati*). The reconcilation is to be found in making the private life simpler and the public possessions richer, by putting 'private' individuals in charge of 'public' properties of common use and enjoyment (like public parks, museums, zoos, childrens' and youths' playgrounds, reading-rooms, libraries, roads, tanks, wells, places of worship, rest-houses, dharmashalas, sarais, almshouses, bathing ghats, hospitals, etc., and inducing them, by the incentives of public honour (and public censure in the opposite case) to lay out their individually-accumulated wealth on these. In this connection the principle of the separation of the four main prizes of life should be very carefully borne in mind. The preservation of the integrity of the central authority (in other words, of the purity of the Legislature), and the inducing of all the individuals composing the community to put forth the best work that there is in them—these are the main problems of government and social organisation. Modern governments and modern collectivist schemes and experiments are all failing to find a solution for them. As said before, that Lenin, in Russia, after extraordinary efforts to abolish private property, has realised that capitalism has to be restored (though, no doubt, with limitations). He is reported to have found out that the peasants avoid working more than will produce enough for their necessary wants, and are not interested in supporting the 'intellectuals', *etc.*, who are necessary for the 'State', unless special inducement is applied. Now the simple old traditional solution, in India, of these problems is the separation of the four main prizes, of life, *viz.*, honor, power, wealth, and amusements, which constitute the main ambitional inducements to strenuous work of correspondingly different kinds. The possibility of combining them, of securing them all, is the one prime cause of all kinds of social and political corruption. Separate them, and you at once minimise the temptations of the central authority, and at the same time provide an adequate (if not excessive) inducement to every worker to put forth his best. Socio-political reform of the affairs of human beings, if it is to be successfully carried out, must not ignore these facts and laws of the Science of Psychology, *i.e.*, of Human Nature.

By taking due account of these laws and facts, it is possible to minimise the disadvantages and pick out the advantages of all the many forms of socio-political organisation, man has tried the village community, the city-guild system, the city-state, the country-state, theocracy or sacerdotatism autocracy and monarchy and despotism, aristocracy and feudalism and militarism, plutocracy and commercialism bureaucracy and oligarchy of many kinds, and finally democracy and collectivism of many shapes and forms—each one only a lop-sided and excessive exaggeration of one constituent and necessary element in the corporate life of humanity—and synthesise them all anew in a truly beneficial form of Self-government or Swaraj.

APPENDIX E.

(*Vide* Part II, paragraph 52.)

Note on the speech of Moulana Abdul Bari of Lucknow made on the 29th February 1920 on the second day of the Calcutta Khilafat Conference.

Moulana Abdul Bari rose and proposed the following resolution :—

> " That this conference declare in clear and unambiguous terms that in case the forthcoming decision of the Peace Conference dismembers the Turkish Empire in any way and places the Jazirat-ul-Arab and all the Holy Places of Islam under non-Muslim control or influence in violation of the requirements of Islam and in utter disregard of the demand of the Indian Mussalmans made from time to time during the last 14 or 15 months, then it will be the religious duty (*farz*) of the Mussalmans to have recourse to every possible means to keep the Khilafate in tact and maintain the position and the dignity of the Khalifa."

He began with the preliminary statement that the time for speech was over and the time for practical work had come. He compared the present position of Islam to that of dying man. Mussalmans were like the family members who are filled with anxiety and they should be ready to do anything possible for the patient. In the past the Muhammadans had not shown enough sympathy with Islam and had they been true Mussalmans they should have been able to overcome any difficulty with the assistance of God. As they have not supported the Khalifa in the last war, they had committed a sin, and consequently their prayers now would not be so acceptable. All Mussalmans would die some day but if they wanted to die a Musssalman death as distinct from the death of an infidel, as every Muslim desired, they must work for the cause of Islam and should not waste time in delivering speeches. There is no question that Sultan Wahid-ud-Din of Turkey is the Khalifa of Islam. The question of his Khilafature could not be disputed on the ground of his not being the Quresh (a family from which early Khalifas were selected). If there should be two claimants for the Khilafate, according to the direction of Islam, the second claimant should be beheaded. He hoped that those dictates would be followed out. He then explained the necessity of having a Khalifa and described how the body of the Prophet was not buried until the Khalifa was appointed. If they did not hear to those dictates of Islam, they would die an " infidel " death. With reference to the Sultan Hosein of Egypt, he said he had informed the British Government that the Sultan should be killed owing to his betrayal of the Khalifa. The Sheriff of Mecca had made a great mistake in revolting from the allegiance to the Sultan of Turkey and Government should realise that a man who had proved faithless to his own master would not be likely to be truthful to them. Indians who have been rewarded by titles such as " Rai Bahadurs, Khan Bahadurs, Shamsul Ulama " might prove serviceable to Government, but those rebels are of a different stamp and would not be satisfied so easily. Turkey used to pay the Arabs two crores of rupees yearly for the upkeep of the Holy Places and yet could not keep them loyal, so it was unlikely that the British Government would be able to satisfy their avarice.

Quoting from the Quran he said that their holy book had said that Mussalmans should never hope for friendship with Jews and Christians. It was not a time now for talking but they should remember these things and do something practical (shouts of " Alla-ho-Akbar "). In the Quran it was said that no kingdom other than the Moslem one would be in Palestine and when that would happen Imam Mehdi would come for the salvation of Islam, and under his leadership Muslims would slay all Jews and Christians in Palestine; even if they tried to hide the stones behind which the world take shelter would call out to give information. Each Muhammadan should become a Saladin to check the flood of non-Muslims encroaching on the territories of Muslims. They must be ready to give up their lives if necessary and their lives and properties were not really theirs but were held in trust to be utilised in the service of God, and therefore they should not hesitate to discharge their duties. Every one would die according to his destiny. He himself was prepared to fight to the end and if he could not kill others, he would prefer that he himself should be killed. If they had had more self respect they would not have hesitated so long to assist the Khilafa; it is the action of an infidel to hesitate. If they gave up their lives in the cause of religion thousands of Muslims would grow out of each drop of blood they shed. Europe by her high-handed proposals to encroach on the rights of Muslims was only hastening her own destruction. He must tell them that now every kind of retaliation had become valid for Muhammadans. The occupation of Palestine could not have taken place had it not been for treachery. Because somebody had been guilty of treachery, that was no reason why they should follow his example. He said that the enemies of Islam were four crores and they were seven crores. (The population of England and the Muhammadan population of India?). Should they have to fight against them, they the Muhammadans. had no guns or cannon but they will have to try to injure them even by throwing bricks. Even if each Muhammadan were to throw a handful of dust at them they would be buried under the heap that would be raised. (The reference here is possibly to the small number of Europeans in India). He advised his audience not to beg for favours any more but to tell Government plainly that they have made a glaring mistake in supporting the Government and fighting against the Khalifa. During the internment of his friends, the Ali Brothers, he had continually sent telegrams to Government protesting against the encroach ment on the holy temple at Mecca. He had intended that as a warning. (This statement received shouts of applause). Whatever might be the mental condition of those who would not support the Khalifa's cause, he was prepared to die cheerfully as the cause is a just one. In order to further the cause of Hindu Muslim unity and to make common cause with the Hindus who were also opposed to Government, he had suggested the prohibition of cow sacrifice. If a Mussalman had not been against Government previous to the time of the Khilafat question he must now become hostile to Government. He was not afraid of the C. I. D.'s as they are little better than menial servants (servants worth two pice) They should be only afraid of God, and they should not be responsible for betraying His cause. If the Peace Terms were unsatisfactory, from that time, God had made every kind of retaliation legal for them. They could sacrifice every Christian's life and property and still get Fatwa. (*i.e.*. religious sanction) and they would not have sinned before God, as Christians had burnt the Muslim's heart. He was ready for all the consequences of his speech and he even practised at home the sufferings of Jail life. Though even if some were blown up with cannon or killed with swords they would still be able to reconstruct the Kingdom of Islam. God was merciful and just and he would help them at the time of necessity. If he could get at his disposal cannon and guns he would be prepared to declare war and burn Christians having saturated them with kerosine oil. If these weapons were not at their hands they should at least throw stones at them. (When saying this the speaker was seen to shed tears and many of the audience also). They did not want any one else's kingdom but they wanted to retain their holy places. It was an outrage to contemplate turning the Turks out of Europe or building a church in place of the mosque at Sophia. All Mussalmans must rise against such intentions and force Christians to give them up. (Prolonged shouts of Alla-ho-Akbar). The Sheriff of Mecca should not have been allowed to retain the holy tomb of Mecca. A rebel should not be in possession of their holy places. Though the Jazirat-ul-Arab, (the area which according to the Koran should be under the Khalifa) was a very large area, Mussalmans only wanted a limited portion of it. He would be a rebel if he allowed any one to seize any portion of Arabia from the hands of Khalifa. With reference to Lord Curzon's agitation against allowing the Turks to remain in Europe Lord Kitchener who held similar views had received a fitting end and he hoped that Lord Curzon would also die in a similar manner. It was a difficult situation for them because if they did not carry out the wishes of Government they would get into trouble and if they helped Government they would be separated from their religion. The Moulana then offered a prayer and asked God why He did not take him out of this world so that he should not have seen with his own eyes the disgrace of Islam. Some of his friends have been fortunate enough to avoid seeing the disgrace by a timely death. If Constantinople were taken away from the Turks, he was sure Imam Mehdi would appear and help the Mussalmans in their difficulty (again shed tears. At this stage the President, Abul Kalam Azad, sent Moulana Abdul Rezak to take away the speaker but he refused to go). He said he was not excited rather he was prepared to die first of them all in defending the cause of Islam. (Shouts came from various people in the hall that they would sacrifice their lives first before it will be necessary for him to do so.) He had no enmity with the Christians except on account of the enmity on the part of the Christians for Islam. Were there any of the audience ready to help the cause of Islam?

This concluded his speech. In response to his last appeal most of the audience stood up and shouted. A large number who were in the neighbourhood of Abdul Bari approached him and kissed his hands.

APPENDIX F.

(*Vide* Part II, paragraph 53.)

Extract from the "Comrade", dated 14th November 1924.

A Historic Appeal.

We publish elsewhere a historic appeal made more than four years ago by the Indian Khilafat Delegation to Sultan Mohamed Waheed-ud-Din, then Khalifa of Islam and Sultan of Turkey. The Draft Treaty of Sevres had already been presented by the Allies to the Turkish Peace Delegation at Paris, and the Delegation was being pressed to accept it would delay. It had, however, to obtain the final opinion of its Government on the Treaty and on its own proposals with regard to it, and had asked for more time, which had been conceded very reluctantly, and in a very niggardly manner. The subsequent history of this Draft Treaty is well known and need not be repeated in any detail. Tewfik Pasha, the Head of this Delegation, who had been the Turkish Ambassador in London when war had broken out, and was a *persona grata* in British political circles because he was not a Young Turk, refused to be a party to the signing of this infamous treaty, and could not be induced by the Grand Vizier, Damad Farid Pasha, who had come in person to Paris, to remain any longer at the head of a Delegation required to sign it. Tewfik Pasha accordingly left Paris, and Rashid Bey, a member of his Delegation, who was believed to be more accommodating and more plain filled his place. Even then the Delegation could not be induced to sign the Treaty, and at last a fresh Delegation composed of persons pledged to sign was sent to Paris. When the Turkish gentleman who was in charge of the Islamic Information Bureau in Paris, established by His Highness the Agha Khan and others, and assisted by the Indian Khilafat Delegation met one of the members of this traitorous Delegation, and asked him for an interview in which he desired to discuss the provisions of the Draft Treaty, he was informed that the discussion could not take place until *after* the signature of the Treaty! The Treaty was accordingly signed in August, 1920, and we all know how the swords of Mustafa Kemal Pasha and his valiant Anadols in three years of hard fighting and patient endurance scored out the worst of its provisions. The publication of the Indian Khilafat Delegation's appeal is not intended to recall old history, but to emphasise once more what Khilafate really means, how for centuries past its essential features were disregarded, and why it is still necessary to maintain it and to revive and reform it. A conference of the World of Islam is being called to-day for the settlement of the future government of the Hejaz, and no doubt this opportunity would be availed of by the representatives of various Muslim people and States that would gather together to confer with each other for a discussion the future of the-Khilafat itself. We therefore propose to express our views on this momentous question in a series of articles in the *Comrade*. The letter that we publish to-day, apart from having a historic value, and being on that account of considerable interest to people, provides a good preface for this series. It has not seen the light of day before, because its publication would have involved the deposed Sultan and Khalifa, Mohamad VI, in trouble with the British if, as was then believed probable, he had not shown this document to the agent of the British Government in Constantinople, immediately on receipt of it.

Copy.

Extract from the "Comrade", dated 14th November 1924.

A HISTORICAL APPEAL.

(From the Indian Khilafat Delegation to the Khalifa).

B-ismi-'llah-ir-Rahman-ir-Raheem,

Hotel Regina,

Paris,

28th May, 1920.

May it please Your Majesty,

The Indian Khilafat Delegation had the honour to address to Your Imperial Majesty on the 11th May a telegram in which we had endeavoured to explain in brief the mission on which we had come to Europe on behalf of the 70 million Mussalmans of India and the 250 millions of our compatriots of other creeds, the nature of the claims that we had been charged to advocate in connection with the Khilafat and the Turkish settlement, and the state of feelings in India and the East generally respecting the same. We had also ventured to express the hope that Your Majesty and your noble and brave distracted and divided nation, would resolutely do your duty not only by Turkey but by Islam, and that the unity of Turkey would soon become a true reflex of the unity of Islam, which stood solidly by Your Majesty's side as it had never stood since the days of the earliest Khulufa.

To-day we beg leave to address Your Majesty in greater detail on some of the points briefly touched upon in that humble message, and the extreme gravity of the present situation for Islam is our only excuse for the importunity that may perhaps be detected in our repeated submissions. For this we confidently trust Your Majesty will extend to us your fatherly forgiveness.

After sending the telegram of the 11th May to Your Majesty we had occasion to meet a prominent and thoroughly disinterested journalist here to whom we gave a copy of that message, and we think it would interest Your Majesty to know what he said to us even before he had read it.

He told us that if he were the Sultan of Turkey to-day, he would forget that he was the ruler of the Ottoman Empire and the head of the Ottoman nation, and only remember that he was the Successor of our Holy Prophet (on whom be God's peace and benedictions) and the Commander of the Faithful, and as such the Servant of the Holy Places and the mandatory of Allah for the Sanctuaries of Islam. He said he would like to appeal to-day not only to the Turks much less only to the small body of people that are in Constantinople, but to the entire Moslem World without distinction of race and country and political sovereignty, and that he would appeal not so much to the brain as to the heart of Islam. If he were the Khalifa to-day, he said, he would make all Islam weep and pray to Allah and seek strength and support in the spiritual awakening thus affected, rather than waste time and energies in futile negotiations with people sunk in gross materialism, to whom neither reason nor sentiment appeals when their immediate interests are concerned. In short, he would stand forth, as no previous Sultan of Turkey had stood forth, as the Champion of the Faith and the Vicegerent of Allah on earth, untrammelled by diplomatic conventions and political artificialities.

This friend of our cause did not know when he gave expression to these ideas that our own humble submissions to Your Majesty were directed to the same end. But having received confirmation of them from such an unexpected quarter, we now feel that we should repeat those submissions with as much emphasis as is compatible with our profound esteem and veneration for Your Majesty.

Islam and not Turkey alone should be the object of our united defence. If the Turks too lay stress upon the obvious danger arising from the dismemberment of the temporal power of Islam, and its reduction to an extent imperilling its spiritual freedom, than they do upon the evils resulting from the dismemberment of the Ottoman Empire, which must be the natural concern of every Turk to-day, then, not only will the dismemberment of that Empire be prevented as the first fruit of our combined efforts, but Islam itself will be secured against the menance of strangulation and death which this infamous treaty, if signed, is expected to spell for it. If, on the contrary, greater emphasis is placed on the necessity of saving Thrace and Smyrna, or the Armenian Vilayet, then we fear even that result may not be achieved, while it may involve the surrender of larger claims and to a Mussalman infinitely more important principles. Not unoften in the affairs of mankind small things have proved the enemy of big things, and the reduction of one legitimate claim, in the hope of placating the adversary and inducing him to be more just and reasonable than he is inclined to be, has many a time produced results quite the contrary of those desired and expected.

The Khalifa is the repository of the sacred Traditions of our Prophet, and, as Your Majesty is aware, according to the most authentic reports, he commanded the Mussalmans on his death-bed not to permit or tolerate any sort or kind of non-Moslem control over any portion of the Jazeerat-ul-Arab, which includes Syria, Palestine and Mesopotamia as well as the region known to European geographers as the peninsula of Arabia. No Mussalman can therefore agree to the exercise of any control by mandatories of the powers in Syria, Palestine or Mesopotamia, and what no Mussalman can submit to consistently with his creed, the Successor of our Prophet can submit to still less. The Arabs themselves have protested against all mandates and protectorates in these regions, so that even the principle of self-determination cannot now be invoked with any success by our political adversaries. In fact, when we discussed this question with some representative Arabs, they readily admitted our well-established contention that, even if they were to determine otherwise, their self-determination in favour of non-Moslem mandates or any other form of control could not be binding on the Mussalmans of the world in clear defiance of the *shari'at* and that obviously the Jazeerat-ul-Arab is not the private property of the Arabs, any more than it is of the Turks, to give away or to retain, but the common heritage of Islam, and subject to the wardenship of the entire Moslem world as a divine trust.

We may mention here that we had clearly stated in our Address to the Viceroy in India that even if the Turks could be made to acquiesce in a settlement of this kind in contravention of the Prophet's death-bed injunction, it would remain as unacceptable as ever to every believing Mussalman.

Turkey cannot, therefore, undertake, consistently with the obligations imposed by Islam, to accept whatever decisions the Allied Powers may be pleased to take with regard to Syria, Palestine and Mesopotamia, any more than she can accept them with regard to the Hejaz or any other portion of the peninsula of Arabia. Nor can Your Majesty renounce in their favour all the rights and titles that Turkey ever claimed over these territories, including those which belong to Your Majesty in virtue of the Khilafat, or undertake to recognise or conform to any and every measure which may be taken, now or hereafter, by the Allies in and concerning these regions. It is obvious that such demands can be accepted only if Your Majesty is prepared to renounce the Khilafat itself, and thus reverse the act of cession, after four long centuries, which enabled Your Majesty's great ancestor, Sultan Selim I, to be recognised by the Moslem world, as Khalifat-ur-Rasul and Ameer-ul-Momineen.

We feel it our duty to submit that Indian Mussalmans, who have always accepted the rulers of the Ottoman Empire as Khulúfa and Commanders of the Faithful without doubt or dispute, are as strong and unwavering supporters of Your Majesty's title to the Khilafat as of any of your long and distinguished predecessors, and that, while earnestly desirous of strengthening the bond which the Khilafat was designed to create and maintain, they will deplore as one of the greatest misfortunes that could befall Islam if anything was permitted to affect Your Majesty's title to it.

After the foregoing submissions, we need hardly trouble Your Majesty with any further appeals against the renunciation of Your Majesty's undisputed and indisputable jurisdiction over all Mussalmans irrespective of the consideration whether they are your own subjects or happen to be on the sovereignty or protectorate of another State. The renunciation of such jurisdiction is the direct renunciation of the Khilafat itself. and neither argument nor appeal is necessary to recommend the categorical and summary rejection of such an unconscionable demand from the Khalifa after innumerable protestations that the war would involve no religious question, and the Khilafat was a subject on which the Mussalmans alone were competent to take a decision.

We may, however, state that we have ventured to place the question of the Jazeerat-ul-Arab in the fore-front of our humble sumbission not because we are unmindful of other equally unconscionable demands that have been made in the draft Treaty, but because it seemed to us just possible that the importance of the inviolability of the Khilafat might not always be kept in view in the present distracted condition of the ill-fated Turkish nation. But even if we had been inclined to ignore the legitimate requirements of the Turks as a nation, which we could not have done consistently with the claims of our Islamic Brotherhood, the needs of the Khilafat itself would have compelled us to offer, as we are prepared to do, every support to Turkey in her vigorous protests against the rest of the provisions of the Draft Treaty. They manifestly seek to deprive you, in spite of the most solemn and repeated pledges of the Allied Powers, of your homelands in Thrace and Asia Minor; they would place your capital at the mercy of your traditional foes, and even then subject it, and, in fact, Your Majesty also, to Allied control; they would rob you for all practical purposes of every kind of resource, financial as well as military, naval and aerial, and, in short leave no vestige of independence even as a sovereign State. It does not, however, seem necessary to go into these provisions at any further length, because they are and must be as unacceptable to every patriotic Turk as they are and must be to every believing Mussalman. The Khalifa to be a Khalifa must be independent, and must possess temporal powers adequate in existing circumstances for the defence of the Faith. But if this Treaty, or, in fact, any treaty like this, is signed, it is clear that Your Majesty will have neither independence nor temporal power left, and lacking these essential qualifications for the Khilafat, Your Majesty will soon cease to be recognised as Khalifa. Already some Arabs have been encouraged to question your title, though they themselves lack these essential qualifications, and cannot therefore be recognised as Khulúfa. But the purpose of those who are opposed to the very existence of the Khilafat, which insists on what they consider to be divided allegiance, but which really demands allegiance to God before allegiance to any earthly Government, Moslem or non-Moslem, will be served all the better if no Moslem ruler remains qualified for the office of Khalifa, and the Faithful are left without a Commander.

If, however, Your Majesty rejects this Treaty in your capacity as a Khalifa, for the obvious reason that its provisions are calculated to destroy the Khilafat and contravene the commandments of Islam, the Moslem World would *ipso facto* be bound to rally to Your Majesty's support, and assist you to the fullest extent of its power, in your efforts to retain your independence and temporal power adequate for the defence of its faith.

As we have already said in our telegram, everything depends upon the kind of response that Your Majesty makes to the iniquitous and impossible demands made in the name of the Allies, and we hope we may suggest without disrespect, that Your Majesty's decision will be the most momentous ever taken by a Sultan of Turkey since Sultan Selim of glorious memory became a Khalifa four hundred years ago. For on Your Majesty's decision will depend the continuance of the Khilafat in his line, and also the uninterrupted and undisputed succession to the Khilafat which has so long been maintained.

But if Your Majesty's decision is what we all confidently expect it to be, you may rest assured of our loyal and hearty support. We have already indicated in our telegram that we in India cannot be satished if our claim is reduced by a hair's breadth. We demand that Your Majesty must retain all the temporal power that was yours when hostilities broke out in November, 1924, and that the territorial *status quo ante bellum* must be restored. We also demand that Your Majesty must continue to be the Servant of the Holy Places as heretofore, and, finally that there must be no sort or kind of non-Moslem control in any portion of the Jazeerat-ul-Arab, which includes not only the peninsula of Arabia, but also Syria, Palestine and Mesopotamia. If these claims are not fully satisfied, it would be futile to expect peace and contentment in India, or the continuance of our undoubted loyalty which has been the mainstay of British rule throughout its history. In that event, the people of India, without distinction of creed and community, have decided to cease all co-operation with Government.

Mr. Gandhi, who had so valiantly and resolutely resisted the encroachments of the South African Government on the liberties of the Indians in that part of the Empire, and achieved such signal success without the use of any violence, is one of the chief leaders of the movement for the defence of the Khilafat in India, and he and other great Hindu leaders have agreed upon a programme of progressive cessation of co-operation and the Mussalmans have decided to work this programme to the end.

The first stage is one that is calculated to bring moral pressure upon Government by the renunciation of titles and decorations conferred upon Indians by the Government, and by resignation of all honorary offices and membership of Legislative Councils. This has already begun, and some frank statements of the reasons for this step being taken have been sent to the Government. But it is clear that those who hunt for titles cannot be expected to join with true patriots in large numbers.

In the next stage, the civil employees of Government will resign their posts, and since most of the work is done by Indians themselves, this is bound to affect the policy of Government and at the very least make it inclined to be less hostile to Islam than it is to-day. In the third stage, the Army and the Police Force will resign, and if even then the hostility of the Government continues, the last stage will be reached, and people will refuse to pay the taxes.

In the event of the failure of this movement, of progressive cessation of co-operation, the Mussalmans have reserved to themselves the right to take such further action as the law of Islam permits and Government has been repeatedly informed that the only alternatives open to a Mussalman in such circumstances are Jehad and Hijrat.

But so exasperated are the Mussalmans that some members of the police force have already sent in their resignations, and have openly stated that they could no longer serve the Government to which they had been so loyal in the past without jeopardising their eternal salvation, and it may be reasonably inferred that the Mussalmans in the Army, when they see the sacrifices their brothers in civil life are making, will not place their loyalty to Government above their loyalty to God.

Another factor of great importance in the present situation is that some Mussalmans have already migrated from India, and we enclose for Your Majesty's information the speech of His Majesty the Ameer of Afghanistan in which he fully approves of our efforts for the Khilafat, and offers his support for the defence of the Khilafat, and promises to give asylum to all the Muhajireen from India. His Majesty's Foreign Minister who is the head of the Afghan Delegation carrying on negotiations with the Indian Government, had already announced this, and now his august master himself confirms that announcement in the most explicit manner. His Majesty is an undoubted Mujahid, whose support of the Khilafat can be fully relied upon, and from his speech it appears that the newly liberated Moslem States of Central Asia will also stand by him in such endeavour. Further, it may be pointed out that the disaffection and intranquillity among the tribes on the North-Western border of India, which have lasted much longer than on any previous occasion, and have absorbed the energies and efforts of an unprecedentedly large force, are due to a very large extent to the hostility of the Government towards the Khilafat. In short, there prevails in India and in neighbouring countries a state of feeling for the Khilafat and its preservation so intense and widespread as has never prevailed for any object for many centuries, and we may safely say that other Moslem lands such as Tunis, Aligeria, Morocco and Egypt, and by no means excluding Arabia itself, will support the Khilafat no less in its defence of Islam. In these circumstances, we submit we were justified in assuring Your Majesty that Islam stood by your side as it had never stood since the last of the Khulúfa-ir-Rashideen passed away.

The unfortunate neglect in the past of the duties imposed and the work demanded by the Khilafat has brought the moslem world to its present deplorable condition, and if we in the present generation also will not make one last and combined effort to retrieve the situation, our children and our children's children will grow up only to curse us and our inglorious memory, and when we march out of our graves on the Day of Judgment to answer for our acts and our omissions, we shall not be able to face Allah and His Prophet whose great trust we shall have so ignominously betrayed.

We cannot but deplore and condemn the separatist tendencies discernible in some parts of the Moslem World, which are undoubtedly subversive of the Brotherhood of Islam and in direct contravention of its teaching and its very spirit. But when we complain of this, we are told that the Turks have themselves to thank for this state of affairs, that their whole outlook at best is national, and that they care little for the Khilafat or for Islam. Non-Moslem critics of position and authority also have begun to ask what the Khalifa himself has done for the Khilafat during the last century or two. Of course, such complaints and criticisms are neither sincere nor disinterested, and besides exaggerating the errors of the past, and taking a wholly one sided view of the matter, they disregard and altogether ignore the distractions of the Turks for so many generations, and show little appreciation of the courage and sacrifice of a noble and brave nation. Nevertheless, it is difficult to silence these critics, and it would be fatal not to confess even to ourselves such truth as there is in these complaints and criticism.

Certainly the Khilafat was always meant to be something higher and greater than merely national sovereignty. And although it is absurd to suggest, as some of the most influential people in Allied Countries are suggesting, that the Khalifa is like the Pope who could be "Vaticanised", and that apparently the Khalifa's sole function in life is to live in retirement like a monk or an anchorite, mumbling his prayers and repeating his beads, it cannot be denied that in the last few generations at least the Khulafa have not asserted themselves as such, and have generally appeared before the world only as Sultan and Padshahs. They were undoubtedly expected to go on the pilgrimage to the Hejaz in person every two or three years, if not, annually, and to make of the Haj a universal Conference of the Islamic World in which its affairs could be discussed in accordance with the divine injunction "*Wa shavirhum fi-l-amar*"; they were expected to interest themselves in the progress of Mussalmans in every country, and to assert themselves constantly in checking the abuses which were undermining the strength of Islam, and in promoting the welfare of the Moslems and the advancement of the Mission of Islam.

But all this is so obvious, and no one is likely to know it so well as Your Majesty yourself, who have inherited the awful consequences of the neglect of your predecessors. Our only object in referring to it is to explain that, because for centuries past the work of the Khilafat was done indifferently, the Mussalmans, who never neglected to remember the Khalifa in their prayers, failed nevertheless to come to his aid in the hour of his need, and made but a poor response to his call. They have, however, realised only too well now, after repeated misfortunes and humiliations, that things cannot be left as they are, and that the bonds of the Khilafat must be strengthened at all costs. Therefore, while, on the one hand, they confidently expect that Your Majesty will rise in this the gravest crisis of Islam to the full height of the Khulafa-ir-Rashideen, they are, on the other hand, themselves prepared also to obey Your Majesty implicitly and to make every sacrifice in obeying your call.

And it will not be out of place to submit that now as ever unity is the greatest need of Islam. Honest differences of opinion must always be tolerated. But only Your Majesty can teach the Mussalmans to-day that to make of one's opinions a fetish, and to be relentless in the pursuit of those who hold different opinions, even when a still more relentless enemy of both is in close pursuit of all without any distinction of persons and parties is the greatest betrayal of Turkey and of Islam. The need of re-uniting all Moslems, specially such as may be disposed to be divided by discord of distrust one from another, within the fold of the true Brotherhood of Islam, is in fact, now greater than ever before, and we fervently pray that Your Majesty may exert yourself in that behalf. And in particular, any misunderstandings that still remain and divide Arab from Turk should be carefully removed. In fact, this is the very moment when all sects and sections of Islam can be welded together, and we have no doubt that Your Majesty must have been deeply touched as are ourselves at the demonstration of the sympathy and support of our Shiah brothers, who realise that the dismemberment of the Khilafat in the present circumstances means the dismemberment of Islam itself. As for the invaluable support given to us by our Hindu brethren, and in fact by all communities of India without any distinction, words fail us to express our appreciation of it, and the only way in which we can demonstrate our gratitude is to pray that we may not disgrace Islam when the time comes to make every sacrifice for the liberation of our Motherland. We have assured our compatriots that we can never think of the subjugation of India to any alien power, Moslem or non-Moslem, and that they will find us at their side in winning Indian autonomy.

We now ask forgiveness of Your Imperial Majesty for the length of this appeal, which is the result of the fulness of the heart and of the grave apprehensions to which every Moslem is a prey to-day. But before we close this humble representation, let us once more assure you, Sire, that you have lying at your feet to-day such vast stores of love and esteem, of affection and reverence as the greatest king in the world may well envy, and it is for you to accept them and make use of them, or spurn them and deem them of less value than the tiny doles of bare justice that may grudgingly be given to you by others with all the show of generous charity. If it had been possible for us to reach the Dar-us-Sa'adat and to touch Your Majesty's feet, we would have begged and beseeched and implored you to make your choice not as the Padshah of Ottoman Turks but as the Captain of Allah's Army of the Moslems of every country and every colour, and as the Successor of the Chief of all Creation and the Last Prophet or God; and we feel certain that with our tears we would have won from you the only answer that patriotism and faith alike demand. But since that is not to be. we have chosen as our great Elchi one who must be even dearer to you than we, your spiritual children, for she is the flesh of your flesh and the bone of your bone. Much is lost of Islam, but its womanhood retains its prestine purity and the readiness to sympathise and suffer with every suffering soul. It is one of these noble women that we have chosen to appeal to Your Majesty in the name of your distant children whom common peril has drawn close to you. She will, we confidently trust, plead their cause as no mother or wife ever pleaded for a son or a husband whose life has been declared forfeit to the Padshah's stern justice, for she is to plead not for the life of a condemned criminal, but for the life of the Khilafat and of Islam. And we hereby charge her in name of the Allah and worships and the Prophet she would please not to give up the advocacy of our cause till victory is won. May Allah give her the eloquence and the persuasion that bind a spell over human hearts and work miracles. May it be given to her to plead as she has never pleaded before, and to win a victory as woman never won in the whole history of the human race.

With every good wish for Your Majesty, for Turkey and for Islam, and with the expression of our homage and devotion we subscribe ourselves,

Your Majesty's dutiful and loving,

Children,

(Sd.) MOHAMED ALI,

(Sd.) SYUD HOSSAIN,

(Sd.) SYED SULAIMAN NADWI; and

(Sd.) ABUL KASIM,

(of the Indian Khilafat Delegation).

APPENDIX G.

(*Vide* Part II, paragraph 75.)

Translation of a Pamphlet entitled "Mutafiqa Fatwa."

Title Page.

Arabic verse:—" Then enquire from the learned men if you do not know ".

75. The Collective Fatwa which was presented before the exalted Ulemas at the grand session of the Jamiat-ul-Ulema-i-Hind held at Delhi was signed by them, after which other signatures were obtained by circulating it to the Ulemas in other places.

In accordance with the decision of the members of the Jamiat-i-Ulema-i-Hind the Secretary of the Jamiat had it printed at the Hamidia Press, Delhi, under the supervision of Munshi Abdul Hamid.

"*The Fatwa*"

In the name of God the most compassionate and merciful.

What do the learned in Theology (ulema-i-din). and the law-givers of the great Shariat say about the following religious proposition :—

1. What is meant by " Mavalat " (co-operation) and according to the religion what kind of " Mavalat " is " haram " (forbidden) with the enemies of Muslim religion, and what kind of " tark-i-Mavalat " (non-co-operation) is obligatory? What is the religious decision about a man who continues to co-operate after knowing the religious commandment on the subject?
2. Is it included in " Mavalat " to be a member of the Councils of the Government of India, to be in the legal profession, to practise as a Mukhtar, etc., to obtain education in Government or semi-government colleges or school or to have one's children educated there, to take help (grant in aid) from Government for education, and to accept honorary Magistracy, and titles conferred by the Government?
3. Is it forbidden for the Mussalman in the present condition to be in the military and other services of the Government which strengthen and consolidate the constitution of the Government?
4. Is it prohibited in the present condition to use the British goods which gives strength to the British nation?
5. Is it permissible by the " Shariat " to have social unity with a non-Muslim who is not inclined to be hostile and also to take help from him in any matter?
6. Is it permissible by the Shariat to accept sound advice tendered by a non-Muslim and to act upon it in order to attain a religious object, which is apparently considered adherence to and following the non-Muslim?

The answer to each of the above questions should be given seriatim in plain and concise language but supported reasons—please answer and you will be rewarded.

THE ANSWER.

" God is helper in reaching the right decision "

Answer No. 1.—The word " Mavalat " in Arabic idiom and the Shariat terminology means love (friendship) and co-operation (helping each other). Its explanation and elucidation is to be found in all books of commentry. "Mavalat" is forbidden (haram) with enemies of Islam in both senses of the word. God has forbidden "Mavalat" totally with enemies of Islam whether it is openly or secretly, paid or honorary. God says (Arabic verse) "God prevents you from friendship and co-operation with those infidels who fought with you in the matter of religion and ejected you from your countries and helped in your ejectment and expulsion. Those who maintain co-operation with such infidels are tyrants".

Any Mussalman who in spite of knowledge of this Commandment maintains "Mavalat" with them will be considered a great sinner and in the words of the Quran a tyrant. God says in chapter (Sura) Maeda (of the Quran) (an Arabic verse) O Musalman do not make the Jews and the Christians (enemies of Islam) your friends and helpers. They are friends and helpers of each other whoever from among you will make them his friend and helper will be counted as of their crowd, as God does not guide the tyrant nation. There is a big and detailed Fatwa by Shah Abdul Aziz of Delhi about "Mavalat" with infidels. The following are some sentences from it :—"In the matter of "Mavalat" with infidels whatever had been written by the law-givers of Islam, it requires some explanation—one should read "Shorah Ain-ul-Ilm" and Ehya-ul-Ulema for it. The purport of it is that "Mavalat", meaning friendship, if it is entertained with them in connection with religion is unanimously "Kufr". If it is in connection with worldly matter, and is optional, it is "haram".

And "Mavalat" meaning helping and co-operation is based upon some prescribed principles and it is this (Arabic) to help in "Kufr" and sin is itself a sin. This decision is unanimous. This proved from the words of God (Arabic verse) "Do not help each other in sin and tyranny"

And this co-operation is sometimes in lieu of payment which is known as services, and sometimes without any wages which is known as help and support. The Commandment in both the cases is identical. That is if the infidels wish to fight with a Muslim or subjugate any country or city of the Mussalmans their service is "haram" and to give them help or support is also "haram" rather it is a major sin. If they fight among themselves or are collecting riches and administering a country which is in their possession from before and they engage a Mussalman in their service for this, it is apparently permissible to serve them for reasons based on the idea that work like tailoring, trading, *etc.*, is permissible with them, and it is also proved from the life of the respected people that they served the idolators. But on deep contemplation it appears that this too is not free from being "haram" especially in these days because their service becomes the cause of many evils in the religion, and the least of these evils is the carelessness and slowness in discharge of religious duties, refraining from preventing them (their employers) from evil deeds and being their well-wishers and advisers, adding to their number, strengthening their grandeur, respecting them beyond limit, calling them "Khudavand", "Sahib" and "Qibla" and expression of great love for them, *etc.*

Answer No. 2.—All these things are included in "Mavalat" because these things apparently create love with the Government and indirectly cause to help them. Therefore on the basis of the Commandment regarding "tark Mavalat" it is incumbent to disassociate from all these acts.

Apart from the Commandment regarding "tark Mavalat" it is obligatory for the Mussalmans to give up these things on account of other evils. The detail of all that had been briefly said is this :—

The following are the reasons for giving up the Councils :—

(a) The Council whether it is legislative or executive has for its object the strengthening of the constitution and the administration of the Government which amounts to an open support of the Government.

(*b*) Laws which are against the principles of religion are often made in the Councils, to move support or to remain silent in spite of power to oppose which is not permissible for any Mussalman (Arabic verse) "The Prophet said that if any of you see an evil enacted you should stop it by your own hand, or if you have not power to do so stop it by your tongue, and if you have not power even of this, do not approve of it in your heart". But the Muslim members of the Council do all this and as a testimony in its support are the past events and the enforcements of the present laws in the country.

(*c*) The English nation is also on the Council which is tyrant and the enemy of Islam and it is made "haram" by the Shariat to have a distinctive seat with such a nation. God says (Arabic verse) "After recollecting do not sit with the tyrants".

(*d*) It is incumbent for the members in Council to take oath of loyalty, obedience and faithfulness towards the Government and in the present condition it is "haram" for the Mussalmans to be loyal, obedient and faithful to the Government willingly and freely. Therefore, the oath of allegiance is "haram" and a major sin.

The reasons for the legal profession being "haram" are as follows :—

(*a*) The members of the legal profession are responsible for maintaining half the constitution of the Government, *i.e.*, the executive branch of the administration and enforce its laws into practice which is a great help of the Government which had been proved to be "haram"

(*b*) Most of the Civil and Criminal laws of the administration are against the laws of Shariat and it is the main duty of the legal practitioner to practise and apply it which is absolutely a sin.

(*c*) All the legal practitioners often simply for the existence of their profession have intentionally to work against the oppressed and in support of the oppressor, which is entirely tyranny and support of sin.

(*d*) In order to bring a case within the legal bounds, most of the legal practitioners intentionally give instructions and induce people to tell lies, which is a great crime. Many legal practitioners are obliged to ignore the commandments of God simply on account of the profession and become careless in the discharge of religious duties.

The reasons to boycott education in Government and semi-Government Madrassas, Colleges and schools are as follows :—

(*a*) The object of this education is either to serve Government or to become a legal practitioner which comes under the forbidden "Mavalat".

(*b*) Besides the above evil, the prevailing education and training lead to other evils such as the predominance of the love of worldly affairs, love for honour, worship of lust, negligence of and carelessness towards religion, *etc.*, and all these things are "haram" Therefore, on the basis of "the means of sin are sin" it is obligatory to refrain from getting and giving such education.

(*c*) The education in college and schools is a course of failure to observe "Farzeain" (compulsory duty) as the necessary religious education which is essential for every Mussalman is generally impossible owing to the present system of education.

(*d*) In tho Arabic Madrassas which are under the control of the Government (whether it is wholly supported by Government or partly, or is only affiliated to its system) besides the above evils there is this evil that the religious education is only acquired for the sake of the worldly gain, which is "haram" according to the "Shariat". In the same way the service of the teachers in these institutions is also "haram" as it is doubly a sin (Arabic) God save us from this.

Different reasons for the acception of grant-in-aid being "haram":—

(a) This is one of the means of "Mavalat" which is forbidden in the present condition.

(b) The real object of education disappears, leading to the above-mentioned evils, therefore on the principle of (Arabic) "What leads to a sin is a sin" this acceptance is "haram".

(c) Intense antagonism which it is obligatory to entertain against enemies of Islam disappears after acceptance of aid—God says (Arabic) "O Prophet, wage Jehad against the infidels and be hard on them". The Prophet's refusal to accept certain presents from the idolators is based upon this, as is explained in the "Fatawah Alamgiri".

Honorary Magistracy and honorary offices are "haram" for the following reasons :—

(a) These officers are a source of help to the Government of India which is "haram"

(b) By virtue of these, decisions have to be given according to the laws of the Government of India which are totally against the laws of Shariat and which is "haram". God says, (Arabic) "Those who give non-Shariat decisions are tyrants".

(c) One has to be slow and careless in discharge of religious duties very often owing to these officers.

To keep Government titles is "haram" for the following reasons :—

(a) The titles are the means of the forbidden "Mavalat". Therefore, to keep them comes under commandment of "Mavalat"

(b) The title-holders have to respect and mix with officials (enemies of religion) which is "haram".

(c) The title-holders beg respect and honour from the enemies of religion which is bad according to Shariat. God says, (Arabic) "People ask for respect at the hands of infidels although all honour is in the hand of God"

(d) The title-holder may be punctual in his prayers and fasting to any degree but he cannot remain hard upon the enemies of Islam which is a religious duty as mentioned above.

Answer No. 3.—All the services of the Government from which it gets help are "Haram" specially the police and the service in the Army are the worst sin, as they have to fire upon their Muslim brothers. God says (Arabic verse) "Whoever intentionally kills a Mussalman will suffer eternally in Hell". The Prophet has said (Arabic), "Whoever took up arms against Mussalmans is not from amongst us". It is laid down in "Mahsud Iman Sarkhasi Vol. X", "If a 'Kafir' King is attacked by another 'kafir' king, in such circumstances it is not permissible for the Muslim subjects to fight for their 'kafir' king, because this would be splendour and grandeur of 'Shirk' (idolatory) and 'Kufr' to help which is "haram"".

Answer No. 4.—It is certainly not permissible to buy goods from the enemies of Islam (British Nation) or to sell goods to them, by which they may acquire strength. The respected law-givers of Islam, writing about the sale of arms to belligerent nations as "not permissible", say that this commandment is not confined only to the arms, but the object is to make the sale of all such articles by which the enemies may acquire strength not permissible, such as steel, *etc.* Therefore, keeping the above noted argument in view, the boycott of English goods is a religious duty, as at the present time the strength which our enemy acquires by trade is much more than that which they can acquire if steel were sold to them. But the use of such things, according to necessity, which it is not possible to avoid and which are indispensable for national purposes, is permissible, on the principle that "if a man is pitched between two evils, he should choose the lesser one" and also on the principle that "necessity makes the forbidden permissible".

Answer No. 5.—It is certainly permissible by the "Shariat" to have political (mulki) and social unity with such non-Muslim who is not at war with the Mussalmans. It is right to be just and equitable to them and also kind and benevolent towards them. God says (Arabic verse), "God does not forbid you to do good and justice towards such infidels who did not fight a religious war against you and did not drive you out of your homes. God certainly loves those who are just". But in the extreme enthusiasm of unity the Mussalman should not do anything which is not permissible by "Shariat" as any such union which produces other evils is not permissible. In these matters this absolute rule of the religious law should be kept in view. (Arabic verse) "It is preferable to remove the evils than to put up with them for the sake of expediency and when evil and expediency coincide, it is often preferable to eradicate the evil." Because the "Shariat" gives more attention to preventing the commission of forbidden acts than to the performance of acts permitted, it is permissible by the "Shariat" to take help from such non-Muslim in religious matters. This proposition is mentioned in detail in the books of "Fiqa", Chapter entitled "The distribution of booty". The Prophet in the skirmishes of the Khyber took help from some Jews against the Jews. In the engagement at Hunain, the Prophet sought the help of one Safiwan-ibn-Umayya who was an idolator. Its details are given in "Fathul Qadir", *etc.*

Answer No. 6.—It is permissible to accept and to act upon the good advice tendered by a non-Muslim which is not against the interest and expediency of religion. In fact this is in accordance with the orders of God and his Prophet. The law-givers of Islam have considered it permissible to follow the leaders of idolators at the time of attacking an enemy during Jehad. The Prophet said "Wisdom is the lost thing of a believer and he should take it from whoever he can get, there is no restriction about it." But it is not permissible and is forbidden to follow the aspirations of idolators. God says, (Arabic verse) "If thou followeth the aspirations of idolators after having knowledge of it, verily thou act as a tyrant". But this should be remembered that it is not permissible for a Mussalman to be under the leadership of a non-Muslim whether wholly or partly. God says (Arabic verse), "God has certainly not made a place for the infidels above the believers." Other details are given in "Tafsir Ahmadaya", by Mulla Jiwan and others.

God knows the best.

(Sd.) ABDUL MOHASIN,

MOHAMED SAJJAD

May God be for him,

Nazim Jamiat Ulema Behar.

Certificates to the effect that the answers were correct were signed by about 120 Ulemas.

APPENDIX H.

(*Vide* Part II, paragraph 98.)

Extract from "Independent" dated Allahabad, the 2nd October 1921.

Mahatma Gandhi has issued the following appeal to the Mussalmans of India :—

To the Mussalmans of India.

Dear Countrymen,—Whilst the arrest of Maulanas Shaukat Ali and Mahomed Ali has touched every Indian heart I know what it has meant to you. The brave Brothers are staunch lovers of their country, but they are Mussalmans first and everything else after, and it must be so with every religiously minded man. The Brothers have for years past represented all that is best and noblest in Islam. No two Mussalmans have done more than they to raise the status of Islam in India. They have promoted the cause of the Khilafat as no two other Mussalmans of India have. For they have been true and they dared to tell what they felt even in their internment in Chindwara. Their long internment did not demoralise or weaken them. They came out just as brave as they went in.

And since their discharge from internment they have shown themselves true nationalists and you have taken pride in their being so.

The Brothers have by their simplicity, humility and inexhaustible energy fired the imagination of the masses as no other Mussalman has.

All these qualities have endeared them to you. You regard them as your ideal men. You are therefore sorry for their separation from you. Many besides you miss their genial faces. For me, they had become inseparable. I seem to be without my arms. For anything connected with Mussalmans Shaukat Ali was my guide and friend. He never once misled me. His judgment was sound and unerring in most cases. With the Brothers among us I felt safe about Hindu-Muslim unity whose work they understood as few of us have.

The Duty of Muslims.

But whilst we all miss them we must not give way to grief or dejection. We must learn, each one of us, to stand alone. God only is our infallible and eternal Guide.

To be dejected is not only not to have known the Brothers, but it is, if I may venture to say so, not to know what religion is.

For do we not learn in all religions that the spirit of the dear ones abides with us even when they physically leave us? Not only is the spirit of the Brothers with us but they are serving better by their suffering than if they were in our midst giving us some of their courage, hope and energy. The secret of non-violence and Non-co-operation lies in our realising that it is through suffering that we are to attain our goal. What is the renunciation of titles, councils, law-courts and schools but a measure, very slight indeed, of suffering. That preliminary renunciation is a prelude to the larger suffering—the hardships of a gaol life and even the final consummation on the gallows—if need be. The more we suffer and the more of   suffer, the nearer we are to our cherished goal.

The earlier and the more clearly we recognise that it is not big meetings and demonstrations that would give us victory but quiet suffering, the earlier and more certain will be our victory.

I have made your cause my own because I believe it to be just. Khilafat, I have understood from your best men, is an ideal. You are not fighting to sustain any wrong or even misrule. You are backing the Turks because they represent the gentlemen of Europe, and because the European and especially the English prejudice against them is not because the Turks are worse than others as men but because they are Mussalmans and will not assimilate the modern spirit of exploitation of weaker people and their lands. In fighting for the Turks you are fighting to raise the dignity and the purity of your own faith.

Non-violence.

You have naturally therefore chosen pure methods to attain your end. It cannot be denied that both Mussalmans and Hindus have lost much in moral stamina. Both of us have become poor representatives of our respective faiths. Instead of each one of us becoming a true child of God, we expect others to live our religion and even to die for us. But we have now chosen a method that compels us to turn each one of us our face towards God. Non-co-operation presumes that our opponent with whom we non-co-operate resorts to methods which are as questionable as the purpose he seeks to fulfil by such methods. We shall therefore find favour in the sight of God only by choosing methods which are different in kind from those of our opponents. This is a big claim we have made for ourselves and we can attain success within the short time appointed by us, only if our methods are in reality radically different from those of the Government. Hence the foundation of our movement rests on complete non-violence whereas violence is the final refuge of the Government. And as no energy can be created without resistance our non-resistance to Government violence must bring the latter to a standstill. But our non-violence to be true must be in word, thought and deed. It makes no difference that with you non-violence is an expedience. Whilst it lasts, you cannot consistently with your pledge harbour designs of violence. On the contrary we must have implicit faith in our programme of non-violence which presupposes perfect accord between thought, word and deed. I would like every Mussalman to realise, whilst the occasion for anger is the greatest, that by non-violence alone can we gain complete victory even during this year.

Nor is non-violence a visionary programme. Just imagine what the united resolve of seven crores of Mussalmans (not to count the Hindus) must mean. Should we not have succeeded already if all the titled men had given up titles, all the lawyers had suspended their practice and all the schoolboys had left their schools and all had boycotted Councils? But we must recognise that with many of us flesh has proved too weak. Seven crores are called Mussalmans and twenty-two crores are called Hindus, but only a few are true Mussalmans or true Hindus. Therefore if we have not gained our purpose, the cause lies within us. And if ours is, as we claim it is, a religious struggle we dare not become impatient save with ourselves, not even against one another.

The Brothers, I am satisfied, are as innocent as I claim I am of incitement to violence. Theirs therefore is a spotless offering. They have done all in their power for Islam and their country. Now, if the Khilafat or the Punjab wrongs are not redressed and Swaraj is not established during this year, the fault will be yours and mine. We must remain non-violent but we must not be passive. We must repeat the formula of the Brothers regarding the duty of soldiers and invite imprisonment. We need not think that the struggle cannot go on without even the best of us. If it cannot we are neither fit for Swaraj nor for redressing the Khilafat and the Punjab wrongs. We must declare from a thousand platforms that it is sinful for any Mussalman or Hindu to serve the existing Government whether as soldier or in any capacity whatsoever.

Boycott of cloth.

Above all we must concentrate on complete boycott of foreign cloth whether British, Japanese, American or French or any other, and begin, if we have not already done so, to introduce spinning wheels and handlooms in our own homes and manufacture all the cloth we need. This will be at once a test of our belief in non-violence for our country's freedom and for saving the Khilafat. It will be a test also of Hindu-Muslim unity and it will be a universal test of our faith in our own programme. I repeat my conviction that we can achieve our full purpose within one month, of a complete boycott of foreign cloth. For we are then in a position, having confidence in our ability to control forces of violence, to offer civil disobedience, if it is at all found necessary.

I can therefore find no balm for the deep wounds inflicted upon you by the Government other than non-violence translated into action by boycott of foreign cloth and manufacture of cloth in our own homes.

INDEX.

GIPD—94(S) DIB—1-12-25—600